This year the publishers will produce many new books on business and management. Many of these will have been written as an attempt to refine and improve the conduct of management and will offer prescriptive solutions designed to show managers why they must change their organizations, and how to manage changes at work. In this crowded market, authors – or 'gurus' – are keen to market their ideas as timely, novel and important. But there are many readers who are unconvinced by the marketing strategy, and argue that the discipline of management is now awash with fads and buzzwords, which in fact limit practice and analysis.

This book reflects those concerns and provides instead a critical-practical account of these so-called fads and buzzwords of management. Building from a critical account of the nature of management, David Collins argues that managerial work is often amorphous and ambiguous, and reveals the ways in which management's fads and buzzwords promise (and often fail) to bring shape and meaning to managers' work.

*Management Fads and Buzzwords* does not dismiss these phenomena however. Instead it takes them very seriously indeed; it offers an account of management that transcends the normal boundaries of organization in order to show the ways in which management 'gurus' damage organizations and, moreover, the fabric of society.

**David Collins** is Lecturer in Management at the University of Essex. He is the author of *Organizational Change: Sociological Perspectives*, also published by Routledge.

# Management Fads and Buzzwords

## Critical-Practical Perspectives

## David Collins

London and New York

First published 2000
by Routledge
11 New Fetter Lane, London EC4P 4EE

Simultaneously published in the USA and Canada
by Routledge
29 West 35th Street, New York, NY 10001

*Routledge is an imprint of the Taylor & Francis Group*

© 2000 David Collins

Typeset in Baskerville by
Florence Production Ltd, Stoodleigh, Devon
Printed and bound in Great Britain by
Biddles Ltd, Guildford and King's Lynn

*British Library Cataloguing in Publication Data*
A catalogue record for this book is available from the British Library

*Library of Congress Cataloging in Publication Data*
A catalog record for this book has been requested

ISBN 0–415–20639–1 (hbk)
ISBN 0–415–20640–5 (pbk)

Made in Kilmarnock

# Contents

# Illustrations

## Figures

## Table

# Acknowledgements

Only the pavement artist can make the claim, 'all my own work'.

In writing this book I have called upon the skills, talent and goodwill of a number of colleagues. It is only right and fitting, therefore, that I should acknowledge the value of their advice and assistance.

First, I owe a debt of thanks to my editors at Routledge. Stuart Hay commissioned this book for Routledge. He managed the project in its initial stages and offered many useful suggestions on the manuscript, which have done much to refine and improve the presentation of the argument. Michelle Gallagher worked initially as Stuart's assistant on this project and, when Stuart moved on, assumed responsibility for the management of this work.

I am also grateful to Michelle Jones of the University of East Anglia who typed the initial draft of the book, and with skill and good humour, (a faculty, which proves difficult to maintain in that institution) converted my pencil scribblings into useful typescript.

I am also grateful to Cliff Lockyer and Bernard Burnes for the detailed advice they offered on the manuscript. Cliff's insight and his encyclopaedic knowledge of the social science literature have done much to improve this work. Similarly Bernard Burnes has also offered constructive reviews of the text, which have helped me to refine my argument and analysis.

The following (authors and publishers) have kindly given permission for the use of copyright material:

American Society for Training & Development for excerpt from 'Self Destructive HRD' by D. Forrest. Copyright © December 1984, *Training & Development* <www.astd.org> Reprinted with permission. All rights reserved.

Blackwell Publishers for the use of 'Pay, Performance and Reward' by C. Lockyer, in Towers, B. (ed) *The Handbook of Human Resource Management*, Oxford 1992.

Curtis Brown Ltd and Granta Books for excerpts from *False Dawn: The Delusions of Global Capitalism* by John Gray, London 1999. Reproduced with permission of Curtis Brown Ltd and Granta Books, on behalf of John Gray. Copyright © John Gray 1998.

Harvard Business School Press for *Managing Across Borders: The Transnational Solution* by Christopher A. Bartlett and Sumantra Ghoshal, Boston 1998 (p. 29).

International Thomson Business Press for 'From Quality Circles to Total Quality Management' by S. Hill, in Wilkinson, A. and Wilmott, H. (eds) *Making Quality Critical: New Perspectives on Organizational Change*, London 1998.

Macmillan Press Ltd for excerpt adapted from *Managing with Total Quality Management: Theory and Practice* by A. Wilkinson *et al.*, London 1998.

Manchester University Press for *Nothing Else to Fear: New Perspectives on America in the Thirties* (eds) S. Baskerville and R. Willett, Manchester 1985. Reproduced with the permission of the editors.

Oxford University Press for excerpt from *Cultures in Organizations: Three Perspectives* by J. Martin, Oxford 1992; *Fuzzy Management* by K. Grint, Oxford 1997. Both by permission Oxford University Press.

Polity Press for excerpts from *Globilization: The Human Consequences* by Z. Bauman, Cambridge 1998; *The Third Way* by A. Giddens, London 1999.

Random House Group Ltd for excerpts from *Managing with the Gurus: Top Level Guidance on 20 Management Techniques* by C. Kennedy, Century Books, London 1996; *Maverick: The Success Story behind the World's Most Unusual Workplace* by R. Semler, Arrow Books, London 1994; *May the Lord in His Mercy Be Kind to Belfast* by Tony Parker, Jonathon Cape, London 1993; *The Witch Doctors* by J. Micklethwait and A. Wooldridge, Mandarin, London 1997; *Managing Across Borders: The Transnational Solution* by S. Ghoshal and C. A. Bartlett, Heinemann, London 1998.

Routledge for excerpts from *Management Gurus: What Makes Them and How to Become One* by A. A. Huczynski, London 1993; *Management Through Organisation: The Management Process, Forms of Organisation and the Work of Managers* by C. Hales, London 1993.

Sage Publications Ltd for *Organizing and Organizations* by D. Sims *et al.*, London 1993.

Simon & Schuster UK for *World Class* by Rosabeth Kanter, New York 1995.

John Wiley & Sons, Inc., for *Organizational Culture and Leadership* by E. Schein. Copyright © 1994 by E. Schein. Reprinted by permission of Jossey-Bass Inc.

W. W. Norton & Company Inc., for *The Corrosion of Character: The Personal Consequences of Work in the New Capitalism* by Richard Sennett, Copyright © 1998 by Richard Sennett; *Silent Depression: The Fate of the American Dream* by Wallace C. Peterson. Copyright © 1994 by Wallace C. Peterson.

Yale University Press for excerpts from *Domination and the Arts of Resistance* by James C. Scott, New Haven 1990. Copyright © by James C. Scott.

# Introduction

The progress of the 'behavioural Sciences' is inexorable and accelerated. You are unlikely to keep up. Should you threaten to catch up, we will define what we gave you as passé and give you something new. Should we run out of new stuff, which is not very likely, we will change the nature of something we have already promoted to you as 'the answer', and which we have displaced with some 'new answer' and then give it to you again.

(Forrest, 1984, p. 54)

There is a new game in town. Rupert Steiner, the editor of *The Sunday Times* 'Prufrock' diary, notes:

THE LATEST executive game sure to relieve boardroom stress up and down the country has recently arrived from across the pond.

It is popular because it undermines the boss, takes little effort to learn and doesn't cost a penny.

The only essential ingredient is a boss so wrapped up in his own ego that he has developed an executive babble to set himself apart from the troops.

Such characters can be found in every office. They are easily identified as they spew out phrases such as 'let's get the big picture', 'get your people to talk to my people', 'we're talking about a paradigm shift' and 'we have a window of opportunity here'.

Players draw up a list of these buzzwords and randomly allocate them on to game cards – there is no limit to the number of people who can play.

The game starts when a meeting is called and players have to check off the key words spouted by the boss.

It has a dual effect of players hanging on their boss's every word and keeping the team awake during meetings.

The first to get a full house is the winner. Participants are permitted to ask leading questions to engineer the response they seek, but shouting 'House' is not recommended – a loud cough usually does the trick!

(*The Sunday Times*, 28/06/98)

It is, of course, unclear whether this tale is true or apocryphal. We do not know whether buzzword bingo is widely played 'across the pond' in America, nor can we know whether buzzword bingo will catch on in Britain, or elsewhere in Europe. Yet it really matters little whether this tale is true or untrue. It matters little whether the game is played or not. In fact I am really quite unconcerned about the empirical validity of this diary entry. So why have I chosen to share buzzword bingo with you?

I have chosen to reproduce this quotation for a number of reasons. At one level I have offered Steiner's rather acidic account of buzzword bingo, because it is amusing, and because it fills me with satisfaction to think that those who embrace and voice neologisms without careful thought, might be subject to ridicule and scorn. But academic analysis must step beyond the whimsy of newspaper diaries. Academic analysis must do more than amuse us and satisfy our taste for *schadenfreude* (shameful joy experienced through the misfortune of another). Of course it can easily fulfil one or both of these needs, but we have a right to expect more from academia.

The quotation from 'Prufrock', then, has been chosen to preface this text because it is amusing; because it appeals to my sense of humour. However, and at a more analytical level, the quotation has been chosen because it reveals (perhaps quite unknowingly), many important aspects and features of organizing and managing, which are often absent from both mainstream and academic accounts of organizations and management. The quotation, then, shows clearly just how many truths may be contained in jest! Thus the quotation exposes a range of key organizational attributes, and demonstrates a range of organizational practices often obscured in mainstream accounts of management and organizations.

For example, Steiner's diary entry gives us insights into the vocabulary of management. Indeed, this diary entry demonstrates the importance and the prevalence of neologisms (often termed 'buzzwords') in the discourse of management. Although it is worth observing that, aside from the term 'paradigm', 'Prufrock' does not actually reproduce any of those terms, which because they excite some hum of chatter, or some 'buzz' of discussion, might be considered to be buzzwords. We might, of course, concede that 'Prufrock' reproduces a number of 'buzz-phrases' for our inspection. But this phrasing is a little clumsy. In this text, as we shall discuss below, we will attempt to avoid such clumsy constructions. Thus we will attempt to analyse the vocabulary of managerialism as it is constructed in the new millennium by analysing the 'fads' and buzzwords of management.

While showing the prevalence of buzzwords in managerial discourse, Steiner's diary also reveals the suspicion of buzzwords, which many, at least in Britain, have. Similarly, 'Prufrock' also demonstrates the mistrust and suspicion which many of us reserve for those who develop management's buzzwords, and for those who repeat these terms.

Yet this 'Prufrock' diary entry does more than, simply, reveal the existence and prevalence of buzzwords as an organizational phenomenon.

Through his whimsical account of the reality of organizational institutions, such as the board meeting, Steiner also reminds us of the extent of, and the importance, of humour at work. Thus Steiner's diary reminds us that organization is a shared, lived experience, where formality and informality, rationality and idiosyncrasy merge. To some extent, therefore, this diary as a whole, might be regarded as an attempt to reclaim the study of organizations and management from a group of 'specialists' who have sought to construct an academic discipline founded upon notions of science and rationality.

It is worth teasing out a few key points from this.

- Commenting upon the academic discipline of 'Organization Behaviour' (OB), Burrell (1997) argues that this attempt to construct, and maintain a rigorous science of OB has resulted in the development of an approach to the study of organizations which deforms rather than informs understanding. Burrell argues that our understanding of management and organizations has been deformed by the tenets of OB, since these refuse to countenance organizational factors and features (such as buzzword bingo), as anything other than non-scientific idiosyncrasies. The up-shot of this, Burrell argues, is that much of OB teaching and learning revolves around a process of collusion and self-denial. Thus he suggests that it is only possible for academics to teach this model of OB, and it is only possible for students to make sense of this account of OB, so long as both teacher and students deny (1) the validity and (2) the complexity of their own experiences of working and organizing.

- Burrell's critical account of OB suggests that the workplace is presented as a strange and serious place when commentators write for a management audience. Sharing Burrell's concerns Sims *et al.* (1993) note that 'Organization Behaviour' textbooks tend to present organizations as humourless and sexless. However, Sims and his co-authors argue that work organizations are, in fact funny, sexy places. Thus, in drawing our attention to boardroom antics, Steiner's diary helps us to see the ways in which many accounts of management and organization ignore the complexity and variety of organizational experience, and so, present us with rather limited and truncated accounts of social action, which limit our ability to perceive the complex realities of managing and working.

- Finally, in this brief attempt to demonstrate the analytical appeal of our opening quotation, it is worth noting that Steiner helps us to see the extent of, and the importance, of 'non-work' at work. Thus we should note that while academic courses on management tend to be constructed around a core concern with 'organizational behaviour', the day-to-day experience of working and managing suggests that 'organizational misbehaviour' is an important, yet under-theorized aspect of organization (Ackroyd and Thompson, 1999). In this respect Steiner's diary is useful, since it helps to remind us of the extent to which people engage in 'misbehaviour', and in 'non-work' (Hales, 1993) activities, as part of the daily rhythm of work.

As this brief listing of attributes demonstrates, the 'Prufrock' quotation represents a worthy starting point for our analysis of 'Management Fads and Buzzwords' since it shows, not only the prevalence of these fads and buzzwords, but also the richly adaptive, and innovative responses which organizational participants craft to survive, and to make sense of these innovations. As such, the quotation forms an ideal platform for this attempt to offer a coherent analysis of management which might allow readers to locate, understand, and so, critique management's fads and buzzwords.

Before we proceed further, however, we must be clear on our key terms. In a moment we will look more closely at two of these: 'fads' and 'buzzwords'. Yet if we are to understand the emergence and prevalence of this vocabulary, we must examine the medium, or conduit, whereby these fads and buzzwords come to be spoken in boardrooms.

Management's fads and buzzwords do not fall like rain. They do not occur naturally. They are *created* and disseminated by groups of people working within an apparatus, which has grown to become an industry in itself. Indeed Crainer (1998) argues that management's fads and buzzwords are now produced by an industry whose core business lies, not in the field of management, but in the fields of media and entertainment.

In the 1980s and 1990s the fads and buzzwords of management have been created and disseminated by a collection of individuals; a fashion-setting community (Abrahamson, 1996), who have come to be known as 'gurus'. Let us look more closely at these 'gurus'.

## The 'Gurus' of Management

The term 'guru' is normally used to refer to a spiritual leader (Pattison, 1997). A 'guru' is (typically) a man of wisdom and enlightenment. Lesser mortals 'sit at the feet' of 'gurus' in the hope that they will receive enlightenment. 'Gurus' solve problems and dilemmas for their followers. Through their words and their teachings, 'gurus' provide answers, and they provide meaning for those prepared to commit themselves to a particular way of life. Jackson and Carter (1998) note:

> The word 'guru' means a spiritual leader, and it derives from the Sanskrit word for venerable. 'Venerable' means worthy of worship, and its Latin origins are connected with Venus, the goddess of love: we should worship our gurus as fountains of love for us.
>
> (Jackson and Carter, 1998 pp. 153–154)

These origins of the term 'guru' make it difficult for some to use the term to describe the group of management commentators who rose to prominence, predominantly in the US during the 1980s and 1990s. Indeed Micklethwait and Wooldridge (1997) observe that many use the term 'guru' to describe management's key commentators, only because they are too mannerly to call these people 'charlatans' in public. This is perhaps a little harsh. The 'gurus' of management are not (necessarily) charlatans. They may well, as we shall see, offer limited accounts of social action at work, and spuriously practical advice on managing and changing organizations, but they do not, I believe, set out to deceive. If they misrepresent their wares, or their capabilities, they do not do so knowingly. They are not, therefore, charlatans, nor are they 'snake oil salesmen' (Hopfl, 1992), deliberately selling remedies and concoctions they know to be useless. They may, however, conform to another stereotype of America's 'old west'. Thus if we must call out the 'gurus', we might do worse than name them as 'carpet-baggers'.

The term 'carpet-baggers' is often used to describe the loose grouping of opportunist capitalists, who roamed America during the depression which followed the civil war. Like the modern management 'guru', the carpet-baggers profited from economic dislocation. These entrepreneurs, like their modern counterparts, were a mobile group. Often they would have no office, and so made use of large carpet-bags which, as they travelled around conducting their business, would become, progressively, more stuffed with cash.

Yet amusing as this comparison may be, the suggestion that 'gurus', like the carpet-baggers, are opportunistic and rapacious in their commitment to capitalism, does little to promote informed analysis of the 'gurus', and their fads and buzzwords. We will not, therefore, pursue this notion of management's 'gurus' as 'carpet-baggers', in spite of the fact that they do seem to have attributes in common!

However, I cannot quite bring myself to call these commentators 'gurus'. Given that the 'gurus' offer limited accounts of organization and social action, I hardly feel it appropriate to label them as enlightened, and as dispensing wisdom. Accordingly, I will distance myself from the term by placing it within inverted commas. Analysing those who create and disseminate the fads and buzzwords of management, and those who commentate upon and shape management, therefore, we will speak of the *'gurus'* of management. But, who are these people that this text would maintain a distance from?

## The 'Gurus' Revealed

Huczynski (1993) notes that the term 'guru', when applied to management, is used to denote an elite, yet diverse grouping, who simultaneously commentate upon management while acting to shape, and to reshape, the forms and practices of management. The term 'guru', then, refers to a diverse grouping and to a complex set of ideas.

Huczynski argues that there are three forms of management 'guru'. These are:

- the academic 'guru'
- the consultant 'guru'
- the 'hero-manager'.

## Buying the Analysis?

When managers purchase a 'guru' text they do not so much buy a book as a piece of the 'guru' (Clark and Salaman, 1996). Reflecting this understanding, Huczynski (1993) argues that when 'gurus' speak to management they speak with the power of belief rather than with the authority of science. Indeed the extent to which managers show a willingness not only to purchase 'guru' texts but to attend seminars and lectures given by 'gurus' (Clark and Salaman, 1998) serves to confirm that 'gurus' are as much celebrity performers as business analysts. Little wonder then, that some commentators have argued that the 'guru' business is as much part of the entertainment business as it is part of business (Crainer, 1998).

Huczynski (1993) observes, however, that the different groupings of 'gurus' which he has identified derive their celebrity status and authority in different ways. The academic 'guru' and the consultant 'guru' derive their authority and appeal, he tells us, from their specialist training.

### The Academic 'Guru'

Academic 'gurus' are highly trained individuals. They are the products of some of America's finest educational establishments. Tutored by some of the finest minds in American academia, many of the academic 'gurus' have themselves risen to take on the mantle of professorship. Based upon this description, Rosabeth Moss Kanter (1985, 1989) and Michael Porter (1985) might be regarded as two of the stars among the community of academic 'gurus'.

### The Consultant 'Guru'

Like their academic counterparts, the consultant 'gurus' also derive their status and authority from their specialist training. Whereas the academic 'gurus' tend to be senior members of faculty within prestigious universities, the consultant 'gurus' are drawn from the senior ranks of America's top consulting organizations. In fact, Micklethwait and Wooldridge (1997) seem to suggest that the top consulting organizations are, increasingly, coming to be viewed as academies in their own right.

Indeed, they suggest that in the future, the passport to professional success may be given to those who have spent time in the top consulting organizations, where now the passport to professional success is granted to those graduating from prestigious universities such as those in America's 'Ivy League'. Thus Micklethwait and Wooldridge suggest that, in the future, it may be necessary to be a 'McKinsey man' rather than be, merely, a 'Harvard man'. Yet, whichever of these two groups rises to enjoy the position of 'top dog', we should be clear that it is their training and their professional position which give weight to the analyses of the academic and consultant 'gurus'.

## The 'Hero-Manager'

Huczynski's third 'guru' grouping; the 'hero-managers' can make no such claim to specialist training and education. Huczynski tells us that the academic and consultant 'gurus' might be thought of as 'medicine men' (and women) – individuals who make use of their knowledge and training to heal and to bewitch. Indeed Clark and Salaman (1996) argue that these 'gurus' perform organizational roles, directly analogous to the roles played by the tribal 'witchdoctors' in tribes such as the Azande of Africa (Evans-Pritchard, 1983). In contrast to this 'witchdoctor' group, Huczynski tells us that the 'hero-managers' should be regarded as sorcerers – individuals who harness and grapple with dark forces which remain beyond their full comprehension. Thus, while academic and consultant 'gurus' analyse and intervene purposefully in organizations to make changes and improvements, the 'hero-managers' are 'dabblers' and 'survivors'.

Hero-managers, then, 'fly by the seat of their pants'. Their status and authority is derived more from their experience and *nous*, rather than from any specialist education and training. If the academic and consultant 'gurus' are highly trained, extraordinary individuals doing extraordinary things (corporate James Bonds) then the hero-managers' appeal and authority, might be viewed as deriving from the fact that they are, more-or-less, ordinary individuals doing extraordinary things (rather like the hero of the *Die Hard* films) (Collins, 1998).

Huczynski notes that labelling these academics, consultants and hero-managers as 'gurus' has a tendency to make the outputs of the 'gurus', what he terms 'guru theory', a fairly broad category. Noting the tremendous growth both in the number of 'gurus' and those in the market for their ideals and services during the 1980s and 1990s he notes:

> the term 'guru theory' is used as a convenient label to refer to [the] different contributions [made by the academic and consultant 'gurus' and by the 'hero-managers] that have been so influential during the last ten years. The label encompasses a rag-bag of prescriptions which include the importance of innovation, more teamwork, more

empowerment of the individual, more employee participation, fewer levels of hierarchy and less bureaucratization.

(Huczynski, 1993, p. 38)

Yet in spite of the fact that 'guru theory' might appear to be a hotch-potch of ideas and prescriptions, Huczynski argues that a common thread runs through 'guru theory'. We will investigate this in more depth in chapter 3; for the moment, therefore, we will analyse 'guru theory' as having three key characteristics. To allow us to highlight differences in American and British attitudes towards the 'gurus' we will label these three characteristics as:

- vision
- active research
- over-the-top.


## *Vision*

The concept of 'vision' highlights the roots of the term 'guru' in religion, and in spiritual and religious teaching. In America the term 'guru' is applied to far-sighted and visionary individuals. 'Vision', in fact, is key to the appeal of 'gurus'.

All 'gurus', if they are to acquire a following, must be able to demonstrate a 'vision' and/or philosophy. This vision should state (either clearly or opaquely) the benefits to the followers of 'buying into' the vision of the 'guru'. Religious 'gurus' (using the term loosely), for example, promise their followers salvation and inner peace, some even promise the opportunity to travel to distant planets! Management's 'gurus' like their religious counterparts, also promise salvation. This salvation, the 'gurus' of management tell us, is to be realized through making commitments to such things as quality improvements, innovation, the search for new customers and so on. Ideally, the vision of the 'guru' should, at the level of rhetoric, over-turn some cherished belief or technique (Clark and Salaman, 1998).

British attitudes to 'gurus' however, are a little more circumspect than the attitudes of the American public. At the risk of over-stating the contrast (and insulting my American friends), it is worth observing that, in comparison to our American cousins, Britons appear to have a more highly developed sense of irony. Thus Britons, and in particular British managers, whom, it seems, have a very real suspicion of abstraction (Huczynski, 1993), tend to be highly suspicious of the 'gurus' and their (quasi) analytical frameworks and models. When British managers use the term 'guru', therefore, they seem more likely to use it in a pejorative sense (firmly encased within inverted commas!).

### *Active Research*

The second of our three key characteristics; active research, draws attention to the extent to which 'gurus' promote management action and active research. Unlike abstraction, action and activity are popular with both British and American managers, perhaps because the active nature of 'guru' advice seems to fit well with the normal pattern of managerial working (see Hales, 1993; Whittington, 1993. Handy, 1988 and chapter 2). Thinking a little more politically, we might also note that managers, if they are to progress, must be able to demonstrate that they have, at least, started some initiative (Collins, 1998; Beaumont, 1995; Grint, 1997). Thus, we could argue that, while managers seem to have a very real suspicion of abstraction, they are positively in favour of action, and so enjoy the active character of 'guru theory', because 'guru' endorsed activity, works, simultaneously, to bring individuals to the attention of their superiors, while differentiating these individuals from their less active, less innovative and less worthy peers.

### *Over-the-Top*

The third characteristic of 'guru theory' we have labelled 'over-the-top' in an attempt to demonstrate further, the differences in American and British attitudes to 'guru theory'. Discussing American attitudes to 'gurus', the term 'over-the-top' is used to convey the, apparent, willingness of American managers to move from active research, to the implementation of 'guru' ideas and templates. During World War I, troops in the trenches referred to assaults on enemy positions as going 'over-the-top' (of their own fortifications). In this sense the term is used to describe the willingness of American managers to enter the fray; to implement the templates and the recommendations of their 'gurus'.

There is, however, another meaning associated with the term 'over-the-top'. In a British context the term may be used to refer to something which is extravagant or outrageous. In this sense, the term 'over-the-top', as well as denoting the willingness of American managers to implement 'guru' ideas, also conveys the understanding, that for many Britons, the analyses and the recommendations of the key 'gurus', are 'over-the-top'; they are outrageous and unhelpful. In common with the British, the French, it seems also have a similar problem with 'guru theory' (Whittington, 1993). Huczynski notes, for example, that for the rigorously trained French manager, Blanchard's and Johnson's *One Minute Manager* (Blanchard and Johnson, 1983) was too glib and superficial (Huczynski, 1993). However, Huczynski notes that the, apparently more pragmatic, Germans, seemed more open to this form of presentation, and so exhibited a greater willingness to embrace the sixty-second prescriptions of Blanchard and Johnson.

Having analysed the term 'guru', let us now look a little more closely at our other key terms; those used to convey 'guru theory'. Let us examine, in a little more depth, the vocabulary of the 'gurus'; let us examine the fads and buzzwords of management.

## Buzzwords

*The Concise Oxford Dictionary* defines a buzzword (choosing to hyphenate the term as buzz-word) as a slogan; or as a fashionable piece of jargon. When coupled with management to form the phrase, 'management buzzword', the term has a tendency to take on a pejorative tone. There is, therefore, a tendency to reject the discourse of management consultants as being *just* buzzwords. There is, as we shall see, some wisdom in this judgement.

Much of what is touted by management's 'gurus' is indeed bland and superficial, if not completely vacuous. Yet superficiality need not be the product of buzzwords. Sociology, for example, might be said to be awash with buzzwords. After all, sociology has its own specialist jargon (so specialist in fact that it often makes use of French and German terms where no adequate term exists in English), and also, seems prone to shifts and movements in jargon. In the late 1970s, for example, the key buzzwords of industrial sociology included the terms Braverman, labour process, Taylorism and deskilling. Currently, industrial sociology's key buzzwords might include the terms discourse, text, narrative and post-modernism. Sociology like the study of management, therefore, might be said to be buzzword-based. Yet no one seriously attacks sociology's key themes as being *just* buzzwords; as being silly and superficial.

The problem for the study of management, therefore, may be not so much the vocabulary of management, as its 'grammar'. Viewed in these terms, the simple existence of buzzwords is not, necessarily, problematic. After all, many 'respectable' disciplines seem to engage, fruitfully, with new and exciting terms, surely deserving of the buzzword monicker. With this in mind, therefore, we might argue that the study of management has been troubled and tortured by fads and buzzwords, because the 'grammar' of management makes the actors unwilling to 'unpack' these ideas so that they might be exposed to critical scrutiny (Collins, 1997). Rather than dismiss the 'hot topics' of management as being *mere* buzzwords, therefore, a properly critical analaysis must look beneath these terms, in an attempt to investigate their construction, and their place within the 'grammar' of management. Through this form of analysis I hope to show the ways in which buzzwords are employed, within certain analytical approaches, to close off truly important aspects of debate.

Instead of dismissing the 'gurus' and their fads and buzzwords as being unworthy of serious study – as being *just* buzzwords – we will take them very seriously. Indeed, we will argue that the works of the 'gurus' might be regarded as a form of science. Unfortunately, however, we will argue that the 'guru' preoccupation with fads and buzzwords, and their willingness to lever these concepts into particular forms of analysis – and into particular 'grammatical constructions' – is constitutive of a 'ready-made' science of management (Latour, 1987) which, in the name of 'practical' endeavour, eschews a concern with theoretical, reflection and reflexivity, which might, otherwise, encourage managers and other social actors to 'wear their own learning with zest and imagination' (Chia, 1996, p. 411).

## A Ready-made Science

Latour (1987; see also Chia, 1996) distinguishes 'ready-made' sciences from approaches to inquiry and analysis which might be termed 'sciences in the making'. Reflecting upon the processes of academic theorizing, Latour reminds us that analytical models are but representations of the world. However, Latour argues (see also Chia, 1996) that such models are, too often, treated not as representations, or as constructs of the mind, but as being, concretely and actually, the world itself. Thus Bateson (1972) demonstrating a similar concern with theory and representation, argues that much of academia has shown a tendency to accept representations of work and managing, in the mistaken belief that they are actually, and concretely, receiving real insights into the lived-experience of working and managing. Thus, Bateson argues that we consume the menu, in the belief that we are enjoying the meal itself.

Through this metaphorical representation of theorizing, Bateson is attempting to alert us to the tendency of sections of academia to make use of a (ready-made) model of 'science' which encourages, in its users, a non-critical, and a non-reflexive approach to the processes of theorizing and analysis. Invoking a slightly different metaphor to that preferred by Bateson, we might venture that 'ready-made' sciences may be thought of as technological artefacts; complex assemblages of parts encased in stout metal containers and embossed with a terse warning – *No user-serviceable parts. Return to manufacturer in case of difficulty.*

Pursuing the limitations of this ready-made, or encased model of academic inquiry, Chia (1996) argues that, when applied to the study of management and organizations, it produces a lifeless, a thin and deathly pale account of all-too-human endeavours. Identifying the key problems and tendencies of a ready-made science of management and organization, Chia argues that:

- Users of the ready-made science of management and organizations are discouraged from thinking, critically about the world, and about the models they employ in their attempts to apprehend it, since these constructs are presented to the users, not as representations, but as the world itself. In this sense the models are presented to end-users as being above reproach. The 'facts' these models generate, it is claimed, speak for themselves. Chia argues, however, that this form of thinking is mistaken. Academic models and the processes of academic inquiry do not, and cannot, speak for themselves. They are the outcomes of human action, and so should be regarded as being contestable and (potentially) controversial. Thus Chia argues that users of theory (and this means each and every one of us), should be encouraged to reflect upon the conceptual 'lenses' we use in our attempts to view, and to apprehend the world, so that we might become aware of the consequences for understanding, which the use of any particular lens must imply.

- Ready-made science encourages us to see the world of management in a fashion which implies a fixity to structures and processes which might otherwise be revealed as complex and dynamic. In this sense, ready-made science encourages a particular 'grammatical' formulation of the problems of management and organization. Thus in Organizational Behaviour courses we study management *not* the processes of managing. Likewise, we are encouraged to analyse organizations as institutions, rather than organizing as a skilled human accomplishment.

- The predominance of passive grammar in academic writing; the rigid separation of subject–verb–object, enforces the analysis of relations *between* apparently separate entities. Thus Chia, in common with this work as a whole, suggests the need for a new grammar of theorizing to facilitate a different type of world view. Indeed, Chia argues that, as we move from a focus upon management and organizations to examine managing and organizing, a new, active, grammar will be required to facilitate the analysis of those complex relations which exist within the passive constructs of management and organization.

- The focus upon practical needs and consequences typical among 'guru' scholarship has a bearing upon the conduct and performance of theorizing. Chia suggests that ready-made science discourages a concern with the inputs of/to theorizing by making a fetish of outputs. The concern with technical and tangible consequences among sections of management academia, therefore – *the need for effective change caused by the imperatives of competition and the quest for total customer satisfaction* – leads users of ready-made theories of management to (1) ignore complexity and (2) serves to silence controversy by propagating the belief that 'facts' speak for themselves and are transparent to all.

In an attempt to overcome the oversights and limitations of the ready-made science of management and organization, Chia encourages a more critical form of inquiry designed to release imagination, and to show 'the power and beauty of ideas' (Chia, 1996, p. 409). Thus while management academia (or at least that district of academia populated by the 'gurus') is keen to present a 'downstream' view of the world that is stable and authoritative, Chia is keen to present an 'upstream' account which, like the mountain streams of my native Scotland, flows more haphazardly as it attempts to navigate the vagaries of a rough and contested terrain.

Armed with this critique of ready-made science, we now have, I believe, a mature and powerful basis upon which to build a critical yet practical (a 'critical-practical') critique. Thus, our analysis of 'ready-made' science, and our analysis of the 'grammar' of management, suggests that, while our title is concerned with management's fads and buzzwords, our analysis must concern itself with the 'grammar', which conveys these terms. Viewed in these terms, it is senseless to seek to debunk fads and buzzwords in isolation, since this form of term-by-term debunking will do little to stem the rising tide of neologisms. Instead, if we are to make a useful contribution to the analysis of management as a complex and contested phenomenon, we must strike at that which sustains and promotes the vocabulary of management. Thus, while our main title deals with management's (new and enlarging) vocabulary, our sub-title should be viewed as an attempt to engage with the 'grammar' of management, which gives force and meaning to the fads and buzzwords that infest the discourse of management.

The analysis contained within this text, therefore, is critical, in that it attempts to interrogate the 'grammar' of management. The analysis contained in the main body of this text, therefore, seeks to unpack the models and constructs which, hitherto, have been presented to us in a ready-made or 'encased form, so that a more 'subjunctive' or 'imperfect' grammatical form, designed to reflect life as it is lived, might be allowed to emerge from the shadows. Yet the analysis is also 'mature' and 'practical'. It can, where appropriate, take onboard certain concerns from the 'guru' analysis. For example, our 'critical-practical' analysis can readily acknowledge that those factors which underscore Kanter's (1985, 1989) analysis of management and change, the threat to (US) corporations, and to the standard of living enjoyed by Americans posed by globalization, are important issues which, in different ways, trouble us all to some degree. Yet, while accepting that 'globalization' is a key and problematic issue, we do not have to accept Kanter's 'grammar', nor do we have to accept her preferred solutions to these problems. What we can do, and what we must do, instead, is look critically at 'globalization' (and other buzzwords), to examine the extent to which the ready-made science of management which often underpins buzzwords closes off useful and stimulating avenues for analysis. Indeed, as we shall see in chapter 11, an 'unpacked' account of globalization is both critical and practical, because it improves our ability to understand, and to locate, the problems associated with such large-scale changes. Similar caveats apply to our use of and analysis of 'management fads'.

## Fads

At one level I must own up to the fact that our analysis of management fads is based upon the rather prosaic realization that the term 'buzzwords', when used on its own, will not quite capture the key and important issues, selected for discussion in this text. Thus while 'culture' and 'empowerment' are buzzwords, Total Quality Management and Business Process Re-engineering are not, properly, buzzwords. They may be 'buzz-phrases', but since 'buzz-phrase' is a rather clumsy conjunction and anyway, is not listed in *The Concise Oxford Dictionary*, the terms 'fads' and 'buzzwords' have been selected in an attempt to capture the key terms applied in management. Of course, we might have adopted Grint's (1997) term, TLA (three letter acronyms), to describe management's 'buzz-phrases'. However this would tend to exclude examples of 'guru-speak' such as MBWA (Management By Wandering Around) and would, in any case, make for a rather clumsy title – *Management TLAs and Buzzwords* – so management fads and buzzwords it is. But what do we mean by the term fad?

A fad, according to *The Concise Oxford Dictionary* is a craze or a peculiar notion. Applied to the discussion of management and to 'guru theory', the term 'fad' tends to be used in a pejorative sense, to denote the senseless adoption of ideas and initiatives for no good reason other than the fact that others have embraced these fads or 'crazes'. There is, of course, something to be said for this line of analysis. After all, managers do seem keener to embrace ideas and initiatives when it can be demonstrated that 'world class' organizations are using them successfully (Grint, 1997). Yet, tempting as it is to dismiss the ebb and flow of management ideas as being due to the whim of fashion alone, this line of argument tends to misrepresent the context of the adoption of management's fads and buzzwords (Abrahamson, 1996; Clark and Salaman, 1998).

Ramsay (1997) for example has observed that management's interest in worker participation is cyclical. Ramsay, however, does not put this variation down to 'fashion'. Instead he argues that this variation occurs due to the changing context of management and work. Thus Ramsay argues that managers become attracted to, and so, renew their commitment to participation schemes when they perceive challenges to their authority and legitimacy. His analysis reveals, therefore, that the most recent iteration of management's historical concern with soliciting worker inputs to the processes of decision-making, empowerment, is no simple fashion item. Furthermore he shows us that empowerment is no 'flash in the pan'. Indeed, Ramsay's work reveals that, since attempts to manage worker inputs to the process of decision-making at work have a long and chequered history (Ramsay, 1997), it would be inappropriate to discuss the current attempts to solicit worker inputs to the decision-making process as being, simply, a fad.

Instead, Ramsay's analysis reveals that questions concerning the best way to secure worker commitment, while maintaining management control, are perhaps the oldest and most central of management's concerns (see chapter 7). Ramsay shows us, therefore, that 'empowerment' (as an attempt to adjust systems of workplace authority and decision-making) is, by no means, a new idea in management circles, and so he shows us that empowerment could hardly be said to be a new craze or fad. However, Ramsay's analysis does alert us to the need to 'unpack' fads and buzzwords, since he demonstrates the peculiarity of the current 'grammar' of empowerment when compared to the more traditional, trade union mediated, system of worker participation which has tended to predominate in the UK (see chapter 7).

Marchington *et al.* (1992) have sought to modify Ramsay's original 'cycles of control' model, arguing that it fails, properly, to account for the reasons why managers may seek out and apply worker participation schemes. Thus Marchington and his co-authors suggest that, as well as analysing external contextual issues (as Ramsay does), we need to examine the inner contexts of the workplace to grasp the micro-politics of empowerment. This alternative analysis of Ramsay's original position is rooted in an understanding that managers, while wrestling with the problems of balancing commitment and control, are more political and less rational than Ramsay allows for. Thus Marchington *et al.* argue that, to understand the empowerment 'fad', we need to analyse a range of factors, both internal and external to the organization.

Yet neither the analysis of Ramsay, nor the alternative position offered by Marchington and his collaborators, argues that in attempting to implement 'empowering' schemes, managers are simple 'fashion victims'. Instead both analyses draw our attention to the material considerations, which shape and condition the willingness of managers to seek out, and to implement, new tools and prescriptions. Thus, attempts to unpack and to unpick the so-called fads of management reveal that it would be wrong to portray managers as the passive victims of fashionable fads.

In using the term 'fad' therefore, we will focus more upon the subsidiary definition offered by *The Concise Oxford*, which these accounts of worker participation make clear. While acknowledging, in Forrest's terms, that progress in the behavioural sciences is indeed 'inexorable and accelerated' (Forrest, 1984, p. 54), we will use the term 'management fad' to denote the tendency of management 'gurus' to proffer (what with undue charity) might be termed peculiar and eccentric accounts of management and organization which retain their plausibility only because the 'gurus' have been successful in enforcing a particular 'grammar', and so, a particular form of 'ready-made' inquiry upon their customers.

This approach to the definition and analysis of management's fads and buzzwords conveys certain benefits. Notably, a willingness to unpack 'guru' concepts assists us in our attempts to locate the 'fads' of business within the larger context of management. Thus while it is tempting to dismiss empowerment, Total Quality Management (TQM) and Business Process

Re-engineering (BPR) as fashionable ephemera, as the lava lamps of management, a dismissive form of analysis, in truth, will not get us very far since it would (1) fail to locate fads in context – presenting them as new departures in thought and practice, (2) discourage us from taking the 'gurus' seriously, which we must do if we are, successfully, to unpack their ideas, and (3) lead us, inexorably, to view managers as hapless, incompetents (see Hilmer and Donaldson, 1996) and as the passive victims of malign consultants (Clark and Salaman, 1998).

Rather than simply insult managers and management, therefore, we will root our discussion, and analysis, of management's fads and buzzwords within an analysis of the nature of management, and within a discussion of the nature of the 'science' of management. Through this, we will attempt to show the ideas and assumptions which, deftly, yet silently, guide the thinking of management's 'gurus'. As we expose and unpick the web of assumptions which guide the ready-made science of the 'gurus', we should be better placed to locate, understand and critique the 'gurus' and their fads and buzzwords. Accordingly the book is structured as follows.

In chapter 1 which follows this, we will attempt to explain the conjunction of the terms 'critical' and 'practical', as these are reproduced in the subtitle of the book. Arguing that the 'practical' accounts of the 'gurus' are both limited and limiting, because of the 'grammar' of management, this chapter attempts to demonstrate the 'practical' benefits associated with the use of a rather different 'grammatical formulation'.

Next, we proceed in chapter 2 to analyse the nature of management. In chapter 2 we develop a view of management, and management control, as being incomplete. Through this we will develop a view of management which highlights the extent of its dependence upon the legitimatory potential of ideology, in its attempts to pursue, and to secure managerial goals.

In chapter 3 we look critically at a range of commentaries on management 'gurus'. Separating these commentaries into three camps:

1    'homages' and 'hagiologies'
2    'redemptive texts'
3    'agnostics' and 'atheists'.

Having outlined the nature and residency requirements of these camps, we will deploy our view of management (as incomplete and ideological) in order to make sense of the three forms of commentary which these camps offer. Arguing that the 'homages' and hagiologies', as well as the 'redemptive texts', operate with a limited and truncated view of the nature of management, we will attempt to demonstrate the insights, on fads and buzzwords, which the 'agnostics' and 'atheists' can offer us through their more reflective and critical accounts.

Taken together, this introduction, and chapters 1, 2 and 3, might be regarded as the 'hub' of the book. Readers are recommended to read these before analysing the subsequent chapters devoted to particular fads and buzzwords. However, having read these first three sections, readers may feel free to wander, with confidence, through the remaining chapters in whichever order they choose.

In chapter 4 we offer an account of culture and cultural management. Tracing the origins and the complexity of this term, we will argue that the 'gurus' of management offer a distorted account of organizational culture, which assumes that organizations, as cultural forms are amenable to managerial control, in part, because they exist in isolation from the wider society. Rejecting this form of analysis we offer organizational culture as a metaphor designed to reveal and to celebrate the complexity of lived experience. Reflecting the importance of this account of lived experience, aspects of my own personal biography – which would normally be rejected as being personal and idiosyncratic – are brought forth to provide an analytical critique of the 'gurus'.

In chapter 5 we deal with the concept of 'excellence'. This term is closely associated with Tom Peters, a well-known and much published, consultant 'guru'. In this chapter we will offer an extended analysis and critique of Peters' account of management and organizations. Chapters 6 and 7 deal with concepts, which have become closely intertwined. Chapter 6 deals with Total Quality Management, while chapter 7 discusses empowerment. Reflecting upon the 'guru' advice and exhortation which has grown up around these concepts, these chapters argue that the 'guru' prescriptions for change are representations which are mocked by empirical inquiry. Chapters 8 and 9 share, in common, a desire to offer an account of management and organization which does not rest upon a process of self-denial. Thus chapter 8 offers an account of business process re-engineering, which uses aspects of my personal biography to challenge the 'grammatical' formulation of BPR. Similarly, chapter 9, which is concerned with downsizing, reflects upon my own personal experience of redundancy to mount a challenge to the account of downsizing, which the 'gurus' are keen to present as rational.

Chapter 10 again attacks the 'grammar' of management to offer an alternative account of 'knowledge work'. Arguing that the 'guru' account of knowledge work is empirically unconvincing, and politically distasteful, an alternative formulation based upon the concept of 'working knowledge' is offered. Finally in chapter 11, we look critically at the concept of globalization. Noting that the 'grammar' of management presents globalization as an imperative, we offer a different 'grammatical' account designed to reveal those ideas and affects which make the grammar of 'globalization' rather more 'subjunctive' and 'imperfect'.

Before we move on to these issues, however, a brief word on the fads and buzzwords themselves is called for. Chapters 4–11 discuss a range of fads and buzzwords. These chapters do not pretend to list *all* the fads and buzzwords of contemporary management discourse. Indeed it would be foolish to attempt this since as the initial quotation from Forrest shows, ideas and orientations in the field of management have a tendency to change quite rapidly. Quite how the technology of management changes is, in fact, the subject of some debate and controversy (Abrahamson, 1996). However it is clear that ideas and practices do change. No definitive listing of fads and buzzwords, therefore, would remain so for long. I must acknowledge, therefore, that my collection of fads and buzzwords is (bound to be) incomplete. Yet, I must also acknowledge that the list is, to some degree, subjective. It is *my* list of buzzwords and fads, and I can claim no scientific authority for its construction beyond noting that, in my experience, these are the terms which currently and variously inflame/ excite/trouble the managers and academics I know.

I trust, therefore, that readers will find the listing, and the analysis, to be both interesting and rewarding, and will be prepared to forgive what they may regard as omissions and over-sights within the listing. Readers who consider it impossible to find such forgiveness in their hearts may, of course, contact me to press for the inclusion of a chapter on any fad or buzzword which they feel it inappropriate to omit. Should such arguments prove persuasive I will commit to including a chapter in a subsequent edition of this book – should such an edition be called for.

# 1 Practical Management and its Critical-Practical Alternative

Over the last few years the market for literature on management has expanded rapidly. Burnes (1998), for example, estimates that each year some five thousand titles are published which, in various ways, offer advice and guidance on how best to run organizations. Similarly, Micklethwait and Wooldridge (1997) have also observed the tremendous market for 'management books'. Choosing to segment the market, they note that two thousand 'guru' titles were produced in 1995.

In part this growth has been due to the mushroom-like growth of formal business and management education which, in Britain, has taken place at all levels: within schools, colleges, 'new' universities, and even within the most traditional of the 'old' and 'ancient' universities. Indeed, such has been the growth of management education in Britain that a few lucky and talented scholars (Laurie Mullins (1996) author of Pitman's *Organizational Behaviour* textbook for one), have become 'best-selling' authors.

Yet, it is noteworthy that, in spite of this growth in the provision of formal management education, a minority of the management literature currently in production is of the scholarly, or textbook variety. Indeed it seems that scholarly works on management now represent the marginal fringes of the market for management books when compared to the mass-market appeal of a group of management commentators often termed the 'gurus' of management (see Micklethwait and Wooldridge, 1997; Huczynski, 1993; Collins, 1998; Kennedy, 1996).

This book has been written because of the mass-market appeal of these 'gurus' of management. Yet unlike many of these texts (see Kennedy, 1996) it is not a hagiology. Hagiologic texts on management, texts which attempt to celebrate the lives and works of the 'gurus' (discussed in more detail in chapter 3) have become widely available as authors, and publishers, have seen opportunities to cash in on the 'guru' phenomenon.

While recognizing the market opportunities within this increasingly important arena, and recognizing too, the market penetration and influence of a few key concepts and commentators, this book articulates a dissatisfaction with the management 'gurus' and their ideas, and so, represents an attempt to do something other than celebrate their wit and wisdom.

Rather than offer genuflection, the book attempts a critical account of the 'gurus' and their works and ideas. With this in mind the book, as a whole, pursues a theme which has underpinned my work for some time now. Thus the book might be considered as part of a project which, sometimes in jest, and at other times quite seriously, I have termed 'management re-education'. Reflecting this project, the book might be considered as an attempt to enter, yet also to *reshape* and to *reconfigure* the market for 'management books'.

In attempting to reshape and to reconfigure what we might term the market for advice on management and managing, this book reflects a concern that, for all the earnest, scholarly activity of much of management academia, students and practising managers appear to receive their management 'education' through rather less formal channels. Thus the book articulates a concern that students and managers seem to derive many of their insights on management, business and commerce, not from academia, nor from their own life experiences, but from popular and populist 'guru' works; works which as we shall see are limited, limiting, and in any sense of the term, partial in the understanding they foster.

This book, then, represents a concern that, increasingly, management education is being forced to dance to the (bland and repetitive) 'tunes' played by 'gurus' such as Kanter (1989), Peters (1988, 1993) and Hammer and Champy (1993) to name but a few, who have, at best, marginal involvement and a marginal interest in the mainstream, critical and academic concerns, which might otherwise underpin 'management education'. Yet in spite of this rejection of traditional academic concerns and cautions (or perhaps because of this!), it appears that it is the 'gurus' who have the ear of management, and the attention of students and would-be managers. So while the 'gurus' thump out their tunes, students chant the shrill lyric; culture, empowerment, quality, re-engineering ... and demand, as 'customers', that these pressing and 'practical' (Collins, 1996) matters be made central to the syllabus (Clark and Salaman, 1998; Abrahamson, 1996).

Of course concepts such as culture, empowerment, quality and re-engineering are, as most conscientious educators would readily concede (although perhaps reflecting a different calculus), important to the analysis of modern management and so should be regarded as important issues in management education. Similarly most educators would acknowledge that the 'tunes' played by the 'gurus', arguments which reflect concerns regarding the globalization of business and the social and economic consequences of restructuring (Collins, 1998), are important issues which require careful and considered reflection, and so should be central concerns in teaching and research. The problem, as we shall see however, is that in receiving their 'education' and 'insight' from the 'gurus', students are encouraged to accept, rather than to reflect upon issues (Latour, 1987), since they are encouraged to use a form of 'grammar', which inhibits reflection and reflexivity.

## The Hungry Spirit?

Reflecting this concern with the vocabulary and 'grammar' of management, Jackson (1996) notes that 'guru' works are: 'generally considered to be too philosophically impoverished, theoretically underdeveloped and empirically emaciated to warrant serious academic scrutiny' (Jackson, 1996, p. 572).

Jackson argues that this 'emaciation' is doubly unfortunate for all concerned (with the exception, perhaps of the million-selling 'gurus' and their affluent, consulting colleagues). First, Jackson argues, the rather limited treatment of management, and of the contemporary developments in management, which is offered by the 'gurus', tends to close off the truly important, and interesting issues and topics, which should be of central concern. As a result of this foreclosure, Jackson suggests that students and managers are seriously constrained in their attempts to understand, and to act upon, their reading of these important developments, and trajectories in management. Yet Jackson also makes the second point that in dismissing 'guru' analyses as shallow and biased, academics have also acted to stymie critical analysis, and so, have denied practitioners the grammar and vocabulary they would require to challenge the 'gurus', and their construction of the world of work.

Noting the importance of providing practitioners with the tools and techniques necessary to challenge the 'gurus', Jackson applauds the efforts of Wilmott (1994) and of Grey and Mitev (1996) in their attempts to provide practitioners 'with the arguments that might enable them to constructively [*sic* ] respond to, and, if possible, resist' (Jackson 1996, p. 587) the 'gurus'. In a similar fashion Abrahamson (1996), in his analysis of 'management fashion' calls for the intervention of academics and business schools, so that the 'consumers of scholarly management rhetorics' (Abrahamson, 1996, p. 279) might be better trained, and so, more discerning in their reading of management's fads and buzzwords.

This book is a reaction to the problems identified above. It is an attempt to question, and to overthrow, the patterns of thinking which foster limiting forms of analysis. It is, in short, an attempt to overthrow the analyses which underpin the fads and buzzwords of management. To this end, the book aims to challenge the 'gurus'. However, and reflecting the discussions of Abrahamson and Jackson, the book, through its challenge, aims to do more than debunk the 'gurus', and their vocabulary of fads and buzzwords. Instead the book attempts to offer a challenge to the 'grammar' invoked by the 'gurus'. Through this challenge, I hope to offer readers a more objective, and critical account, of the key ideas and concepts, variously discussed and deployed, by a range of key management commentators.

The book, therefore, readily concedes that much of the vocabulary of the 'gurus' is, indeed, worthy of analysis. However, while acknowledging this fact, the text attempts to go beyond the normal managerialist confines of 'guru' analysis; and beyond debunking, to offer a a challenge to the 'grammar', which gives force and meaning to the fads and buzzwords of management. Together with our preface, therefore, this chapter, and the two chapters which follow, are intended to provide a means by which readers might locate, reflect upon, and so, better understand the concepts which they are being urged to implement, or indeed which they may have had enacted/enforced upon them by others.

As distinct from the largely uncritical, and often largely acontextual, celebrations of management offered by the so-called 'gurus' of management, this text will attempt to offer a critical, objective, contextual account of contemporary developments in management. As part of this programme, the book will also attempt to locate, so that we might better understand, those factors, which underpin the developments in management, which we have witnessed. Through this project, it is hoped that students and managers might be better placed to understand the complexity, and ambiguity, which surrounds social action at work. In this way, the book has as one of its key aims, the attempt to establish the usefulness (indeed the indispensability) of a critical and contextual account of the 'guru' phenomenon, and of the concepts and strategies which the 'gurus' would seek to apply. As an initial step on this journey, the remainder of this chapter will attempt to outline the significance of the 'critical-practical' conjunction of the book's sub-title. Accordingly, the remainder of this chapter is structured as follows.

In the next section we will pause to examine the extent of the 'guru' phenomenon, so that we might better understand the extent to which both managers and 'management education' have changed. This analysis should also allow us to examine the pace with which management discourse, and 'management education', continue to change. From here, we will move on to examine some of the critiques made of the 'gurus' and their works. While acknowledging the validity of a great deal of this criticism, we will begin to analyse the critiques themselves. In chapter 3 we will offer a more detailed analysis and critique of the 'gurus' and their commentators. In this chapter, therefore, we will offer only the briefest of critiques. Just enough of a critique, in fact, to allow us to pin-point the basic, conceptual limitations and over-sights of those works which, themselves, have set out to critique the 'gurus'.

In pinpointing the limitations of the 'guru' analysis, and the limited nature of the critiques made of the 'guru' works, we will argue that, often, these critiques remain limited and incomplete, because they do not build from a properly coherent and theoretically grounded model of managing and organizing. Accordingly, this chapter will attempt to offer a more rigorous theoretical account of managing and organizing. Indeed, it will conclude by attempting to show the inseparability of theory and practice, and so, will set the scene for our later 'critical-practical' account of the management 'gurus' and their fads and buzzwords.

Let us begin, then, with a brief reprise of the modern 'guru' phenomenon.

## The Resistible Rise of the 'Guru'?

Huczynski (1993) has observed that any analysis of management's 'gurus' must acknowledge that 'gurus' are not simply a phenomenon of the 1980s. Instead Huczynski reminds us that F. W. Taylor, the father of an approach to the design and management of work, known as 'scientific management' (Collins, 1998; Thompson and McHugh, 1995) is properly regarded as a 'guru' because of the influence he has had on management thinking and practice, through his publications, and also through his lectures and consulting activity. However, while it is quite correct that we should trace and acknowledge the importance of the 'guru' founding fathers, we must also acknowledge that the 1980s represent a period in which managerial interest in 'gurus' went into 'over-drive' (Micklethwait and Wooldridge, 1997; see also DuGay and Salaman, 1992; Clark and Salaman, 1998).

Micklethwait and Wooldridge note that the management 'guru' business has been booming since the early 1980s. Indeed they have observed that the 'guru' business seems to be one, if not the only properly legitimate form of business activity, which does not seem to suffer from cyclical variation. They observe that by 1996 the market for business books was worth some $750 million dollars per year. In addition Micklethwait and Wooldridge estimate that, currently, US firms are spending vast sums of money on consultancy activities. Indeed they estimate that US firms spend $20 billion on 'outside advice' each year.

The year 1982 represents, probably, the birth date of the modern 'guru' phenomenon. That year saw the publication of Peters' and Waterman's *In Search of Excellence* (Peters and Waterman, 1982) which, almost overnight, catapulted two management consultants to fame and fortune. Clark and Salaman (1998) have observed that *In Search of Excellence* sold 122,000 copies in its first two months of publication: 'Within one year it had sold more copies than any other book except the *Living Bible* in 1972 and 1973. The book has sold more than 5 million copies world-wide' (Clark and Salaman, 1998, p. 140).

In 1983, the year after the publication of *In Search of Excellence*, business books, many of them written by management consultants, began to appear on the US 'best-sellers' list, and for a period in 1983, business books occupied the top three positions in this listing. In 1985, Iacocca's account of his managerial career (Iacocca with Novak, 1986) became the best-selling business book of all time (Micklethwait and Wooldridge, 1997). Iacocca, however, faces stiff competition from a host of new and emergent 'gurus'. For example, according to Crainer (1998), Steven Covey has sold some six million copies of his book *The Seven Habits of Highly Effective People* (Covey, 1989). Confirming Covey's success, Clark and Salaman (1998) observe that *The Seven Habits of Highly Successful People* has spent four years on the *New York Times* best-seller list.

Indeed the influence of management 'gurus' is such that their reach now extends beyond matters concerning management and the economy, so that they now seem to influence the polity as well! Thus Micklethwait and Wooldridge (1997) have observed the influence of certain management 'gurus' upon key politicians. For example, Newt Gingrich the (now former) Republican leader of America's House of Representatives and Bill Clinton, the American president, have each called upon key business 'gurus' for advice on 'leadership' and campaign management (*The Sunday Times*, 20/12/98). Yet in spite of these impressive sales figures, and in spite of the influence which 'gurus' clearly exert, they are not without their critics.

Micklethwait and Wooldridge (1997) note, for example, that the publisher and business magnate, Rupert Murdoch, has observed that for all his reading of the management 'guru' texts, he has learned little of significance from these works. Similarly, if a little more forcefully, Micklethwait and Wooldridge offer the opinion of a senior colleague at *The Economist* who states that the 'guru' works are '99 per cent bullshit. And everybody knows that' (Micklethwait and Wooldridge, 1997, p. 4).

### Are the Gurus Mad?

In comparison to the judgement offered above, Burnes (1998) presents a similar, if more reserved and academic form of critique. Burnes notes that the 'gurus' tend to develop programmatic approaches to key management problems. Such programmatic accounts Burnes terms 'recipes for organizational success'. Analysing the works of the 'gurus', and the recipes for organizational success, which these works promote, he is led to ponder the value of the 'guru' recipes. Finding little to recommend these recipes he asks himself (and us): are the recipes for organizational success mad, bad or just dangerous to know?

Burnes observes that recipes for organizational success are (or should be), at some level, models of management and organization. In crafting his analysis of 'guru' works, therefore, Burnes suggests that we would require (at least), two key features of a model of organization and management.

First, any sensible model would have to be based upon a theoretically rooted understanding of organization and management which, for the purposes of research, would serve to underpin a coherent and rigorous methodology, which could be used to develop valid hypotheses and/or research results. Second, Burnes also argues that a theoretical model of organization and management, if it is to be considered adequate must:

- acknowledge the existence of other, competing models
- be able, either, to withstand or to incorporate criticisms made by other actors and scholars, who may elect to deploy competitive models.

Using this understanding as the basis for his analysis of the 'gurus', Burnes notes two key, yet often unacknowledged, problems associated with the 'gurus' of management. Echoing Guest's (1992) demolition of Peters' and Waterman's *In Search of Excellence*, the first key problem Burnes notes is that many of the 'guru' texts are poorly researched. Indeed he notes that many of the 'guru' works seem 'to have only a scanty research base and serve merely to express their author's opinions, however one-sided' (Burnes, 1998, pp. 105–106).

Burnes does concede that there is a second strand of 'guru' work which might be considered to be more respectable, since its methods and techniques conform more fully to the canon of social scientific research. Yet, and this is the second problem he identifies, those works that are more clearly rigorous and theoretical in orientation may be, and often are, contested by other approaches. Burnes notes, however, that this contest is seldom acknowledged by the 'gurus'. Thus he observes that, even those 'guru' works which might be considered to be adequate, at the level of methodology, are inadequate theoretically, since they fail to understand, or to concede, that they are based upon constructs, attributes, indicators and benefits which are contestable and contested.

Burnes' analysis, reveals, therefore, that one strand of guru work is limited. It is inadequate both theoretically and methodologically. This strand he is dismissive of. Indeed discussing the work of Lewis Carroll (1989) he notes that managers swayed by such forms of analysis would, surely, have to have expended considerable energy and resources on working to deny what life and work experience (Burrell, 1997) teaches us all: that other people do not tend to think and act as we do. Thus quoting Lewis Carroll he notes that managers who attempt to follow the works of the 'gurus' would, surely, have to work hard to deny their experiences, in order to believe impossible things!

The second strand, the researched strand of guru work, Burnes also criticizes. While he concedes that these works are more adequate in the methods of research they deploy, he draws attention to the theoretical and conceptual weaknesses which these works display. Thus Burnes articulates reservations concerning what we might call 'the quality end' of the 'guru' market since, he argues, even these more adequate works remain rooted in rather limited theoretical discussions, which fail to acknowledge their own limits or the strengths of other, often competitive, accounts.

In an attempt to summarize and pass judgement on the popular 'guru' accounts of management, Burnes, as we have seen, poses three questions in one. He asks: Are the 'guru' models and accounts of management, mad? Bad? Or, just dangerous to know?

Quite correctly, I think, Burnes rejects the charge of madness. Charging those who disagree with us as 'mad' is an unhelpful basis for critical and constructive discussion (see chapter 5). Thus Burnes concedes that the 'gurus', and their ideas are not 'mad'. The 'guru' models may be flawed and unhelpful. But the 'gurus', he warns us, are not 'mad'.

However, Burnes seems less tolerant of those who actually purchase the works, merchandise and services of the 'gurus'. Thus while Burnes refuses to label the 'gurus' as mad (perhaps he is swayed by their business acumen and entrepreneurial zeal), he seems willing to countenance the idea that the sanity of those managers who follow the 'gurus' might be questionable. Burnes, then, seems to suggest that in the market for 'guru' services the customer may indeed be king: 'mad' King George III.

### Bad?

If the 'gurus' and their works are not mad, are the 'gurus' and their works then, to be regarded as just 'bad'? For Burnes some of the 'guru' works, their ideas and conceptualization of management, business and commerce must be considered to be 'bad'. This judgement he reserves for the variety of 'guru' works which, as we have observed, tends to lack a sound basis, either for its argument or for its analysis. Indeed, as we have seen, Burnes argues that this strand of 'guru' work, as well as having theoretical inadequacies, also tends, either, to have no research base, or is founded upon research (if indeed the activity merits the term), which lacks a proper methodological foundation.

Countering the mode of analysis and presentation – that is, the 'grammar' – preferred by the 'gurus', Burnes argues that prescriptions for organizational effectiveness, if they are to be practical, 'have to be based on a critical evaluation of available options rather than merely a reflection of . . . personal biases' (Burnes, 1998, p. 105). In this way, Burnes offers careful theoretical analysis and research, constructed to reflect theoretical reflection and reflexivity, as a means of overcoming bias. Objective research, then, Burnes tells us, must have a sound theoretical basis, which is used to underpin a rigorous, yet reflexive, methodology.

As we have seen, Burnes does concede that some of the guru works do appear to have a more rigorous methodological grounding, and for this reason he seems unwilling to label all guru works as just 'bad'. However, Burnes does observe that those works which do have a stronger basis in research, those which exhibit a more considered approach to the question at hand, often remain weak because of the nature of the constructs they deploy. Thus Burnes notes that even the better 'guru' works tend not to acknowledge that the constructs used to underpin and to report the research activity undertaken, might, with some credibility, be contested. However, since there are forms of 'guru' work which exhibit some degree of rigour at the methodological level, Burnes seems unwilling to castigate 'guru' works as being plainly 'bad'. Yet, we should not imagine for a moment that Burnes' reluctance to label 'guru' works as 'bad', implies that the converse applies. 'Guru' works might not be plainly bad. However, no stretch of the imagination could make them 'good'. Thus, we should note that, even at their best, 'guru' models of organization often exhibit a poverty of thought which, all too often, leads managers and consultants to embark on spurious courses of action. This poverty of thought, as we have seen, has its foundation in a 'grammar' of management, which:

- fails to develop a theoretical model of work and organization
- fails to unpack theoretical constructs and ideas
- has a tendency to treat particular theoretical accounts of organization, as if these represent *the* definitive account.

The result of these failings, Burnes argues, is that competitive theoretical modellings to those preferred by the 'gurus' are not allowed the privilege of a hearing. This is a point echoed by Gold (1998).

Discussing management, and the problematic nature of favoured 'guru' constructs, such as 'organizational goals', 'effectiveness' and so on, Gold observes that 'guru' models of management and organization constitute, what might be termed, a 'ready-made' science (Latour, 1987). Gold argues that the 'gurus' present their representations of the world *as if* these were clearly, and concretely, reality. Thus, 'guru' models are offered as being natural, transparent and self-evident in their truthfulness. But they are not. They are, merely, representations of reality, which fail to allow for the fact that people will tend to hold, and/or commit to models of organization, and to constructions of organizational processes which may conflict with those proffered by the 'gurus'. For Gold, the failure to concede the existence of this contest is rooted within a particular (ready-made) conceptualization of organization and management. In short, Gold tells us that 'guru' forms of analysis hold fast to a conceptualization of organization and human interaction, which tends to quash dissent at a social level, while denying the virtues of abstraction at the conceptual level, because they assume organizations to be stable and unified. Furthermore, these representations assume that organizational processes (such as effectiveness, excellence and quality) are measurable, and are enduring in being measurable.

Discussing Britain's penal system Handy (1997) notes how the 'grammar' of managerial attempts at representation tend to quash dissent and discussion. Reflecting on performance indicators as an attempt to manage markets and market imperfections, Handy notes the difficulties which many organizations (although we should properly root decision-making as being the province of actors!), will have in developing measures of performance. On the management of prisons he notes that we cannot measure performance until we are clear on objectives. In attempting to improve the management of Britain's prisons, therefore, he observes a key problem. He tells us that, as a society, we have not yet decided whether 'the purpose of prison is to punish, to deter or to rehabilitate the inmates.' (Handy, 1997, p. 19).

Prison management in Britain, then, has at least three valid sets of performance measurements, each dependent upon how we represent the purpose of incarceration. So for example, right wing politicians may argue that Britain's prisons will be improved by intensifying the punishment of prisoners. Thus right wing politicians may argue that prison is 'too soft' as evidenced by high rates of 're-offending'. Some might be inclined to argue, therefore, that prison regimes will be more 'effective', and recidivist behaviour less likely, where the experience of prison is made harsher and more disciplinarian. Yet for others, such 'improvements' in prison management would be viewed as destructive and retrograde steps. Those who judge prison performance on the ability of incarceration to reform thinking and behaviour, for example, may be more likely to argue that prison regimes, based upon trust, are more effective than those based upon discipline and control (Boyle, 1977), and so, would tend to argue that prison regimes should be based less on discipline and more on therapy and education.

Which, if either, of these two camps is correct is, of course, open to debate. However, an awareness of the existence of this debate, at least, allows us to see that any recipe for success in prison management is likely to be more fraught and difficult than is conceded by the 'gurus' in their discussions of market 'needs' and effectiveness.

Reflecting upon the limitations of 'guru' advice which this example from Handy illustrates, Gold is rather shocked to find that the essential impracticality of 'guru' representations and prescriptions actually seems to boost the marketability and market presence of the 'gurus'. In any other marketplace we could expect consumers to reject and/or discard those goods and services which disappoint their expectations. Thus we might have expected that the inability of the 'gurus' to develop stable measures of performance and effectiveness would lead managers to reject 'guru' products. Indeed we might have expected that experience would teach managers that 'guru' analyses are flawed because they fail to acknowledge the ambiguous and problematic character of organizing. However, Gold observes that the failure of the 'gurus' to acknowledge the problematic, and ambiguous nature of such a thing as 'effectiveness', leads managers not to reject the 'gurus', but to seek yet more support from them. Thus Gold seems to argue that, since managers accept the 'grammar' invoked by the 'gurus', they lack the tools to unpick, and to expose the limitations of 'guru' analyses, and so tend to blame themselves for problems which become defined as problems of implementation.

Rather than reject the 'gurus' and their blandishments, therefore, Gold argues that managers accept the ready-made science of management as valid, and so, turn the blame for failure inwards. Thus managers seem to seek out more innovative forms of action from the 'gurus' when confronted with what they seem to regard as *their personal* failure to achieve, generally acceptable and operationally useful measures of 'effectiveness'. Gold notes, therefore, that when confronted with failure, an outcome not explained within the confines of 'guru' models of management and organization, managers 'resort to the pursuit of ever-more adventurous ideologies, sets of techniques and even fads to bring events under their control' (Gold, 1998, p. 108).

Wilkinson *et al.* (1997) offer a similar account of the nature of 'guru' constructs in their analysis of Total Quality Management (TQM) and employee involvement. Wilkinson *et al.* note that the advocates of TQM present it as being unequivocally 'good', leading to major benefits for organizational members. Thus they observe that the advocates of TQM present managers and employees with a range of bouquets:

- education
- empowerment
- liberating
- delayering
- teamwork
- responsibility
- post-Fordism
- blame free culture
- commitment.
                              (Wilkinson *et al.*, 1997, p. 800)

Wilkinson *et al.* (1997) observe, however, that, working from the same source material, other scholars have unpicked the web of assumptions which underpin TQM, to produce a rather different representation, and a rather different set of 'facts'. Thus Wilkinson and his co-authors suggest a complementary body of 'brickbats', which exist as a counter-representation of TQM. Accordingly, the bouquets and brickbats are reproduced in Table 1.1.

The problematic thing for practising managers, however, is that it is not only 'clever' scholars who are capable of unpicking the accounts of management and organization proffered by the 'gurus'. Of course, as Jackson (1996) observes, practitioner challenges to 'guru' accounts (thanks, in part to the silence of academia), have a tendency to be limited and are often easily deflected by the slick performances of the 'gurus'. Nevertheless, the point remains that brickbats do not just exist in the learned academic

*Table 1.1* Bouquets and brickbats

| Bouquets | Brickbats |
| --- | --- |
| Education | Indoctrination |
| Empowerment | Emasculation |
| Liberating | Controlling |
| Delayering | Intensification |
| Teamwork | Peer group pressure |
| Responsibility | Surveillance |
| Post-Fordism | Neo-Fordism |
| Blame free culture | Identification of errors |
| Commitment | Compliance |

*Source*: Wilkinson *et al.*, 1997, p. 800.

press. They exist and can be found in everyday discourse. Indeed, they exist, and are part of our own personal biographies (Burrell, 1997). Hamper (1992), for example, in his biographical account of 'working on the line' for General Motors (GM) offers an amusing account of his own personal 'brickbat' to GM's, quality management, 'bouquet'.

## GM's Quality Cat

Like the account of Wilkinson and his colleagues, Hamper's discussion of working for General Motors focuses upon a system of 'quality' management. Indeed Hamper's 'brickbat' is deployed against management's attempts within the Flint, Michigan, plant to encourage workers to 'commit to quality'.

Hamper unpicks GM's account of quality management by comparing management's representation of TQM, against his experience of management practice in the Michigan plant. In this way he sets his discussion of 'quality' within a larger discussion of GM's working methods and managerial priorities. Noting that GM's managers and supervisors seemed obsessed with maintaining continuity of production, Hamper observes that management's conversion to, and obsession with 'quality', did not quite mesh. He notes: 'Up until this time, the maxim had always been Quantity. Quantity and Quota. Herd them trucks out the door. Quick, quick . . . Quicker' (Hamper, 1992, p. 111).

Yet he clearly understands why GM had come to endorse the new vocabulary of quality: 'Evidently, GM was finally sniffin' the wind. Americans didn't give a shit about how fast and how many units [cars and trucks] you could zoom out the back door. They just wanted a vehicle that didn't begin to disintegrate the moment it rolled off the showroom floor' (Hamper, 1992, p. 111).

Hamper understands, however, that to achieve force and meaning, management's fads and buzzwords require a particular form of grammar built around imperatives. Reflecting upon the management of TQM, he shows how the 'grammar' of TQM was outlined to employees:

> Quality represented buyers. Buyers meant sales . . . Quality could change the tune and serenade the buyer out of a buck. For living proof all one had to do was glimpse over at Lee Iacocca, the born-again pom-pom boy of Quality High who was currently splattering himself all over media land with galvanic jabber along the lines of 'WE BUILD THEM RIGHT OR WE ALL EAT DOGFOOD!'
>
> (Hamper, 1992, pp. 111–112, original emphasis)

Yet, it seems that GM's managers felt the need to bring their 'grammar of imperatives' to life. In order to encourage GM's employees to commit to the new quality-oriented system of working, management decided upon the need for a 'quality mascot'. They invested in a large cat suit and ran a competition, among staff, to name the new 'Quality Cat' who would tour the workplace exhorting employees to 'build it as if they owned it'.

> Howie Makem [the name chosen for the Quality Cat] stood five feet nine. He had light brown fur, long synthetic whiskers and a head the size of a Datsun. He wore a long red cape emblazoned with the letter Q for quality. A very magical cat, Howie walked everywhere on his hind paws. Cruelly, Howie was not entrusted with a dick.
>
> (Hamper, 1992, p. 113)

Yet few of Hamper's workmates find the cat to be magical. Most, it seems, find his presence insulting. Hamper, too, finds Howie insulting. He is insulted because he knows that for all the talk of 'quality', GM remains 'quantity' obsessed. What Hamper terms a 'Howie Makem backlash' (Hamper, 1992 p. 155) develops, and GM's management quietly drop Howie from the scene. Some time later, however, Hamper is informed that Howie's head has been discovered and he resolves to resurrect Howie and develop his own counterblast, his own brickbat against management's 'quality' bouquet. 'It was my resolute intention to swipe the spare cat head, paint the eyes a violent red, attach large fangs to its overbite and carve the word QUOTA on its forehead' (Hamper, 1992, p. 155).

Where Howie Makem exhorted quality, Hamper's cat would seek to offer a representation of TQM which Hamper clearly feels is more accurate in the light of his experience. Like GM's management, therefore, Hamper's cat would rail against lost production and downtime. Hamper claims that with Howie Makem's transformation complete, he as:

> the Quantity Cat, would set out to terrorize all those who were responsible for assembly line downtime. How many times had I heard the woesome lament: 'For each minute the line is down, the company

loses another $10,000.' I would fix all that. I would call myself Howie Rakem, Quantity Cat . . . No man would dare shortchange the coffers knowing that Howie Rakem was on the prowl.

(Hamper, 1992, pp. 155–156)

So far we have analysed two of the three questions which Burnes (1998) has posed regarding recipes for organizational success. We have checked these recipes for 'madness', and with the assistance of Gold, Handy and Hamper, we have examined the raw ingredients of the recipes, and have checked them for 'badness'. Let us now consider whether they are 'dangerous to know'.

### Dangerous to Know?

If the gurus are not 'mad', and if their works, while clearly limited and partial are not unequivocally 'bad', Burnes ponders, are they just dangerous to know? Responding to his own question, Burnes is quite clear in his response. 'Guru' works are dangerous. They offer a spurious legitimacy to certain forms of action and, furthermore, stress action above reflection. *Ready, Fire, Aim!* might serve as an adequate summary of this.

Yet, 'guru' ideas and prescriptions are not just dangerous to know because of their consequences for organizations. 'Guru' prescriptions are dangerous because these models and ideas affect larger communities, beyond the boundaries of the organization. Indeed Burnes (1998) contrasts the idealism of Handy's (1989) account of 'the shamrock organization' – an account of organizations which variously notes/advocates the division of employees into three key groupings; a group of core employees, a fringe of contracted employees and a third, lumpen, peripheral grouping – with Hutton's (1996) concern that such organizational policies will lead to widespread inequality, poverty and to the social problems which tend to follow in the wake of inequality, poverty and dependency. Thus while Handy, at least in his 1989 work, muses on the organizational and competitive benefits of the shamrock organization, Hutton's work exhibits a concern with the societal implications of such a policy. Indeed Hutton is concerned about the development of a 40:30:30 society. A society where 40 per cent of people have well-paid, secure jobs; with the middle 30 per cent having employment in insecure jobs, while the final 30 per cent suffer from unemployment or chronic under-employment, and so, exclusion from the decent housing and education which others have in abundance (see chapter 9).

Micklethwait and Wooldridge (1997) also observe problems with the 'guru' industry, although their critique is much more focused upon organizational concerns than the wider and more socialised critique of Burnes (1998). In this sense we could say that Micklethwait and Wooldridge offer a more limited line of argument which concerns itself, mainly, with the organizational consequences of 'guru' prescriptions. From this perspective we might say that Micklethwait and Wooldridge offer two-thirds of Burnes' critique. Thus for Micklethwait and Wooldridge, 'guru' accounts of organizations and management are *just* 'bad'.

Micklethwait and Wooldridge note that while management, 'good' management, is vital, much of what is written on management is just not very profound. Indeed, they observe a catalogue of problems with 'guru' models and prescriptions.

1   'Guru' models lack a reflective quality, and so, lack a dynamic for development and improvement. 'Guru' models, we are told, are 'constitutionally incapable of self-criticism' (Micklethwait and Wooldridge, 1997, p. 15).

2   'Guru' accounts lack a clarity of thought and clarity of expression. Indeed they make so much use of jargon and acronyms that commentators on 'gurus' have been forced to develop their own acronyms to cope. Grint (1997) for example, noting that the 'gurus' of management seem keen on abbreviations such as MBO, TQM and BPR has, in turn, adopted the acronym, TLA (which stands for Three Letter Acronyms), in order to facilitate an effective summary and economical analysis of the 'gurus' and their works. Bemoaning this taste for jargon Micklethwait and Wooldridge argue that 'guru' works obfuscate when/where they should educate.

3   'Guru' accounts and 'guru' prescriptions present the common-sense and common-place as if these represent new discoveries or new trajectories. Indeed Micklethwait and Wooldridge argue that 'gurus' are the prophets of futures which are already here. While we can agree with the sentiments which Micklethwait and Wooldridge voice here, it might be more accurate to say that 'gurus' have a tendency (1) to present, quite unwarrantedly, their ideas and their analyses as new departures, distinct from what has gone before, or (2) have a tendency to revisit, quite unknowingly, arguments and forms of analysis which previous generations of scholars, invoking a different 'grammar', have discussed and rejected. The case of 'empowerment', as chapter 7 will show, is a good example of this first tendency, while the case of 'knowledge work', as chapter 10 will show, is a clear example of this latter tendency.

4   'Guru' ideas are faddish and often contradictory. Indeed on the question of faddishness, Micklethwait and Wooldridge (1997) observe that the life-cycle of 'guru' ideas seems to be collapsing (see also Grint, 1997). They suggest, in fact, that while, at one point, 'guru' ideas might have had a ten year life-cycle, the more recent 'guru' offerings have a shelf-life of only one year. Hilmer and Donaldson (1996) confirm this to some extent, although they observe a two year shelf-life for 'guru' ideas and prescriptions.

A fifth line of criticism may be added to the four points detailed above. This criticism is implicit, to some degree, in the work of Micklethwait and Wooldridge and is explicit in a range of other commentaries (Thackray, 1993; Grint, 1994; De Burgundy, 1995; Clark and Salaman, 1998)

5    'Guru' ideas, and the templates for action which the 'gurus' promote, often produce disappointing results. The promise of the 'gurus' falls well short of expectations, and there is good reason to believe that 'gurus' may actually do more harm than good (Abrahamson, 1991). Henderson (1998) for example, argues that the Boston Consultants' famous market matrix encouraged managers to abandon markets long before their potential was spent. Similarly, we might note that it has been estimated (although Hammer and Stanton (1995) dispute this) that around 70 per cent of Business Process Re-engineering projects fail (Grint, 1994; De Burgundy, 1995). Yet, aside from the disappointment of these failures we might also do well to note that Hammer, the 'guru' of downsizing, has been attacked by Strassman (1994; see also Grint, 1998) who claims that BPR as espoused by Hammer (1990) shows a callous disregard for humanity and for the suffering caused by re-engineering (see chapters 8 and 9). Echoing these themes of failure and betrayal, Guest (1992) observes that, for all the problems with their analysis, Peters and Waterman (1982) show, quite clearly, that the successful American organizations of the late 1970s and early 1980s had scrupulously ignored the consultancy advice which had been dispensed by the 'gurus' of earlier decades (see chapter 5).

## Summary

This section has been designed to spell out the ways in which the 'grammar' of management influences the articulation of management ideas and concepts. Demonstrating that 'guru' models of management are representations, which may be contested in a variety of ways, we have been at pains to point out the benefits for analysis of unpacking the ready-made science of management, which the 'gurus' sell. Making use of academic and 'biographical' examples, we have attempted to show how a critical account of the 'grammar' of management offers the means to undermine management's fads and buzzwords. Thus, we have argued that a critical and theoretical model of human interaction and organization, is central to mature and reasoned choice-making behaviour. In the next section, therefore, we will look a little more closely at the question of management theory.

## Management Theory

Micklethwait and Wooldridge (1997), as we have seen, have observed that much of what passes for theorizing in management is just 'bad'. Looking for ways to excuse this poverty of thought they speculate that, given time, management theory may develop into a more robust (and respectable) body of thought. Thus Micklethwait and Wooldridge seem to suggest that management's 'bad' theory may be a symptom of immaturity, and so, they appear to suggest that, in the fullness of time, 'management' may develop a more coherent and generally accepted body of theory. This, as we shall see below, is misguided since it seems to accept a grammar built upon imperatives – *the needs of the organization, the need for quality, the need for change, the needs of the academy* – as a valid representation of the complexities of human experience and interaction. Speaking both academically and biographically, my knowledge of concepts and my experience of organization, suggests that it is unrealistic to expect that one single theory, or body of theorizing, might be able to speak to the experiences, and satisfy the drives of all those involved with work organizations. Could we for example, expect to happen upon, or to create a body of management theorizing that would satisfy all those who work in, as well as all those who research and commentate upon, organizations? Indeed could we not argue, with equal veracity, that in the study of social phenomena, a key indicator of theoretical maturity might, in fact, be diversity of opinion and ideas rather than unanimity? As contributors to *The Economist*, would Micklethwait and Wooldridge attempt to place such a conceptual and theoretical straitjacket around the discipline of economics?

Reflecting, in part, questions which Micklethwait and Wooldridge allude to, that is, what is 'management theory' for?, how is 'management theory' to be used?, Lee (1987) has suggested that management teaching and theorizing should be redirected to develop 'appropriate theory'. Recognizing the complexity of organizations, and so, the problems of codifying managerial behaviour, Lee argues for the development and propagation of 'appropriate theory' which, it seems, is a simplified discussion of management and organization. Actually I prefer the term 'management-lite' to the term 'appropriate theory' since this better expresses its key characteristics.

## Appropriate Theory: *Management-Lite*

According to Lee, 'appropriate theory' has three key characteristics:

1  It offers a reasonable, that is a management practitioner-accepted account, of reality.
2  It exists to aid practitioners in the development of personal conceptual frameworks.
3  It supports the attainment of practical goals.

Putting a little more detail on these characteristics, in an attempt to explain their desirability, Lee argues that 'appropriate theories' are theories which, while we know them to be partial are, nonetheless, useful since they offer reasonable, practitioner-accepted accounts of reality, which offer a basis for practical action.

Anthony (1987) has been, rightly, scathing of this notion of 'appropriate theory'. He asks, can a theory we know to be 'wrong' really be useful? Indeed, and reflecting our concern with 'ready-made' science, we might ask, why should we accept, in a ready-packed form, the collection of ideas which Lee, alone, has decided is necessary for 'success' in management?

Reflecting upon the implications of 'appropriate theory', Anthony asks, would we in any other field teach students something we knew to be wrong? Would we teach students of medicine 'appropriate theory'? No, we would not. And we would not call a medical practitioner schooled in 'appropriate theory' a doctor. We might, however, call such a person 'a quack', 'a danger to humanity' or 'an offence to good sense'!

In an attempt to move from such fruitless pursuit of 'good' management theory, the section that follows will try to show that we do not so much require a theory of management, as a means to understand, and to locate management, within a larger discussion of organizations as complex phenomena. To this end the following section will offer, not an account of management and 'management theory', so much as a basic exposition of sociological theory, which might illuminate, and underpin, our understanding of management. In this way, we will work to develop a critical account of management and, in so doing, will attempt to show the practical benefits of such endeavour.

## A Sociological Account

Within a more general exposition of sociology and sociological theorizing, Smelser (1994) makes an important observation on the nature of sociological thinking, which has key implications for the analysis of management. When we study management and organization we study, or we should study, human interaction, albeit within certain institutional circumstances and contexts. If we are to make sense of this human interaction, we will require some model of humanity, which can explain relations and actions in this context. In short, we will require a model, which can offer an account of, and an explanation for, action, within certain structures. Sociological thinking has the capacity to offer such an account of action in context, and so, it might be argued to offer a useful basis for our discussion of management.

Smelser notes that while (sociological) theorizing is most useful, it is also inescapable. Addressing both his colleagues and his students, Smelser notes:

> In discourse we typically refer to sociological theory as an entity and to sociological theorizing as a recognizable activity. We write articles and books and teach courses on the subjects, and some of us say we

specialize in theory. Such statements are misleading in one sense. Every item of empirical research in our field – however narrowly defined and circumscribed – is rooted in general propositions about human beings and society and contains the seeds of abstract reasoning and normative evaluation. These elements are often hidden or implicit, but never absent. For this reason theory should be regarded as an integral *aspect* of sociological inquiry, rather than a separate entity.

(Smelser, 1994, p. 1, original emphasis)

Noting that sociological theory is a complex and contested area, Smelser likens theory and the process of sociological theorizing to a mosaic. But if sociological thinking is so complex and diverse, and is notable for the contest evident between theorists, can we really offer a general sociological account of management? The answer, I believe, is yes. In spite of the contest evident in sociological thinking (Collins, 1998) sociological models, however contradictory, must build from accounts of action in context, and so, tend to share certain fundamentals. What follows, therefore, is an attempt to spell out these fundamentals.

## Locating Management

Theories of 'management' are in various ways accounts of human action and interaction within particular (workplace) contexts. Theories of 'management', therefore, must model both human action and interaction, but in setting this in context, theories of management must also make some attempt to study the nature of organizations. Thus a theory of management, if it is to be illuminating, must attempt to model:

• the nature of human action and interaction
• the nature of work organization.

Yet, if our theory of management attempts to model only these features of work and working it will be incomplete. Why? Because organizations do not exist in isolation. Organizations, of course, are pervasive aspects of modern life. We have seen, for example, that 'guru' theorizing on management extends beyond the boundaries of the workplace to exert an influence on political strategy, and on the *management* of government. Yet, as Goldthorpe *et al.* (1968) note, organizations are as much pervaded as they are pervasive.

Organizations influence the wider society, yet they are also influenced by the wider society. This must imply, therefore, (although some would disagree; see Donaldson, 1985) that in order to understand management, organization and organizations, we must be prepared to 'exit the factory gate', so that we might locate work organizations within the context of the wider society. Our theory of management, or more properly, our sociological account of action within particular contexts, must, therefore, be multi-layered and must be able to account for:

- the nature of human action and interaction
- the nature of work organization
- the wider society.

Let us examine a 'practical' account (Collins, 1996) of these three key features as this tends to be presented by the 'gurus' of management. When we have completed this 'practical' discussion we will, then, attempt to unpick the web of assumptions which bind and limit this ready-made account of 'practical' matters, by offering a reflexive, 'critical-practical' account of management, so that we might discern the benefits of critical thinking and reflective action.

## *A Practical Account of Management*

'Guru' works, as we have seen, tend to offer advice on how best to run organizations (Burnes, 1998, 1996). In this respect, 'guru' accounts of management and organizations market themselves as offering 'practical' guidance to managers, on how best to run and/or change organizations. Burnes' critique of 'guru' recipes reveals, however, the limitations of these works. Indeed Burnes' critique draws attention to the fact that 'guru' accounts of management and organization offer a poor basis for action, because they are weak both theoretically and methodologically.

Reflecting this criticism, this section on 'practical' management will attempt to demonstrate that the 'guru' accounts of management should, properly, be called 'spuriously practical' accounts, since, in stressing practice above reflection, and in viewing 'practical' matters, as existing prior to, and as taking precedence over theoretical concerns (Collins, 1996, 1998), 'guru' accounts of management offer a spurious legitimacy to certain forms of action. Thinking back to Handy's prison example, we could say that, most often, the 'guru' account of 'practice', and 'practical' matters operates, *as if,* society had resolved the question concerning the purpose of incarceration, and so, assumes the existence of a natural, obvious and self-evident 'practical' agenda. Yet as the prison example shows, this is unrealistic. Indeed, we should note that 'practical' issues and 'practical' agendas for action are not natural occurrences obvious to all. 'Practical' matters are constructed by actors and reflect, in part, the concerns and orientations of these actors (Du Gay and Salaman, 1992; Jackson, 1996; Clark and Salaman, 1998). In any sense of the term, therefore, 'practical' agendas build from partial analysis.

## A Partial Agenda?

'Practical' agendas for action are partial. A 'practical' agenda as conceived by the 'gurus' of management, represents a particular ordering of information and, furthermore, represents a particular ordering of priorities. Any particular agenda for 'practical' action, since it filters information in order to promote particular forms of outcomes, therefore, must be considered to represent, however loosely, a concern with abstraction and with theory. Viewed in these terms, 'practical' matters are, at root, and are inescapably, theoretical matters. Like the theoretical constructions, which (must) underpin any particular version of practice, therefore, 'practical' matters are contestable and, as a result, are contested within organizations.

To earn its monicker, therefore, any truly practical account of management and managing, if it is to serve its purpose and identify areas for action, must first be able to explain, and to account for, some degree of contest over 'practice' and 'practical' matters. Indeed as Handy's analysis makes clear, any model, which fails in this respect, will be hard pressed to offer constructive suggestions on the management of organizations.

With this point in mind, let us examine the (spuriously) practical accounts of management before turning to examine more 'critical-practical' perspectives, which may be used to illuminate, and to rationalize, the conflicts evident in the analysis of management and its practical concerns. This brief account of 'practical' management will reflect our multi-layered model of organization, and so, will 'drill down' from the 'wider society', through a consideration of 'organization' to consider the 'model of humanity' evident in the works of the 'gurus'.

## The 'Gurus' Take!

'Practical', 'guru' accounts of management and change tend to argue (though given the difficulty of establishing this as fact, perhaps we should say, they assert) that society is changing, and now changing faster, than in any other period in the history of humanity. These accounts (see Collins, 1998; Dawson, 1994) tend to argue that, as technologies and markets change, so organizations and society more generally will experience change and turbulence. To misuse Marx, all that was solid melts into air.

The turbulence, which the gurus find at the level of the national and global economy, is said to lead to similar forms of change and turbulence at the level of organizations. Indeed, the 'gurus' invoke a particular form of grammar to give force and meaning to their accounts of change. Thus, changes in markets and technologies are said to cause imperatives for change within organizations. Kanter (1989), for example, tells us that organization *must* become fast and flexible: lean but not mean. Handy (1989), likewise, has warned us that organizations will/must change. Indeed

Handy's shamrock account suggests that in reducing the permanent workforce to a small core, and in hiving off work to contractors, or to a peripheral fringe, we may have to curb our tendency to speak of organizations (concrete things) and may instead have to focus upon 'organization'.

This concern to move the focus of management from control to coordination; and from managing business-as-usual, to leading radical change is a theme common to all the key 'gurus'. Thus Peters (1988) has encouraged managers to embrace 'chaos' and to 'get crazy' (1994). Senge (1990), meanwhile, has encouraged managers to make organizations more 'learningful' so that leaders might tap the skills of workers.

Not surprisingly, these organizational changes, brought forth in response to competitive imperatives, are said to lead to a requirement that we, as individuals, modify our expectations, and change how we act and interact. Kanter (1989), for example, tells us that we *must* modify our expectations with regard to our working lives. She warns us that organizations can no longer make the commitment to offer us a job for life. Yet keen to 'accentuate the positive', she tells us that good managers; those who will master change (1985), will work with employees, and in developing employee skills and talents for mutual benefit, will ensure that we, as employees, remain attractive in the labour market. Thus Kanter tells us that we *must* trade 'employability' for the traditional career. Handy (1989) echoes this. We will, he tells us, have a number of careers. Indeed we may, simultaneously, have a number of 'employers', each making use of just some of the skills in our 'portfolio'.

The future the 'gurus' envisage for us, then, should be clear. If we harbour doubts; we should not. The 'gurus' are unequivocal. Change is here and is here to stay. We are told, therefore, that we should wise up and get on board! Indeed, reflecting Pattison's (1997) analysis of the religious imagery deployed by the 'gurus', we might say that the 'gurus' tell of the coming of a great flood, and warn us that those who fail to board the ark will, surely, perish in the deluge.

In attempting to establish this line of argument the 'gurus', clearly, offer a multi-layered form of analysis. It is a line of analysis which invokes a particular grammatical construction in an attempt to show the (unavoidable) implications for society, for corporations, for management, and for each of us as individuals, of the changed and capricious environment of business. Yet, while this argument seems plausible, in part, because it resonates with much of our day-to-day experience, and while it offers a range of 'practical' outcomes (couched as managerial imperatives) we must ask; is it truly useful? Once unpicked, does this 'grammar' offer a useful summary and explanation for events? Does it offer a prescription based on thoughtful analysis? Indeed will a single prescription cure all ills?

Let us unpack the ready-made science of the 'gurus' in order to attempt a critical-practical analysis in response to these questions.

## A Critical-Practical Analysis

In Shakespearean plays the wisest man at court is often 'the fool'. Perhaps this is why Peters (1994) has encouraged managers to do 'crazy' things. I doubt this, however, since while Peters' 'crazy managers' are encouraged to throw off the traditions and strictures of management, avoiding 'paralysis by analysis' (Peters and Waterman, 1982) in the search for opportunities and creative solutions, the Shakespearean 'fool' is, in contrast, a careful analyst.

Shakespeare's fool is a man able to link levels of analysis. We might say that the fool possesses a 'sociological imagination' (Wright-Mills, 1973); a way of seeing which facilitates movement between the private and the public; between troubles and issues 'to provide . . . cohesive assessments [and] comprehensive orientations' (Wright-Mills, 1973, p. 14). In these terms, the 'fool' is a man who is able to judge political moods, yet at the same time, the 'fool' remains a shrewd judge of character. The fool, then, is a critical thinker, able to link levels of analysis. Through his capacity for critical thought and reflection, the 'fool' offers his master useful and practical advice.

'Gurus' as we have seen, offer 'practical' advice on how best to run organizations. Yet their advice is 'spuriously practical'. It is weak conceptually, theoretically and empirically, yet has a certain immunity to criticism because the users of 'guru theory' (Huczynski, 1993) are discouraged from questioning the assumptions which underpin it. Once unpicked, however, it becomes apparent that rather than offering guidance to management, rather than offering a cohesive assessment of the very real problems of managing, the 'guru' practical advice serves only to befuddle and to overwhelm managers in a welter of contradictory advice (see chapter 3).

As distinct from the 'spuriously practical' advice offered by the 'gurus', what the field of management requires, instead, is something more critical; something more provoking of thought; something which exercises the sociological imagination, to provide a more comprehensive orientation. Arguably what the study of management requires is a 'fool' in the Shakespearean mould. We could say, then, that what the study of management requires is, not more 'gurus' in the mould of Peters and Covey, but the intervention of someone, or better still, some body of thought,[1] which might risk unpopularity, by challenging the 'court' specialists, and their privileges and assumptions, so that eyes and ears may be opened to different ways of seeing, and to different ways of thinking. Management's fool then, like Shakespeare's court fool, would look critically, to link levels of analysis and in so doing, would be able to provide truly practically, relevant, insight and analysis. Management's 'fool', if you will, would offer 'critical-practical' advice.

As a contrast to our 'practical' account of the 'gurus', let us don the jester's cap, to offer a 'critical-practical' analysis of the 'gurus' and their message for change.

## The Context of Business

The 'gurus', as we have seen, invoke an argument built upon imperatives for change. They all take as their departure point the fact that the competitive environment of business is now much changed. They argue (see Dawson, 1994) that a combination of economic and technological change has altered fundamentally, and forever, the essential nature of business and competition. Thus, the 'gurus' argue that, a range of technological and competitive imperatives are driving changes within, and between organizations. There is of course some wisdom in this account of change. Thanks, largely to the Japanese, I now expect the products I buy to be of a high quality. Thanks also to the Japanese, I now expect that products will change and will be improved year-on-year. However, we misrepresent the nature and processes of change where we assume that 'imperatives', remorselessly and unavoidably, force particular outcomes upon organizations, and upon our lives. For example, in spite of the availability of a whole host of alternative products, my preferred car is a Mini Cooper, which aside from the incorporation of a fuel injection system, remained essentially unchanged in over thirty years until production ceased with the new millennium.

If competitive imperatives cause irresistible forces for change, why (until 2000 at any rate), was Rover still able to sell the Mini Cooper, in spite of the existence of any number of 'super-minis' which are known to be cheaper, faster, more comfortable and more sophisticated products? Now, while marketing experts may offer a range of reasons for this state of affairs, at the level of organizational analysis, the persistence of a healthy market for the Mini Cooper seems to suggest that the forces of competition and change do not strike all with equal ferocity. The case of the Mini Cooper seems to suggest that rather than accept, as self-evident, the existence of competitive imperatives, we might be better advised to analyse those factors which may intervene to deflect, reshape or blunt what the 'gurus' have assumed are the unstoppable forces of competition, globalization and technological change (see *The Daily Telegraph*, 21/08/99, for an interesting account of the decision-making processes which led Rover to scrap production of the Mini). In short, the case of the Mini seems to imply a need for a more 'subjunctive', or 'imperfect', form of grammar. Indeed, this account of the non-imperative of 'imperatives', implies that we should investigate the complex socio-political processes of management and change rather than assume the effect of certain disembodied forces. As we shall see, this movement must imply a change of focus. The move from a consideration of the *environment* of competition so that we might, instead, study the *context* of business (Collins, 1998, 1998a).

Moving our focus from the analysis of environment (an *ad hoc* backdrop of business and economics indicators) to study context (a richer and more complex form of analysis which acknowledges continuity within change, and which attempts to link action and structure (Pettigrew, 1985, 1987; Dawson, 1994)) should allow us to raise some important, and critical questions, which cast shadows over the 'encased', practical accounts of the 'gurus'. These critical questions, as we shall see, have important practical implications.

## The Benefits of Contextualism

A contextual analysis of business offers a qualitatively different account of management and organization compared to accounts prepared by management's 'gurus', which focus upon *the environment*. Environmental forms of organizational analysis tend to assume that *the environment* enforces itself upon businesses and individuals. Thus changes in the environment of business are said to force changes upon organizations. Environmental changes, therefore, are said to cause imperatives for change. A contextual form of analysis, however, with its focus upon the complex socio-political processes of management, encourages us to analyse continuity and change, structure and action, together. In this way, a contextual account of managing encourages a more sensitive form of analysis, which allows actors to make choices, and to buck the so-called imperatives of the environment.

In common with the environmental account of business, contextual forms of analysis do, of course, argue that what might be will be conditioned by what is. Yet a contextual form of analysis refuses to portray social actors as the victims of change. Thus, while environmental accounts of management assert that action is formed by wider changes in the environment, a contextual account acknowledges that action is *informed* by wider changes. Thus a contextual account of management argues that actors may harness, or change aspects of context, to their own advantage. For example, Pettigrew (1985) in his account of ICI, shows that the managers of ICI were far from being meek victims of the environment. Indeed Pettigrew shows how managers attempted to engineer crises in the business 'environment' in order to initiate change. Similarly De Lorean (Wright, 1980) argues that General Motors (GM) did not meekly accept changes in its competitive environment. Indeed De Lorean's insider account of GM shows that when faced with new competitive challenges in the market for NATO contracts, GM's managers chose to alter the environment – by attempting to bribe those who were in a position to award contracts!

What the 'gurus' call *the environment*, therefore, does not force change upon actors. Instead, we should note that actors work within a context, and through their actions, work to *shape* this context. This suggests then, that in spite of the pace of technological change, and in spite of the apparent tendencies towards the globalization of business, the nature of competition will be shaped more by actors, than by the disembodied forces which the 'gurus' assume to be operational.

A contextual form of analysis suggests, therefore, that the so-called imperatives for change, will tend to be mediated by a range of factors. In this way a contextual analysis, a critical-practical analysis, might help us to realize (and to rationalize in terms of choice-making activities), the differences evident between, say, Nike's management of its US-based design teams (a carrot and stick, though mainly a carrot approach) and the management of its Vietnamese production facility (mainly and literally, a stick approach) which Boje (1998) has observed. Indeed, a contextual analysis of Boje's account of Nike's violent system of management may be deployed to prick the conscience of management and its commentators.

As distinct from the 'gurus' environmentally focused form of analysis, Boje's acount of Nike reminds us that within a contextual form of analysis, managers must take responsibility for their actions. *The environment* does not cause an imperative to bribe government officials (Wright, 1980), nor does it cause an imperative to inflict physical harm upon employees. Instead a contextualist reading of Boje's work reminds us that Nike's managers must be viewed as selecting a form of factory management, and workplace discipline, which chooses to (or condones) the assault of employees. This form of analysis also has implications for the next level of analysis on our schema: the organizational level.

## The Nature of Organization

The 'gurus', as we have observed, have argued that changes in the competitive environment cause imperatives for change within organizations. Yet a contextual analysis reveals the extent of managerial choice in such matters, and so reveals a diversity of organizational forms and trajectories. Clegg (1993) offers an interesting, discussion of this.

Clegg begins chapter 5 of *Modern Organizations* in a biographical vein, by offering an account of his lunch. Clegg, it seems, likes bread, cheese and pickles for his lunch. Indeed he is fussy about his bread and cares little for the bread sold in the US. This he calls 'industrial bread' (Clegg, 1993 p. 107). Clegg's taste in bread leads him (and us) to an interesting question; if there are competitive imperatives then why is all bread not made in the fashion of the American 'industrial bread' which he dislikes? If there are, indeed, competitive imperatives would we not expect all bread to be made as it is in the US, in large factories owned by conglomerates? If there are competitive imperatives we could expect that: 'efficient and successful firms in similar industries, cross-culturally would adopt the same type of strategy and structure irrespective of their location' (Clegg, 1993, p. 108).

He continues:

> so, how is French bread possible? How has the market dominance of conglomerate oligopoly bread manufactured by firms like Goodman

Fielder Wattie or Rank Hovis McDougall been avoided? Why should it be that in France the equivalent of these 'manufacturers' control only about 10 per cent of the market whereas in other countries, such as Britain and the United States, it is far closer to 100 per cent?

(Clegg, 1993, p. 108)

Clegg's analysis of bread manufacture, then, effectively demolishes the argument that all organizations face similar competitive imperatives, and so, will converge in terms of structure, strategy and policy. Put plainly, there can be no 'competitive imperatives' where managers can exercise choice over systems, structures and strategies!

So much then for the argument that all organizations are alike. Yet we must still address the related critical-practical question: just what are organizations like?

For the 'gurus' of management, organizations are essentially co-operative. Both strands of 'guru' work – that strand which touts opinion as research, as well as the more rigorously researched variant (Burnes, 1998), share the assumption that organizations are, essentially, harmonious and co-operative. (Fox, 1985; Huczynski, 1993). There is, of course, something to be said for this. Edwards (1986) notes, for example, that organizations, on a day-to-day basis, do tend to exhibit co-operative social relations. However, if we are to offer practical perspectives on, and practically useful accounts of management, we must at least acknowledge that there exist, competitive accounts of management and organization, which dispute the essential harmony, which the 'gurus' assert as the 'state of nature' within work organizations (Collins, 1998). The problem, with 'practical' and co-operative accounts of organizations, however, is that in asserting co-operation as the state of nature, they must work to deny the validity of lived experience, since they have great difficulty in incorporating, and in explaining, many of the key and day-to-day aspects of modern organizations. For example, if organizations are co-operative how then, do we explain the existence of trade unions? If the workplace is so harmonious and co-operative why is it that workers feel the need to combine to represent their interests? If the workplace is harmonious, why do we have statutes designed to protect workers from harassment and discrimination?

Of course, 'guru' forms of analysis may attempt to explain away organizational features such as trade unions, as distractions. There is the obvious temptation in 'guru' analysis, therefore, to argue that workers are misguided, and join trade unions in the erroneous belief that they need protection from management. However, this is not a very persuasive line of argument when trade union membership is numbered in millions. Alternately, advocates of unitary (Fox, 1985) accounts of organizations, might be tempted to argue that trade unions are some form of historical residual, like the human appendix or the male nipple, trade unions might be considered to be the vestigial remains of times past, some hangover from the early, 'bad old days' of management. In this sense, unitary thinkers might argue that trade unions are a spent force and need no longer be regarded as being worthy of serious study. This may explain why few, if any, of the 'gurus' even mention trade unions in their account of organizations (Collins, 1998; Furnham, 1997). However, we cannot be sure why trade unions are omitted from 'guru' analyses, since the assumptions of these models are never shared with us!

If I am correct in my unpacking, and the 'gurus' have indeed decided that trade unions are superfluous to management studies, then we must acknowledge that the 'gurus' are of course, perfectly at liberty to conclude that trade unions are superfluous to management studies. Yet we must also note that others, more keen to discuss their assumptions in public, are equally at liberty to argue that trade unions are, and will remain, worthy of serious study (see Marchington, 1995). Yet the key point for a practical analysis of organization and management is surely this: where such debate and controversy exists, practical accounts of management, if they are to live up to their marketing, must make some attempt to discuss the relative merits of competing arguments. After all these arguments cannot be wished out of existence, so any decision-maker – whether manager, politician or trade unionist – will have to accept the existence of some level of dissension. The problem, however, for the 'guru', practical account of management is that its tendency to omit, or to dismiss, those aspects of organizations which it finds impractical, unimportant or just plain tedious, does little to develop practical insight on the nature of management, or on the nature of work organizations. Thus while it is only right that we should concede that trade union membership in Britain has declined significantly from its 1979 peak of some 13 million to its current level of around 7 million (*Labour Market Trends*, May 1999), we must also acknowledge that this current membership level represents a significant minority of the workforce (Beaumont, 1995) which continues to exert an influence on both organizational and governmental policy in Britain. The 'gurus' of course, may find unions troublesome or inconvenient for their analysis. But would we not expect 'practical' and useful accounts of management to flag, and to analyse, those matters that are troublesome?

It should be clear then, that 'practical' accounts of organizations cannot simply ignore those things they find uninteresting, nor can they ignore those elements deemed to be less than constructive. Instead if it is to be 'practical', a model of management must be able to account for the assumptions which underscore analysis and shape analytical concerns. So-called practical accounts of organization, with their focus upon co-operation and management, however, fail to explain their analytical focus, and so fail to explain why persistent features of organizational life and persistent institutions, fundamental to organizational practices (such as trade unions) are omitted from so many 'practical' analyses. Thus we might ask:

if organizations are co-operative why do certain groups of Nike's employees suffer beatings at the hands of managers (Boje, 1998)? On more managerialist terrain we might ask: if empowerment is truly important, and if empowerment is to be a key managerial goal, how will an account of organization which fails to consider the wider context, or which fails to explain the role which trade unions play in workplace decision-making, assist managers in restructuring authority at work (see Baruch, 1998; and for rejoinder Collins, 1998b)?

A critical-practical account of organization, then, through its willingness to unpick the ideas of the 'gurus' offers a fuller analysis of work in context. Since it refuses, either to side with or to flatter management, it has the capability to offer insights on organization which illuminate important (though often complex, and sometimes discomfiting) dimensions which should be central to the consideration of practical matters. Through this account of contest and dissent, critical-practical accounts of work and management may be used to demonstrate the essential *impracticality* of the particular, 'practical' account of organizations and their environments offered by the 'gurus' (Collins, 1996). Let us, then, conclude our critical-practical account with a brief analysis of the final dimension, which we observed as being necessary for a sociological account of management. Let us examine, briefly, the nature of human action and interaction.

## Behaviour and Action

Our critical-practical account has cast doubts on the idea that there are competitive imperatives, which impact upon all organizations, forcing them to adopt particular forms and policies. Thus in spite of apparent globalizing market imperatives, we have been able to uncover considerable organizational diversity. There is one area of business, however, where convergence is clear for all to see: the 'guru' business itself!

Thousands of 'guru' titles are produced each year. Yet in spite of this number of titles, and in spite of the apparent diversity of these works, the books penned by management's 'gurus' actually exhibit distinct similarities (see Waters, 1998). The texts, for example, offer similar accounts of management and economics. These 'guru' works define organizations as unitary structures within complex business environments and offer remarkably similar prescriptions for change (Huczynski, 1993; Grint, 1994). Crainer (1998) has suggested that much of this convergence may be due to the growing tendency for guru works to be 'ghost-written'. Yet, shocking as this may be, we might be inclined to forgive the 'gurus' and their ghost-writers, if they were to offer thoughtful and sensible accounts of human action at work.

Alas, I do not feel that forgiveness is due to the 'gurus' or to their 'ghost-writers'. Indeed I would call down a plague on each of their many houses, villas, converted barns and country estates, since having alighted on a particular notion of 'practical' advice, the 'gurus' seem unable to allow for the fact that others may hold distinctive and often competitive notions of 'practical' advice. For example, any form of 'practical' advice as regards management and the processes of management, must contain some account of human action. Any form of 'practical' management, if it is to allow managers to work with, and through others, must have something to say about human action and interaction. As such any 'practical' account of management would have to be based on some model, or at least some notion, of the important features of human psychology and the human condition. Putting this another way, we could say that since management, to a large degree, is about controlling and motivating goal-directed behaviour (Buchanan and Huczynski, 1997), any practical model of management would have to offer some analysis of human goals and motivations.

The 'gurus' of course, do say something on this. But this is precisely the problem. They say *something*; their advice is partial, it is misleading, and so, it is impractical.

The study of human action and interaction is, of course, a complex and contested area of knowledge. When we commit to investigating the debates on human psychology and action, therefore, it becomes terribly difficult to offer 'practical' advice on the terms recognized by the 'gurus', since different models of human psychology and action exist, and each of these models yields radically different forms of advice.

On the highly practical question of designing payment systems, for example, Lockyer (1992) notes that systems of payment, if they are to direct and motivate behaviour must both build from, and tap into, those factors which motivate individuals. The problem, which Lockyer reveals, however, is that a grammar built upon imperatives does little to inform action. Thus Lockyer notes that while the advocates of human resource management argue that it is imperative that we change payment systems, empirical (and biographical) accounts of social psychology, suggest the need for a different form of 'grammar', because of the existence of various and competitive accounts of human motivation, which would tend to yield quite different trajectories for 'practical' management. However, Lockyer observes that, rather than consider, carefully, the tensions and contradictions inherent in the management of payment and reward systems, the 'practical' advice offered by the 'gurus' of human resource management (HRM) tends to quash discussion and considered reflection. He notes:

> HRM in its haste to promote the commitment and involvement of the employee to the organization and often away from the trade union – has ignored much of the knowledge and wisdom of the past. Frequently the operationalization of HRM payment schemes is flawed by internal confusion, contradiction, superficiality, and an ignorance

of those factors, both internal and external to the organization, on which appropriateness and effectiveness of payment systems depend.
(Lockyer, 1992, p. 238)

Lockyer, then, is critical of some of HRM's key proponents. Indeed, by demonstrating the divisions between a number of models of human psychology and motivation, Lockyer shows the spurious and impractical nature of the 'guru' exhortations to design and to implement performance appraisal systems of payment and reward.

Unlike the 'gurus', Lockyer's analysis is not glib and it does not offer easy solutions. While I would baulk at calling any of my former tutors, 'fools' (even in the Shakespearean sense), we should note that far from being impractical, Lockyer's critique, and his advice to examine, and to re-examine, a host of factors central to the design and implementation of payment systems (often ignored by HRM's 'gurus') is, in fact, highly practical. The caution and reflection he counsels, for example, helps to explain to managers why the management of payment systems is so fraught and problematic. Yet, at the same time, Lockyer's analysis is geared to limit the upset and disruption, which we could expect would be associated with managing changes in remuneration and reward systems. In this sense, Lockyer's analysis, and his counsel to reflect upon, and to unpick HRM, is 'practical', but by a form of calculus somewhat removed from that of the 'gurus'. It is 'critical-practical' in its intent and in its outcome because it seeks to undermine the 'grammar', which facilitates the vocabulary of management's 'gurus'.

In the remainder of this book we will attempt to build a 'critical-practical' account of the 'fads' and 'buzzwords' put forward by the 'gurus' of management. Starting from a sociological account of management, which attempts to link the three levels, and dimensions, of analysis noted above, we will attempt to provide the 'consumers of scholarly management rhetorics' (Abrahamson, 1996, p. 279) with the ability to locate, understand and critique the 'gurus'. On these terms the text is not anti-management, yet neither is it a homage to 'management' (as many 'guru' texts tend to be), nor is it a hagiology to the 'gurus' (as some of the commentaries on the 'gurus' have tended to be; see Kennedy, 1996). Instead this work is intended as a critical account of management and organization, which through the careful deconstruction of the ready-made science of the 'gurus', is designed to offer useful insights to careful scholars, and to thoughtful managers alike.

## Summary

This chapter has attempted to demonstrate the importance of adopting a theoretically grounded approach to the study of management. By offering a brief critique of the prescriptions and ideas of the popular 'gurus' of management, it has attempted to expose and to unpack the assumptions of the 'gurus', in order to demonstrate the limits of their 'practical' approach. The chapter has argued that the vocabulary of management takes its force and meaning from a grammar founded upon imperatives. Accordingly, it has sought to construct an alternative account of management fads and buzzwords, which is based upon a 'non-imperative grammar'.

Rooting an alternative approach to the analysis of management, within a sociological form of analysis, the chapter has attempted to demonstrate the merits of what has been termed a 'critical-practical' account of management. It is this critical-practical perspective which we will use to underpin our analysis of management fads and buzzwords. However, before we can do this we must first consider, carefully, the nature of management. Accordingly, in chapter 2, we will pause to consider the nature of management, so that we might be able to understand, and to locate those factors which shape and condition management thought and practice.

## Note

1    My preference for 'the fool' as a body of thought is informed by Orwell's account of the fool, since Orwell seems to suggest that, as an individual, the fool will be powerless to resist larger forces and movements which, ultimately will swallow him and his quest for decency.

   Discussing the work of Orwell, Atkins (Atkins, 1971, *George Orwell: A Literary Study*), notes that in his attempts to fight for 'decency' Orwell did not see himself cast in the role of fool: 'The Fool was a Chestertonian figure who really held out no hope for the world of decency [while acting for change] the net would be closing in on him and he would be powerless to resist it' (Atkins, 1971, p. 2).

# 2  The Nature of Management

## Introduction

So far we have attempted to explain the limits of the 'guru' account of management and organization. Using the analyses of Latour (1987) and Chia (1996) we have argued that the works of the 'gurus' are limited, and remain limiting, because users of 'guru theory' (Huczynski, 1993) confront a ready-made science of management which actively discourages reflection and reflexivity. As an attempt to overcome the limitations of this approach to the analysis of management and organization, a 'critical-practical' alternative has been offered. Through an analysis of 'practical' management and its 'critical-practical' alternative, we have attempted to show how the 'grammar' of management gives force and meaning to management's fads and buzzwords, and through this analysis, have attempted to highlight (1) the need to unpack and to unpick 'guru theory' and (2) the inseparability of theory and practice.

In this chapter we will continue with the theme of unpacking as we attempt to unpick the concept of management. Accordingly, this chapter will argue that we must locate *and* understand the nature of management itself, if we are to make sense of the fads and buzzwords of the consulting industry. We must then, as we shall see, do more than 'explore' the fads and buzzwords of management.

Perhaps an analogy will help. Generally argument by analogy is unhelpful since such forms of argument seldom bear close scrutiny. The analogy offered below, therefore, is presented merely as an illustration; as an attempt to demonstrate the purpose, and the central arguments of this chapter, in an understandable and (hopefully) a memorable fashion.

## 'Exploring' Management?

Explorers visit. They climb peaks; they hack through jungles; they sketch maps; take snapshots and collect artefacts. Sometimes they collect humans as artefacts. Explorers visit and when they return home, they tell wild tales, at court, of the strange sights and peoples they have encountered.

This is the problem. What explorers find is strange to them and remains strange because, often, no real attempt is made to understand, and to locate the artefacts, practices and peoples they have discovered.

As we shall see, numerous explorations have been made of 'management'. We know for example, that managers seem to have a preference for certain forms of activity. We know that managers spend a lot of time in meetings. We know that the working pattern of managers is fragmented and disjointed. We know that often, managers lack a formal education in management, and we know that managers tend to be male (Rees, 1996; Hales, 1993). Yet while all this is known, and has been uncovered through 'exploration', much remains which is unknown within this framework. This 'exploration' informs us that 'managers' exist and that managerial activity has a frenetic character. But if we confine ourselves to this 'exploration' alone, we will be in danger of accepting modern management as a natural phenomenon, whose existence was inevitable. Thus, a simple exploration of management would tend to lead to a timeless analysis.

Of course, this analysis would, it is true, tell us something of management activity. However, we would know little of the nature of management, how it has developed and how it may change. To understand the fads and buzzwords of management, therefore, we must do more than 'explore' these fads and buzzwords and we must do more than simply 'explore' 'management'.

Sometimes when explorers return home to tell their tales of far-off lands, missionaries and zealots are dispatched overseas to visit these lands. Where the explorers roved and climbed, the missionaries settle because their role is to make the strange, familiar. Missionaries do this, however, not by attempting to comprehend what is strange to them, but by attempting to convert what is strange to what they know; to what they prefer and feel comfortable with. Missionaries, then, do not explore; they civilize. Missionaries gather souls. And the history of the missions suggests that while missionaries prefer to harvest the souls of the living, they will, where necessary, kill that which is mortal to allow the immortal soul to flourish.

Management has its 'explorers'. It also has a zealot band of missionaries. Like the religious missions, management's missionaries come with messages of salvation through education (Pattison, 1997). In common with the religious missions, the missionaries of management do not have to trouble themselves, to locate and to analyse what they find, because they have come to change and to convert. And this is the problem. Where 'explorers' simply miss much of what is important, the missionaries misunderstand or misrepresent what they find, since they are driven by the belief that the ways of the mission, and of the missionary, represent a preferable set of practices and a preferred way of life. For example, Deal and Kennedy (1982) in their discussion of corporate cultures, and the need to understand and to manage cultures, bemoan as they see it, the tendency towards relativism!

Currently management's 'missionaries' bring messages of salvation (Pattison, 1997) through the pursuit of empowerment and delayering (Hilmer and Donaldson, 1996). Previously, the missionaries of management promised salvation through such routes as science and scientific management (see Huczynski, 1993).

This book has a purpose, but unlike the zealots and missionaries of management it is not 'on a mission' since, ultimately, the missionaries of management come to know even less than the 'explorers'. While the explorers learn only a little from their travels they, at least, learn something. The 'missionaries' however, come to teach. They do not come to learn, and so, they work over time, to deny the existence and validity of 'native' knowledge and experience, gathered over generations (see Hilmer and Donaldson, 1996).

Aside from 'explorers' and 'missionaries' there is a third grouping, sometimes dispatched to foreign climes. This group we will call 'researchers', for convenience. Researchers attempt to understand. They do this by attempting to uncover notable aspects and features of the phenomena they study. They ask questions and engage in forms of activity designed to offer insight. While missionaries work to change, and to overthrow that which is 'native', or that which is deemed to be in need of reconstruction, researchers tend to choose a different path.

Unlike the missionary who works to implement, and so, must work to privilege a particular belief system, the researcher may well adopt a position at some distance from both the natives and the mission (Pocock, 1988) in order to ask: What happens when systems collide? What is the nature of the indigenous system? How does 'the mission' seek to change 'the native'? Is the missionary discourse stable? Is the discourse all-encompassing or does it change according to its setting? To what extent do the natives adopt, reject or modify the discourse of the mission? Have the natives always lived as they do now? Why do we have missionaries?

Or in more secular terms; what is the nature of management? Do managers attempt to implement 'guru' ideas? How can we explain the rise of the management 'guru'? Is it possible to reject the 'gurus' and maintain a place within management?

Eschewing the position adopted by 'the missionaries' of management, and rejecting the limited understanding of management offered by management's 'explorers', this chapter will attempt to research the nature of management. Through this analysis we will attempt to locate, both management, and the practices of managing, as social phenomena which have developed historically. We will use this departure point to make sense of management, and to allow us to analyse the contemporary discourse of management.

Accordingly, the chapter is structured as follows. We begin by raising the question: What is management? This as we shall see is a crucial undertaking, yet it is a question, and a dimension for analysis, curiously absent from many contemporary discussions of management and managing (Collins, 1998).

By considering the question 'What is management?', we will be better placed to (1) understand the complexity of management, (2) comprehend the problematic nature of managing, and (3) recognize the attraction which the 'guru' fads and buzzwords hold for management. This analysis of the nature of management will be used to underpin and to inform our discussion of management's fads and buzzwords in the chapter which follows this, and in the remainder of the book as a whole.

Let us begin, then, by asking the question: What is management?

## Management and Managing

Mary Parker Follett, perhaps one of the earliest commentators on management, defines management as 'the art of getting things done through people' (quoted in Rees, 1996, p. 1). Apparently accepting this as a useful summary, Rees offers his own version of this definition of management. Management he tells us: 'is "getting work done through others"' (Rees, 1996, p. 1). Heller (1972) too, seems to accept this as a useful summary of, and departure point for, the discussion of management, since he offers a remarkably similar definition.

At one level, of course, this is a perfectly adequate and sensible description of management. Managers after all, are paid to organize, to command, and to control the work of others. It seems sensible to suggest, therefore, that management is, indeed, about achieving results through people. But does this, so-called definition really tell us much? In fact, does it tell us anything about management and managing? Probably not, because as we shall see, it obscures more than it illuminates.

Mary Parker Follett has recently been rediscovered and rehabilitated within management circles. Some years ago Follett would have been considered a curiosity; part of the prehistory of modern management (Thompson and McHugh, 1990). However, in recent years a number of commentators (see Sheldrake, 1996; Graham, 1995) have revisited the work of Follett in an attempt to show the continuing relevance of Follett's philosophy of management.

Sheldrake (1996) observes that the key to comprehending Follett's work is to understand that: 'Follett was not a "business woman" or a conventional academic. Instead she was a political, social and management thinker who derived her early inspiration from involvement in social work in her native city of Boston' (Sheldrake, 1996, p. 73).

As a result of this orientation, Follett's supporters tell us that she was equipped to deal with a range of issues and phenomena, which had tended to be neglected in discussions of management. Follett's advocates, for example, argue that, somewhat in advance of her time, her discussion of management and managing showed a concern with groups. They argue that this concern with groups reflected Follett's experiences of civic politics and decision-making. Thus we are told that Follett's interest in civic politics and decision-making led her to argue that commercial management should be refocused to concentrate on channelling conflict, in order to secure and to maintain group consent. Indeed, she argued that this approach to management would encourage individuals to turn from the pursuit of their selfish and self-interested goals, in order to define and to pursue the goals of the larger collective. As Sheldrake observes, Follett's whole philosophy of management turned upon the idea that: 'through the clash of ideas, participants in a group, enterprise or by extension, a whole society would come to recognise their own interest in the wider interest rather than the narrow confines of the self' (Sheldrake 1996, p. 77).

For Follett, then, management was to be regarded as participative. Thus Follett argued that management turned upon the ability to channel group activities, and group conflicts, in order to harness the constructive potential contained within these. Sheldrake tells us: 'She began by accepting the complexity of social situations and focusing on the working groups and the need to integrate its efforts within the productive whole' (Sheldrake, 1996, pp. 77–78).

This account of Follett's approach to management, of course, contrasts quite starkly with Taylor's analysis and account of management (Taylor, 1911; Braverman, 1974). Indeed, where Follett's analysis shows a concern to foster participation, and to unite and reunify the conduct of managerial matters, Taylor's analysis is built upon 'separation'.

Taylor argued that, left to their own devices, workers toiled inefficiently because they based their practices upon custom and tradition. Taylor argued, therefore, that managers should take onboard the responsibility for the redesign of work, to ensure the overthrow of these troublesome craft traditions. Thus Taylor advocated the implementation of a more efficient form of working, based upon the analysis of 'time and motion', which he termed 'scientific management'. As compared to Follett, Taylor's preferred form of working, and Taylor's preferred system of management, paints a rather bleak picture of humanity. Where Follett sees the potential for individuals to work collectively for the greater good, Taylor tends to see only self-interest. So, where Follett sees the opportunity for a collaborative system of working, where all contribute to the processes of managing, Taylor works to ensure the rigid separation: management from workers; planning from execution.

Both Follett and Taylor, of course, have their critics. Indeed those who have attempted to rehabilitate Follett as a 'prophet', have themselves been subject to academic scrutiny (Calas and Smircich, 1996). What we have to ask is this: Can a definition of management, which so easily incorporates quite different notions of management, be useful? Can a definition of management which simply states that management is 'getting work done through others', and so accepts simultaneously, and without comment, the competitive visions of management put forward by Follett and Taylor, really be considered as a useful starting point for analysis? Probably not. Indeed this contest, disguised within the definition of management as 'getting work done through others', suggests that far from attempting to develop a simple definition of 'management', we should, instead, work to understand the complexity of management, its concepts and practices.

Accepting that we should, indeed, attempt to understand management in all its complexity, Hales notes a key problem. This is a difficulty, which confronts all those who would attempt to analyse the nature of management. Hales notes:

> Few modern phenomena so patently pervasive and systematically scrutinised as 'management' have been so beset by ambiguity, confusion and, at times obfuscation. In its English usage the term 'management' denotes, *inter alia*: an organisational function, an organisational stratum, an occupational group, an organisational process, an interpersonal process and an intra-personal process (self management), each with their own associated body of knowledge and set of skills. The term is employed as both noun and verb, descriptively and normatively, approvingly and pejoratively.
>
> (Hales, 1993, p. 1)

For Hales, therefore, the concept of 'management' is essentially ambiguous. Indeed, quite unlike the glib discussions offered by Rees (1996) and by Heller (1972), Hales' analysis shows management to be complex and somewhat lacking in shape (De Cock and Hipkin, 1997). Thus Hales notes that 'management' is simultaneously, verb and noun; a function and a process; a body of knowledge and a set of techniques. Perhaps unsurprisingly, given this complexity, the literature on management, itself, mirrors these amorphous and ambiguous qualities, and so exhibits a considerable diversity of form and process.

It is worth examining this diverse literature in a little more detail.

## Accounts of Management and Managing

Generally, student-oriented texts on 'management' (see Mullins, 1996) trace the origins of modern management thinking and writing to a few key commentators. This group of commentators – we might call them the 'usual suspects', since they form the initial 'identity parade' of so many management textbooks – would include Taylor (1911), Fayol (1949), Follett (1941) and Barnard (1938). Hales captures this rather well. He notes: 'If all philosophy is a set of footnotes to Plato, management theory is, in large measure, a reply to Fayol's original memo' (Hales, 1993 p. 3).

Fayol's conception of management sets out the management functions, which he considered would be required by organizations. This conception of management is somewhat formulaic. Indeed it might conveniently be summarized (and committed to memory) as *PO3C*. Thus for Fayol management is a process involving:

- planning
- organizing
- commanding
- co-ordinating
- controlling.

Yet, while Fayol is clearly regarded as one of the founders of management thinking, his account of the functions of management tells us little *about* management and managing. Taylor's managers for example clearly plan, organize, command, co-ordinate and control (Taylor, 1911; Braverman, 1974). Yet Follett's managers, acting quite differently, also engage in all these tasks.

Since Fayol's *PO3C* formula fails properly to discriminate between these philosophies, it must be viewed as doing little to illuminate the diverse processes of management. However, Fayol's formula does allow us to see, in relief, the limitations of Rees' preferred definition. Far from offering a useful summary of the nature of management, therefore, Rees' definition serves only to highlight the fact that the nature of planning, organizing, commanding, co-ordinating and controlling advocated by Taylor and by Follett, in their attempts to get work done through others, are in fact radically different.

If we are to locate and understand management, therefore, we must go beyond the definition offered by Rees, and we must do more than summarize the general processes of management. This has led some to attempt to analyse what managers actually do at work.

### What Do Managers Do?

Recognizing the limitations inherent in analysing 'management' as a range of abstract processes, a number of authors have attempted to look more closely at what managers actually 'do'. Largely these accounts of what managers 'do' are practical manifestations of the abstract categories/ processes of work identified by Fayol. Mintzberg (1973), for example, views managers as fulfilling a number of roles. Managers, he tells us, in carrying out their work, take on 'interpersonal' roles, 'informational' roles and 'decisional' roles. Kotter (1982), in a similar fashion, notes the multi-dimensional character of managerial work. Thus Kotter notes that managers set and implement agendas, and to accomplish this must build and use networks.

Noting differences, as well as similarities in the works of eight key scholars who have attempted to study what managers 'do', Hales (1993) concedes that in comparison to Fayol's formulaic account of management, these scholars do help to illuminate the essential complexity of management. What we routinely call managerial work, therefore, is revealed by these scholars as encompassing a range of tasks. At its most basic, then, management might be thought of as involving some combination of specialist-technical work and general managerial-administrative work. Indeed, Hales points out that the accounts of the processes of managerial work, offered by the likes of Mintzberg and Kotter, serve to draw our attention to the fact that managers spend a considerable part of their day in meetings and in 'networking'. In this way, the studies of what managers actually do at work, serve to highlight a lack of definition as regards the duties and processes of the managers. Noting this as an important issue for the study of management, Hales argues that a key part of the content of managerial work seems to be concerned with negotiating the boundaries of management action. Thus Hales suggests that managers must attempt to give shape to their roles, while attempting to inscribe meaning upon their activities. It seems sensible to suggest, therefore, that the ideas and techniques proffered by the management 'guru' industry may hold an attraction for managers, because they seem to promise to bring meaning and shape to the processes and problems of managerial work.

For the moment, however, we will continue with our analysis of the available literature on management, since analyses of the process and content of 'management' have led some (Sayles, 1964; Stewart, 1976) to study the form of managerial work. Studies of the 'form' of managerial work show its frenetic character, and have led some to argue for the redesign of management.

## The Form of Managerial Work

Managerial work is focused upon contact and communication. Managers, it seems, spend a lot of time in meetings or engaged in more *ad hoc* forms of communication, both with peers and with subordinates. The time the manager actually spends in the office, therefore, is likely to be filled with interruptions. Small wonder then that accounts of the form of managerial work portray it as frenetic, disjointed and reactive. If in the state of nature the life of man is *nasty, brutish and short*, then the life of the manager, it seems, is *noisy, busy and short-termist*.

Luthans and Davis (1980) argue that accounts of the form of managerial work pinpoint the need for major changes in management. Appalled at the frenetic and reactive character of managerial work, they argue that management would be more efficient and effective, if managers could only act a little more proactively. Others however (see Kotter, 1982) do not see the frenetic character of managerial work as representing managerial incompetence. Instead, they argue that the essential nature of managerial work – its ambiguity and its search for congruence – causes managers to adopt such forms and patterns of working.

Kotter (1982) argues, therefore, that managerial work is frenetic by nature. Managers are drawn into reactive patterns of behaviour because this is the very nature of managerial work. Thus Kotter argues that the work of the manager is characterized by meetings, negotiations, networking and by reactive forms of action and decision-making because, if managers are to achieve any success in dealing with complex and ambiguous problems, they must cultivate and maintain a network of contacts and supporters. Hilmer and Donaldson (1996) however, suggest that both Luthans' and Davis' damning account of managerial work, and Kotter's more forgiving version, misrepresent the form of managerial work. Thus Hilmer and Donaldson argue that managers are much more reflective and cerebral than these authors allow for. Hilmer and Donaldson concede that while at work, managers may well be subject to constant interruption and do seem to dash from meeting to meeting. However, they warn us that this does not mean that managers are not reflective practitioners. Nor does it imply that managers lack proactivity. As a former manager, Hilmer would probably concede that, sometimes, it can be difficult to find the time or the space to think things through when at work. Yet both Hilmer and Donaldson have observed that managers do not only work when 'at work'. Indeed, they cite the case of Geneen (the former head of ITT) for example, who each night would take reams of documents home *for analysis* (see also Geneen with Moscow, 1986). Hilmer and Donaldson suggest, therefore, that studies of the form of managerial work tend to misrepresent the extent to which managers reflect upon and plan their activities, future plans and actions when at work. In addition they also argue that managers engage in reflection and planning when they are not 'at work'; when they are in the bath, in bed, on the golf course, or increasingly, in their own private studies.

However, while these studies of the processes, content and form of managerial work serve to illuminate aspects of 'management', and while these studies help us to understand management as a complex, political activity, they do not actually do much to illuminate the nature of management, since they do not allow us to locate or to contextualize management and its development. For example, the accounts of management discussed so far tend to accept management as a natural phenomenon, when historical forms of analysis reveal management to be a recent, upstart construction (Child, 1981). Furthermore, the accounts offered so far tend to begin from the starting point that 'management' (the organizational function and organizational, interpersonal and intrapersonal process) is equivalent to what 'managers' (the organizational stratum and occupational grouping) do! But 'management' is not just what 'managers' do. Much of 'management' is performed by people who never get to glory in the title 'manager', and if we fail to allow for this fact, we will cloud our analysis.

In an attempt to offer a clearer analysis Hales (1993) provides an account of 'managing through organization'. This account of managing through organization might be considered 'critical-practical' inasmuch as it seeks to alter the grammar applied to the analysis of 'management'.

## Managing Through Organization (MTO)

Hales' (1993) account of 'managing through organization' offers a distinctive perspective on management. Indeed it would probably be more appropriate to say that Hales offers a distinctive perspective on managing and organizing. Rather than focus upon organizations and management as things, as objective concrete identities, therefore, Hales is more concerned to analyse organizing and managing as processes. Noting that 'management' as a proper noun used to describe a particular occupational grouping is a recent addition to the English language, which acts to separate, (somewhat falsely), 'managing' from 'working' and 'management' from 'workers', Hales tells us that his MTO analysis:

> examines the nature of the management process and shows how it has become separated from the work process and dispersed through different managerial jobs. Consequently, management has become not simply the management of work, but the problematic and contested management of other people, a characteristic exhibited in the content and form of managerial work.
>
> (Hales, 1993, p. xviii)

It is worth considering this quotation in a little more depth before considering the MTO framework.

## The Separation of Management

For Hales 'management' has become *separated* from 'work'. Fayol (1949), Follett (1941) and Barnard (1938), as we have seen, all variously detail the functions of the manager. Managers plan, organize, command, co-ordinate and control (*PO3C*) the activities of others. Management, then, is something distinct and separate from 'work'. This 'separation' of managerial work is probably best described by Taylor (1911).

Taylor, as you will recall, showed a concern with efficiency and control. He argued that the traditional practices, processes and rhythms of craft working were inefficient and inappropriate for modern factory production. Thus Taylor was concerned that industrial development, and advances in material prosperity, were being delayed because managers had allowed workers to retain discretion over the practices, processes and rhythms of work. In order to overcome such inefficiencies, Taylor argued that management would have to take responsibility for the design and allocation of work. Using principles designed by Taylor, and labelled by him as 'scientific management', managers were exhorted to analyse the work rhythms and processes of craft working, so that inefficiencies might be removed through the systematic and scientific process of job design.

Taylor's 'scientific management' led to increased specialization at work. In the name of efficiency, traditional craft principles were broken up by 'scientific management'. Thus instead of having one skilled craftsman perform the whole range of production tasks, Taylor advocated that work tasks and processes should be broken into component parts and then re-allocated, piecemeal, to a number of workers.

Under Taylorized forms of working, therefore, specialized workers engage in the fabrication of components or sub-assemblies. Each worker is dedicated to a fraction of the production process previously performed by skilled craftsmen. Yet by working together, these relatively unskilled workers produce more output than could be produced by each skilled craftsman performing separately the whole range of production tasks. Under Taylorism, however, cost-savings occur not only through the increased throughput of work which specialization allows. Cost-savings also occur because managers no longer have to reward highly skilled individuals. Taylorist principles, therefore, allow management to 'deskill' work. This deskilling, built upon specialization and upon the division of labour, represents the cornerstone of Taylorism (Braverman, 1974).

However, it is not only workers and work processes which become more specialized under Taylorism. Using Taylorist principles of work design and allocation, the organization as a whole becomes more specialized. As attempts are made to secure and to maintain a separation between 'managers' (who have responsibility for designing and allocating work) and 'workers' (who have responsibility for executing work tasks as designed and allocated by management), so specialist groups of work-study engineers, and middle managers are brought forth, to develop, and to maintain, the new system of work design and work allocation. Thus under Taylorism, the complex division of labour on the shopfloor is mirrored by the development of a division of labour within the ranks of management.

In many accounts of management this 'separation' between managing and working is discussed as a natural feature of the social organization of production. Fayol (1949), Barnard (1938) and the other 'founding fathers' of modern management, for example, discuss the separation of 'management' from 'working' *as if* this must be the case; *as if* this is a natural product. But it is not. Hales argues: 'Management as a separate function is a socially contingent phenomenon which has come to appear as a technically necessary one' (Hales, 1993, p. 8). Indeed when we consider Taylorism a little more carefully, and a little more critically, the socially contingent nature of management under Taylor's 'scientific management' becomes apparent (Thompson and McHugh, 1995; Littler, 1982; Braverman, 1974).

Critical accounts of Taylorism and of Taylorized production systems, for example, show that managers found it difficult to secure and maintain a separation between 'management' and 'working'. Workers, for example, would connive to restrict output (Taylor referred to this as systematic soldiering). They would absent themselves from work, either individually or collectively (by organizing strikes). Equally they might sabotage equipment and/or output (Beynon, 1979). Often they would simply quit to seek work elsewhere – Ford's River Rouge car plant, for example, had a quit rate running in excess of 300 per cent in 1913 (Beynon, 1979).

The separation of management, then, carries no sense of inevitability. Indeed the process is complex, problematic and difficult to maintain. Hales notes that the process: 'Was contested and resisted . . . for this and other reasons, the separation of management functions may be diverted, incomplete or, indeed reversed' (Hales, 1993, p. 6). Together with this analysis of the *separation* of management, Hales also notes the *dispersion* of management.

## The Dispersion of Management

The *separation* of management implies a division between 'management' and 'working', and between 'managers' and 'workers'. Yet, as we saw in our brief discussion of Taylorism, management itself also exhibits some degree of separation. We have 'office managers' and 'plant managers', 'marketing managers' and 'production managers', 'manufacturing managers' and 'human resource managers', 'junior' and 'senior' managers. All of these 'managers', manage. Yet no one manager performs all of the management tasks and processes required. Instead each performs an aspect of the overall function of management which is dispersed throughout the organization. Indeed it is worth observing that, since the division of labour is often contested, the separation of 'management' from 'working' is likely to be incomplete (Goodrich, 1975). In this sense, and with the separation of management incomplete, 'management' will be dispersed throughout the organization as a whole and not just throughout the 'management' hierarchy. In the study of industrial relations, for example, it is common-place to observe that collective bargaining, the process by which the contract of employment is *jointly authored* by management and trade unions, enhances the rights and the dignity of workers, since the process of forming and maintaining the collective bargain, places limits on management prerogative (Flanders, 1970). Viewed in these terms, the institutions concerned with collective bargaining might be viewed as 'dispersing' factors, which place limits on the separation of management.

Indeed, this reading of Hales' analysis seems to suggest that the dispersion of management makes the separation of management problematic to achieve, and problematic to maintain. In an attempt to give management both shape and meaning, therefore, Hales argues that managers attempt to call upon institutional resources, and organizational symbols, in an attempt to bolster the separation of management. Thus, Hales argues, that management should be viewed as achieving its effect *through organization*. Let us examine this third aspect of Hales' analysis of management.

## MTO

Our analysis of the content of managerial work demonstrates the extent to which management seems to hinge upon communication and interaction. For Hales, this implies that managing is a social process. Managing, as most commentators would concede, is a process conducted through the interaction of human agents. Managers, however, do not just 'pass the time of day' in their various interactions. While managers' interactions are social, they must also be viewed as political, since through their meetings, discussions and interactions, managers attempt to influence and to shape the behaviour of others, so that they might be 'persuaded' to work in pursuit of certain objectives. Management, then, is a social and a political form of activity. Indeed, the analysis of Kotter (1982) suggests that management is social and political by nature.

This makes managing problematic. Managers, for example, may fail in their attempts to 'persuade' others to pursue those objectives which they feel are important. Equally, managers may be successful in securing consent for, and even commitment to their plans, only to find a gulf between their hopes and achievements. McLoughlin and Clark (1994), for example, discuss managing technological change at work, as a process whereby managers act as the creative mediators between the potential hoped for, and the actual outcomes realized through the change process. Scott (1994) shows a similar gap between plans/hopes and outcomes in his study of the attempts of British managers to develop, and implement a system of management commonly referred to as 'human resource management' (HRM).

Case studies of management, therefore, reveal the complexity of management and its problematic nature. However, these case studies also demonstrate that, in their attempts to secure management (separated), discretion over planning, organizing, commanding, co-ordinating and controlling, managers and other actors (Abrahamson, 1991) have sought to institutionalize organizational arrangements designed to facilitate, and to legitimate particular forms of activity.

## Summary

Summarizing our discussion so far, it is worth reminding ourselves that Hales' analysis, in comparison to earlier discussions of the functions, processes and forms of managerial work, unpacks the concept of management, to offer us a clearer and more integrated account of the nature of management. Compared to these earlier discussions, Hales' analysis does not require our view of management to be timeless. Indeed he demonstrates that management as it appears to us today is not 'natural'. Management has developed and has changed through time, and Hales' analysis allows us to trace these developments. Contrary to the forms of analysis promoted by the founding fathers of management (and retold in countless OB textbooks), Hales' analysis also shows us that management has become increasingly 'separated' and 'dispersed', as capitalist economies have developed large scale organizations, and as these organizations have developed complex hierarchies to secure co-ordination.

This analysis of the separation and dispersion at work assists our analysis of management in a number of ways. First, it allows us to see the complex, socio-political nature of management, since it allows us to see the contests over, and within the 'separation' of management. Second, this account of the separation and dispersion of management also allows us to see the potential for conflicts within the ranks of the occupational strata, which we, quite carelessly, term management. Third, Hales' account suggests that managers might be viewed as actors who must attempt to create meaning from ambiguity, so that some structure may be placed upon organizational tasks. Thus managers might be viewed as social actors who, themselves, must struggle to create meaning while attempting to be symbols for others (Hatch, 1997). Finally, as we shall see below, Hales' analysis also allows us to understand how, and why, the management process might take different forms in different places, and at different times.

## The MTO Framework

An understanding of the problematic nature of management endeavour shapes Hales' MTO framework. Echoing Fayol's (1949) initial *PO3C* formula, Hales offers his own MTO framework for the analysis of the management process, forms of organization and the work of managers. Thus Hales argues that the process of management 'subsumes five conceptually distinct, if, in practice, intertwined elements' (Hales, 1993, p. 2). He argues, therefore, that the process of managing work, in general terms, involves:

- deciding/planning what is to be done
- allocating time and effort
- motivating or generating effort
- co-ordinating and combining disparate efforts
- controlling what is to be done and ensuring this conforms with the original plans/intentions.

This framework, which we might summarize as *PAM2C*, Hales offers as a general framework for analysing different forms of the organization and management process. Taylorism, or 'scientific management', for example, might be expressed within this *PAM2C* framework as follows:

- *Planning*: Centralized. There is a clear separation between 'management' and 'workers'. 'Management' claims a monopoly on planning and designing the activity of workers.
- *Allocating*: Through a complex division of labour. Time and effort are allocated through a complex division of labour which sub-divides tasks.
- *Motivating*: Extrinsically. Taylorism is based on the assumption that workers do not seek intrinsic satisfaction from their work. For Taylor, workers are motivated by high wages.
- *Co-ordinating*: Externally. Much of the co-ordination of activity within a Taylorized system of working is achieved through the physical flow of work itself. Thus workers are co-ordinated and paced by the speed of their machines or by the pace of the production line as a whole. Beynon (1979) for example, shows how managers in the Ford plant he studied, not only co-ordinated activity but sought to extend and increase worker effort by, surreptitiously, increasing the speed of the production line. Beynon also shows, however, how employees worked together to restrict the ability of management to practise 'speed up'.
- *Controlling*: By rule. Under Taylorized systems of working, workers toil within a detailed system of rules. The contract of employment spells out these rules as a set of duties and practices, and spells out, too, the penalties and punishments consequent upon failure to observe these rules. Here we see clearly, *management through organization*. The recalcitrant employee does not face his/her manager. The recalcitrant employee is not called to account by any, one, manager. Instead the recalcitrant employee confronts the organization as a system of power. While the employee's immediate manager may take responsibility for discipline, the manager fulfils this role by virtue of the position held within the organization. As an individual the manager may have little personal power to control and discipline his/her subordinate. The manager's disciplinary power is organizational. It is achieved through the particular institutional arrangements of the organization. The organization, then, is an instrument, and the manager must strive to be its architect and symbol. The concept of management, therefore, achieves force and meaning from the grammar of management studies, while the practices of managing achieve shape, form and significance via particular organizational arrangements. In short, management achieves its effect through organization.

This account of Taylorism, or scientific management, may be contrasted with accounts of organization, which have variously been described as representing Japanese management (Dore, 1973), clan management (Ouchi, 1981) or as representing organizational 'excellence' (Peters and Waterman, 1982).

## MTO: 'Japanese' Management

In comparison to Taylorized forms of management, which attempt to establish and maintain a rigidly 'separated' form of management, 'Japanese' management is said to offer a reintegrated approach to management. For some (Wickens, 1987) this 'Japanese' approach represents an *anti*-Taylorist or 'post-Fordist' approach to working and managing, since it is said to attempt to tap worker skills and talents by seeking to reunite the conception and execution of work. Other commentators, however, (Garrahan and Stewart, 1992; Collins, 1995; Boreham, 1992; Tomaney, 1990) articulate misgivings over the extent to which 'Japanese' management is truly 'post-Fordist' either in its aims or in its practices. In a related fashion, another group of scholars has suggested that the notion that there is a peculiarly 'Japanese', or Asian, form of management is crude (*The Economist*, 25/07/98) and may serve to disguise the varieties of management practice within any one Japanese organization (Kamata, 1983) and across the Japanese economy as a whole (Sethi *et al.*, 1984).

While accepting the validity of much of this criticism, we will nonetheless use the MTO framework to analyse 'Japanese' management because this comparison (1) offers a useful, if idealized, contrast to our discussion of Taylorism, (2) allows us to see how a different approach to managing and organizing represents not the absence of control but, rather, a different form of management facilitated *through* a different form of organization, and (3) because discussions of 'Japanese' management tend to lead to calls for more 'organic' (as opposed to 'mechanistic') approaches to management. Since such calls for more 'organic' forms of management can be found within the work of all the key 'gurus' of management (see Collins, 1998), we can learn much about the 'gurus' and their analyses, by examining this notion of 'Japanese' management, in spite of its conceptual and empirical flaws.

The MTO framework for 'Japanese management' according to Hales, is as follows.

*   *Planning*: Decentralized. Unlike Taylorism with its rigid separation of 'management' and workers, and its rigid separation of conception and execution, Japanese organizations are said to reintegrate the process of management into aspects of the process of work. Decisions concerning the planning and design of work, therefore, are not the sole prerogative of management. Instead these decisions are decentralized and take place in a consultative (empowered), fashion to allow management to tap into the skills and talents of workers.
*   *Allocating*: Through group decision-making. Unlike Taylorism with its complex and specialized division of labour, 'Japanese' organizations are said to exhibit low levels of individual job specialization. Work groups may specialize in certain tasks and/or processes, however,

within the group there is an expectation that individuals will be able to work flexibly; performing a variety of tasks.

- *Motivating*: Internally. Unlike Taylorism and its assumptions regarding workers' orientations to work, 'Japanese' organizations are said to motivate intrinsically and 'internally'. Thus workers do not need 'the carrot' of high wages to perform their work appropriately. Nor do they need 'the stick' of the 'functional foreman' because, to a large degree, workers are said to have adopted the norms and values of the organization as their own. Thus workers through their teamworking motivate themselves and one another. This, of course, does not mean that workers are not rewarded. They are. However the rewards are deferred and reflect the importance of normative and cultural influences. Thus rewards are linked to loyalty (pensions and promotion) and seniority (a career path).

- *Co-ordinating*: Mutually. Unlike Taylorism where much of the co-ordination of work is enforced externally via machine-pacing, 'Japanese' organizations are said to be co-ordinated, mutually and through teamworking and liaison. Team leaders play a pivotal role in this (Graham, 1994; Bratton, 1991) both informally; working to ensure co-operative relations within teams on an *ad hoc*, day-to-day basis and more formally; by taking responsibility for team briefings and forms of problem-solving activity such as 'quality circles'.

- *Controlling*: Normatively. Unlike Taylorism where workers are formally controlled by a complex set of regulations and procedures and are subject to detailed and personal supervision (see Hamper, 1992), 'Japanese' organizations are said to operate more on the basis of trust. Workers do experience some degree of personal supervision, however, this supervision tends to be subsumed within the rhetoric of teamworking (Parker and Slaughter, 1988), and so tends to be presented as coaching rather than as surveillance (Grant, 1994; Winfield, 1994). It is worth observing, too, that the importance placed upon workers holding key norms and values may allow management to move the focus of control outwith the organization. Thus, detailed recruitment and selection practices designed to deliver what might be termed 'normatively appropriate' workers, may allow management to set a 'control hurdle' at the stage of recruitment which, if it filters individuals effectively, may allow managers to dispense with more visible forms of imposed control within the workplace. We see again, therefore, the ways in which 'Japanese' management achieves its significance, and its effect, through an institutionalized pattern of organizational arrangements.

The MTO framework, and the differences it highlights between Taylorist and 'Japanese' organizations, therefore, allows us to contrast different forms of management. Furthermore, the MTO framework allows us to see how management controls in different ways; achieving its effect through organization. But what we have not been able to rationalize clearly so far, is why management, why MTO, might change its form and processes. Why have we seen an apparent shift from Taylorized, or Ford-style management, towards 'Japanese' or more 'organic' forms of management? This we will address in the section that follows.

The work of Child (1981) offers both a convenient summary of our discussion of the Management Through Organization (MTO) framework, and a useful means of analysing the changing discourse of management.

## Child's Play

Child offers a three-fold framework for the analysis of management. Sharing Hales' (1993) concern that 'management' is more than what 'managers' do, Child argues that the concept of management, as we now understand it, refers simultaneously to three interrelated aspects. Management, then is:

- an activity
- an elite social grouping
- an ideology.

### Management as Activity

Management is, self-evidently, an activity. It is something men and women do, and in the modern era, it is something that men and women are employed by others to do. The roots of the term 'management' are ancient and refer to direction; to manipulation; to the activity of the hand. As the *PO3C* and *PAM2C* frameworks show, management is a process. Indeed these frameworks show that management is a social and a political process. Yet while 'management' is an activity, not all of us are allowed to be 'managers'. Indeed the term, management, is often set aside to describe an occupational stratum or sub-grouping. There must be more to the study of management, therefore, than the analysis of its processes.

Let us look more closely at this elite grouping.

### Management as Elite

Hales (1993) argues that 'management' has become increasingly 'separated' from 'work'. Increasingly, he observes, 'management' has come to denote an organizational sub-stratum or an occupational grouping. Noting the recency of this 'separation', Child (1981) observes that this focus upon 'management' as a distinctive grouping is a comparatively new phenomenon. Indeed Child argues that managers, as we now recognize them, as a distinctive occupational grouping, are 'a historically unique and short-lived group' (Child, 1981, p. 33).

Yet, if the origins of management are ancient why, in recent times, has a specialist and separate grouping, which claims a monopoly on the term, management, developed? To answer this question we must consider a little history.

In a sense we could say that much of the study of history is, in fact, the study of 'management'. For example, the building of such ancient wonders as the pyramids must presuppose management. Any construction project on this scale must presuppose, surely, some exercise of control and direction. Likewise the co-ordinated movement of livestock, men and materials associated with notable historical events such as the Roman conquest of England and the Norman conquest of England in 1066 must also presuppose some management system. Indeed, we might say that the Norman invasion of England implies not only management, but some form of management accounting as evidenced by the 'Domesday Book'.

Hilmer and Donaldson (1996), in fact, might even be prepared to take this line of argument somewhat further. In fact Hilmer and Donaldson suggest that a reading of Scottish history shows the weakness of the 'clan' concept of management which has become popular with management's 'gurus' (see Ouchi, 1981). Commenting on Scotland's 1745 rebellion, which culminated in the Battle of Culloden, Hilmer and Donaldson argue that the defeat the Scots suffered, at the hands of the English, is explicable in terms of the different 'management' systems employed by each of these armies.

Hilmer and Donaldson argue that the loose clan structure of the Scots army caused a fatal lack of discipline. This lack of discipline, they tell us was exploited by the commanders of the English force, who employed bureaucratic forms of organization (see Hatch, 1997). This bureaucratic management system, Hilmer and Donaldson tell us, was the key to England's success. Thus, they argue that the clear command and control structure employed by the English force, allowed for a more disciplined form of action in the English ranks, which enabled the English commanders to see off the uncoordinated attacks mounted by the individual clans which made up the Scottish army.

But if management is truly ancient, and if management is an activity practised by all of us to some degree: we 'manage' our time, we 'manage' our money and now through the likes of Oprah and Jerry Springer, we are exhorted to 'manage' our relationships – how can it be that 'management' is now viewed as the prerogative of a social elite?

To some degree the emergence of management as a social elite is a product of the 'separation' of management. However, and as we saw above, management's separation is the outcome of a socially contingent process; it is not the outcome of a technically necessary process. To understand the emergence of 'management' as a social elite, therefore, we must be able to analyse management in terms of power and control. This, as we shall see, demonstrates the importance of Child's third aspect of management; management as ideology.

## Management as Ideology

The existence of 'management' as an elite presupposes the operation of an ideology. If a group is to arise from the population as a whole, and if that group is to maintain its elevated position, it will require some means to justify its position. This is the role of ideology.

Ideologies justify the social status of elites and, furthermore, serve to legitimate the actions of elites. Discussing the work of Bendix (1956), Anthony (1977) describes management ideology as: 'Those ideas which are espoused by or for those who exercise authority in economic enterprises' (Anthony, 1977, p. 1). This conception of ideology helps us to explain management's current elite social status. Indeed it also allows us to understand why those who controlled and directed the construction of important political and religious projects, such as the pyramids of ancient Egypt were regarded, socially, as being of little importance.

Ideologies of management build from and reflect ideologies of work. Management as a social grouping, therefore, will be important, and will occupy an elite social position, only when/where work is regarded as being an important and worthy aspect of life. Where work carries little importance, management too, will be unimportant.

In ancient Egypt, ideologies of work were ideologies of anti-work because Egyptian theology regarded work as a curse. The gods of Egypt, it was believed, had set aside those who were worthy and important, and did not require that these groups should work. Ancient Egypt's social elites, therefore, did not work. The elites prayed and made war on others. Those 'overseers' (remember management is not so fully 'separated' in this time as to allow us to use properly the term management to describe this stratum), charged with directing and controlling the work of others, therefore, could not constitute a social elite, since their involvement in the process of production demonstrated their low birth and low social standing. Thus the theology and ideology of ancient Egypt had a profound impact upon the nature and form of 'management'. Indeed, the divisions in the fabric of ancient Egyptian society, which our analysis reveals, may help us to understand why history recalls only certain forms of 'management'. For example, history records in considerable detail, the names of those who 'managed' military campaigns long ago, but it does not tend to record the names of those who 'managed' the construction projects of this era.

Management as we currently understand and experience it in Britain, in Europe and in America clearly constitutes a social elite (Abrahamson, 1991; Pattison, 1997). For many groups in western society, high levels of remuneration may be regarded as both an outcome and indicator of social elitism. Viewed in these terms the moneys paid to management indicate its elite social status.

Indeed in comparison to most 'workers', managers are paid vast sums of money (and earn fortunes from share options and bonus payments). *The Sunday Times* (25/10/98), for example, reports that the median level of pay for the chief executives and chairmen of FTSE-100 companies in Britain is £1,035,227 (which compares with a median figure of £823,146 in 1997). This, of course, does not imply that each of these top 100 executives pockets a cool million each year. Some have to get by on as little as £300,000 a year which compares rather unfavourably with Jan Leschly who, as the FTSE-100's highest paid executive, received around £27.5 million in 1998.

However the elite social standing of managers extends beyond the simple fact of their wealth. Being wealthy, of course, does much to elevate one's social standing, so, when managers are paid annual sums in excess of a lottery player's wildest fantasy, it is surely little wonder that management and managers attract attention, and sometimes, a fan base. Yet managers constitute a social elite in our societies, because, together with our voyeuristic interest in their bank accounts, we also demonstrate an interest in their work and in their ideas. In short we seem to want to learn from (and not only about) managers. Thus we buy the biographies of senior managers, we buy the analyses of management's 'gurus' and we make managers the subject of comic-book heroics (see Francq and Van Hamme, 1994).

'Guru' texts and the biographies of hero-managers (Huczynski, 1993), as we saw in our introductory discussion, are big business. These works have been purchased by millions of people – and read by many. However, the media appeal of management's 'gurus' is not confined to the published word alone. Some of the 'hero-managers' (Harvey-Jones, the former head of ICI for example) have enjoyed multi-media success, having produced both books and television programmes for the BBC, while some of the 'gurus' (Tom Peters, for example) have produced syndicated newspaper columns and video cassettes, as supplements to their books.

The rewards accruing to 'management', and the obvious concern to learn from, (and about), management demonstrate the importance of this grouping as an organizational elite and as a social elite more generally. As compared to the 'overseers' of ancient Egypt, management's current elevated social standing must be indicative of a changed ideology of work.

For Weber (1958), this change in attitude reflects the overthrow of earlier belief systems by the Protestant concern that man might become closer to God by labour (see also Giddens, 1991). Thus Weber argued that the Protestant belief that man might worship God in a job well done, served to promote and facilitate a transformation in attitudes to work which was required for the development of capitalist social relations of production.

Gramsci (1976) offers a slightly different analysis of this in his discussion of Americanism and Fordism. Thus Gramsci draws our attention to the importance of prohibition in ensuring the supply of disciplined bodies for factory systems of production.

But why should managers require particular attitudes from workers? Why should managers require an ideology, when their position as a distinctive occupational grouping, and as a specialist organizational sub-stratum gives them the right to issue commands?

## The Need for Ideology

So far we have learned a few things about management. We have learned that the aims and processes of management are ambiguous. Furthermore, we have learned that the boundaries of management activity are permeable and moveable. We have learned too, that management is primarily about control. However, the nature of management, and the nature of the employment relationship, makes this control activity problematic.

Fayol's (1949) *PO3C* framework, as we have seen, highlights the importance of control, in the conduct of management. Similarly Hales' (1993) MTO framework shows the importance of control within management. However, Hales shows that since management is properly viewed as a social-political process, relying on networking and persuasion as much as command and control, managers often find it problematic to secure and to maintain control over the co-operation of others.

A properly social and political view of management, therefore, reveals that attempts to control others will be incomplete, and in some sense, will be self-defeating. For example, we observed that under Tayloristic production methods, managers attempt to secure control over workers and the process of work (1) by claiming a monopoly on decision-making, (2) by specifying, through the contract of employment the duties of workers, and (3) by employing machinery and techniques of production designed to pace the work of employees. Yet the story of Taylorism, as a system of production, is not one where managers simply impose a system of working on employees. Instead sensitive analyses of Taylorism produced by academics (Friedmann, 1967; Blauner, 1973) and by novelists (Torrington, 1996) show the fluidity of power relations, and the ability of workers to resist, to challenge and to reverse managerial prerogative within these particular systems of control.

Hamper (1992), for example, shows that while Taylorist systems seek to specify the roles and tasks of employees, the employees themselves, may use the contract *against* management. So where a contract of employment clearly specifies the job of an employee, the employee can quite legitimately refuse management's *order* to move to another work-station, or to work 'flexibly'. In a similar way, we can see that employees may use the contract of employment to turn in minimal, or minimum, levels of performance. For example, the employees may choose rigidly to work to contract, doing only that work specified in the contract, and doing the work exactly as specified. Under such circumstances, variously called 'work to contract' or 'work to rule', employees make use of what is supposed to discipline and control them, in order to challenge management.

Confronted with such problems, management groups have tended to attempt to supplement direct control of the labour force with less overt strategies of control (Gramsci, 1976; Meyer, 1981), which are designed to give shape, meaning and symbolic significance to managerial endeavours. These less overt strategies of control turn upon ideological appeals. As Anthony (1977) shows, these ideologies espouse the interests of those who own and control economic enterprises. They serve: 'to justify both the way in which work is managed and, indeed, the fact that it *is* managed – by others' (Hales, 1993, p. 68, original emphasis).

Ideological appeals may take different forms. The ideology surrounding Taylorism, for example, is couched in the language of science. Under Taylorist systems of management, the processes of working are managed by specialists, who are skilled in the ways of 'scientific management'. Left to work scientifically, the doctrine of Taylorism states that, managers achieve technical efficiency. More is achieved from less, and so managers and workers achieve mutual benefit and material prosperity. As distinct from the ideological appeal of Taylorism, the ideology of 'empowerment' achieves its force and meaning from a 'grammar' which is couched in terms of a nationalistic competitive imperative (Collins, 1998; Pattison, 1997), which argues that human capacity *must* be freed from the chains of Taylorism, if competitive success/salvation is to be realized (Collins, 1998, 1998a).

These examples demonstrate the ways in which managers make use of organizational arrangements, and an ideologically loaded 'grammar' to facilitate their activities. Thus managers use institutions, in tandem with the 'grammar' and vocabulary provided by their 'gurus' in their attempts to inscribe meaning upon the rhythms and processes of management. Through this inscription, managers hope to animate and orientate (Weick, 1995) their subordinates towards managerial goals.

Yet, while ideological appeals do much to facilitate managerial power, they do not make managers all-powerful. Ideologies, therefore, give shape to management, but only in a tenuous and temporary fashion. Indeed, the contest between Taylorism and the ideology of empowerment, and the subversion of the ideology of Taylorism by the ideological appeal of 'empowerment' (Collins, 1995a) demonstrates that ideologies are not stable. Ideologies of work are a key part of the system of managerial control. They reflect, therefore, the problems and tensions associated with attempts to control the efforts and manners of others. As a system of control, therefore, ideologies are temporary, because they are incomplete.

Confronted with a challenge, ideologies tend to be adapted and modified. Indeed, it is worth noting that the 'gurus' of management have become key players in this process of modification and regeneration. Thus the models and prescriptions of/for management, which have been developed by the 'gurus' since the 1980s might be viewed as recent episodes in a chain of historical events which stretch back over the history of management. In this sense the fads and buzzwords propagated by the 'gurus' reflect the essentially problematic nature of managing, since they represent attempts to give shape and significance to an increasingly fraught and complex process. Modern 'guru' accounts of management, therefore, seek to supply techniques, and arguments, which bring a shape to management (De Cock and Hipkin, 1997), while explaining the social significance of the managerial role in seeing off fierce foreign competition (Pattison, 1997).

However, these 'guru' accounts often overstate the extent to which the nature of managerial control is changed by 'guru' analyses. For example, we saw in our MTO analysis of Taylorism and 'Japanese' management, that in spite of the protests of its supporters, 'Japanese' management does not represent the absence of, or the end of management control. Rather, and reflecting the different context and history of Japan, the MTO framework shows that 'Japanese' management achieves its effect through a different form of organizational arrangement, and derives its meaning from an ideology, often expressed in terms of duty and accountability (Collins, 1999).

Despite the protests of the 'gurus', therefore, the transplant of 'Japanese' management to Britain, and America, has to be viewed as reflecting a modification in management, and not a fundamental change in its character or processes. These modifications reflect, in part, the changed competitive context of these states during the 1970s and 1980s. For example Fukuda (1988) shows that, in reacting to a variety of political and economic crises, the economic and political elites of a range of western countries have argued that there is a need to learn from, and to adopt 'Japanese' management practices if we are not (as the 'gurus' would have it) to perish (Pattison, 1997).

Kanter has offered a similar ideological platform for, and endorsement of management. Building a powerful ideological platform both for management, and for her own particular views on management, Kanter (1989) has argued that far-reaching changes in US management practice represent the only means to safeguard the 'American Way of Life' against the damage which might be done to it by foreign competition.

Yet we need not accept the 'grammar' and vocabulary of the 'gurus'; we need not accept the ideological statements, which have been created to bolster and to support management and its 'gurus'. 'Guru' analyses, as we have seen, use a 'grammar' of imperatives to silence dissent. However, we need not be victims of the 'gurus' (Jackson and Carter, 1998). Given the right tools, we can overcome this attempt at victimization. Thus, we can use a more critical form of scholarship to undermine the 'gurus'. Equally, however, we can use insights derived from our own, lived experience to unpack, and to unpick 'guru' analyses.

Hamper (1992) as we saw earlier is skilled in the art of unpicking management ideology. Through his biography he shows how the ideology associated with the 'gurus' of management, which unlike Taylorism, is built more upon nationalism than on science, is presented to (and interpreted by) employees. Indeed he shows clearly the ideological message behind management's call for such things as quality and commitment:

> Quality represented buyers. Buyers meant sales ... Quality could change the tune and serenade the buyer out of a buck. For living proof all one had to do was glimpse over at Lee Iacocca, the born-again pom-pom boy of Quality High who was currently splattering himself all over media land with galvanic jabber along the lines of 'WE BUILD THEM RIGHT OR WE ALL EAT DOGFOOD'.
>
> (Hamper, 1992, pp. 111–112, original emphasis)

Based upon his experiences with General Motors, however, Hamper argues that the new ideological articulation and affirmation of management lacks substance. In spite of the new ideological affirmations of quality, Hamper knows, deep down, that the managers of General Motors remain 'quantity' obsessed. Similarly academic research studies have shown that for all the talk about 'Japanese'-style management and its overturn of Taylorism, the patterns and processes of 'Japanese' management remain firmly Taylorist (Garrahan and Stewart, 1992; Boreham, 1992).

Our discussion of Management Through Organization, therefore, allows us to see how, and why, management might attempt to change its spots. Furthermore, our analysis demonstrates the manner in which management through organization, as the institutional affirmation of managerial prerogative, modifies to reflect the shifting foundations of ideological representation.

In short, our analysis reveals that ideologies of management change when they are challenged, either from below, or by the competitive marketing activities of other 'gurus' (Abrahamson, 1991). In addition, the MTO framework helps us to understand why management remains open to challenge, since its more qualified 'grammatical construction' allows us to see that management, as a system of control, is incomplete and self-defeating. Furthermore, it is worth noting that this account of 'grammar' and ideology, also allows us to see the limited extent to which 'Japanese' MTO has really changed from the basic principles of Taylorism. Indeed, our three-fold view of management, management as activity, as elite and as ideology, may allow us to begin to rationalize why management has come to constitute such an important elite despite the fact that its form and practices, as espoused in 'Japanese management' seem to have changed very little from the principles of 'scientific management'.

Thus our three-fold view of management facilitates the unpacking of the preferred, 'guru' account of managing:

- *Activity*: Apparently little changed in its basic nature from Tayloristic principles. Minor 'de-separation' of management yet maintained/increased focus upon timing and specification of work. (Fucini and Fucini, 1990; Graham, 1994).
- *Elite*: Management in spite of the pessimism of Hilmer and Donaldson (1996) occupies a privileged position in mainstream society. Its influence spreads beyond simple business matters to influence government, the arts and culture. Many managers as we saw above, are richer than Croesus, while some also enjoy a celebrity status. Richard Branson, the iconic head of Virgin, for example, is as famous, if not more famous than the musicians signed to the Virgin record label which he created.

So how can we explain management's newly acquired and recently elevated standing (Keat and Abercrombie, 1991; Collins, 1998) as a social elite? How is it that through the 'gurus', managers now enjoy the status of 'leaders'? How is it that we have come to view management in heroic terms (see the adventures of Largo Winch, the millionaire in blue jeans, as told by Francq and van Hamme, 1994)? How is it that we have come to see management as something, reinvented – protecting the nation, liberating talent and potential, when in truth, it is little changed either in terms of form, process or substance from the Taylorist principles of mechanized mass production?

The answer lies, at least in part, in the understanding that management now has a grammar, and a newly invigorated ideology – fostered and promoted by the media, and by governmental actors and agencies – which, in spite of a base level of academic dissent, has served to bring new meaning to the ambiguities which dog management. Indeed, we could argue that the tools and techniques associated with initiatives such as Total Quality Management (see chapter 6) and empowerment (see chapter 7) have done much to promote a new symbolism, which portrays managers as both important and heroic.

The 'gurus', of course, have played a key role in all this. Indeed it is the 'gurus' who have sought to provide form and meaning to the processes of management. It is the 'gurus' who have been foremost among those who have worked hard to portray managers as national standard-bearers, carrying the hopes of the nation, within a managerial ideology built upon some mix of neo-liberalism and nationalism (Collins, 1998).

Reflecting this view of the 'gurus' and their importance, we will look towards these important commentators in the chapter which follows. Yet, since the bulk of this book will be dedicated to a critical analysis of management's 'gurus', via a discussion of the terminology they have promoted, the following chapter will pause to consider those who have variously discussed and analysed the works of the 'gurus'. Thus, rather than consider the 'gurus' themselves, we will instead look to a range of accounts written about the 'gurus'. We will offer comment upon those who have themselves, commented upon the commentators of business. Through this I hope to show (1) the ideological set-up and appeal of the 'gurus' and (2) the limitations both of the 'gurus' and of many of the commentaries offered on the 'gurus' and their works.

## Summary

This chapter has attempted to explore the nature of management. Based upon the knowledge that we will be unable to understand properly management's fads and buzzwords until we know something of the nature of management, this chapter has attempted to unpack 'management' so that we might witness this as a complex and ambiguous phenomenon. Rejecting as over-simplified and unhelpful, the normal definition of management as 'getting things done through others', this chapter has argued, instead, that the processes of management resist simplistic attempts at codification. We have contended that the nature of management can seem opaque, because the processes of management tend to lack shape and definition. Recognizing the ambiguous and amorphous character of managerial work (De Cock and Hipkin, 1997), we have used the works of Hales (1993) and Child (1981) to examine both the development of management and its varieties.

Noting that, at root, management reflects a concern to control, which is incomplete, and self-defeating, this chapter has analysed the role of 'ideology' in management's attempts to secure control. Indeed, we have suggested that the analyses offered by the 'gurus' are attractive to managers, and achieve a market presence, because they promise to give shape to the processes of management while diminishing the ambiguities inherent in management decision-making. Thus, we have argued that the key function of the 'gurus' is to provide managers with ideological accounts of managing, which explain, and justify the conduct of management. Pursuing this ideological theme we have also argued that the recognition of management's need to revise and revisit its ideological appeals for control, allows us the means to understand, and to rationalize (1) changes in management discourse and (2) the stability evident within such changes. Thus the chapter concluded by suggesting that the 'new' ideological appeals of the 'gurus' may actually work to disguise stability, and to forestall more fundamental changes in the forms and processes of management.

# 3   The 'Guru' Industry

## Introduction

This chapter will discuss what might be termed the 'guru' industry. Indeed it will offer a framework which might be used to classify and to analyse the various contributors to this industry. Since this chapter, and the framework it offers, builds upon our discussion so far, it should be helpful to spend just a few moments recapping.

In the introduction we spent some time spelling out the key terms used in our analysis. Thus we discussed the first half of this book's title, so that we might be able to understand the variety of ways in which the terms 'guru', fads and buzzwords might be interpreted. Having spent some time analysing the various ways in which these terms might be used, the introduction then attempted to explain that, while this text seeks to take issue with management's fads and buzzwords, it aims to do more than simply debunk the collection of fads and buzzwords presented in this text. In short, the book seeks to go beyond the mere debunking of a managerial vocabulary, because this activity alone will do little to forestall the production and propagation of the new terms which would quickly replace those we had successfully debunked. It is worth reminding ourselves, therefore, that for this text, the fads and buzzwords of management are problematic because they build from a 'grammar' of management, which is, itself, constitutive of an approach to 'thinking' about work which discourages reflective analysis and reflexive action. Thus, in an attempt to encourage a more reflective and reflexive form of study, we spent some time elaborating upon the need to unpack the concepts and ideas which the 'gurus' have been keen to present to us as transparent, and so, unremarkable.

Pursuing this theme of unpacking, our chapter 1 then moved on to examine our subtitle. Building from an analysis which attempted to show the extent of the 'guru' phenomenon (now firmly encased in inverted commas), we argued that 'guru' accounts of management are both limited and limiting, since they fail to offer a developed, and academically useful, account of organization. Thus the chapter argued that, in their haste to supply their customers – not their clients (Burrell, 1997) – with practical assistance and guidance, the 'gurus' have alighted upon a peculiar notion of 'practical' advice which eschews critical reflection and reflexivity.

In an attempt to overcome such a narrow and (spuriously) 'practical' orientation, chapter 1 offered a sociological account of management as a more useful basis for analysis. This sociological description of management was presented as offering a multi-layered account of action; (one which allowed us to locate social action within an organizational context, and which, in turn, allowed us to locate organizations within the context of the wider society), which, it was argued, facilitated a critical account of management. Using this critical account of management to unpack the (spuriously) practical one offered by the 'gurus', chapter 1 concluded by spelling out the benefits, for analysis and action, of adopting a different 'grammatical' approach, designed to offer the foundations of a 'critical-practical' perspective.

Adopting this notion of the 'critical-practical' as our core theme and concern, we then proceeded, in chapter 2, to offer an account of the nature of management. Arguing that many studies of work and organization neglect to analyse management, critically, we maintained that an analysis of the nature and form of the management process helps us to understand, properly, the complexity of management, and the problematic nature of managing.

This current chapter builds upon our discussion so far, in order to analyse the 'guru' industry. Taking our cue from the introduction, we should spend a little while examining this term.

## The 'Guru' Industry

Crainer (1998) argues that the 'gurus' of management constitute an industry. However, he argues that we often have a tendency to misunderstand the nature of the services which these 'gurus' supply. Thus Crainer argues that the 'gurus' of management are not so much part of commerce and industry as a part of the entertainment industry. This is a point echoed by Hopfl (1992) when she argues that 'gurus' might be compared to the performing 'snake-oil salesman' of America's frontier days (see also Jackson, 1996).

In this chapter, however, we will use the term 'guru' industry in a slightly different sense. Where Crainer uses the term to refer, directly, to the 'gurus' of management, we will use the term 'guru' industry to refer to a group of writers and commentators, who live in the shadow (or in the reflected glory) of the 'gurus'. In this sense the term 'guru' industry refers to the (diverse) grouping of writers and commentators who have grown up around the 'gurus', and whose market presence is, in some sense, dependent upon the 'gurus'. Those active in the 'guru' industry then, are not themselves 'gurus'. However they exist symbiotically with the 'gurus', and have drafted works which, in various ways, comment upon, or distil the ideas of the 'gurus'. Those familiar with the sociological literature might like to think of the 'guru' industry as analogous to the 'Braverman industry', the huge body of literature, conferences and careers (see Eldridge, 1983) which grew up around Braverman's *Labor and Monopoly Capital* (1974).

In comparison to the works of the 'gurus' of management, the writing offered by those working within the 'guru' industry is much more varied and diverse. To make sense of these diverse contributions, to understand the differences between writers, and to understand those factors, which underpin the differences we find, we will require some form of framework, which might be used to separate and to classify those active in the 'guru' industry. Indeed the complex and fast-changing nature of the 'guru' industry makes an analytical framework vital to our endeavours, since in the absence of an analytical framework we would surely be swept away by the sheer size and weight of the 'guru' industry.

We would do well to note, therefore, that the 'guru' industry, like the market for 'guru' products and services more generally, is large and fast-growing. No account of the 'guru' industry, therefore, could be exhaustive or encyclopaedic. In fact, given the speed at which this industry and the publishing industry move any account of the 'guru' industry risks being 'dated' almost as soon as it is drafted. The search for an 'ultimate guide' to the 'gurus', therefore is an illusion, a fool's errand.

With this in mind, this chapter does not pretend to offer an exhaustive bibliography of the 'guru' industry. Instead, the chapter offers a framework designed to allow readers to analyse and to locate both current *and future* contributions to the 'guru' industry.

We will develop this framework in our next section.

## A Framework for Analysis

'Gurus', as we saw in our initial discussions, are properly defined as wise men (and women) who deserve our veneration (Jackson and Carter, 1998). However, in both the introduction and chapter 1 of this book, we questioned the wisdom of the 'gurus' of management. Arguing that the 'gurus' offer partial and limiting analyses of organizations and management, a decision was made to place the term 'guru' within quotation marks. Pattison (1997), however, offers us a reason to persist with the 'guru' monicker despite our initial misgivings.

Discussing the similarities between (management) theory and theology, Pattison tells us that he has selected the term 'guru' to describe the key, and influential commentators on, and shapers of management since he finds that in their rhetoric and mode of operation they have so much in common with the religious prophets of the bible. Clark and Salaman (1996), it is worth observing, offer a similar, if more profane religious analogy in their discussion of 'the management guru as organizational witchdoctor'.

Pattison argues that the management 'guru', like the religious prophet, 'conjures up a dualistic, polarized world' (Pattison, 1997, p. 139). The religious prophet offers a vision of a world polarized between good and evil; heaven and hell; salvation and damnation. In a similar fashion the management 'guru', 'conjures up a dualistic, polarised world in which businesses are either conspicuously successful or conspicuous flops' (Pattison, 1997, p. 139). Yet the 'guru' account of the business world does not begin and end with description. To qualify as a 'guru', prescription must be coupled to description. Thus in common with the religious prophet, the management 'guru' offers 'easy-to-grasp principles of salvation' (Pattison, 1997, p. 135).

Discussing Peters', *Thriving on Chaos* (1988), Pattison argues that, in this work, Peters 'clearly reveals his charismatic, prophetic nature' (Pattison, 1997 p. 135). *Thriving on Chaos*, Pattison tells us, is 'a work full of religious style, insights and language' (Pattison, 1997, p. 135).

Caricaturing Peters' argument only slightly, Pattison suggests that *Thriving on Chaos* may be summarized as follows:

- The 'promised land' is under threat. Fierce competitors from foreign shores threaten the 'good life' enjoyed by Americans.
- This foreign challenge has arisen because those in charge of American industry have failed to realize that the 'old order' is passing away. This old order was built upon rationalist planning. However, the emergent, 'new order' resists rationalism. The future, therefore, can no longer be mapped, planned for, or guessed at by extrapolating from the past, because the 'new order' is 'chaotic'.
- Salvation is at hand. Those who would protect the 'promised land'; rising up to meet foreign invaders need to embrace the 'new order'. To embrace the 'new order' individuals must 'convert' from rationalism with all the zeal that can be mustered, in order to meet the challenges which 'chaos' brings.
- Do not delay! Tomorrow it may be too late to change. 'Convert' now!
- Great rewards await those with 'faith'. Those who 'convert' to 'chaos' shall be able to reap and manipulate the terrible forces of 'chaos'.
- Those who fail to 'convert' will die.

Reflecting Pattison's analysis of Peters, and recognizing the importance of religious imagery and allusion within the works of the 'gurus' of management more generally, the framework developed here for the analysis of the 'guru' industry will employ religious imagery and allusion.

The framework for analysis offered in Figure 3.1, is a continuum. This continuum divides the 'guru' industry into three key groupings. Moving from right to left these three groupings represent:

- a grouping, that has produced a range of 'homages' and 'hagiologies'
- a grouping that has produced, what might be termed, a range of 'redemptive' texts

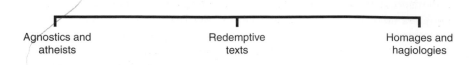

*Figure 3.1* The 'guru' industry

- a grouping (from but not of the 'guru' industry) which might be regarded as comprising 'agnostics' and 'atheists'.

Let us examine each of these groupings in turn.

## Homages and Hagiologies

Many of the contributions to the 'guru' industry adopt a highly deferential approach to the 'gurus' of management. Indeed a number of texts in the 'guru' industry seem to be written as devotions to the 'gurus'. In these texts, the 'gurus' of management seem to be regarded as somehow, other-worldly and almost worthy of worship (Jackson and Carter, 1998). Texts exhibiting such features, I have termed 'hagiologies'. Let us examine a sample of these hagiologies.

Kennedy's *Managing with the Gurus* (1996) aims to offer, as its sub-title tells us, 'top level guidance on 20 management techniques'. It attempts to supply this 'top level guidance' by distilling from the works of the 'gurus', the key ideas and insights which Kennedy seems to believe 'top' managers require in order to remain successful. The argument of the book, then, is really quite simple and goes something like this:

A number of thinkers and scholars have written a great deal about management which today's managers should be aware of. The problem, however, is that today's 'top' managers are too busy, and too hard pressed, to devote their valuable time to the mundane task of reading these important works. To alleviate 'top' management of the burden of reading any whole book, therefore, Kennedy has taken it upon herself to read the key and important texts, and having read these works, has selected the key and important passages which 'continue to resonate' (Kennedy, 1996, p. 1).

Analysing the works of the 'gurus', with an eye on the practical function of management, Kennedy considers these extracts to be like 'torch-beams' (Kennedy, 1996, p. 2) designed to 'inspire and aid people struggling with the disciplines of management' (Kennedy, 1996, p. 2). To this end Kennedy offers the following structure:

After a brief preface, she spends a few moments detailing the lives of her forty-three 'gurus'. We are told their dates of birth (and where appropriate the date of death), and we are offered a small biography, which spells out the notable achievements and accomplishments of each. Following this, Kennedy then takes us on a tour of twenty chapters where, following a brief introductory discussion written by Kennedy, extracts from the works of these forty-three 'gurus' are reproduced, in order to provide illumination and inspiration on topics such as 'the craft of management', 'culture', 'motivation', 'quality' and 're-engineering'. This book I have labelled a hagiology because of its mode of presentation. However, as we shall see, it would probably be more accurate to say that the book is, in fact, some mix of martyrology, hagiography and hagiology.

Discussing the *Lives of the Saints*, Baring-Gould (1914) notes that: 'A MARTYROLOGY means, properly, a list of witnesses. The Martyrologies are catalogues in which are to be found the names of the Saints, with the days and places of their deaths, and generally with the distinctive character of their sanctity, and with a historic summary of their lives' (Baring-Gould, 1914, p. xi). In this sense, we can see that in listing the 'gurus' and their accomplishments, Kennedy's text bears similarities to the traditional, religious, martyrologies. Indeed *Managing with the Gurus* might be thought of as a secularized *Lives of the Saints*.

Yet Kennedy's text is not just a martyrology. It does not just chronicle the lives of its secularized witnesses. Together with a brief martyrology, Kennedy also offers us her own brief account of the 'gurus' and their wit and wisdom. In this sense Kennedy's work is also hagiologic. In fact Kennedy's work is part martyrology (since it details the lives and accomplishments of the 'gurus'), and part hagiology (since each chapter offers an initial discussion of the 'gurus' and their works which has been penned by Kennedy). However, for the most part Kennedy's work might be considered to be a hagiography since it reproduces, verbatim, extracts from the works of the 'gurus', apparently in the hope that we, lesser mortals, might aspire to the virtues which the 'gurus' extol.

Yet, however we choose to label Kennedy's work whether as martyrology, hagiology or hagiography, (hagiology, I believe represents a reasonable compromise since, according to *The Concise Oxford*, hagiologies are that branch of literature dealing, broadly speaking, with the lives of the saints), her intention is clear. Kennedy's aim is to improve the practice of management by making the (saintly) wit and wisdom of the 'gurus' more generally accessible. Yet while many of us might accept this desire to educate and to inform, as laudatory and would wish to commend Kennedy, I find that I cannot offer praise since, on close inspection her text appears flawed and marred by over-simplification. Indeed a number of rather damaging critiques may be tilted at Kennedy.

### A Fall from Grace?

Kennedy's secularized 'Lives of the Saints' is marred, perhaps unsurprisingly, by a trinity of errors. Her account of management's 'gurus' fails to consider three issues, which should be central to any analysis of management and its 'gurus':

1   What is a 'guru'?
2   What is the nature of management?
3   Does a linear account of management, and the supposed 'development' of management thought and practice represent, adequately, the history of management thought?

Let us deal with each of these in turn.

## What is a 'Guru'?

Kennedy's brief martyrology lists forty-three 'gurus' of management. Selections from the works of these 'gurus', as we have seen, form the bulk of *Managing with the Gurus*. Kennedy's intention in providing these extracts is clear. She hopes that hard-pressed managers might learn from the 'gurus', and so, improve the practice of management. She argues, however, that her book should not be regarded as a crib guide, providing ready access to essay-writing material for the dilettante student. Thus she protests that her book is designed to inspire others to read, in full, the works of the 'gurus'. She argues: 'There are some books no manager or student of management should be without, and I hope the extracts selected here will impel readers to bookshop [*sic!*] or library to search them out' (Kennedy, 1996, p. 2).

Yet it appears that Kennedy does not follow her own counsel, since on inspection of the extracts she reproduces, it soon becomes apparent that she does not always return to the original sources, in spite of the fact that she would 'impel' others to do so. Alongside (or perhaps even above!) the forty-three 'gurus' Kennedy lists, therefore, we should add the names of Pugh (1990) and Thomas (1993) as (hidden) 'gurus', since a range of the 'guru' extracts reproduced come second-hand from these scholars. In fairness to Pugh and Thomas, therefore, we should make it clear that there are, for Kennedy, not forty-three, but forty-five 'gurus' of management.

So what separates these saintly individuals from the thousands of others who have written about, and through their writings have sought to shape management thought and practice? Or putting this another way, is it only modesty which excludes Kennedy from the listing?

Baring-Gould (1914) in setting the scene for his sixteen-volume account of the *Lives of the Saints* notes a problem which confronts anyone who would compile a hagiology. The problem, in short, is one of selection. He notes:

> In writing the lives of the Saints, I have used my discretion . . . in relating only those miracles which are most remarkable, either for being fairly well authenticated, or for their beauty or quaintness, or

because they are often represented in art, and are therefore of interest to the archaeologist. That errors in judgement, and historical inaccuracies, have crept into this volume, and may find their way into those that succeed, is, I fear inevitable.

(Baring-Gould, 1914, p. vii)

In a similar fashion, any listing of the 'gurus', and indeed any listing of their preferred fads and buzzwords, is likely to suffer from what others may regard as errors of omission. This much was acknowledged in our earlier discussion, and is acknowledged in my earlier account of *Organizational Change* (Collins, 1998). Yet while acknowledging that not everyone will agree with our criteria for selecting the 'gurus' of management, we must, if we are to separate forty-three (or forty-five) special individuals, make some attempt to explain the significance of this grouping. If we cannot articulate what makes a group special, then we have no right to set it apart.

To be fair to Kennedy we should acknowledge that in the second edition of her 'Guide to the Management Gurus' (Kennedy, 1998) she does make some attempt to pinpoint what it takes to be a 'guru'. 'Gurus' she tells us: 'generate original, durable thinking on the hard matter of managing people and resources' (Kennedy, 1998, p. xvi). But, far from disposing of the issue, this simply suggests more problems. In particular this presents three key questions:

- Can the likes of Hamel (Hamel and Prahalad, 1994; Hamel, 1996) who has been active in the 'guru' market, only since the mid-1990s really be judged to have made a durable contribution?
- Can Peters' contribution be considered durable (see chapter 5) given his propensity to reinvent his work?
- Where we can prove that the ideas of a 'guru' lack novelty, should that 'guru' be struck from our list (or defrocked)? For example, Handy's quest for meaning within capitalism (Handy, 1997) is hardly a novel concern. In fact the problem of alienation was central to the work of Marx in the nineteenth century (Tucker, 1978). Should we, then, strike Handy from our list of 'gurus' and replace him with Marx? Similarly, when someone finally presses the charge that BPR is not 'new', will this mean that Hammer (Hammer and Stanton, 1995), for all his sales and influence will no longer be ranked among the 'gurus'?

Still on the question of designating 'guru' status we should also acknowledge tensions and contradictions between the works of Kennedy. For example, we should note that whereas Kennedy's 1996 text, lists forty-three (forty-five) 'gurus', her 1998 text lists only forty 'gurus'. Similarly, we should note that many of the forty-three (forty-five) listed in the 1996 text do not make it into Kennedy's 1998 listing.

Yet, in neither text does Kennedy offer any clear rationale for her choice of 'gurus'. Indeed the tensions and contradictions between her 1996 and her 1998 listings simply add to the confusion as regards Kennedy's definition of a 'guru'. It is difficult to escape the conclusion, therefore, that Kennedy presents, not so much a useful collection of 'gurus', as an arbitrary collection of management scribblers.

Of course, we should be fair to Kennedy and acknowledge that a number of those writers and thinkers she singles out for special attention would be regarded by most thoughtful commentators as 'gurus', thanks to the influence of their accounts of management, and of the templates for management action which they proffer. Thus, most thoughtful commentators would probably acknowledge that the likes of Kanter and Peters are, respectively, representatives of the academic 'guru' and the consultant 'guru' cadre (Huczynski, 1993). Others however, are a little more problematic. Most UK managers, I feel, would probably place Harvey-Jones on their 'guru' listing. However, I feel less certain that their American counterparts would consider Harvey-Jones influential enough to qualify as a 'guru'. Indeed Huczynski, a UK-based commentator, would be inclined to consider Harvey-Jones, a rather minor 'guru' of the 'hero-manager' variety.

It is only right to acknowledge, therefore, that within her 1996 collection of forty-three (forty-five) 'gurus', Kennedy lists a core of writers popular and influential enough to qualify for 'guru' status within any sensible listing of management's 'gurus'. Yet, outside this core group (of Harvard Scholars and McKinsey-ites), it becomes increasingly difficult to condone Kennedy's collection. For example, together with the leading lights of Stanford and Harvard (who together fill seven of the forty-three 'guru' slots), Kennedy allocates two of the available slots to scholars from England's Ashridge College. Thus Kennedy seems to imply that a minor business school in the south of England currently supplies almost 5 per cent of the world's management 'gurus'!

Of course, this is not to imply that Messrs Campbell (Campbell and Tawadey, 1990) and Sadler (1992), the academics from Ashridge College whom Kennedy lists, are not worthy and committed scholars. However, in the absence of any explanation regarding the basis for the selection of these 'gurus', we are left to wonder why Ashridge is singled out for such praise, while notable scholars from schools (such as Warwick, Strathclyde and Cranfield) rated as 'excellent' by those charged with the execution of the 'Research Assessment Exercise', which grades Britain's universities, should receive no mention at all. Similarly we should note that Kennedy's 'guru' selection, makes for rather strange bed-fellows. Thus in her discussion of 'the changing organization' she reproduces extracts from Weber (via Pugh, 1990) and Jaques (again via Pugh, 1990) side-by-side with contributions from Peters (1988), Kanter (1989) and Barnard (1938).

In the absence of any comment from Kennedy, readers could be forgiven for assuming that the contributions of these commentators mesh, to form a consensus on the nature of organization, and upon what Kennedy takes to be the changing nature of organization. So, readers could be forgiven for thinking that Weber, Jaques, Peters, Kanter and Barnard are 'gurus' of the same ilk. But they are not. Indeed the cautious, reflective and sociological scholarship of Weber and Jaques sits ill with the prescriptive 'guru' templates for action offered by Peters, Kanter and Barnard.

In summary, then, we should note that Kennedy's failure either to think through or to articulate her 'guru' category, causes major problems for her analysis which, ultimately, renders her work unconvincing, and so, unhelpful. Indeed given Kennedy's willingness to elevate what (with respect to the scholars of Ashridge) must be considered to be minor figures to the status of 'guru', and given her tendency to lump together quite diverse forms of scholarship, we must wonder whether she has any clear understanding of the 'guru' phenomenon.

Similar conceptual problems also loom large in her account of 'management'.

### The Nature of Management

Given that Kennedy fails to consider, carefully, the 'guru' phenomenon it should not surprise us that she also fails to consider either carefully, or critically, the nature of management.

Management, Kennedy implies, is an 'art'. This term is often used to describe what Kennedy would term 'the craft of management'. Yet, as we have seen, this terminology actually tells us little about management or managing. Indeed there is the suspicion that when writers refer to management as being an 'art' they are, tacitly, admitting how little, with certainty, can be said about the day-to-day practice of management. Thus when a writer states; 'management is an art', s/he is really saying 'management is difficult to codify, it is complex and it is problematic'. This, however, begs the question; 'why is management so complex; why is managing so problematic?

Unfortunately Kennedy can offer no meaningful response to this question. In keeping with the 'guru' account, she might be prepared to venture that managing is complex and problematic, because of the capricious nature of the environment of business, and the pace of organizational change. Yet this would surely imply two things which do not bear close scrutiny.

1   That managing is simple and straightforward where the environment of business is stable.
2   That everyone accepts the 'separation' of managing and working, as self-evident and natural, with the result that there is no legitimate space for conflicts over the nature and scope of management practice.

Our discussion of the nature of management in chapter 2 demonstrated the complexity and the novelty of 'management'. Indeed by moving from the position which states that management may be either 'science' or 'art', we have been able to analyse the upstart construction which is management, as a 'separated' and 'dispersed', activity; as an organizational elite; and as an ideology. Chapter 2 revealed, however, that for all its complexity, we may with some effort, comprehend 'management' as a social-political phenomenon. Indeed deploying the analysis developed in chapter 2 allows us to see the ideological appeal of Kennedy's art metaphor.

Thus the analysis contained in chapter 2 helps us to see that describing management as an art form offers, curiously enough, only a two-dimensional view of management. This two-dimensional account promotes a view of management as a special elite, and as a skilled activity while, simultaneously, removing any searching or difficult questions about control, ideology and symbolism from the analysis. Yet, since Kennedy's analysis of management lacks a third dimension, her description of 'management as art', does little to explain how, and why, management has moved, apparently, from a concern with scientific matters, to embrace ideologies built, not on 'art', but upon notions of nationalism, (Collins, 1998). This, under-theorized account of management and managing is rooted, in part, in the tendency to assume that 'progress' is evident in management thought and practice.

### Progressive Management?

Notions of 'progress' figure strongly in Kennedy's account of management and managing. Adopting the 'grammar' of the 'gurus', she makes continual reference to 'old-style' organizations, and argues that these out-moded patterns of organization and thinking, inevitably, will be supplanted by more up-to-date patterns of organization. Apparently taking her cue from the natural scientific community, she implies that 'management' progresses and develops as a result of new discoveries. Indeed she pinpoints ten key moments in the evolution of management (Kennedy, 1996, pp. 38–40). While she makes no real effort to spell out how, and why, the thought and practice of management might change, the implication is clear: management proceeds on the basis of discovery; 'old' ideas are discarded when it can be demonstrated that 'new' ideas offer better explanations and solutions.

Central to this battery of 'new' ideas, Kennedy tells us, is empowerment. However, not all share Kennedy's conviction regarding the efficacy of empowerment in the context of business management. Indeed a range of authors (see Collins, 1994) have noted that it is difficult to establish that empowering schemes are new. In a similar way, we should also note that it is difficult to establish that empowering schemes actually lead to meaningful changes in systems of workplace decision-making. Yet in spite of this, empowerment, for Kennedy is a 'fact'. (Apparently facts exist within the subjective domain of art!) Indeed, empowerment, for Kennedy, is the key and defining feature of the new-style organization, which, inexorably will replace the 'old-style' bureaucratic and Taylorist organizational form. Yet the history of management (that is, the history of management as a contested and increasingly separated phenomenon, rather than the 'history' of management as an 'art') does not support this progressive, evolutionary argument. Huczynski (1993) for example, notes that Mayo and his human relations school (often presented as the antithesis of Taylorism) did not overthrow scientific management (see also Hatch, 1997). Indeed Huczynski notes that managers were keen to embrace Mayo's ideas, because his ideas on social organization, leadership and satisfaction seemed to offer managers the means to correct, by way of a supplement, the perceived deficiencies of Taylorism. As I have written elsewhere: 'Human relations [thinking] did not replace scientific management. Instead it merely revised it some degree. Management thought and practice, therefore, did not move from Taylorism to human relations. Instead what we get is Taylorism with a human relations topping!' (Collins, 1998, p. 18).

Close analysis of Kennedy's *Managing with the Gurus* reveals, therefore that, in spite of her intention to educate, Kennedy supplies little insight, because she accepts the pre-packaged; 'encased' model of management prepared for consumption by the 'gurus':

- She fails to explain the central feature of her analysis since she chooses to assume rather than define her 'guru' grouping.
- She is unwilling to analyse the nature of management, and so, she is unable to analyse the nature of management thought and practice.
- Through her willingness to construct a hagiologic account of the 'gurus' of management, she repeats and compounds the errors, evident in the stunted and spuriously practical accounts of management and organization produced by the 'gurus'.

Yet in all this, Kennedy is not alone. Crainer (1998a), for example, in his 'ultimate' guide offers a hagiologic account of the 'gurus' of management, which, to some extent, mirrors the problems identified in Kennedy's account.

### Crainer: King of the 'Guru' Industry?

In one sense, Crainer's *Ultimate Business Guru Book* (1998a) is superior to Kennedy's hagiology. Yet, in another sense Crainer's book is very much worse, even than Kennedy's. Let us have the 'good news' first. Let us examine the 'positive' aspects of Crainer's work, before we look to the 'negative'.

On the plus side for Crainer, we should acknowledge that, unlike Kennedy, he does attempt to offer a definition of 'guru', and some guidance regarding the allocation of the term. We should note, however, that this 'analysis' takes place largely at an implicit level. Indeed, it is in his sub-title that Crainer expresses, most clearly, the difference between a 'guru' and a mere writer. Thus 'gurus' shape management thought and practice, and so, in his sub-title Crainer promises us an analysis of '50 thinkers who made management'.

To be fair to Crainer we should also acknowledge that, unlike Kennedy, he does not pretend to offer a definitive listing of management's 'gurus', (although this does seem to render his title meaningless). Crainer notes that, to some extent, all 'guru' listings could be accused of subjectivity, bias and error. In an attempt to mitigate these problems, therefore, Crainer supplements his group of 50 shapers of management, with an appendix containing the names of 62 more 'thinkers with strong cases for inclusion' (Crainer, 1998a, p. 265) in the main text. However, we have to wonder why Crainer limited himself to 112 names, and we have to wonder, since he fails to spell this out, just how a writer might press a case for inclusion!

Yet, we said we would stress the 'positive' in Crainer's work, so we should note that, unlike Kennedy who fawns over her 'gurus', Crainer, at least initially, appears to express some degree of scepticism regarding the 'gurus' and their works. Pondering the phenomenal growth of the 'gurus' he notes: 'The sheer mass of new material suggests that quantity comes before quality. There is a steady supply of new insights into old ideas. Management theorizing has become adept at finding new angles on old topics' (Crainer, 1998a, p. xiv). Yet alongside these 'positive' aspects we must also weigh some rather obvious 'negatives'. The first 'negative' we should note concerns the contradictions in Crainer's analysis.

### Contradiction

Above, we noted a certain degree of scepticism in Crainer's work. Indeed we noted in his work, a degree of scepticism as regards the value of the 'gurus'. However, when we look closely it becomes apparent that this scepticism is half-hearted. Crainer blusters in his introductory comments, yet, in the main body of the text it soon becomes apparent that Crainer's attitude to the 'gurus' is much like Kennedy's.

On the dustjacket of his book, Crainer informs us that, since every good manager is just too busy to read the 'gurus' (yet dare not admit ignorance of these works to colleagues and peers), he has decided to offer an 'ultimate' guide, which will sift out and select the key points which every manager should know. Thus Crainer's overall aim is much like that of Kennedy's. Unlike Kennedy, however, there is no real hagiography here. Rather than reproduce extracts from the works of those who have 'made' management, Crainer prefers to offer his own commentary. Yet, while Crainer's account eschews hagiography, his overall tone is clearly hagiologic, since in spite of his initial scepticism, Crainer is very supportive of, and devoted to his 'gurus'. Any criticism which Crainer voices in the main text is muted, therefore, and it is clear that, for all his initial protestation regarding the 'gurus' of management, he employs the term 'guru' entirely without irony.

## Misapprehension

A second point of criticism, which may be made of Crainer, builds from this first 'negative' noted above. On the dustjacket we are told that the best companies, those that are winning, follow the 'gurus'. The inference we are meant to make here is clear. Those who fail to follow the 'gurus' (and those who fail to part with £15.99 for Crainer's book) will fail; they will be left behind, (and they will look stupid at conferences). Yet it is difficult to establish that successful organizations are, in fact, beholden to the 'gurus' for their success. Indeed Guest's (1992) analysis seems to suggest that, if anything, the 'gurus' are more closely associated with business failure than with business success. Thus Guest argues that Peters' and Waterman's (1982) discussion of 'excellence' demonstrates, quite clearly, that the successful companies of the early 1980s had, scrupulously, avoided the advice (to integrate and to 'conglomerate') peddled by 'gurus' in the 1970s. Crainer's willingness to 'bend the knee' before his 'gurus', therefore, seems to blind him to the errors and limitations which we might have expected would have been exposed by an 'ultimate guide'.

## Misbegotten

A third point of criticism, which might be made against Crainer, is that he misrepresents the nature of management. Like Kennedy, Crainer holds a view of management that is based upon notions of 'progress'. It is a view of management where 'old ideas' are bowled over by 'breakthroughs'. So, for example, we are told that the transition from Taylorism to Mayo's human relations thinking represents a swing from 'science' to 'art' in management. Similarly, Crainer tells us that Mayo's work was concerned to rehumanize the workplace. Yet other commentators have failed to find the 'neutrality' of science, or of art, in Mayo's work and, furthermore, find little humanity in his analysis of the workplace. Thompson and McHugh (1990), for example, argue that human relations approaches were not driven by 'progress', nor were they driven by 'humanity'. They argue, instead, that human relations approaches were driven by a number of situational problems. They 'arose from attempts to grapple with the recruitment and motivation problems deriving from the increasing size of the labour force and a new industrial relations situation shaped by declining loyalty and rising unrest' (Thompson and McHugh, 1990, p. 75). It seems clear, therefore, that Crainer's devotion to his 'gurus', and the ideology they represent, actually limits his ability to understand management, and the role which 'gurus' play in shaping the thinking and practices of management. This leads us to our fourth and final criticism of Crainer.

### Misaligned

Both Kennedy and Crainer, as we have seen, offer hagiologic accounts of the 'gurus'. Kennedy, as we have seen, is happy to sit at the feet of the 'gurus' while Crainer protests, initially, before taking his place in the worshipful congregation. The problem being that Crainer does not seem, overly, keen on serving the 'gurus'. Indeed, one might speculate that, rather than critique the 'gurus' in any meaningful way, Crainer would much prefer to step out of their shadows. After all he is, according to his dustjacket, 'the world's leading commentator on business gurus', so it can be only a short hop to 'guru' status! Our fourth point of criticism, then, is this: Crainer's text is misaligned. It is hagiography masquerading as criticism.

Summarizing the nature and character of 'guru' hagiologies, then, we should note that hagiologic accounts of the 'gurus' of management do little to unpack the 'guru' concepts of management and managing. They accept both the 'grammar' and the vocabulary of the 'gurus', and so do little to improve our understanding of the fraught and problematic character of managing. What then of the 'homages'?

### Homage to Management?

Pugh's and Hickson's *Writers on Organizations* (1996) represents, probably, the best known of a range of books which might be considered as 'homages' to management. Now in its fifth edition, this book might be thought of as the 'industry standard' for homages. But what separates a homage from a hagiology?

For some, the dividing line may be fine and difficult to perceive. Yet there is, I believe, a demarcation. The 'guru' hagiologies are devotions to the 'gurus'. 'Gurus', it seems, are special men and women, talented and charismatic, who exist not just to teach; they exist to 'save' management. 'Guru' hagiologies then, elevate the 'gurus' and to some extent, denigrate those who would/should follow the 'gurus'. Pugh's and Hickson's 'homage', however, is a little different.

Pugh's and Hickson's 'homage', unlike the bluffer's guides produced by Kennedy and Crainer, has a serious educational intent. Unlike the hagiologies, which require students and managers to suspend their critical faculties and 'follow' the 'gurus', Pugh's and Hickson's text is written as a teaching tool, to encourage a more critical appraisal on the part of the reader. In this sense, Pugh's and Hickson's text envisages a more balanced relationship between student and teacher, between reader and author –

not you will note, reader and 'guru'. However, the Pugh and Hickson text is clearly managerial in its focus and in its intent, and it is this that makes Pugh's and Hickson's text, and others like it (see Mabey and Mayon-White, 1993), a homage to management.

A homage to management, therefore, offers a celebration of managing, and of the skills and talents of managers. The interests and orientations which a homage expresses are managerial. Indeed a key aim of a homage to management must be regarded as the attempt to improve management. Yet within these homages no real attempt is made to unpick management. No attempt is made to consider the 'separation' of management (Hales, 1993) or the contests and conflicts, consequent upon any attempt to manage the *social* organization of production. Thus, (for what the authors of these works fail to say as much as for what they say), their collections of writers and ideas must be considered as 'homages' to management; as formal acknowledgements of their allegiance to managerialism (Thompson and McHugh, 1995).

What then of our second grouping: the redemptive texts?

## Redemptive Texts

In a sense, that segment of the 'guru' industry which I have labelled 'redemptive texts' might equally be thought of as 'homages' to management, since the redemptive texts demonstrate a clear managerial orientation, and in many ways, represent celebrations of management. Yet the accounts offered by such writers as Hilmer and Donaldson (1996) and Micklethwait and Wooldridge (1997) are not simple homages. These texts, as we shall see, are driven by a sense of frustration and dissatisfaction regarding the 'gurus' and their analysis. This sense of frustration changes the tone and presentation of these works, transforming them from simple homages into redemptive texts. Thus, unlike the hagiologies and homages presented above, Hilmer's and Donaldson's and, to a lesser extent, Micklethwait's and Wooldridge's text have been written to save management, not from fierce competitors, but from the 'gurus'.

### *Management's Redeemers?*

In the introduction to *Management Redeemed*, Hilmer and Donaldson (1996) tell us that they have written their book together, because they are 'mad' (Hilmer and Donaldson, 1996 p. ix). Now, for those who have engaged in debate with Donaldson regarding his commitment to 'positivist' organization theory (Donaldson, 1985, 1996) this might seem an overdue admission, so it is important that we finish the quotation; Hilmer and Donaldson are, they tell us, mad, 'mad as hell' (Hilmer and Donaldson, 1996, p. ix). They are angry because of what they see 'happening to the practice of and writing on management, namely, the substitution of dogma

– platitudes, homilies and fads – for careful, sustained professional manage-ment' (Hilmer and Donaldson, 1996, pp. ix–x).

Hilmer and Donaldson are arguing, therefore, that the 'guru' phenom-enon, and the extent of the market for 'guru' products and services, is a cause for concern, since the gurus' over-simplify and distort the very real problems of managing in the 1990s. Ultimately, they tell us, this tendency towards over-simplification will undermine, both the practice of manage-ment and the ongoing prospects for success in those organizations where managers follow the advice of their 'gurus'. For Hilmer and Donaldson, then, the term 'guru' would tend to carry deeply ironic connotations.

The 'gurus' of management (although Hilmer and Donaldson do not use this term) are a cause for concern, therefore, because:

- They produce 'fads'.
- They promote a fixation with 'technique'.

Hilmer and Donaldson never quite get around to telling us what a 'fad' is. Indeed they never quite get around to telling the managers, they would redeem, how to spot a fad. However, Hilmer and Donaldson are clear on one thing – fads in management are bad news.

With the benefit of hindsight it is relatively easy to spot a 'fad'. Fads have a short lifespan, while, by implication good and sound ideas persist. This, of course, represents a rather simplistic and non-Kuhnian (Kuhn, 1970) account of the development of ideas, yet we can, I think, concur with Hilmer and Donaldson – management fads are a bad thing. They are bad because they are based on scant research and on poor models of organization, which encourage peculiar approaches to management. In a related fashion we should also acknowledge that fads cause problems for management, and for managing, since each new fad tends to contra-dict and/or reverse the fad preceding it. Thus Hilmer and Donaldson argue that managers flit from one fad to another, leaving havoc, chaos and any number of really 'mad' people behind them. So why do managers embrace these fads?

Hilmer and Donaldson argue that managers embrace fads, because (1) the 'guru' sales pitch is seductive and (2) because managers put their faith in technique rather than in their own skills and experience. However, Hilmer and Donaldson tell us that this faith in technique is misplaced. New fads and techniques, they tell us, come around every other year. Each new fad, they warn us, claims to re-invent the world; and each new technique claims to fix the problem identified by this new worldview. Hilmer and Donaldson argue, however, that this claim is pure folly. Managers, they tell us, do not have to disregard the past in order to embrace the future. Indeed they argue that managers should scrap the fads of management, and should instead, use their *own* analytical skills and their *own* knowledge of history and the environment, to meet the very real challenges of managing. Thus Hilmer and Donaldson argue that the 'gurus' of management peddle an anti-management message. The 'gurus' and their fads, we are told, disrupt and damage organizations, and their focus upon technique belittles the skills, talents and training of those who have worked hard to become managers.

In an attempt to reclaim management from the clutches of the 'gurus', and in an attempt to redeem managers from their dual fixation with fads and techniques, Hilmer and Donaldson set out to 'debunk' the fads of management. These fads, they tell us, may be collected under five headings. These headings, Hilmer and Donaldson argue, represent 'false trails'. They are, I suppose, paths less travelled – and for good reason.

We will look, briefly, at these five 'false trails'; however, since the remainder of this book deals with a range of fads and buzzwords, we will offer just a few words of comment on Hilmer's and Donaldson's 'false trails' and delay our own critical analysis until later chapters.

The five 'false trails' identified by Hilmer and Donaldson are exhortations to:

1 flatten organizational structures
2 develop a bias for action; and a suspicion of reflection, abstraction and analysis
3 deploy 'new' techniques when confronted by problematic issues
4 scrap hierarchy in favour of 'clan' management
5 increase the surveillance and supervision of top management in order to improve accountability.

Debunking each of these in turn, Hilmer and Donaldson argue that:

1 Radical restructuring and delayering deliver only modest cash savings while damaging, severely, the competitiveness of organizations.
2 Careful analysis and reflection is the key to sound management.
3 Fads and other new techniques are limited and flawed, both in their understanding of management and in their ability to improve organizations.
4 Bureaucracies are flexible means of controlling and directing complex systems.
5 Supervisory boards do not improve organizational competitiveness.

In comparison to this bold attempt at redemption, Micklethwait and Wooldridge (1997) have produced a text, which, while its aim is, clearly, to deliver management from the 'gurus', is more ambivalent as regards the role and value of the 'gurus'.

### Children of a Lesser God?

Micklethwait's and Wooldridge's (1997) *The Witch Doctors* is presented as offering an account of the insights and oversights of the key management commentators. We are informed that these 'gurus', or as the authors would have it, these 'witch doctors', are 'the unacknowledged legislators of mankind' (Micklethwait and Wooldridge, 1997, p. 5) and should be a key area for analysis because they 'are laying down the law, reshaping institutions, refashioning our language and, above all, reorganising people's lives' (Micklethwait and Wooldridge, 1997, p. 5). However, Micklethwait and Wooldridge are not entirely comfortable with this. Indeed they argue that while we (and they do mean all of us), need to make sense of the insights which the 'gurus' offer, we also have to be aware that not all of what the 'gurus' say makes sense.

Micklethwait and Wooldridge offer four key criticisms of the 'witch doctors' of management (see also, chapter 1) They argue that:

- The form of analysis offered by the 'witch doctors' is 'constitutionally incapable of self-criticism' (Micklethwait and Wooldridge, 1997, p. 15). In this Micklethwait and Wooldridge seem to imply that 'witch doctor' ideas and analysis lack the capacity to develop. Wittgenstein (Monk, 1990) expresses this well. In a letter to Rush Rhees he notes just how much of a wrench thinking can be. Yet he also implies that an absence of reflection and self-criticism might be considered a form of sickness. He notes: 'Thinking is sometimes easy, often difficult but at the same time thrilling. But when it's most important it's just disagreeable, that is when it threatens to rob one of one's pet notions and to leave one all bewildered & with a feeling of worthlessness. In these cases I and others shrink from thinking or can only get ourselves to think after a long sort of struggle. I believe that you know this situation and I wish you lots *of courage*! though I haven't got it myself. We are all *sick* people' (quoted in Monk, 1990, p. 474, original emphasis).

2   The 'gurus' employ jargon and obscure terminology which does little to clarify or to convey their ideas and analysis. Indeed Micklethwait and Wooldridge seem to suggest that 'gurus' use jargon in an attempt to protect their work from criticism, and from more searching forms of analysis. Thus Micklethwait and Wooldridge seem to suggest that the 'witch doctors' use jargon, not because they are poor writers, but because *they are keen to make their work delphic and cryptic* (see Wolfe's (1994) account and critique of McLuhan).

3   The 'witch doctors' base their arguments and analyses not on rigorous research, but on 'common-sense'. Thus the analysis of the 'gurus' has a tendency to be skewed, slight and partial.

4   The ideas and analyses proffered by the 'witch doctors' are faddish and often contradictory. Thus Micklethwait and Wooldridge note that organizational analysis, and so, organizations swing between a focus

upon 'commitment' to a focus upon 'flexibility', without pausing to ponder the contradictions and reversals implied in a switch from policies, ostensibly designed to foster commitment, to policies associated with redundancy.

Overall, Micklethwait and Wooldridge offer a damning critique. Their analysis has the ring of a general critique. Indeed it sounds like a generalized attack on the whole 'guru' phenomenon. If 'witch doctors' are 'constitutionally incapable' of over-turning their pet notions and prejudices, why should we listen to them at all? Can there be any insight within such oversights? Apparently yes.

In spite of the trenchant and generalist tone of their critique and in spite of the contradictions this causes for their own analysis, Micklethwait and Wooldridge seem to insist that theirs is a specific, not a generalist critique. So, in spite of the fact that 'witch doctors' constitutionally lack the ability to develop and to think through their ideas, only some 'gurus' are bad. So Drucker is 'good' while Hammer and Champy are, let's say, worrying. 'Knowledge work' seems a sound idea while 'Globalization' is mocked as a management concept.

Viewed in terms of this 'specific' critique, Micklethwait's and Wooldridge's book (which to be fair offers a rich, 'insider' account of the 'gurus') must be viewed as a 'redemptive' text. It is an attempt to deliver management from *bad* 'gurus' and an attempt to nudge managers towards the bosom of *good* 'gurus'. However, in spite of this desire to save management from the 'gurus', so that managers might receive a better press, and so that management might develop as a respectable and rigorous discipline, the redemptive texts have a tendency to 'do down' management and managers, because short of portraying managers as the dopey and the duped, they lack the means to explain why managers, in any sense of the term, buy the 'guru' analysis. This problem is clear to see in Shapiro's (1998) account of management's 'guru' fixation.

### Fad Surfing

Shapiro's *Fad Surfing in the Boardroom* (1998) is billed in its sub-title as an attempt to give managers 'the courage to manage in the age of instant answers'. In this sense, the book seems to conform to the 'redemptive' text category in our model of the 'guru' industry. When planning this chapter, however, I must confess that my initial framework did not include Shapiro's text within the main body of the diagram. Shapiro's text appeared on the diagram, but not on the line. Instead the initial diagram placed Shapiro and Furnham (1998) floating in 'space' around the diagram, in an area which I would have labelled to denote the slightness of these analyses. On reflection, however, I decided that this judgement lacked charity, and so, realized that the work of Shapiro and this work of

Furnham's do, properly, constitute 'redemptive' texts. They are indeed, slight works – flawed and lacking in insight – but they are 'redemptive' texts nonetheless. Let us, then, look more closely at Shapiro's work.

## Testing the Water

To be fair to Shapiro it is clear that she knows her market. She tells us that all of her chapters are brief:

> in keeping with my belief that many readers of business books are tired of long chapters. They all start with a definition meant to be humorous and, I hope, provocative, since I'm convinced that the best way to meet a fad is with tongue tucked firmly in cheek. And they also contain a number of stories, examples and quotations, all of which I chose solely to illustrate the points I wished to make.
>
> (Shapiro, 1998, p. xv)

Or put another way we could say that the text is one part Christmas cracker, and one part *Reader's Digest*.

Each of Shapiro's chapters is designed to offer deliverance and to galvanize managers with the courage to, 'just say no' to fads. Yet like management's other redeemers Shapiro does not tell us how to spot these fads, or what might separate a 'fad' from a 'good' idea. In addition there is also some room for suspicion regarding her commitment to delivering management from fads, and from the consultants who develop and propagate these fads, since she is a consultant.

Yet even leaving my suspicions to one side, there are at least three key problems with this text.

1   Reviews of Shapiro's text heap praise upon it. August journals such as *The Independent, Personnel Today* and *The Financial Times,* according to the book's cover, have praised Shapiro for her 'sharp' writing; for the power of her attack; and for her wry humour.

    This is high praise, but I can find no power in her attack, since her text betrays no real interest in unpacking the ready-made vision of management put forward by the 'gurus'. Furthermore, we should note that Shapiro's writing style, in spite of the praise heaped upon it, does little to convey insight, because its 'grammar' and style are almost identical to that of the 'gurus'. Indeed, we would do well to note that while Kanter and many other 'gurus' have a taste for metaphor (Collins, 1998), Shapiro has a taste for mixed metaphor. She tells us, for example, that managers adopt a cookbook approach to management, and so, tend to operate on auto-pilot!

2   Shapiro's aim, it seems, is to disempower the fad industry so that managers might be empowered to manage once more. So Shapiro

would drive managers from the arms of the fad industry to where, exactly? Into *her* arms it would seem. So what does she offer? How does her analysis overthrow that promoted by the fad industry?

In keeping with the analysis developed by Hilmer and Donaldson (1996), and with the analysis developed by Micklethwait and Wooldridge (1997), Shapiro suggests that fads are bad for business, because they encourage managers to flit between contradictory imperatives, and because they encourage a fixation with technique, to the extent of denying the skills and judgement of managers. Yet in spite of this critique, Shapiro operates with a model of management and organization which, essentially, is identical to that employed by the 'gurus'. Her work is managerialist. It is a unitary (Fox, 1985) approach to modelling organizations. As such it takes the organization (and its supposed needs) as the unit of analysis, and so invokes a 'grammatical account' of management, which presents a top–down, closed-system, asocial and acontextual view of the workplace (Collins, 1998).

In common with the other 'redeemers' of management, therefore, Shapiro misrepresents the nature of management, and so fails to construct the 'critical-practical' account of management and managing, which is necessary in order to make sense of the 'gurus'. Shapiro, then, rejects the fads which the 'gurus' produce, yet accepts all the other aspects of their modelling and analysis! This, ultimately, and I suspect, contrary to her intentions, makes for a rather curious outcome. Apparently *breaking the laws of physics*, the would-be redeemers of management have managed to produce a unitarist account which is hostile to management! This feat is apparent in their treatment of fads and faddishness.

3  Each of the redeemers of management, as we have seen, has argued that fads are bad for organizations. Yet none of them explains, adequately, why managers should be attracted to fads, and why managers might be prepared to implement the changes suggested by these fads. Using Shapiro's analogy we could say that management's redeemers fail to offer any useful explanation as to why 'fad surfing' has become a key boardroom practice, nor do they explain why the 'surf' of fads tends to rise and fall; flooding, then abating only to flood again.

Hilmer and Donaldson (1996) suggest that managers are duped by consultants. Shapiro implies that managers lack the courage to challenge the 'gurus'. Yet in spite of the concern of Hilmer and Donaldson, that the 'gurus' diminish management as a craft, and represent an anti-management rhetoric it is, in fact, they who come across as anti-management since their explanation for 'fad surfing', in common with Shapiro's, is built upon the argument that managers are dim yet opportunistic.

Micklethwait and Wooldridge, to be fair, do offer a slightly more sophisticated and slightly less anti-management explanation for 'fad surfing'. They imply that management is an immature discipline, and so easy prey for charlatan consultants (i.e. managers are dim and under-educated in management matters). However, they also acknowledge that changes in the nature of government, and in the nature of organization have, in engendering turbulence and uncertainty, worked to drive managers into the arms of the (*bad*) 'gurus'.

Yet, as we shall see, such attempts at redemption still represent a rather passive account of the 'guru' phenomenon, which portrays managers as the duped and the dopey. Furthermore, as we proceed across our continuum, it will become clear that the redeemers offer only an 'externalist' account of 'guru' work (Abrahamson, 1996), which fails to recognize that the social scientific weaknesses noted in the 'guru' works may, in fact, be the key strength which encourages managers in their pursuit of fads.

We shall suggest in a moment that the 'agnostics' and 'atheists', active in the 'guru' industry provide a more useful (and in many ways, a less anti-management) account of the managerial pursuit of fads and buzzwords. However, before we attempt this we should pause to offer just a few words on, our final 'redeemer', Adrian Furnham (1998).

### Management's Boswell?

Furnham's, *The Psychology of Managerial Incompetence* (1998) is, according to its sub-title, *A Sceptic's Dictionary*, and so offers an *A to W* of what Furnham perceives to be the key organizational issues of the day.

Over-riding this text is the concern that the key organizational issue of the 1990s has been neglected by most managers. Thus Furnham implies that while most managers seem to regard such things as empowerment, TQM or BPR as the key organizational issues of the moment, they are, in fact, misguided. The key issue for managers and their organizations (*note the unitarism*) Furnham tells us, relates more to the role which management's 'gurus' perform in propagating fads. Like the other redeemers, therefore, Furnham hopes to save management through his 'sceptical dictionary'. Thus he observes that: 'Many managers are fashion victims who follow the self-appointed gurus to destruction' (Furnham, 1998, p. 13). However, as we saw earlier, this represents a rather passive account of the 'guru' phenomenon which portrays managers as meekly accepting, rather than constructing (Abrahamson, 1996; Jackson, 1996), the fads and buzzwords of management.

Accordingly, we should note that, in spite of his stated intention to be 'sceptical' rather than 'cynical' (Furnham, 1998, p. 13) Furnham's essentially anti-management account of the 'gurus' and his peculiar brand of 'info-tainment' provides little in the way of insight or social commentary. Thus Furnham's dictionary does little to examine the nature of management, and so can offer no useful account of the 'gurus' as a ready-made approach to the problems of managing.

Perhaps we could have expected more from a professor. Perhaps not. This is his thoughtful contribution to the debate on 'English-ness' and 'English culture' (masquerading as a debate on 'British-ness') precipitated by *World Cup '98* and the behaviour of English hooligans during this tournament: 'I genuinely think that to be British *[sic!]* is a huge advantage in life. You are brought up with tolerant, reasonable, intelligent people with a wonderful history *and nothing to be ashamed of.* (Treneman, A., *The Independent, Weekend Review*, 25/07/98, p. 9, emphasis added).

Contrasted with Paxman's account of 'The Joy of Thuggery', Furnham's account of 'the British' seems rather silly. Thus whereas Furnham sees 'the British' as tolerant and reasonable, Paxman unpacks the excesses of nationalism to reveal the essence of 'English-ness' in a qualitatively different sense:

> Why does a minority of the English population think that the only way to have a good time is to get disgustingly drunk, to shout obscenely and to pick a fight? The only honest answer is that this is how a part of the English population has always been. *Far from being ashamed of their behaviour, they see fighting and drunkenness as part of their birthright. It is the way they proclaim their identity.*
>
> (Paxman, J., *The Sunday Times, News Review*, 11/10/98, emphasis added)

Let us see if the 'agnostics' and 'atheists' of the 'guru' industry can rival the wisdom and insight of the redeemers. Let us look first at the 'atheists'.

## The Atheists of the 'Guru' Industry

The 'atheists' of the 'guru' industry do not really 'believe in' the 'gurus'. In fact they do not really believe in 'management'! Indeed this suspicion of 'gurus' and of 'management' defines the atheists. However, we should note that, as a group, the 'atheists' of the 'guru' industry represent a rather large and eclectic gathering. The atheists represent (if you will forgive the pun), a 'broad church' and would occupy the upper reaches of Burrell's and Morgan's (1979), now famous, paradigmatic grid. We will do little more than mention the analyses offered by two of the key writers working within these traditions – mostly for reasons of economy.

For the 'atheists' of the 'guru' industry, the 'gurus' of management would tend to be viewed as forces working to secure the domination, and so, the alienation of workers within capitalist social relations of production. For example, Gramsci's work (1976) while not directly concerned with 'gurus', would tend to suggest that 'gurus' are representative of a capitalist ideology. Thus Gramsci's analysis would suggest that, in presenting a plausible, ready-made account of management and working, which reflects the dominant interests of capitalist society, the 'gurus' work to legitimate, and to maintain the power of dominant groups, both at work, and in the wider society: 'through the creation and perpetuation of a belief system which stresses the need for order, authority and discipline, and consciously attempts to emasculate protest and revolutionary potential' (Burrell and Morgan, 1979, p. 289).

Gramsci referred to this process of ideological control as 'hegemony' and argued that such things as schools, the family and the workplace, all played roles in the development and perpetuation of this unobtrusive power. Viewed in Gramscian terms, therefore, the project of the 'gurus' would be seen as revolving around an attempt to recreate and bolster the ideology required to ensure labour discipline. Thus Gramsci's analysis would tend to draw attention to the 'grammar' invoked by management's 'gurus'. In this way, a Gramscian analysis of the 'gurus' would highlight the nationalist rhetoric at the heart of the 'guru' analysis, and would argue that notions of nationalism, and of nationalistic crisis, are used by the 'gurus' and by the ruling class, to redirect worker protest away from their own ruling class to attack some, socially constructed, mystified foreign threat.

Notions of discipline are also central to the analysis of Foucault (1991). Unlike Gramsci, however, Foucault does not envisage that power is centred to serve the interests of a ruling class. Instead Foucault views power as a complex web, integral to all social relationships. Foucault's work shows a concern with the 'exotic' (Fincham and Rhodes, 1999). His work, for example, shows an interest in the periphery of society; a concern with clinics, prisons, barracks and workhouses. Through this analysis of the 'exotic', however, Foucault provides a new and different view of that which is familiar. Thus Foucault argues that barracks and workhouses are very much like modern work organizations since they exercise similar forms of disciplinary power, which are based upon routine and surveillance.

Experts, Foucault tells us, play a key role in the maintenance and extension of this disciplinary power. Experts construct discourses. These discourses, for example, subject people to investigation, to training and to examination. Yet these investigations do not 'test' people; the investigations 'construct' people. Thus when a psychiatrist decides that a 'patient' (a particular construction of the person) is schizophrenic, this empowers the psychiatrist to incarcerate that individual. However, the 'problem' and the category (the schizophrenia and the schizophrenic) have both been *created* by the discourse.

A Foucauldian perspective on the 'gurus' of management would, I suppose, spend a fair amount of time discussing the term 'guru'. Could any professional, secular, grouping ask for a more powerful discourse than to be granted a spiritual presence on top of specialized training?

In a similar way, a Foucauldian analysis would analyse the discourse of the 'gurus', stressing its ability to construct particular rationalities. Thus a Foucaldian analysis would tend to draw attention to the manner in which 'gurus' construct particular notions of 'empowerment' (Collins, 1996a), 'effectiveness', 'quality', 'world class performance' and so on. In a similar way, a Foucauldian analysis would also draw attention to the extent to which such initiatives (again noting the preferential construction implied even in this term), increase the examination and surveillance of employees at work.

While Foucault, like Gramsci, would see the overthrow of such forms of power, Foucault's position, unlike Gramsci's, tends to be much less optimistic about the ability of individuals and groups to throw off the 'normalizing judgements' of disciplinary power. However, what these two 'atheists' of management have in common is a radical orientation which demonstrates a concern with freedom and emancipation. This concern with emancipation leads the 'atheists' of the 'guru' industry to challenge the 'grammar' of the 'gurus', and underscores their (atheistic) concern and suspicion regarding the power of the 'gurus'.

In contrast, the works of those writers I have labelled as 'agnostics', represent more of an ironic account of the 'gurus' and their supposed mastery of the business world. As such, the accounts developed by 'agnostics' tend to be less concerned with the transformation of society.

## The 'Agnostics'

As you might expect, it can be difficult to grasp quite what the 'agnostics' of the 'guru' industry believe in. The writers of the hagiologies clearly 'believe in' the 'gurus'. The 'redeemers', meanwhile, protest that they believe in management. The 'atheists', in turn, protest that they believe in 'humanity', and so would work to transform those things that emasculate the potential of humanity. But what do the 'agnostics' believe?

Agnostics, generally, believe that material matters are all that we can be sure about. Thus agnostics would argue that the value of 'faith' and the wisdom of 'having faith', which is stressed in religious teaching, is uncertain and unknowable. Agnostics, therefore, concentrate on secular matters, and so exhibit disdain for religious matters. In a similar way, the 'agnostics' of the 'guru' industry are disdainful of the 'gurus' of management since, they argue, having faith in the 'gurus' is, in a sense, immaterial. Huczynski (1993) has argued, for example, that the 'guru' phenomenon has been carried by some (misplaced) belief in the power of the 'gurus' to improve organizations, which is not confirmed by rigorous, material forms of analysis.

Thus whereas the 'atheists' attack the 'gurus' of management, because they dominate and subjugate humanity, the 'agnostics' tend to attack the 'gurus' because they are unscientific. Huczynski's *Management Gurus* (1993) is, perhaps, the key agnostic text in this area, and so we will analyse its key features and arguments.

## The Real King of the 'Guru' Industry?

Echoes of Huczynski's, 'scientific' critique of management's faith in the 'gurus', can be found in the redemptive texts discussed earlier. Thus Hilmer and Donaldson (1996) employ empirical techniques in their attempts to debunk the 'gurus'. However, where Hilmer and Donaldson would knock down the 'gurus' to rebuild management, Huczynski demonstrates no real interest in reconstruction. As an 'agnostic' concerned with material matters, it is enough for Huczynski to knock down the 'gurus', since this demonstrates the conquest of 'religion' by 'science'. For the 'agnostic', then, debunking is an end in itself.

Noting that by the normal standards of academic inquiry, the works of the 'gurus' are questionable (see also Collins, 1998; Burnes, 1998) Huczynski is led to ponder why the market for 'guru' products and services is so buoyant. Given that the 'gurus' of management offer similar, yet limited accounts of organization and management, how are we to explain the sustained level of demand? How are we to explain this, scientifically unsound, devotion to the 'gurus'?

### How to be a 'Guru'?

In *Management Gurus: What Makes Them and How to Become One*, Huczynski (1993) notes that, in spite of the, apparently, diverse and eclectic nature of management writing, key families of ideas have persisted, and have been reproduced over time. He argues that these families of ideas have characteristics in common which set them apart from their less successful counterparts. In this way, Huczynski notes that the key families of management ideas demonstrate crucial similarities in approach and orientation. From this he is also able to show the nature of the ideology of management which underscores these idea families.

Noting that the works of the modern 'gurus', such as Kanter and Peters, are but the latest in a long line of successful (that is marketable), management ideas, Huczynski argues that successful ideas develop an audience, and a market, by focusing upon presentation. Successful ideas, then, have a good sales pitch. But what makes for a good pitch?

### A Good Pitch

For a product to sell it has to appeal to us and satisfy some sort of need. Huczynski tells us that the successful management ideas of any particular period are those that are pitched to address the needs, and where appropriate, the fears of management. We can see for example, that in building upon fears of Japanese economic dominance, the works of Kanter, Peters and other 'gurus' of management resonate with, and reflect popular beliefs and dominant ideologies. Thus Huczynski warns us that we should not think that the most popular ideas are, in some sense, the state of the art of management thinking. Indeed Huczynski argues quite the opposite, as does Grint (1994) in his study of business process re-engineering (BPR).

Huczynski argues that the key management ideas which have served to shape western management, have not been those which demonstrate a sound methodological or empirical base, nor have the popular and persistent ideas shown any real theoretical development over the 'out-dated' ideas they were supposed to replace. Instead Huczynski shows that the key, and persistent, ideas are, in fact, bastions of arch conservatism whose authors display a common social and political orientation, while their works display a common (and pseudo-theoretical) grounding, which is seldom exposed to critical scrutiny. Indeed, and budding 'gurus' should note, Huczynski's work makes clear predictions as to what form of 'guru' work is likely to fail.

Huczynski argues that a management idea is unlikely to attract a following, and so is likely to fail to persist over time if it is new; if it challenges management's current beliefs, and if it can be interpreted as saying unflattering things about the role or conduct of its target audience. It is hardly surprising, therefore, that in discussing some of the more popular 'gurus', this book has already uncovered remarkable similarities in the content and tone of their work.

## The Ingredients of 'Guru' Success

Over-turning the negatives listed above we can discern the characteristics which seem to be necessary for 'guru' success. The key and persistent ideas of management, therefore share:

1   An understanding of the world of work which:

   • is communicable and memorable
   • is individually focused
   • has a malleable vision of human nature
   • is legitimating of management activity and the role of management and managers.

2   An intellectual focus which enhances the status of management which has:

   • a focus upon co-operation
   • some potential for managers to tailor the ideas and pronouncements of the 'guru' in question
   • a leadership focus

- some potential to allow managers to develop a feeling of being in control, in a world remarkable for its upheavals and dislocation.

3    A practical appeal and application which:

- consists of a number of steps or principles
- claims universal applicability
- carries some authority or proof
- carries the promise of improvement and/or turnaround.

It is worth examining these three key characteristics in a little more detail.

## Modelling the World of Work

Successful models of the world of work are pitched to improve memorability. In particular Huczynski observes that the best 'guru' ideas consist of only a small number of ideas and, ideally, should lend themselves to expression by an acronym, such as MBO (Management By Objectives), BPR (Business Process Re-engineering) and so on.

On the content of the model of the world of work itself, we can see that, in assuming that behaviours, structures and strategies can be changed, the model expresses the idea that managers have the right (often in fact the duty) to bring about change. We should note, too, that in having the necessary skills to achieve change, managers are the salvation of our society. Obviously, then, 'guru' ideas portray managers as having a necessary and legitimate role to play both at work and in the wider community.

## The Intellectual Focus

The intellectual focus of 'guru' models must build upon the assumptions made about the world of work, to describe the processes and the role of management within organizations. In this way, the intellectual focus should express above all, a commonality of interest between management and workers. Having established this basic harmony and commonality of interest, the model will receive an ideological boost, since it will be able to portray managers as performing an entirely legitimate, leadership role. Even in times of recession when workers are laid off, or are being made redundant; even during times of industrial strife when management may seek to hire an alternative workforce; even during times when we might expect the relationship between management and workers to be remarkable for its conflictual nature, the intellectual focus of the model serves to deny any role for conflict and instead, encourages us to think of organizations as places where skilled managerial leaders work together with committed employees.

Huczynski also notes that the successful management 'guru' will develop an idea which, while it portrays managers as leaders within harmonious organizations, must allow the audience to add to, or in some sense, tailor the content to some degree. Huczynski argues that this tailoring improves 'ownership' of the model. Indeed it is worth observing that this tailoring, which is probably better thought of as interpretation, must surely improve 'ownership', since the act of interpreting and applying the model must lead to its modification, and in this way, 'tailoring' must surely act to enhance the resonance between the model, and the dominant ideologies and problems of the time. This quality of being open to interpretation also demonstrates that if an idea is to be acceptable to its managerial audience, it should not in fact be truly novel. Instead it appears that successful ideas are, in fact, open to interpretation since they clearly build upon the current stock of managerial knowledge. Indeed Huczynski (1993) and Grint (1994) argue that for an idea to attain general acceptability, it should not require management to scrap their existing intellectual framework or stock of ideas.

## A Practical Appeal

Huczynski's third feature clearly builds on the first two characteristics while, again, confirming the role and potential of managers. The works of the 'gurus', Huczynski notes, all claim some form of authority or proof. Some 'gurus' as we have seen, tend to play on their years of experience, and on the quality of their track record in business. Academic 'gurus' on the other hand, tend to claim that their ideas and prescriptions are useful and valid, since they are based on the results of their research activity. However what is, perhaps, most notable about the works of the 'gurus' is their willingness to package their ideas in a ready-to-use format. Thus, Huczynski notes that all 'gurus' demonstrate a willingness to spell out a (limited) range of steps which, they claim, summarizes the outputs of their research/experience, while pinpointing the steps that managers must take in order to mimic the successful practices which the research has uncovered.

Grint and Huczynski offer a persuasive analysis and account of the 'guru' phenomenon. Some have argued, however, that Huczynski's (1993) and Grint's (1994) account of the 'gurus', and their ideas, tends to misrepresent the factors internal to organizations which might encourage managers to seek out, and to take up, 'guru' advice. Thus Jackson (1996) has argued that there is a need to supplement the 'externalist' critiques of Huczynski (1993) and Grint (1994) with an 'internalist' critique.

Jackson has observed that, while the 'resonant' arguments of the 'externalist' critiques have, quite rightly, observed that popular 'guru' ideas have sympathetic resonances with cultural and symbolic factors, with economic and spatial factors, and with political and temporal factors, such forms of argument fail to analyse, properly, the dramatic power of the 'gurus'. Thus Jackson, perhaps pushing on an open door, has argued that his preferred, 'internalist' critique allows us to see more clearly that, in fact, the debunking of the 'gurus' as unscientific may do little to diminish the appeal of their analyses, since 'gurus' address managers' 'sense of self' rather than their sense of the scientific. Contrary to the line of argument put forward by the authors of the 'redemptive' texts discussed above, therefore, Jackson demonstrates that managers do not passively accept the 'gurus'. Instead managers work to 'construct' the 'gurus' and, in turn, 're-engineer' their sense of self. He argues:

> Management gurus are both products and producers of managers' needs to define, judge, reconcile and preserve themselves ... Contemporary gurus ... speak to and shape the manager's self-concept through a variety of media, first by threatening that self-concept and then by offering an alternative vision in the name of survival and self-actualization.
>
> (Jackson, 1996, p. 586)

Grint (1997) echoes elements of Jackson's 'internalist' and 'dramatic' account of the 'gurus' in his five-fold account of the 'gurus' and the waves of TLAs (three letter acronyms) which they promote.

## Waving or Drowning?

Reflecting on the 'waves of fashion' which have, recently, crashed over management, Grint (1997, for more detail see Grint, 1997a) offers five different approaches geared to understanding 'this cornucopia of change' (Grint, 1997, p. 731). Of these five approaches, two, we are told, represent rationalist (externalist) accounts, two offer emotional (internalist) accounts, while the final explanation 'is itself a mirror of fashion' (Grint, 1997, p. 731).

Let us examine each of these in turn.

### Wave One: Rational Ideas

Grint's first explanation for the waves of managerial fashion offers the simplest and most clearly rationalist approach. Thus he argues that one way to explain these innovations in management would be to reflect the belief that they work! One explanation for the successive waves of TLAs, therefore, would be that managers act rationally, and innovate in order to keep ahead of competitors in a fast-changing environment. However, as the 'redeemers' of management have attempted to show, through their debunking of management's fads and buzzwords, this 'efficient-choice perspective' (Abrahamson, 1991, 1996) does not offer a particularly appealing explanation for managerial innovation since it is difficult to demonstrate that 'guru' ideas contribute to organizational success.

## Wave Two: Structural Requirements

Grint's second explanation for the waves of change in management suggests that managerial waves alternate between normative and rational concerns. Thus he notes that managerial waves seem to alternate between 'soft' and 'hard' approaches. Mapping these changes in managerial ideology against Kondratieff (1935) long waves of economic and technological development, (phases of economic development spurred by periods of capital accumulation or technological development which last for approximately fifty years), Barley and Kunda (1992) suggest that swings in economic development are matched by swings in management. Thus the expansion phase of a Kondratieff wave seems to promote a rationalist ideology, while the decline of any particular Kondratieff wave seems more closely associated with normatively based approaches to management (see chapter 4).

Grint's second wave, which might be termed a 'structural requirements' explanation, therefore, suggests once again that managers act rationally in the pursuit of management's fads and buzzwords. The structural requirements explanation, therefore, suggests that those managers who identify, properly, the managerial ideology appropriate to the phase of economic development steal an advantage over rivals who fail to innovate. Thus the structural requirements explanation suggests that 'rational' managers move between different approaches, in an attempt to tailor the form and style of management to the phase of economic development.

## Wave Three: Charismatics

Grint's third explanation for the succession of managerial waves focuses upon the inadequacies (real or otherwise) of the leaders of organizations. Noting that it is the senior members of organizations who choose to implement new waves in management, Grint argues that we should attempt to understand those factors which influence, and impact upon the sense-making, and choice-making activity of senior managers. Thus Grint argues that we must, when discussing the take-up of fads, acknowledge the extent to which charismatic 'gurus' encourage senior managers to respond emotionally, politically, and so, selfishly to managerial waves. As Grint notes:

> one should note the significance of being regarded as a fashion-setter rather than a fashion-taker. If part of the attraction of the consultant as charismatic is that some of the charisma may rub off on those who are first to use the latest technique then we might explain the desire of CEOs to throw themselves on to the experimental altar.
>
> (Grint, 1997, p. 733)

## Wave Four: Distancing

Grint's fourth wave is informed by a reading of Veblen (1994). Discussing the work of Veblen, Grint argues that material abundance has a tendency to blur boundaries and status divisions in society. Building from Veblen's analysis, Grint argues that high status groupings have a tendency to develop new forms and patterns of consumption, in an attempt to distance themselves from lower status groups. For example, wealthy and fashion conscious consumers patronize 'exclusive' forms of design and 'exclusive' holiday destinations. However, should these labels and resorts become affordable to the masses, the higher status grouping will quickly define them as passé and move on to other, still, 'exclusive' forms of consumption, in order to distance themselves from lower status manners and ideas.

Grint argues that this general tactic of social distancing might help to explain the willingness of managers to embrace new fads. Thus Grint suggests that, both within and between organizations, managers might adopt new ideas in order to mark themselves out as better than the rest. Thus as distinct from the previous explanations the distancing account: 'has less to do with the performance of the consultant or the logical promise of radical business improvements and more to do with the emotional significance of internal status and identity construction in the face of increasing complexity.' (Grint, 1997, p. 735).

## Wave Five: An Institutional Account

The fifth, and institutional argument to explain the waves of management fads, suggests that managers are subject to normative pressures at work. Grint argues that senior managers are expected to be leaders. To be a leader one cannot simply manage. One must have vision. One must be at the cutting edge of ideas. Thus Grint suggests that, even though managers may be perfectly aware of the limitations of an idea, and may be perfectly aware that any new idea (or fad), stands only a limited chance of being successful in the workplace, the truly aspirant manager cannot risk being viewed as using last year's technique, and so is pushed by normative pressures to embrace each new wave. Thus Grint's institutional argument, contrary to the argument of Hilmer and Donaldson (1996) suggests that managers may not be the hapless victims of malign, management consultants. Instead Grint's institutional argument suggests that managers patronize consultants and indulge faddish ideas, even when they understand these to be flawed, because there are status and career benefits associated with being at the head of the pack.

These five waves of explanation work to build a bridge between 'externalist' and 'internalist' explanations for the character of 'guru' ideas and for their success(ion), and so, offer a useful complement to Huczynski's mainly 'externalist', 'agnostic' analysis.

Huczynski's analysis, of course, does not represent the only 'agnostic' account of the 'gurus'. Indeed we could spend some considerable time analysing a range of agnostic-type contributions. Rather than become bogged down in this, however, we will pause to examine only the 'agnostic' account offered by Burrell (1997) before offering a brief concluding discussion.

## Pandemonium

Like Huczynski, Burrell does not believe in the 'gurus'. In fact, quite unlike Huczynski, Burrell shows a distinct lack of patience with the 'gurus'. Selecting Charles Handy as his *bête noir* (mainly I suspect because of the linguistic possibilities which this allows him as a student of language and humour), Burrell makes numerous references to limitations inherent in 'Handy pocket theory' (Burrell, 1997, p. 27) and to the attempts made by 'Handy flea bags' (Burrell, 1997, p. 47) and by 'Handy wipes' (Burrell, 1997, p. 85) to clean up, or to obscure, the true nature of organization and our anxieties regarding organizational life.

However, whereas Huczynski's agnosticism leads him to stress the social-scientific, material world, Burrell presents us with a view of the material world which is profoundly anti-scientific (or at least anti-scientistic). In this sense Burrell's work, while clearly an attack upon the 'gurus' of management, is somewhat different from Huczynski's agnosticism, since it might also be read as an attack upon the rationalistic study of organizations.

Burrell's *Pandemonium* (1997) is interesting to read, yet it is a challenge to write about. In fact Burrell seems to warn us not to analyse his work too closely, or with too much pomp. After all, he tells us that his work is a 'lubidrium', which he defines as 'a playful toying with ideas' (Burrell, 1997, p. 28). Yet, while apparently warning us off, Burrell, simultaneously, seems to dare us to analyse his work, by raising the possibility that we might, if we possess the courage, navigate through *Pandemonium* however we please. So let us risk a brief analysis.

## Shit Happens

Life, Burrell tells us is notable for its shit. Discussing cities, Burrell draws our attention to the amount of shit, both human and animal which, in previous eras, would have lain all over the city streets. Indeed Burrell notes that during the hot summer months the stench of the city would be so foul, that the wealthy city-dwellers would retreat to the mountains, or to the country to escape it. It is worth observing, therefore, that while shit is a notable feature of life, life isn't shit, not for all anyway.

Readers may baulk at my usage of the term 'shit' (there I have used it again). Some may find the term shocking and unnecessary. Yet this is exactly Burrell's point. He warns us that we neglect the 'profane' at our peril, and so, he has elected to focus upon that which is 'profane' in order to show the intellectual costs of our ignorance of 'shit'.

Building upon this analysis of shit, Burrell argues that a key element of the appeal of the 'gurus' is their willingness to obscure the dark side, the shitty, profane aspects of organization. However, he warns us that the 'Handy wipes' of 'guru' theory will not clean up the problems of organizing and managing others. 'Handy wipes' may, of course soothe the anxieties of organizational elites, but they will not, and cannot, alter the nature of the social organization of production since, he tells us, 'Handy pocket theory' offers only a narrowly pragmatic and ego-centric view of the world.

In an attempt to counter these ego-centric tendencies, Burrell argues for a 'retro-organization' theory which, he tells us might be employed to reveal the (Kingdom of) 'Pandemonium' that is hidden within (the text-book and 'guru' sanitized accounts of) modern organization. Thus Burrell warns us that while 'gurus' focus upon business success, his retro-organization theory shows us that it is business failure which is the norm! Similarly, Burrell warns us that while 'gurus' focus upon globalization, and on the salaried employees within these globalizing corporations – as if these are the only forms of organization, and the only forms of 'work' – the truth is that by the year 2000 there would be two billion peasants on the globe. This compares to the one-third of a billion on the planet in the year 1500!

Through his analysis of shit and pandemonium, through his analysis of the profane, Burrell seeks to reverse modern organization theory (and the grammar and vocabulary which conveys it) in favour of retro-organization theory. Thus, he argues that peasant organization should be an important area for analysis, not least because peasant organization exerts a profound influence on other forms of organization.

Burrell's agnosticism, therefore, leads him to attempt to overthrow the 'gurus' of management; to overthrow 'Handy theory' so that we might understand, properly, the profane complexity of managing and management, and the inability of the 'gurus', the 'redeemers' and the 'hagiologists' to grasp this 'profanity'. In this sense the agnostics of management offer a 'critical-practical' account of management's fads and buzzwords which is designed to allow us to locate, to understand and to critique.

We shall now attempt to carry this account forward into our analysis of the fads and buzzwords which we have selected.

## Summary

This chapter has offered an analysis and exposition of what I have termed the 'guru' industry. Breaking this 'guru' industry down into three main market segments, this chapter has analysed (1) 'hagiologies' and 'homages', (2) 'redemptive' texts and (3) the accounts offered by the 'atheists' and the

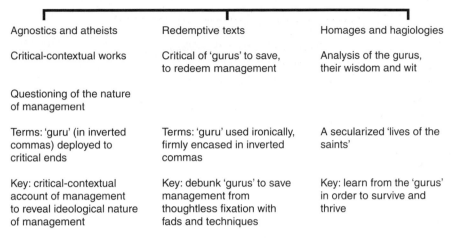

| Agnostics and atheists | Redemptive texts | Homages and hagiologies |
|---|---|---|
| Critical-contextual works | Critical of 'gurus' to save, to redeem management | Analysis of the gurus, their wisdom and wit |
| Questioning of the nature of management | | |
| Terms: 'guru' (in inverted commas) deployed to critical ends | Terms: 'guru' used ironically, firmly encased in inverted commas | A secularized 'lives of the saints' |
| Key: critical-contextual account of management to reveal ideological nature of management | Key: debunk 'gurus' to save management from thoughtless fixation with fads and techniques | Key: learn from the 'gurus' in order to survive and thrive |

*Figure 3.2* Exploring the 'guru' industry

'agnostics' of the 'guru' industry. The key features of each of these accounts is represented in Figure 3.2.

In chapter 2 we argued that, to understand fully, the fads and buzz-words offered by the 'gurus' we must, first, understand the nature of management as a separated and contestable phenomenon. Indeed, we argued that the 'gurus' of management are unable to locate, or to pierce the key issues confronting management, and managers, because they misrepresent the processes of managing, because they owe an allegiance to a truncated model of management, frozen at that point which defines managing, simply, as getting work done through others, and which assumes the practices of managing are transparent and self-evident to all.

Through our criticism of the 'hagiologies' and 'homages', and through our criticism of management's redeemers, it should be apparent that these devotions to/celebrations of management offer limited, and often distorted forms of analysis and argument, which lack logic, because they fail to grasp management as a contested, multi-dimensional phenomenon. Thus the first two segments of the 'guru' industry could be argued to limit and distort our understanding of management, since they offer only a two-dimensional view of management as activity, and management as elite.

In order to improve our understanding of management, we have argued that it is necessary to transcend this two-dimensional view of management, to embrace a three-dimensional account: management as activity, elite, and as ideology, which allows us to see, properly, social contests at work, and the attempts made by management (and the state, and the 'gurus') to maintain, to secure and to advance forms of managerial control.

Through their critical and contextual accounts of management, the 'atheists' and the 'agnostics' of the 'guru' industry offer dynamic accounts of management, and furthermore, offer us the basis for dynamic analyses of the role(s) which the 'gurus' play in the performance (however interpreted) of managing and organizing.

Let us now embark upon our 'critical-practical' analysis of the fads and buzzwords of management which have been selected for analysis.

# 4  Culture

## Introduction

As we saw in our introductory discussions, the field of management studies is not alone in making use of buzzwords. The discipline of sociology, to cite just one familiar discipline, also makes extensive use of buzzwords – terms that excite a hum of discussion and debate. In the 1980s the buzzwords of sociology and of social theorizing more generally, changed quite profoundly. The 'old' buzzwords of sociology – terms such as Braverman, Taylorism, Marxism and deskilling – were undermined by a 'new' collection of buzzwords. These 'new' buzzwords, gathered under the banner of post-modernism (both with and without the hyphen (Hassard, 1994)), include terms such as Foucault, Derrida, narrative and discourse, and have ushered in the 'linguistic turn' in sociology, and the development of 'litero-philosophy' (Merquior, 1985, p. 13). The 1980s as we have seen, also represent a period of profound change in the study of management. Indeed, while social theorizing embarked on its linguistic turn, the 'gurus' of management toiled to effect what might be termed the 'cultural turn' in management thinking.

The linguistic turn in social theorizing has led to many changes in the conduct of social scientific theorizing (Hassard, 1994). However, these changes do not amount to a *volte face*. Indeed the 'linguistic turn' in sociology has been contested to some degree. Habermas (1984, see also Best and Kellner, 1991), for example, has argued against post-modernism and has protested that the 'modernist project' so maligned by the post-modernists has not, yet, run its full course. In a similar fashion, Best and Kellner (1991) have argued that the post-modern critique is: 'excessive, abstract and subversive of theoretical and political projects that remain valuable' (Best and Kellner, 1991, p. 257).

Like the linguistic turn in social theorizing, the cultural turn in management has also led to some degree of change in management thought and practice. However, unlike the case of social theorizing, the cultural turn in management has excited comparatively little in the way of controversy or contest. Indeed the idea that cultures can, and should be managed, now represents a rather orthodox belief for a range of actors concerned with management. For example, Deal and Kennedy (1982) have argued that 'strong' cultures are vital for business success. Hofstede (1991) with perhaps just a little more feel for contingent issues, has argued that if a business is to succeed its culture must be matched with its strategy. Perhaps most famously of all, Peters and Waterman (1982) have argued that managers should take responsibility for the cultural management of their enterprises, and have argued that managers must match the 'hard-s' factors of strategy with the 'soft-s' factors of culture, if they are to achieve business success.

Clearly, many managers have taken this advice on board and have sought to change, or to intervene in their organizational cultures (see, for example, Brown, 1998). Some managers, however, seem to have embraced the concept of culture in a more literal fashion. For example the management of Chanel invoke the term 'culture' as an *aide memoire* for front-line sales staff.

Thus, just out of sight of the customer, Chanel's staff receive the following inspiration:

**C**ustomer approach
**U**se open questions to find out customer needs
**L**isten to their needs – introduce products and demonstrate
**T**ackle customer objections by reinforcing 'Chanel plus'
**U**nite with customers to get commitment to buy
**R**emember to introduce complementary products
**E**nd sale.

However not all use the term culture in such a positive and up-beat manner. Indeed some scholars have argued that the managerial advocates of cultural management and culture change, either misunderstand or misrepresent the concept of culture (Wright, 1994; Ackroyd and Crowdy, 1990; Morgan, 1986; Ackroyd and Thompson, 1999). Thus, a range of scholars have argued that the managerialist discussions of culture and cultural management, which have been prepared by the 'gurus', have a tendency to quash informed debate on the concept of culture, and on the prospects for cultural management, because they lack either the will or the skill to unpack the contests which surround this complex construction (Martin, 1992; Feldman, 1986; Smircich, 1983).

To be fair, however, we should also acknowledge that a number of managerially oriented writers have highlighted some potentially negative consequences of 'culture'. Yet where critical academics highlight problems with the management of cultures, because they observe conceptual and methodological problems in the study of cultural matters, managerially oriented writers tend to see problems, not with the conceptualisation of culture, but with particular formations of culture. For example, Deal and

Kennedy (1982) highlight the negative consequences of 'weak cultures'. Pearn *et al.* (1998) have observed the tendency for organizations to develop 'blame cultures' and have advocated 'ending the blame culture' which, they argue, restricts corporate success by inhibiting risk-taking. Similarly, senior police officers in Britain have increasingly come to discuss problems of policing in cultural terms. For example, police force managers have argued that many constabularies are now 'compensation cultures': social formations where cash settlements for illness and injury have come to be viewed as a form of perk, or pension supplement (*The Guardian*, 27/10/98).

This division between the concerns of critical academics and the preoccupations of management's 'gurus' has resulted in a state of affairs where, in spite of the misgivings voiced by a range of academics, most management writers seem either to ignore or to be unaware of the conceptual and methodological critiques made of 'cultural management', and so, tend to discuss 'culture' in a positive manner, even while attempting to encourage managers to change the cultures of their organizations. Mink (1992), for example, clearly sees opportunities in cultural management, and so, has encouraged managers to engage in 'transformational leadership'. Others, such as Oren and Bell (1995), have employed an even more up-beat and metaphorical form of analysis, as they have encouraged managers to transform their organizations from a 'Wile E. Coyote' culture to a new-style 'Roadrunner' culture!

Yet, it is not only managers and their 'gurus' who have embraced this new lexicon. Politicians, for example, have recently come to express their political aims and ambitions in 'cultural' terms. Thus Mrs Thatcher's political project has been expressed in terms of an attempt to rekindle the 'enterprise culture' of Britain (Keat and Abercrombie, 1991; Du Gay and Salaman, 1992). However, politicians have not always been able to secure control over this mode of expression. Hughes (1993) for example, has employed the metaphor of culture to criticize the impact which, he claims, Mrs Thatcher's great ally, Ronald Reagan, has had on public life in America. Railing against the therapeutic discourse evident in day-time television, and in the self-help books which both promote and underpin these confessional programmes, Hughes argues that America has transformed from the 'culture of contentment' identified by Galbraith (1993) to become a 'culture of complaint'.

Reflecting this broad spectrum of interest in the concept of culture, this chapter will attempt to unpack the concepts of culture and cultural management. Through this process of unpacking, I hope to offer readers a means to locate, to understand and to criticize management's focus upon 'culture', and the importance of managing culture. Accordingly the chapter is structured as follows.

Noting the upsurge of interest in 'cultural' matters, we begin by attempting to understand why management, and its 'gurus', have come to focus upon culture, and we will investigate why the 'gurus' of management have come to view cultural matters as the key to competitive success. From here we will examine, in more depth, the concept of culture employed by the 'gurus' before proceeding to offer a more general 'critical-practical' critique of the culture buzzword.

## Explaining the 'Cultural Turn'

Discussing the concept of culture Hofstede (1986) notes: 'IDEAS arrive when their time has come. The idea of "organizational" or "corporate" culture, since the early 1980s, has acquired the status of the dominant buzz-word in the US popular and academic literature' (Hofstede, 1986, p. 253). While accepting this statement as an accurate chronology for the upsurge of interest in cultures and cultural management, this section will endeavour to look more closely at the 1980s in an attempt to explain why the concept of culture has emerged to become, perhaps, the central motif in modern management thought and practice.

At one level, of course, we should acknowledge that the concept of organizational, or corporate culture was not discovered in the 1980s. Indeed history reveals many 'cultural' studies of management and, further-more, demonstrates that managers, long before the 1980s, had shown an interest in anthropological concepts such as culture. For example, the Hawthorne studies, conducted between 1927 and 1932 might, at one level, be interpreted as studies of organizational culture.

Wright (1994) discussing the 'anthropology of organizations', has observed the social anthropological leanings of Mayo and his Hawthorne research colleagues. She notes, for example, that Mayo, a close friend of Malinowski and Radcliffe-Brown, the leading anthropologists of the time, (see Kuper, 1993) actually recruited a student of Radcliffe-Brown's so that the Hawthorne research team might employ anthropological techniques to make sense of the workplace as a social system.

Employing Radcliffe-Brown's, then, recently developed notion of the social system, the Hawthorne research team attempted to analyse the relationship between the formal system of the workplace and the, less visible, informal system which, they observed, characterized relationships between peers and workmates. However, Wright notes that, whereas anthropologists studying third world systems had attempted to show that 'exotic' social systems were underpinned by shared ideas which, while often different from our own ideas and values, could be shown to be logical, the anthropology employed by the Hawthorne researchers did not interpret the informal system of the workplace which they uncovered as logical. In fact, the Hawthorne researchers argued that the informal system of the workplace was driven by 'sentiment', and so was to be regarded as non-rational in the face of management's 'rationalism'.

Wright (1994) does concede that the informal system noted by Mayo contrasted, starkly, with the formal system of the workplace which had been designed by management. The formal system of the workplace, for example, was designed to reward high levels of output. Indeed it would be more accurate to say that the formal system of rules and incentives 'was designed to make it to the workers' advantage to strive continually to increase output' (Wright, 1994, p. 7). Yet in spite of this, Mayo and his colleagues observed that workers seemed to limit their output and, perhaps even more surprisingly, Mayo and his colleagues observed that workers chose to under-report their output levels; choosing to disguise the level of output which they had achieved.

This tendency to restrict output and to under-report production troubled the Hawthorne researchers. The notion of the social system, which they had taken from Radcliffe-Brown's work on anthropology was underpinned by notions of common consensus. Yet the Hawthorne studies seemed to demonstrate conflicts between the formal system, designed by management, and the informal system developed by work-groups, and so, seemed to suggest either a breakdown of consensus, or the absence of a common consensus between groups at work. However, the Hawthorne researchers, it seems, could not allow this. Relativism might be the order of the day for exotic, third world anthropology, but it was a quality, which it seems did not permeate through to these anthropological studies of the workplace. Thus the observation that workers refused to join the company's incentive scheme, and the observation that workers routinely maintained production norms below their maximum, possible levels of output performance, was not allowed a 'logical' explanation, or an explanation based upon material experience. Instead the Hawthorne researchers seemed to consider that the workers' restriction of output served to demonstrate, only, the non-rational nature of the informal system as compared to the (obviously), rational nature of the formal system.

The workers' restriction of output, and their tendency to under-report the levels of output achieved, therefore, was to be regarded as non-rational and illogical, since such forms of action ran counter to the formal system and, consequently, were contrary to the economic interests of workers paid on piece rates. Yet, what the researchers did not seem to realize, or could not allow for, was that the dual systems of the workplace might both be rational. By focusing upon the formal system as the only plausible and rational account of the workplace, therefore, the Hawthorne researchers failed to understand the complexity of the workplace, and so misunderstood the contours and rhythms of the workplace culture at the Hawthorne plant. Thus the Hawthorne researchers' insistence that management's preferred approach to organizing and motivating employees was definitively rational, obscured the plain fact that the economic interests of workers might be better served by restricting output, since this strategy would smooth market fluctuations and would keep workers continuously employed, whereas full compliance with management's formal system tended to lead to periods of 'short-time' working, or to temporary lay-offs which, of course, restricted worker income quite severely.

The Hawthorne studies of 'cultural' management and their omissions and assumptions, therefore, tell us much about management and its interest in culture. They show us, for example, how management hoped to control and direct worker 'sentiment', so that this might be harnessed to the long-term (and rational) goals of those charged with co-ordinating the enterprise. In a similar fashion, we also see how this desire to harness, and to control, the social system led researchers to focus on one particular agenda in the belief that only their agenda could be rational.

We should note, therefore, that the Hawthorne researchers' attempts to enforce a common consensus, to enforce one social system upon the dual system evident in the workplace, has a tendency to portray management as the sole receptacle of rationality; and has a tendency to portray managers as the sole arbiters of rationalism within a unitary social system. Somewhat ironically, however, this representation of complex cultural formations actually serves to make the social system of the workplace opaque, since in portraying management as rationalists within a sea of 'sentiment', the Hawthorne research denies the possibility that the actions of the informal system might be perfectly rational, in spite of the fact that these actions may reflect a different agenda from that preferred by management.

Unfortunately this anti-relativist position, in spite of its flaws, and in spite of its arrogance, has proved to be a persistent theme in the study of organizational cultures. Indeed Deal and Kennedy (1982) tell us, as they preface their account of corporate cultures (and how-to manage them), that they 'think that society today suffers from a pervasive uncertainty about values, a *relativism* that undermines leadership and commitment alike' (Deal and Kennedy, 1982, p. 22, original emphasis). Clearly, then, through their anti-relativist tendencies, the Hawthorne studies continue to influence contemporary studies of organizational culture and have done much to shape and, unfortunately, to distort the preferred analytical approach adopted by the 'gurus' of management.

However, and in spite of the self-promoting activities undertaken by Mayo, we should note that the Hawthorne studies, flawed as they are, were not the earliest 'cultural' studies of the workplace. The Hawthorne studies, of course, do tend to be portrayed as discovering the informal side of organization, and so, tend to claim the social analysis of the workplace as their own. However, earlier studies of the workplace, which are often portrayed as ignoring the social side of enterprise, might equally be interpreted as having an interest in the informal systems of the workplace, and so, might be viewed as 'cultural' (if not cultured!).

## Taylor-ed and Cultured?

Taylor's discussion of 'scientific management' (1911) is often portrayed as flawed because, its detractors claim, it failed to analyse or to understand the interaction between technical and social systems at work. Yet this is something of an exaggeration.

Taylorism you will recall (see Collins, 1998) is a body of thought developed to transform work practices and work organization. Dating from around the beginning of this century, Taylorism, or scientific management as it is sometimes known, is based upon four key principles:

1   the science of work study
2   the scientific selection of staff
3   mutuality and co-operation
4   the division of labour.

As we have seen, Taylor argued that, left to their own devices, workers toiled inefficiently, working according to tradition rather than to the rhythm of scientific efficiency. To overthrow this inefficiency, Taylor argued that management should take responsibility for work design and for staff selection. Working according to the principles of scientific management, Taylor argued that management would be able to secure co-operation for a mutually acceptable, yet scientific division of labour (for more detail, see Thompson and McHugh, 1995; Braverman, 1974).

The history of Taylorism, of course, is a story built upon conflict rather than co-operation, since Taylor, using the ideology of science, seemed unable to secure consent for the 'separation' of conception from execution; management from working, which his 'scientific management' required (Hales, 1993). For some, notably the researchers of the 'human relations' school, Taylor's failures and the conflicts associated with Taylorism have been interpreted as being reflective of a larger failure to conceive of the workplace as a social system, peopled by workers who have emotional needs, and a need for intrinsic satisfaction, over and above the economic drives and extrinsic rewards, which Taylor had assumed held sway. Yet this understates Taylor's knowledge of the prevalence and importance of group regulation at work. Indeed much of Taylorism represents an attempt to intervene in work processes so that traditional group norms might be changed. As such, Taylor's work has clear affinities to accounts which promote the management of cultures and social systems.

It is true, of course, that Taylor took a dim view of many group practices. Yet the absence of relativism in Mayo's work, and in the work of Deal and Kennedy suggests that, in holding to this dim view of group norms and practices, Taylor is hardly atypical among the scholars of 'culture'. It is also true, of course, that Taylorism assumes that workers are motivated by extrinsic factors, and so, unlike the advocates of cultural management (Deal and Kennedy, 1982; Peters, 1994, 1997) Taylorism sees no real need to manage 'emotional' aspects of working. Yet it would be a distortion to say Taylor showed no interest in the processes of work-group regulation. Indeed in his concern with 'soldiering' (restriction of output, where the pace of working is set and policed by the work group), Taylor demonstrates his understanding of the efficacy of group norms and values. In this sense, Taylor's work shows a keen awareness of cultural matters, and perhaps beyond Mayo's understanding, shows a keen aware-ness of the interaction, and the conflict possible, between the formal system designed by management and the informal system developed and main-tained by workers.

It seems clear, therefore, that however negative the interest and intent, Taylor (with no less relativism than Mayo), showed an awareness of the importance of understanding the social system of the workplace. Thus if we locate interest in the management of culture as a phenomenon of the 1980s we will actually misplace the chronology of 'cultural management' by at least seventy years.

Yet, while this discussion of the works of Taylor and Mayo serves to demonstrate the long history of cultural management, we must concede that by the 1980s, 'culture' had moved from the exotic periphery of management studies, to become one of management's central and ortho-dox concerns. By the early 1980s, therefore, the notion that the social system of the workplace should be understood in cultural terms had become common-place in a whole host of both, populist and academic books and journals. Indeed as distinct from Taylor's preferred approach, managers were now extorted to work with and through teams; with and through 'cultural' matters to ensure competitive success. So what had changed?

## A Cultured Approach to Management

The 'gurus' of management argue that 'cultural' matters hold the key to corporate success. Indeed it would not be an overstatement to say that for the 'gurus' of management, 'cultural' matters offer both an explana-tion for corporate performance (or under-performance), as well as the means of securing improvements in performance. However, and in spite of the 'gurus' faith in single factor explanations (see Hilmer and Donaldson, 1996), an appropriate explanation for management's interest in all things 'cultural' is multi-factorial, and involves a consideration of a range of economic, political and social matters. These factors are clearly inter-related. It is difficult, therefore, to offer a clear and readily intelligible analysis, which captures the complex interaction of these factors. For ease of analysis however, we may separate the various influences, so long as we bear in mind that this separation is, to a degree, artificial.

### *Economic Influences*

The 1980s represent for American (and European) managers, a period of economic change and dislocation (Huczynski, 1993). This period of economic change, which saw crises in areas of industry and commerce, where America's superiority and predominance had been assumed (Iacocca with Novak, 1986) led to some degree of introspection on the part of management. Indeed, we could say that the economic depression, which marked the early 1980s, caused a crisis in western management that challenged the practices and symbols associated with management in America. Viewed in these terms, it would not be too much of an exaggeration to say that, in many ways, the economic problems of the early 1980s led actors to seek out some means of imparting meaning and significance to a form of complex work, now beset by crisis.

Of course, we now know that it did not take these social actors long to find 'gurus', initially, in the shape of Peters and Waterman (1982), who in the name of 'excellence' provided managers with the 'grammar' and vocabulary deemed necessary to situate and escape from economic damnation (see chapter 5 for more detail).

Pascale and Athos (1986), consulting colleagues of Peters and Waterman, capture this sense of crisis and dislocation rather well. In common with Peters and Waterman, Pascale's and Athos' text might be interpreted as an attempt to persuade American managers that they were not, simply, bad managers. Indeed both of these texts might be interpreted as attempts to renew and to reinvigorate the strengths of American management, while learning from the new competitors who had arisen to challenge American industry – principally, the Japanese. Yet while Pascale and Athos were keen to stress that 'good' American managers were already embracing good practice (evident in so-called Japanese managerial practice), they were equally keen to attack the sense of complacency which, they argued, had caused American management to fail to renew itself. Thus Pascale and Athos framed their explanation for the success of America's (Japanese) competitors as an impending crisis for 'the American way of life' (see also Kanter, 1985, 1989). Discussing 'the Japanese mirror' which they would use to reflect on American management they observed the following:

> In 1980, Japan's GNP was third highest in the world and, if we extrapolate current trends, it would be number one by the year 2000. A country the size of Montana, Japan has virtually no physical resources, yet it supports over 115 million people (half the population of the United States), exports $75 billion worth more goods than it imports, and has an investment rate as well as a GNP growth rate which is twice that of the United States. Japan has come to dominate in one selected industry after another – eclipsing the British in motorcycles, surpassing the Germans and the Americans in automobile production,

wresting leadership from the Germans and the Swiss in watches, cameras, and optical instruments, and overcoming the United States' historical dominance in business as diverse as steel, shipbuilding, pianos, zippers, and consumer electronics. Today, Japanese wages are slightly higher than those in the United States, and the cost of doing business in Japan – with imported raw materials, expensive real estate, and crowded highways – is decidedly higher. American executives complain of extra costs that stem from occupational safety regulations and pollution controls. While initially lagging, Japan's standards in these areas are now among the most stringent in the world. Some of us rationalize the disparity by emphasizing the problems stemming from the Arab oil crisis of 1974. While all other industrialized democracies have experienced inflation and a decline in productivity growth as a result of higher petroleum costs, Japan, which imports all of its oil, has maintained a very low rate of inflation, has increased productivity, and has by most accounts proven a more competitive trading partner in the past five years than ever before.

Despite the advantages of a homogeneous population, and those related to culture to be explored herein, there is no simple way to dismiss Japan's success. If anything, the extent of Japanese superiority over the United States in industrial competitiveness is underestimated. Japan is doing more than a little right. And our hypothesis is that a big part of the 'something' has only a little to do with such techniques as its quality control circles and lifetime employment. In this book we will argue that a major reason for the superiority of the Japanese is their managerial skill.

(Pascale and Athos, 1986, pp. 20–21)

Of course, the Asian crisis of 1998 makes all this sound just a little hollow, especially as newspapers have reported major job losses in Japan (*The Times*, 31/03/99) and the rescue of Nissan by the French firm, Renault (*The Economist*, 26/03/99). Nevertheless it is important to note that in the 1980s the message was clear. Since Japan lacked physical and material advantages, Japanese economic success, it was argued, must be built upon managerial excellence, on the capacity to engage in cultural management at the level of the workplace, and at the level of the team. The 'gurus' of management argued, therefore, that the reinvigoration of the American economy would go hand-in-hand with the development of a renewing, culturally based approach to management.

To achieve this renewal, American managers (obviously) would need help and guidance; most of all they would need that all-American virtue, self-help (Freedland, 1998) and, of course, books crafted by experts to facilitate self-help (Hughes, 1993).

### Help and Healing

Periods of crisis and dislocation are by no means alien to the United States. In fact the United States, together with the rest of the developed world has experienced a range of economic and socio-economic crises – the depression of the 1930s being one of a host of examples which continues to shape analysis and debate (*The Sunday Times*, 29/09/98). What is, perhaps notable about the United States, however, is its reaction to such events.

Writing in 1985, Baskerville and Willett capture this well. They note that in the face of social crises Americans seem to exhibit a tendency to embrace individualist, 'how-to' and 'self-help' books, in spite of the fact that, in the view of Baskerville and Willett, some more critical (-practical?) form of social commentary might provide a more useful, and a longer-term basis for social change and renewal. Their book begins:

> to those who remember the Great Depression, to those even who have merely read of its privations, the following words will have a familiar ring to them: '17,000 Washingtonians have queued outside 16 area churches for up to five hours in the relentless heat for a hand-out of government surplus food and vegetables ... Hundreds were turned away empty-handed'. This description was written not in 1933 but in 1983, adding texture and meaning to figures published by the Bureau of Census which revealed that 34.4 million Americans were living below the poverty line. Revivals of *You Can't Take It With You* (a farcical thirties endorsement of individualism) were being produced in both New York and London, providing the ironic counterpoint to a reality which saw the United States in the grip of the worst economic recession since the Second World War.
>
> Much has altered in the two years since: the unemployment rate has fallen as dramatically as the budget deficit has widened; the public mood has lightened; and President Reagan has received an electoral endorsement to rival that given to President Roosevelt in 1936. The pressure for change has proved both controversial and irresistible. Critics may rightly argue that the intellectual response to adversity in the eighties has been feeble, muted and above all conservative when compared to the ferment and clamour of the thirties; but it has not been negligible. It can be argued, for example, that supply-side economics has a sounder intellectual basis than the half-hearted spending policies of the early New Deal; that the tax-reform proposals of populist Congressman Jack Kemp are every bit as radical as the 'share our wealth' schemes of Senator Huey Long. Even so, many Americans, unconvinced by the nostrums and panaceas on offer, are clearly willing to trust the soothing words of leadership before the ambivalent complexities of intellect. In so doing, they find themselves

caught once again between an optimistic hope that the future will be better, and a nagging fear that just round the corner yawns a fathomless abyss.

(Baskerville and Willett, 1985, p. 1)

We can see, then, that Baskerville and Willett capture both the contours of the recession of the early 1980s and the response to crises such as recessionary downturns in the US. Through this Baskerville and Willett show us that it is the interpretation of, and the reaction to, economic events and circumstances that is significant in explaining the emergence of social changes, such as the rise of the 'gurus' and their vocabulary of cultural management. Thus Baskerville and Willett remind us that, if we are to make sense of economic events, we must attempt to analyse how the actors involved actually make sense of these economic matters. To our economic explanation of the 'cultural turn' in management, therefore, we must add a political dimension.

### Political Influences

Economic changes do not, themselves, cause changes in thinking and practice. Economic changes, of course, may do much to facilitate changes in thought and practice. Thus, economic turmoil in Germany during the 1920s and 1930s seems to have done much to facilitate Nazism, but it would be a simplistic over-statement to say that Germany's depression caused Nazism. Instead, to explain historical developments such as the rise of Nazism, and the 'cultural turn' of management we have to ask: how do economic changes make changes in practice palatable? How and why does Nazism become persuasive? How and why does 'cultural management' become *the answer?*

To answer our question on cultural management (and to some degree the question concerning our illustrative example of the rise of Nazism) we must analyse the role(s) played by politicians and other influential groupings in interpreting economic crises, and in crafting strategies to resolve these crises.

The economic turbulence of the 1980s, which we noted above, finds its reflection in profound changes in political policy and political leadership, particularly in Britain and the US. As distinct from the Keynesian policies, which had formed the backbone of economic management in both Britain and America since at least World War II, the Republican administrations in America and the Conservative administrations in Britain, embraced a radically different policy agenda. Whereas Keynesian economic management attempted to manipulate the level of economic activity, in order to maintain stability in both price levels and in levels of employment, the monetarist agenda, embraced by governments on both sides of the Atlantic, argued that inflation should be the key policy item such that governments might, for a time, have to allow the rate of unemployment to rise so that a long-term equilibrium might be achieved (Burton, 1982; Hayek, 1978). Or, more plainly, politicians argued that Keynesian economic policies, through their stress on seeking consensus with organized labour, had damaged the economic viability of western economies, making them inefficient, over-staffed and prone to rigidity (Minford, 1982; and for an alternative view, Burkitt, 1981). To solve these problems politicians argued that the cosy, consensus-oriented and union-friendly (or union-enslaved) policies of previous administrations would have to be abandoned in favour of radical and far-reaching forms of change. Thus Britain and America experienced a policy of deregulation (and re-regulation in the case of union activity (see Beaumont, 1993; Kessler and Bayliss, 1992; MacInnes, 1989)) designed to facilitate fundamental changes in economic management.

Given the economic crises of the 1980s and this reaction to it, we should not really be surprised to learn that the change-oriented, deregulation policies associated with Thatcherism, and with Reaganomics, at the level of the economy, facilitated similar agendas for change in industrial and commercial management. Indeed the 'grammar' used to convey, and to promote the Thatcherite economic policies of the 1980s is, in many ways, indistinguishable from the language of the 'gurus'. Thus, both politicians and 'gurus' have expressed their projects in 'cultural' terms as necessary, and unavoidable missions to change cultures in order to reorient the economy and to rekindle the spirit of enterprise (Keat and Abercrombie, 1991; Du Gay and Salaman, 1992).

Yet, while economic and political changes make the 'imperative grammar' of culture and cultural management 'thinkable', they do not necessarily make this rhetoric feasible. Taken together, therefore, our discussion of the economy and the polity do not in themselves, provide a fully coherent explanation for management's 'cultural turn'. After all previous Conservative administrations in Britain had publicly voiced the *need* to control trade unions and the *need* to deregulate the economy (Crouch, 1982). Yet these calls had failed to secure a policy of deregulation, in the face of trade union opposition. To fully comprehend the 'cultural turn' in management, therefore, we must address the social and institutional changes which shape, and which in turn, are shaped by changes in the economy and polity.

### Social Influences

As early as 1958 the Inns of Court Conservative and Unionist Society in Britain, had published a pamphlet complaining that Britain's trade unions were 'over-mighty' (Crouch, 1982). To remedy this state of affairs the pamphlet, entitled *A Giant's Strength* argued that, amongst other things, the right to strike should be restricted and that trade unions should be accountable, at law, for the actions of their members. Elements of these changes were, of course, incorporated in the trade union legislation enacted in Britain during the 1980s (see Blyton and Turnbull, 1994). So what we must ask is this: why did it take at least twenty-one years to move from pamphlet to policy?

To answer this we need to consider the following; what factors changed between 1958 and 1980 (the date of the first of the Thatcherite Employment Acts), to make economic deregulation and trade union regulation possible? Here a number of factors, together with the economic recession of the 1980s, are implicated. While we can do little more than sketch these influences it is, nevertheless, worth drawing attention to the changes in the structure of industry and employment; the decline of employment in coal, steel and in ship-building, for example (see Edwards, 1995), which weakened the 'big battalions', and the local organization of the trade union movement, so leaving unions disadvantaged in the contests which ensued with key private sector employers (see Melvern, 1986) and with the government and its public sector managers (see Sirs, 1985; and MacGregor, 1986), over redundancy, regulation, technological change and 'cultural change' more generally.

As this brief sketch shows, a range of factors have served to promote, and to facilitate the 'cultural turn' in management. Indeed our sketch illustrates that we can only make sense of this 'cultural turn' as an attempt to change, and to regenerate the economies of Britain and America, when we are able to locate this economic project within changes in wider social and political factors. Having sketched these changes, let us now turn to examine the concept of culture within the context of management.

We begin the following section by showing the rather unreflective approach adopted by the 'gurus' when discussing the concept of culture, before moving on to offer a more critical form of analysis designed to unpack the 'guru' construction of culture.

## Culture's Culprits

Discussing the virtues of 'strong' organizational cultures Deal and Kennedy (1982) define culture as: 'the way we do things around here' (Deal and Kennedy, 1982, p. 4). This is an awful definition. It is an attempt at definition which does little to clarify ideas or concepts. It is an attempt at definition which does nothing to contextualize the key concept(s). It is, therefore, a definition which does little to promote analysis, or to guide reflection. As a consequence this 'definition' does little to inform or to illuminate discussion.

Yet while Deal's and Kennedy's account of culture as 'the way we do things around here', is truly awful, it works fairly well as an allusion. For this reason, and because this 'definition' is popular with students and managers alike, we will use Deal and Kennedy as the 'launch vehicle' for our, critical, analysis of the concept of (organizational) culture.

Deal's and Kennedy's 'definition' of culture draws attention to culture as a pattern of action. Indeed, the concept of culture, in many ways, might be thought of as a metaphorical attempt (Morgan, 1986) to say something about the complexity of human action and interaction within certain contexts (see also Hatch, 1997). Viewed in these terms, cultures are formed, are maintained and develop, or change, on the basis of human interaction. As Martin notes:

> *As individuals come into contact with organizations, they come into contact with dress norms, stories people tell about what goes on, the organization's formal rules and procedures, its informal codes of behaviour, rituals, tasks, pay systems, jargon, and jokes only understood by insiders, and so on. These elements are some of the manifestations of organizational culture. When cultural members interpret the meanings of these manifestations, their perceptions, memories, beliefs, experiences, and values will vary, so interpretations will differ – even of the same phenomenon. The patterns of configurations of these interpretations, and the ways they are enacted, constitute culture.*
>
> (Martin, 1992, p. 3, original emphasis)

Unlike Deal's and Kennedy's, preferred, analytical approach, Martin's account of culture shows the importance of adopting a relativistic stance towards the study of action and interaction at work, since her account of culture draws attention to the fact that the perceptions of organizational members – even of the same phenomena – will tend to differ! Yet at this stage, Martin's account of culture is mainly descriptive, drawing our attention to the existence of such things as rituals and 'in-jokes', within organizations (see Sims *et al.*, 1993). However, there is more to the study of culture than description alone. Indeed there would be little in the way of managerial interest in the study of organizational culture, if the concept allowed only for the description of organizational phenomena and human interaction. Thus we should acknowledge that cultures, in the allusion offered by Deal and Kennedy are not just patterns *of* action, observable phenomena amenable to description, they are also patterns *for* action, forms of action underpinned by a constellation of norms and values which, to some degree, guide our thinking and our routines.

Viewed in these terms, as a pattern of action, and as a pattern for action, the concept of culture, and the idea that cultures can be managed represents, apparently, a powerful tool for management. As it has been interpreted by management writers, the concept of culture promises managers that they will be able to manipulate, not only the actions of their employees, but also how employees think and feel about their work, their careers, and their customers. Thus the idea of cultural management seems to promise managers that by manipulating employee beliefs they will be able to build organizations that will be successful in the long term. Indeed Deal and Kennedy, apparently oblivious to the

National Socialist overtones of their project, tell us that they hope to instil a new law for business: 'In Culture There is Strength' (Deal and Kennedy, 1982, p. 19).

For managers struggling to match their competitors in the early 1980s this was, no doubt, a welcome motto. In a simplistic and readily under-standable way, this motto promised managers that, like their Japanese counterparts, they too, could learn to manipulate the values and beliefs of employees. Furthermore, the motto seemed to promise that once control of the organizational culture had been attained, once a 'strong' culture had been established, the business would, more-or-less, take care of itself, since the organization would become flexible, adaptive and open to change.

This line of argument, however, is built upon a range of rather dubious assumptions. Key among these assumptions are the ideas that:

- cultures form templates for thinking, feeling and acting
- the organization represents the appropriate unit for analysis when studying culture(s).

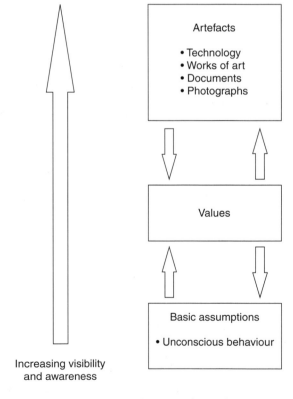

*Figure 4.1* Schein's model of culture. *Source*: Schein (1985)

Let us pursue these assumptions through an analysis of Schein's discussion of culture.

### Culture's Layers

In comparison to Deal and Kennedy, Schein's (1985) approach to the analysis and management of organizational culture is based much more clearly upon an attempt at definition. For Schein, the term culture:

> should be reserved for the deeper level of *basic assumptions* and *beliefs* that are shared by members of an organization, that operate unconsciously, and that define in a basic 'taken-for-granted' fashion an organization's view of itself and its environment. These assumptions and beliefs are learned responses to a group's problems of *survival* in its external environment.
>
> (Schein, 1985, p. 6, original emphasis)

Based upon this definition, Schein argues that cultures may be thought of as having different levels, or layers, and offers a diagram, similar to the one reproduced in Figure 4.1, to aid analysis.

## Artefacts

The top layer of Schein's diagram deals with cultural artefacts. These artefacts, things such as photographs, documents, technologies and works of art, Schein tells us, are visible manifestations of cultures. Through an analysis of cultural artefacts we can learn much, or at least we can make educated guesses, about human action and interaction in certain contexts (Collins, 1998). For example, an open-plan office architecture might be interpreted as an artefact associated with 'cultures' which promote free-flowing and *ad hoc* forms of communication. Conversely, forms of architecture which work to exclude certain types, or classes, of employees from particular areas the Vice Chancellor's corridor, the 'executive washroom' – might be viewed as artefacts which facilitate the interpretation of social action within more formal, more hierarchical, forms of culture.

Together with such 'visible' artefacts, however, we might also include such things as speech patterns. Reflecting upon his attempts to understand the politics and sectarianism of Northern Ireland, Parker (1993) for example, reflects upon the importance of speech and language codes in deciphering the norms and values of social life in Northern Ireland. It is worth quoting from this at length.

Parker notes:

> however irrelevant and unimportant it seemed to me, a middle-class English agnostic pacifist, I soon and quickly started to learn what first

and most mattered in Northern Ireland today – which is that no relationship can proceed unless certain basics are clarified to begin with.
The first thing you need to know about someone as soon as you meet
them – and they equally need to know about you – is whether each
or both of you is Protestant or Catholic. To be 'neither' is not sufficient. You can be 'neither' now but in that case what matters is 'where
did you begin?' Or in other words, what were your parents, where
were your grandparents? What is your *origin?* This must be, and almost
unfailingly is, established within the first minute, or at the most, two.
Once on a social occasion my wife happened to tell someone she'd
never met before that her ancestors had been in the siege of what was
known as Londonderry in 1689. It was true: but jokingly though she'd
intended it, immediately came the only half-humorous response:
'Where were they? Inside the city or besieging it?'

The need for knowledge of someone's present faith or antecedents
isn't for the purpose of expressing empathy or antagonism, but purely
so that any following conversation can continue with greater ease.
Once you know whether you share a common background, or you
do not, thereafter you can avoid saying the wrong thing, or wrong
word, to unwittingly [*sic!*] cause offence.

Anyone born and brought up in Northern Ireland can do this effort-
lessly, practised since birth: almost by extra-sensory perception, it seems
at times. More than one person told me casually and in passing,
making nothing of it because it seemed quite normal, that they could
usually tell at first glance merely by looking at someone what they
were. I found this incredible – until before long, I became aware I
was trying to do it myself: and, when I sometimes got it right, was
coming to regard it as a skill. Then even more incredibly, came the
discovery after a while, that I was beginning to *want* to know, and
bothering to try to find out. I started to ask myself why I cared.
Curiosity of course, was the answer, no more than that. But what
happened then to its all being 'irrelevant and unimportant'? No really
it was just curiosity, that's all. Honestly no more than that. But tell
yourself whatever you like: you do wonder, you do listen, you do
notice, and you want to find out. Insidiously it pervades, it corrodes
you. It really does.

Because of such things as these. If you are Protestant and 'British',
you'll always call the second biggest city in Northern Ireland
'Londonderry': if you're Catholic and/or Nationalist, you'll only refer
to it as 'Derry'. Nationalists and Catholics speak of 'the North', Ireland
or, intentionally aggressive, 'the Six Counties'. 'Northern Ireland' and
'Ulster' are Protestant terminology: and to speak of 'the Province' in
front of a Nationalist is provocative, even if it wasn't intended . . .
Catholics and particularly Republicans never talk about 'the Troubles'
– they use the blunter 'the war' or 'the struggles'. Even in the *minutiae*

of pronunciation there are giveaways: the Department of Health and Social Security's initials are pronounced 'DHSS' by Protestants, but by Catholics 'D Haitch SS'. So too with the IRA: more correctly 'The provisional IRA', its members are only called the 'Provos' by Protestants: to Republicans, Nationalists and Catholics they're 'the Provies', the slightly changed sound with its more moderating softness perhaps revealing something else as well. These are only some of the more obvious pointers. But in every conversation there'll come the faintest of suppressed grimaces, or the slightest flicker in an eye, if a 'wrong' word is used revealing you to be one of the 'others'.

(Parker, 1993, pp. 3–5, original emphasis)

Schein warns us in his definition, however, that we should not think that the analysis of artefacts, and observable patterns of behaviour (however diverting), exhausts the study of culture, since to understand cultures we must see through these visible phenomena, to study the norms and values which underpin such things as the creation of works of art, the structuring of speech and the lay-out of work space, which all serve to shape, and to regulate, human interaction.

Schein argues, therefore, that in order to understand cultures we must be able to account for, and to explain, the patterns of interaction we reveal through description. Thus Schein warns us that we must move from the description of action and artefacts, to a point which will allow us to understand how culture, as a pattern for action, works to influence the artefacts of any given society. The next level of Schein's diagram, therefore, is concerned with values.

### *Values*

Value judgements build from belief systems and, in turn, shape norms. At the risk of over-simplification we can illustrate this as follows: A *belief* in a Christian God, and in the sanctity of Christian commandments, leads Christians to hold certain *values*. These values mean that for Christians it is *wrong* to steal (and to murder, and to covet, and so on). The Christian code of values and the consequent belief that certain forms of thought and action are wrong, therefore, leads to certain *norms* or standards of behaviour, such that God-fearing Christians will be law-abiding and will not steal; will not murder, and above the requirements of statute law, will not covet.

Beneath the layer of values there is another level in Schein's diagram. This deepest and, least visible level, Schein refers to as the level of basic assumptions. These basic assumptions, Schein's definition tells us, are located in the 'unconscious', and shape our norms, values and beliefs. In this sense, Schein's definition argues that 'basic assumptions' shape how we think, feel and act; in a fashion that is, to a large degree, mysterious to us.

## 'Basic Assumptions'

Schein's model of culture is popular with both the practitioner and the academic community. In part, this popularity may be due to the fact that Schein's model offers an academic veneer and justification for Deal's and Kennedy's promise. We can see, for example, that in defining culture as relating to 'an organization's view of itself' (Schein, 1985, p. 6), Schein has developed a managerialist (Thompson and McHugh, 1995) and consensus-oriented view. Thus Schein argues that the organization should be the subject of analysis, while securing the organization's needs for survival (so little chance of relativism here!), should be the objective of cultural studies of the workplace. In a similar way, we can see that in rooting the study of culture in the mysterious realm of the unconscious, Schein (either deliberately or unwittingly) adopts a tactic central to the *modus operandi* of the management 'guru'. Thus in rooting cultural norms and values as part of the mysterious and 'unconscious', Schein, it might be argued, mixes just enough hocus-pocus to make this simplistic prescription; that cultural change is like collective mental programming, delphic enough to seem profound.

Feldman (1986) is, rightly, scathing of Schein's account of, and prescription for, managing culture change. He notes:

> Using one of the most misunderstood concepts in the social sciences, Schein defines culture as existing in the hidden 'unconscious'. The problem is that the term 'unconscious' does not refer to a place, but is a linguistic device to *describe*, not *locate*, mental phenomena.
> (Feldman, 1986, p. 87, original emphasis)

Perhaps the main problem with this device is that it implies that organizational cultures – patterns of and for human action and interaction – are not amenable to the normal tools of social-scientific analysis. After all, if cultural assumptions are rooted in 'the unconscious', how are we to study these? Indeed we might allow ourselves to wonder how Schein has been able to force the understanding of culture as a multi-layered phenomenon from his own 'unconscious'. We might wonder what extremes of training, what powers of transcendence might be required to reveal the 'unconscious'? Alternatively we might simply discard 'the unconscious' as a device which serves only to obscure the nature of social action (Feldman, 1986; Collins, 1998).

With 'the unconscious' exposed as a device (and a rather poor device), to describe mental phenomena, Schein's analysis of culture, and his prescriptions for managing culture can be shown for what they are: spuriously practical accounts of human action, and interaction, which deform rather than inform our understanding. Indeed with Schein's 'unconscious' exposed as a device, it should be apparent that the models of Deal and

Kennedy, of Schein, and of a whole host of other managerialist authors are just that: models, human constructions which reflect human (in this case, managerial) drives and afflictions, more than they reflect any set of 'needs' or any notion of reality (Chia, 1996). In fact, the work of Martin (1992) demonstrates that these managerialist accounts of organizational culture represent only one of a range of possible constructions for the interpretation of organizations, as cultures.

## Three Perspectives on Culture

Martin (1992) warns us that, as is the case with theoretical models more generally (see Collins, 1998), we should not discuss models of culture as being 'right' or 'wrong'. Inevitably, she notes, certain theoretical models, and so, certain modellings of culture will appear as preferable to us. However, she warns us that our preference for certain constructions does not imply that other, less preferred, models should be regarded as 'wrong'. With this admonition in mind we will make use of Martin's work to illuminate three different perspectives on culture before proceeding to analyse the problems and paradoxes inherent in managerialist (and often *anti*-relativist) discussions of organizations as cultures.

### An Integration View

Managerialist accounts of organizational culture conform to what Martin would refer to as an 'integration view' of culture. An integration view of culture stresses the extent to which cultural norms and values ensure social cohesion. In the work of Deal and Kennedy (1982), for example, culture is said to act like a social glue, which allows *organizations* (as the unified subjects of analysis) to meet competitive challenges, and to cope with uncertainty. In a similar fashion Schein's (1985) notion of culture, as a form of collective mental programming, and Hofstede's (1991) notion of culture as being 'software of the mind', vital to corporate survival, also point to the integrative function of culture. Harrison's (1995) discussion of organizations as task cultures, role cultures, power cultures and person cultures, similarly, draws attention to the *function* which culture performs in allowing different types of organizations to match, and to meet the challenge, which their environments throw at them.

From an integration perspective the management of culture, and the management of cultural change is fairly easily accomplished. Indeed, if culture is, in some sense, the software of the mind, or is some form of collective mental programming, then it would appear that all management must do is to re-code, or re-wire the organization; informing people of the newly desired collective beliefs so that changes in belief systems may occur (Feldman, 1986). Thus from an integrationist perspective, the process of cultural management and change is a process hinged upon managerial

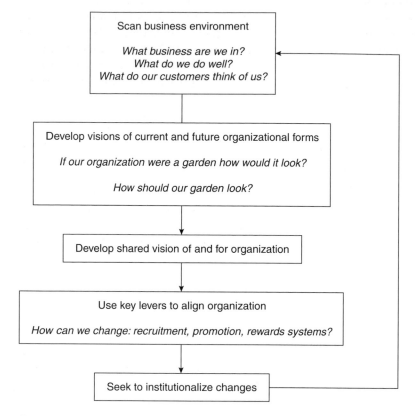

*Figure 4.2* An integrationist account of cultural management and change

leadership. It is a process where skilled, committed (and rational) leaders diagnose the 'need' to change, and then set about changing the values and attitudes of employees (towards 'customers' for example) so that long-term organizational success may be attained.

Schematically this process may be represented as in Figure 4.2. This integrationist view, which is popular with managers and with their 'gurus', however, is called into question by what might be termed a differentiation perspective.

## *A Differentiation Perspective*

Martin notes that in spite of the fact that integrationist accounts constitute something of a 'guru' orthodoxy, a differentiation perspective may be used to attack the integrationist – culture as the social glue delivering business success – perspective. Thus a differentiation perspective on organizational culture would argue that integrationists focus only upon harmony, and so, see norms and values only as centripetal forces for *organizational* good. For differentiationists, however, such a consensus-oriented account of culture represents a distortion of the nature of human interaction, / and so, a distortion of the nature of organization. Differentiationists, therefore, would tend to argue that, in spite of the fact that many forms of human organization are notable for their tendency to exhibit harmonious social relations, we must allow for the fact that conflicts exist with, and within 'harmony'. A 'differentiation' perspective on culture, then, in comparison to the unitary account of the 'integration' perspective, is built upon / a plural understanding of human motivations and of human action. In this sense the pursuit of a shared vision, developed by a rationalist senior management, becomes problematic. This is a concern reflected in the work of Ackroyd and Thompson (1999) on 'misbehaviour'. Discussing the notion of cultural change, they argue that management writers confuse behavioural 'tractability' with behavioural 'corrigibility'. Thus Ackroyd and Thompson argue that, while behaviour at work is properly regarded as tractable, as being open to influences which may effect marginal changes in behaviour, it would be wrong to view organizational behaviour as corrigible, since this would be to assume that patterns of thinking and behaviour could be permanently adapted to conform to managerial expectations.

Reflecting these concerns over the efficacy of shared visions in complex social formations, a plural, or pluralist, modelling of organization, and culture, would seek to overthrow simplistic notions of organizational needs. Rather than assume that organizations, as concrete things, have needs, the pluralist account offered by the differentiation perspective acknowledges, explicitly, the understanding that organizational goals are, in fact, / created and promoted by certain groups (such as the 'gurus'). Accordingly, the so-called needs of organizations should be viewed as conscious creations oriented to address the drives and ambitions of certain dominant individuals and groups. Unlike the 'integrationists, who study 'organizations', therefore, differentiationists might be more inclined to study 'organization' (Hatch, 1997; Chia, 1998, 1998a), the complex process of co-ordinating actors and action. In this regard, differentiationists would be inclined to reject the idea that we may meaningfully study organizations as concrete, stable and harmonious entities. Reflecting this focus upon organization, and in contrast to the account offered by the integration perspective, differentiationists would argue that the drives and ambitions which actors exhibit, ( may conflict with the drives and ambitions of other individuals, and of other groupings, who may understand the so-called 'needs' and 'mission' of the organization, in a radically different way. A differentiation perspective on culture, therefore, would argue that the needs, goals and mission of the organization cannot be viewed as being natural and self-evident. Equally, a differentiation perspective would argue that since the drives and ambitions of any one grouping may conflict with the norms and values of other groups, to a considerable extent, it will often be meaningless to talk of (the) organization as a single culture. Under these (common) conditions we require a differentiated, or multi-cultural viewpoint, which can acknowledge the existence of sub-cultures – distinctive constellations of norms and values, variously drawn into conflicts with other groupings – within (the) organization.

Within the differentiation perspective, therefore, we do not have as a necessary assumption, the idea that the norms and values of individuals and groupings will coalesce to provide a basis for business success. The differentiation argument, of course, does not rule out the idea that consensus and commonality might develop or might, to some extent, be engineered. However, what a differentiation perspective does draw attention to, through its study of conflict with, and within, harmony, is the idea that a model which assumes harmony will tend to distort, and so mislead us, on the very dynamics which it promises to manage. However, the differentiationists do not have it all their own way.

### *A Fragmentation View*

Just as differentiationist scholars remain unconvinced by integration accounts, so scholars persuaded by a 'fragmentation' perspective remain unconvinced by the differentiationist attack on those who view cultures as the glue vital to business success. While acknowledging, and indeed confirming the importance of studying the conflicts associated with human action and interaction, fragmentationists would tend to argue that the differentiation perspective sees the world too clearly. Thus the fragmentationists would argue that while the differentiation perspective, quite correctly, analyses the conflicts between, and within, sub-cultures, it quite wrongly assumes that these conflicts have clearly defined battle lines. Fragmentationists, therefore, would argue that life, even organizational life, is much more complex and ambiguous than the other schools allow for. In this way a fragmentation perspective draws attention to the flux and ambiguity which is characteristic of many forms of social networks and understanding. In this sense, with cultural formations viewed as complex and ambiguous social formations, the notion that culture might be managed to engineer business success becomes rather dubious.

Taken together the differentiationist perspective – which argues that cultures exhibit conflicts and uncertainties making them problematic to manage – and the fragmentationist perspective – which argues that cultures are complex, ambiguous, more-or-less opaque, and so, virtually impossible to manage – raise a range of problems and paradoxes for the managerialist account of cultural management. In the following section we will pursue these.

# Culture's True Consequences?

A number of rather damaging points of criticism may be levelled against the managerialist accounts preferred by the 'gurus'. Over the next few pages we will deal with just four of the key points. These critiques are offered both to show the limitations of the 'guru', 'practical' account, and to show the benefits for action and reflection, of a more 'critical-practical' account.

## A Social View

The metaphor of culture, when applied to the analysis of organizations is, at one level, an attempt to acknowledge the complexity and multi-faceted nature of organizations (Morgan, 1986) It is somewhat ironic, therefore, that managerialist accounts of culture, penned, ostensibly, to explore organizations as cultural forms, offer only what might be termed a White, Male, Management (WMM) account of cultures.

Discussing the extent to which the training, experience and identity of the researcher influences both the questions chosen to research and the conduct of this research, Martin (1992) notes the tendency within discussions of cultural management to produce, not just a management view (as the integration perspective does), but a White, Male, Management view. Indeed in the work of Deal and Kennedy (1982) we have White, Male, Management Consultants (WMMCs) studying White, Male, Managers' stories and recollections, with the result that we are presented with a rather superficial and simplistic account of complex social formations. As McCrone (1992) notes in his discussion of 'Scottish culture', superficial and simplistic forms of analysis which masquerade as discussions of culture offer an account 'of personalities rather than people, of events rather than processes' (McCrone, 1992, p. 18).

Thus most accounts of culture and most accounts of managing culture have a tendency to discuss personalities – a work-crazed Geneen; a tough-talking Iacocca, an avuncular Hammer (?) – and to trade anecdotes, rather than engaging in meaningful discussions of peoples, processes and social action. Would we, after all, accept a collection of war stories as offering a definitive account of American history, or Apache culture (Debo, 1993)?

Since we would reject an account of Apache culture which focused solely upon the hostile activities of Geronimo's 'renegades' (Debo, 1993), we must also reject the simplistic account of organizational culture put forward by the 'gurus'. Thus we should acknowledge that the work-focused WMM or WMMC view, preferred by the 'gurus' fails to acknowledge key dimensions of work and organization which are central to a social-cultural understanding of the workplace. For example, Deal's and Kennedy's WMMC account of culture fails to recognize the extent to which 'non-work' (Hales, 1993; Sims *et al.*, 1993; Ackroyd and Thompson, 1999) is characteristic of 'working'. As Sims *et al.* note:

Looking at organizations purely as places of work is almost as naive as looking at sex purely as sexual intercourse. Our sexuality is a central part of our personality. We all have sexual desires, anxieties and fantasies and we spend some of our working time talking, joking and thinking about sex. The graffiti in toilets and lifts, the pin-ups in lockers and workshops, the sex gossip and casual conversations provide ample evidence that sex is very much on people's minds during their time at work.

(Sims *et al.*, 1993, p. 145)

On humour and joking, other important elements of the 'non-work' performed at work, they make a similar point. Thus, in spite of the fact that humour is central to our experience of life and work, and in spite of the fact that Britons claim a different sense of humour from their 'European' and American cousins, no real attempt is made to examine the cultural role, and the cultural contours of humour in the (integration) accounts of culture prepared for managers. *Sotto voce* integration accounts may claim that humour provides a function in organizations; pulling people together to give them shared understanding, and over time a common heritage. Yet if you are female; if you are black; if you are black and female; if you are gay, or if you are 'normal' yet find racism and sexism to be offensive, your experience of workplace humour is likely to resonate to a fragmentationist tone.

On the serious nature of management studies Sims *et al.* note:

Most organizations are serious places. People go about their business with deliberate seriousness. they fill in forms seriously, they answer phones seriously . . . An air of no-nonsense fills organizational spaces.

From time to time humour makes a tentative appearance. A joke in the middle of a stuffy meeting or a cartoon on an office wall lightens the atmosphere and raises a smile. But books on management and organizations [including those which purport to study organizationl cultures!] have not paid much attention to such phenomena.

(Sims *et al.*, 1993, p. 158)

### *Pattern or Template?*

We observed in our discussion of the managerialist accounts of culture, that 'gurus' and practising managers developed an interest in the concept of culture because success in cultural management seemed to promise to deliver competitive salvation, if not competitive success. Thus we observed that, to some degree, culture forms a pattern for action and so exerts an influence on how we think, feel and act. Yet we are not slaves to culture. Cultural norms and values, in spite of Schein's notion of mental programming, do not form templates for behaviour. Indeed cultural 'rules' are notable for being 'negotiated'. For example Malinowski, in his anthropological investigation of the Western Pacific, observed that in spite of cultural rules and conventions regarding reciprocity and gift-giving, the Trobrianders should be viewed as living, calculating, *individuals*. As Malinowski observed: 'whenever the native can evade his obligations without the loss of prestige, or without the prospective loss of gain, he does so, exactly as a civilised [*sic!*] business man would do.' (quoted in Kuper, 1993, pp. 24–25).

Scott (1990) offers similar illustrations concerning the extent to which cultural 'rules' are negotiated. Indeed, Scott's work suggests that the returns accruing to the culture changing endeavours of management might well be far less rewarding than managers might have hoped, since his analysis suggests that any new roles, and any new rules, implemented in organizations, would be just as 'flexible' and just as negotiable as the old! Thus Scott confirms the point made by Ackroyd and Thompson (1999) that while behaviour may be tractable, it is not corrigible.

Reflecting upon the negotiated nature of such complex patterns of thinking and action, Scott (1990) observes:

> the pastoralist Tutsi, who were feudal lords over the agriculturalist Hutu in Rwanda, pretended publicly that they lived entirely on fluids, from their herds – milk products and blood – and never ate meat. This story, they believed, made them appear more awesome and disciplined in the eyes of the Hutu. In fact, the Tutsi did like meat and ate it surreptitiously when they could. Whenever their Hutu retainers caught them in flagrante delicto they were said to have sworn them to secrecy. One would be astonished if, in their own quarters, the Hutu did not take great delight in ridiculing the dietary hypocrisy of their Tutsi overlords. On the other hand, it is significant that, at the time, the Hutu would not have ventured a public declaration of Tutsi meat-eating and the public transcript [the official version of the truth] could proceed *as if* the Tutsi lived by fluids alone.
>
> (Scott, 1990, pp. 50–51, original emphasis)

In a similar way, Scott (1990) observes that while we, as outsiders, are encouraged to think of the cultural prohibitions attached to caste as being 'set in stone', subordinate groups and elites seem only too willing to conspire in the contravention of cultural norms and prohibitions which we have been encouraged to view as inviolable. He notes:

> Officially contact between [high-caste Hindus and untouchables] is governed by the elaborate rituals of relative purity and pollution. So long as this public reality is sustained, many Brahmins apparently feel free to violate the code privately. Thus, an untouchable procurer delights in manoeuvring his high-caste customers into eating with him

and using his clothes, and they appear relatively unperturbed, providing this behaviour takes place offstage.

(Scott, 1990, p. 51)

Yet we need not confine ourselves to 'exotic', anthropological examples. In our everyday lives we see many examples of the negotiation and re-negotiation of cultural norms and values. Such activity suggests that culture is far from being the template for thinking, feeling and acting which the integration perspective implies. As I have written (perhaps just a little too biographically) elsewhere:

> In each of our own lives we can all, I am sure find instances of . . . cultural renegotiation and modification. For example we might 'fiddle' our expenses, or 'fiddle' an insurance claim, perhaps because the company is 'fair game'. We may, in spite of legal and religious prohibitions, and in spite of the frowns of our elders, argue that fiddling the company is acceptable because this form of individual action against a large company is not regarded as being 'real' theft in our eyes. Equally we may choose to procure resources from our place of employment (pens, stamps, a desk, a computer) based upon a similar understanding that such actions should not really be considered a theft. However, and in spite of such acts of theft, we will probably regard ourselves as up-right, law abiding and culturally speaking, mainstream.
>
> (Collins, 1998, p. 119)

### *Cultural Desert?: Cultural Island!*

Managerialist accounts of culture management and cultural change discuss organizations as if managers were solely and completely the architects of their own destiny, and the destinies of all those employed within the organizations (see Martinez-Lucio and Weston, 1992, for a discussion of this applied to HRM).

This, however, is an arrogant over-statement of managers' capability to manipulate and change organizations. At one level this faith in managerial control seems to imply the existence of definite and impermeable boundaries which seal organizations (and cultural management programmes) from the influence of the wider society (Martin, 1992). This, however, conflicts with the lived experience of organization (which cultural studies are supposed to capture).

Organizations do not exist in a vacuum. Organizations, of course, are pervasive features of modern life, but they are also pervaded. They are shaped by the wider society as much as they shape society. Thus it is difficult to establish the existence of clearly defined boundaries around organizations. For example, I recall as a child growing up on the fringes of Kilmarnock that, twice a day, groups of old men would congregate and would then set off together towards town. I call these men 'old', not in a disrespectful sense, but because as a young child that is how men aged sixty-five and over appeared to me. As I grew up, the reason for this congregation, and the reason for this shared journey became apparent. These 'old' men, I now realize, formed something of a senior citizen elite. They were former employees of the whisky blender Johnnie Walker and Co., and as retired former employees they had the right to present themselves at the plant twice a day, at which time they would be offered, without charge, a 'nip' of whisky.

Where, then, does Johnnie Walker, the company, begin and end? Since the company maintains such close links with its retired ex-employees (who are now sent a generous ration of whisky to save them the, twice daily, walk) might there not be a case for saying that the boundary of Johnnie Walker and Co. extends well beyond the factory gate? Indeed this example shows how difficult it can be to establish (either concretely or analytically) an organizational boundary.

Overall this policy of gifting whisky to retired ex-employees of Johnnie Walker and Co. suggests the limited usefulness of the 'cultural island' perspective, evident in the integration account, since it seems clear that aspects of Johnnie Walker as a cultural formation extend beyond the plant gates and into the wider community, into the homes of retired ex-employees, into the lives of their spouses; into my childhood memories . . . and into this book!

The 'cultural island' perspective, which views organizations and their cultural formation in isolation, therefore, seems facile and unhelpful. It fails to acknowledge, for example, that, in spite of management's tendency to prolong the working day, we are allowed home at night and when we return in the morning, we will have a perspective on managing and organizing informed by our experience of the wider society. These wider experiences as we noted above may lead us to bend and to rene-gotiate the cultural norms of the workplace. Equally our experience of the wider society may lead us to reject management's plans or even to 'blow the whistle' on some form of wrong-doing, which the policies and procedures prevalent in the organization (a manifestation of its culture) may otherwise promote or condone.

### To Have and To Hold?

Managerialist accounts of culture, as we have seen, are arrogant and 'over-socialized' (Clegg, 1993), since they assume that managers can change systems and structures while altering how people think of these things. When discussing culture and cultural change this form of thinking is facilitated by the assumption that organizations *have* cultures (see Ogbonna and Wilkinson, 1988). Ackroyd and Crowdy (1990; see also Morgan, 1986), however, are dismissive of this line of argument. They argue that organizations do not *have* cultures. Instead they warn us that organizations *are* cultures and that the metaphor, of organizations as cultures, has been coined to suggest the complexity, the disorganizing and unmanageable characteristics of organizations. Forging an implicit comparison between an integrationist account and their preferred modelling of culture as a differentiated (if not fragmented) phenomenon, Ackroyd and Crowdy note:

> 'managing culture' is only possible if it is regarded as something an organization 'has' – that is a variable (or variables) that can be manipulated. In other words, that culture is accessible to control through the ability to change such things as payment and information systems; or even more superficially, through the use of such things as mission statements and corporate image. If, on the other hand . . . an organisational culture is what an organisation 'is', that is, the common values and beliefs which have emerged from people's shared experiences, then it is much less obvious that organisational cultures are amenable to control.
>
> (Ackroyd and Crowdy, 1990, p. 3)

Pursuing this theme of differentiation/fragmentation Ackroyd and Crowdy note:

> People act out their work roles in a manner that is highly dependent upon their customary definitions and understanding of their task and its meaning. These meanings are embedded in quite distinctive class, regional and national cultures.
>
> (Ackroyd and Crowdy, 1990, p. 3)

Finally on this theme we should note that the assumption that organizations 'have' cultures leads to a rather curious and illogical position. If an organization can 'have' a culture, then, this would seem to suggest the possibility of a situation existing, or arising, where an organization 'has' no culture. This is implicit in Schein's (1985; see also Feldman, 1986, 1989) account of culture and leadership, and is clear and explicit in Ogbonna's and Wilkinson's (1988) account of change management in the UK supermarket industry. Thus Ogbonna and Wilkinson suggest that high levels of staff turnover may make for weak ties, and poor affective linkages among supermarket employees such that supermarkets may, in effect, not have organizational cultures. Yet this represents a rather non-sociological, (a WMM), and integrationist account of organizations as cultures, and so, represents a distortion of the social experience of working.

By turning our back on this simplistic and integrationist account, to embrace the more complex accounts offered by the differentiation perspective, and by the fragmentation perspective, it becomes apparent that the supermarket studied by Ogbonna and Wilkinson *is* a culture. To suggest otherwise would be to conjure a picture of carnage and war, since, if we were to say that an organization truly 'had' no culture, we would describe a state of affairs where social regulation and negotiation would be absent, since no code of values, beliefs or norms would exist to pull the population together, and in this sense we would confront a violent *dis*organization!

Thankfully the fragmentationists and the differentiationist offer us some means to correct such a misapprehension. Thus where the integrationists see an absence of culture, differentiationists see what they had expected to see – people within structures being drawn into disagreements and into factions, due to their differing drives and experiences. Similarly the fragmentationist would see, not an absence of culture, but people being drawn into issues and disagreements which, because of the ambiguity of life and experience, they must attempt to make sense of, while pursuing a theme or defending a corner, whose significance might not be fully apparent either to themselves or to others.

Taken together these four points of criticism do a great deal of damage to the simplistic, managerialist account of culture as an organizational variable which lends itself to management.

## Summary

This chapter has sought to locate, and to contextualize, the factors underpinning the 'cultural turn' in management. Locating management's interest in cultural matters as a product of a range of economic, political and social changes the chapter proceeded to analyse the concept(s) of culture deployed by management's cultural 'gurus'. Looking critically at the concept of culture invoked by the 'gurus', the chapter has argued that this conceptualization represents an integrationist account of culture. Having outlined the challenges to this form of thinking which have been laid down by differentiationist and fragmentationist accounts of culture, the chapter then concluded by outlining four key criticisms which may be made of the 'practical' accounts offered by the 'gurus'. Through this analysis and exposition, this chapter has attempted to offer a 'critical-practical' account of culture, and of managing culture which is intended to draw attention to the limitations of cultural management, both conceptually and in practice. Through this analysis, the chapter has aimed to illuminate the potential pitfalls that await those who would blindly follow the advice of management's specialists.

# 5 Excellence

## Introduction

The year 1982, as we have seen, represents, in many ways, the birth date of the modern management 'guru'. In this year Tom Peters, together with Bob Waterman, a consulting colleague from McKinsey, began to refashion (some would say, debase) the 'grammar' and the lexicon of management. Thanks to Tom Peters (and others), the 'grammar' of management practice is now couched in imperatives. The vocabulary of management, meanwhile, has come to focus upon an enlarging range of fads and buzz-words. Excellence is one of the main pivots upon which this new management vocabulary turns.

The concept of 'excellence', as applied to the world of business is a complex, yet seldom analysed concept. Accordingly we will examine the excellence buzzword in this chapter in an attempt to analyse its meaning(s), the context of its formation and its limitations.

We shall accomplish this examination through an analysis of the main works of Tom Peters. This analysis of Peters' thoughts on management, and managing, will attempt to unpack the key assumptions underpinning Peters' managerial project. From here we will examine the changes evident in Peters' work, while offering an examination of the analytical stabilities evident within his, otherwise, chimerical account of management and managerial leadership.

So that a balance may be struck between exposition and analysis, this chapter will offer a chronological account of Tom Peters' discussions of management as these have been presented and developed in the range of books to which he has contributed (either as sole author, or as co-author). We could, of course, have chosen many vehicles for our analysis of Peters and his views on management. We might, for example, have included Peters' many syndicated newspaper columns as part of our analysis. But since these columns are (however loosely) based upon his books, the inclusion of these columns in our account of Peters and his work seems an unnecessary duplication of effort. Equally we could have offered an analysis of Peters 'in motion', had we the inclination to attend his seminars and 'skunkwork camps'. By the same token we might have chosen to include, let's call them, the Tom Peters franchise products, such as *The Tom Peters Business School in a Box* (Goldberg *et al.*, 1995).

However, we must draw a boundary around our analysis at some point, and so this chapter will focus upon the books which Peters has either written, or co-written. This does not mean, however, that we will ignore Peters' more dramaturgical (Jackson, 1996) contributions. Through an analysis of Peters' books we can, in fact, gain key insights into Peters' seminar presentations since a number of Peters' works, especially his later works (Peters, 1994, 1995, 1997) are derived from his seminars, and have been designed as an attempt to mimic the free-flowing, organic nature of such forms of interaction. Limiting our analysis to Peters' key and major texts, therefore, should not unduly restrict our discussion. We will not, however, analyse the 'school in a box' (Goldberg *et al.*, 1995). We are primarily concerned with the work of Peters, and so, there is little to be gained from the analysis of a text which, although it bears his name, has not been authored by Tom Peters. At a more prosaic level it is also worth acknowledging that we have enough text from Peters' own hand available to us, and so do not need to analyse his 'fellow travellers' at this stage. Our chapter begins, therefore, with an account of Peters' first, and perhaps most (in)famous mass-market publication on management, *In Search of Excellence* (Peters and Waterman, 1982).

## In Search of the Excellence Phenomenon

*In Search of Excellence* (or *ISOE*, for short) was developed from an in-house research project conducted by a number of McKinsey employees. Written around the turn of the decade, *ISOE* was published in America in 1982. This, as we shall see, was a period of upheaval and re-evaluation in America.

From 1981 to 1983 America endured a deep business recession. This downturn in business activity was the worst America had suffered in five decades and led to street scenes which many thought (or hoped), had been consigned to an earlier period of history. *The Observer* (quoted in Baskerville and Willett, 1985) for example, noted that in Washington DC 17,000 people had queued for up to five hours to receive food handouts. Similarly the American Bureau of Census Statistics published figures which show only too painfully the social impact of this economic dislocation. Thus the bureau noted that in 1983, 34.4 million Americans were living below the poverty line (Baskerville and Willett, 1985).

By the early 1980s, therefore, there was for many Americans, the feeling that things were going badly wrong in the home of the brave. This feeling was reinforced by the impression that America, and Americans, were suffering while others, (mainly the Japanese) prospered. Thus the concept of 'excellence', and the appeal of *ISOE*, was forged not by recession alone, but by an understanding that other nations seemed immune to the recessionary problems which seemed set to despoil, and bankrupt, both American industry and the American polity.

Fears regarding Japanese economic success and the growing dominance of the Asian economies more generally had, of course, been troubling a number of commentators and many, ordinary, Americans before the recession of 1981–1983. As early as 1970 Kahn had published *The Emerging Japanese Superstate* which argued that Japanese per capita income would exceed the per capita income of the US by the year 2000 as Japan rose, inexorably, to become an economic superpower. However, by 1978, Kahn had revised his forecast and was now suggesting that the Japanese economic mission to catch up with the west would be accomplished by 1980. This led a great number of people to ponder the reasons for the success of the Japanese economy.

The Japanese economy, as we have seen (see chapter 4), has virtually no natural resources. It has no coal-fields and no oil reserves. Indeed Japan is short of most things, including land. It is the size of just one American state (Montana), but it has a population roughly half that of America's. Lacking natural resources, Japan imports all its key resources. Yet in the 1970s and 1980s it ran a trade surplus with almost every developed economy in the world. This led many to argue that Japan's economic success was predicated upon its superiority in management. In particular, it was argued that Japanese economic success was cultural at root.

Japanese managers, it was argued, had become adept at managing organizational cultures (Fukuda, 1988) and it was this approach to management which had given Japan its economic advantage. In the early 1980s, therefore, there seemed two routes available to American management: either they could work *like* the Japanese or they could work *for* the Japanese (Fucini and Fucini, 1990).

Rejecting such forms of argument and analysis as distorted and unhelpful (and no doubt as unpalatable), Peters and Waterman elected to write a text which they hoped would both demonstrate, and celebrate, the quality of American management. Thus *ISOE* was conceived as an attempt to educate American managers in *American* management, and so, was designed to stimulate American managers to adopt the practices of a range of 'excellent' American corporations.

## 'In Search of Excellence'

*ISOE* is based upon a simple, yet plausible idea; that successful organizations have something in common. Indeed Peters and Waterman suggest that it is what these organizations have in common that (1) explains their business success, their excellence, and (2) sets them aside from less successful, less-than-excellent, corporations.

Using the, now famous, 7-S framework developed by McKinsey and Co., (see also Pascale and Athos, 1986) Peters and Waterman argued that their 'excellent' organizations had developed methods which allowed them to strike a balance between the 'hard-s' and the 'soft-s' factors of strategy. Finding the appropriate balance between the 'hard-s' and the 'soft-s' factors of business strategy, Peters and Waterman argued, was the key to competitive success. Indeed, they argued that the slippage of corporate America had occurred because of imbalances in the American approach to management. These imbalances, they argued, had developed in the approach to management which had emerged in American during the 1950s and 1960s. Thus Peters and Waterman argued that in the post-World War II era, many American managers (and the American military – see p. xviii of *ISOE* for a brief discussion of the 'warning' of Vietnam) had become fixated upon the 'hard-s' factors of business *strategy*, *structure* and *systems* and had lost sight of the importance of *staff*, *style*, *skill* and *superordinate* goals, the 'soft-s' factors required to breathe life into strategies, structures and systems.

Peters and Waterman argued, therefore, that 'excellence', measured mainly in financial terms, would be achieved if managers could develop the skills and insights necessary to bring out the, (latent), best in American management. The search for excellence, therefore, was designed to regenerate American management and to turn the tide against the Japanese. In these terms excellence is the outcome of finding a balance between:

- *Strategy*: the strategic goals and mission of the organization
- *Structure*: the organizational structure developed to facilitate communication and co-ordination
- *Systems*: the policies and procedures of the organization

which American corporations and America's military planners had become fixated with, and the under-developed 'soft-s' factors of:

- *Staff*: the nature of the organization's staff
- *Style*: the preferred approach adopted by managers as they work with and through others
- *Skills*: the distinctive capabilities of the firm
- *Superordinate goals*: the guiding concepts; the significant symbols used to orient organizational members in the achievement of organizational goals.

As this framework shows, excellence is primarily a managerial product. Indeed, it is to be regarded as the outcome of a balanced approach to management. Excellence, therefore, is not a technological attribute, nor is it something dependent upon a patented process. Instead, it was argued that excellence is rooted in the ability of skilled managers to get the best out of committed employees. Excellent companies, therefore, would not be confined, only, to particular sectors of the economy. Indeed Peters and Waterman were keen to argue that excellence was not just the domain of high tech and highly fashionable business concerns. Highly traditional and, apparently, unfashionable sectors of industry and commerce were promised that they, too, could achieve excellence if they worked to ensure that strategy and staff, structure and style, systems and skills were melded by managerial leadership to meet the demands of customers. In this sense Peters and Waterman argued that excellent companies (even those from quite different industrial and commercial settings) would share attributes in common. Each would have a culture (see chapter 4) displaying the following.

- *A bias for action*: Excellent companies, Peters and Waterman argued, engage in traditional planning activities, but they are not bound by these. An excessive reliance on traditional forms of planning, and a reliance upon 'hard' data analysis, they argued, delays effective decision-making and discourages risk-taking. Thus Peters and Waterman observed that excellent companies avoid 'paralysis by analysis' by scrupulously avoiding the use of committees, and by refusing to accept that all decisions have to be backed by 'hard' data analysis. Instead of making excessive use of committees, Peters and Waterman argued that excellent companies maintain a bias for action; a willingness to try out new ideas; a willingness to take risks. This commitment to action, they argued, is maintained by excellent companies because these organizations form *ad hoc* groupings of people who 'love' to innovate and experiment. This tendency to action, they suggested, might be contrasted with other companies who seem to form committees with a brief to *talk* about experimentation.
- *Close to the customer*: Excellent companies, Peters and Waterman argued, gear their innovation, and their strategies, structures and systems to meeting, and exceeding, the expectations of the customer. Where a product or a system failed to satisfy customer needs, the excellent organization, Peters and Waterman argued, would have a means of identifying this, and would have a channel to ensure that this information was fed back to the appropriate personnel within the organization, so that the problem would be remedied.
- *Autonomy and entrepreneurship*: Excellent companies value entrepreneurship. To encourage enterprise, to encourage people to develop and to try out new ideas, excellent companies, Peters and Waterman argued, try to ensure that departments and units remain small enough to allow for *ad hoc* exchanges and informal networking. From such forms of exchange, Peters and Waterman argued, new ideas and new products would be developed which would keep the company close to the customer.
- *Productivity through people*: While it is easy to mouth the words that people are the organization's key asset, Peters and Waterman argued that excellent companies pay more than lip service to this idea. Thus

excellent companies work to ensure that people are recognised and rewarded for their contribution so that they, in fact, feel valued.

- *Hands-on, value driven*: Leaders of excellent companies are just that. They are leaders, not managers. In an attempt to refine the concept of leadership, Peters and Waterman argued that leaders are visible. They lead by example. Maintaining close contact with staff and with customers, leaders work to foster key values (customers first, zero defects) which, we are told, bind people together in the pursuit of common goals.

- *Stick to the knitting*: Excellent companies, Peters and Waterman argued remain focused upon the key skills of the organization. Contrary to the trend towards the construction of huge, conglomerate, organizations, Peters and Waterman argued that excellent organizations thrive because they understand where their strengths lie, and build upon these strengths to delight their customers.

- *Simple form, lean staff*: Excellent companies are staffed by skilful, innovative and committed men and women. In an attempt to maximize the potential of their staff, excellent companies, Peter and Waterman argued, adopt simple, team-based structures, designed to maximize interaction, and so, innovation. Since the organization is value driven, and staffed by competent and committed employees, the organization does not need to invest (divest?) money in the development, and maintenance of a complex bureaucracy designed to oversee the efforts of others. Instead the excellent organization is able to adopt a simple (team-based) form and is able to operate, successfully, with a lean staff geared to meeting the needs of customers.

- *Loose–tight properties*: Excellent companies confront and conquer a key paradox. Excellent companies value innovation and risk-taking, and so, they reward free-thinking people who have the courage, we might say, to reinvent the wheel. Yet to reap the rewards of innovation, to ensure that innovation remains customer-focused, a system of control is required. In seeking to channel and to control innovation, however, managers run the risk that they will actually stifle innovation. To overcome this paradox, excellent companies, Peters and Waterman argued, work carefully to ensure that staff understand the organization's values and are oriented to achieving these. In order to encourage innovation, therefore, the managers of excellent organizations make use of a loose system of management. Yet because the organization is value-driven, managers may employ this system of management, safe in the knowledge that the trust this places in their co-workers and subordinates will not be abused since the core values of the organization serve to integrate and to focus the diverse and autonomous contributions made by the various teams throughout the organizations. Thus excellent companies reward loyalty and commitment by granting freedom and autonomy!

As we have seen in earlier chapters, Peters and Waterman have sold millions of copies of *ISOE*. There can be few managers who have not (at least pretended to have) read it. On its own terms *ISOE* is a persuasive, perhaps even a seductive piece of work. After all who could disagree with the idea that successful companies direct their efforts towards meeting customer needs? Who could disagree with the idea that companies that desire innovation from their staff must be prepared to reward innovation? Who would disagree with the idea that companies need to strike a balance between the social and the technical, between the 'soft-s' and the 'hard-s' factors, if they are to achieve excellence?

Yet in spite of all this seduction, and in spite of the fact that *ISOE* seemed to spell out a cogent action plan for American management, and for the survival of corporate America, there are key problems with the analysis offered by Peters and Waterman. Indeed Guest (1992) has argued that *ISOE* is 'Right Enough to be Dangerously Wrong'.

## Dangerously Wrong?

In a paper entitled 'Right Enough to be Dangerously Wrong', Guest (1992) captures both the empirical and theoretical limitations of *In Search of Excellence*, while at the same time exploring the ideological appeal of the study. Guest notes that criticisms of *ISOE* may be divided into two camps: namely, methodological criticisms and conceptual criticisms.

### *The Methodological Critique*

*ISOE* attempts to distil, from a sample of highly successful US firms, what it is that separates the successful organization from its less successful counterparts. To separate the successful from the less-than-successful, we require some form of sampling technique. Guest argues, however, that there are problems with the sampling technique adopted by Peters and Waterman. Indeed Guest argues that the sampling techniques adopted by Peters and Waterman are *ad hoc* and lack an objective methodology.

Guest notes that in preparing *ISOE,* Peters and Waterman selected an initial group of seventy-five companies for analysis. These companies had previously been identified by McKinsey staff as being 'highly regarded' in their industries. Peters and Waterman tell us that they then went on to conduct interviews in about half of these highly regarded companies. As an aside we should note, however, that this 'half' actually amounted to thirty-three companies.

From the original grouping of seventy-five, Peters and Waterman tell us that they subsequently rejected thirteen companies as failing to reflect the pattern of European business. Analysing the remaining sixty-two, Peters and Waterman tell us that they decided that, based upon an analysis of a range of financial performance indicators, thirty-six companies could be judged to be 'excellent'. However by 'boosting' the scores awarded for innovation, Peters and Waterman finally decided upon forty-three excellent companies. From this grouping Peters and Waterman elected to conduct interviews in twenty-one of these companies. To supplement this sample of twenty-one, however, Peters and Waterman decided to study a further twelve companies which they describe as 'near misses' on their criteria of excellence.

Looking more closely at Peters' and Waterman's sample of 'excellent companies', Guest has argued that it is unsystematic and lacks objectivity. For example the initial selection of seventy-five companies, which was conducted by the McKinsey consultancy firm, appears to have been rather *ad hoc*. Thus, we should note that the sampling technique adopted by Peters and Waterman may have omitted a number of qualifying organizations from the study. Furthermore, we should note that a range of the qualifying attributes selected by the authors seem highly subjective and resistant to objective measurement. For example, Peters and Waterman seem quite cavalier in their treatment and measurement of qualifying organizational attributes such as innovation, blithely 'boosting' the scores attached to this attribute in order to add to their sample of 'excellent' organizations.

Together with such design problems, Guest also observes that the data collection techniques adopted within the study are questionable. Indeed the information gathered on the, so-called, excellent companies appears to have come from an *ad hoc* grouping of senior executives and journalists, and seems to have excluded those who would really know what it was like to work within these excellent companies. Surely it would have been better to base the analysis of the management of excellent companies upon a representative sampling of the organization's employees?

No doubt these employee, insider, accounts would have offered, at least, an interesting complement to the accounts offered by the senior executives and by the journalists interviewed by McKinsey staff. Indeed, it is worth pondering whether 'ordinary' employees would have been able to confirm the willingness of the CEO to live up to the eight attributes of excellence. Would these employees have been able to confirm that the CEO did indeed, reward innovation? Would these employees have been able to confirm his/her willingness to praise staff skills and to praise initiative?

The truth is, we do not know. So we cannot confirm that excellent organizations do balance the 'hard-s' and the 'soft-s' factors of business, and so, we cannot say that Peters and Waterman were able to confirm their excellence thesis.

Together with this methodological critique, we should also consider the conceptual problems which Guest has identified.

### *The Conceptual Critique*

At the conceptual level Guest observes that, implicitly, the excellence literature assumes that managers are entirely the controllers of their own destiny. Thus *ISOE* fails to acknowledge the range of contextual and environmental influences which intervene in the conduct of business, and which impact upon the opportunities for business excellence and success. Indeed in assigning organizations to a category marked 'excellent', it is unclear whether, what Peters and Waterman have trumpeted as excellence in management, leading to business success, might more usefully be considered as business success built upon technology, a patented process, geographic advantage, trade protection, or any one of dozens of environmental and contextual factors. Furthermore, in addition to noting that a number of Peters' and Waterman's companies have subsequently fallen from grace (the criticism which students recall), Guest also notes that the authors fail to discuss whether in fact, all of the eight attributes of Peters' and Waterman's excellent organizations are, in fact, necessary for excellence. Might it be the case, for example, that, say, six of the eight attributes of excellence might be sufficient for business success?

Leaving aside the other caveats for a moment we can see that in the Peters and Waterman framework this might be a distinct possibility, since there is a certain duplication among their eight attributes. For example the first and third attributes, and to a lesser extent the seventh attribute, all deal with issues of structure, while attributes number two and six deal with customer service, market niches and so on.

Overall, then, we can see that *ISOE* is a rather poorly conceived, and poorly executed piece of work. Yet in spite of these failings Peters has gone on to make more millions and has gone on to write subsequent books on management and leadership. Let us turn to examine Peters' first follow-up work, *A Passion for Excellence* (Peters and Austin, 1985).

## A Passion for Excellence

*A Passion for Excellence* (*PFE*, for short) might be considered as the 'new testament' revision to the 'old testament' of *ISOE* . Like the Christian 'new testament', *PFE* is an extension of *ISOE*, yet in other ways it offers a revised account of excellence, and promotes a slightly different template for management (and for salvation). Thus in *PFE*, excellence in business is said to stem from just two key attributes:

1   taking exceptional care of customers
2   innovating constantly.

Peters and Austin argue that if organizations commit to taking exceptional care of their customers, and commit to innovation as the only constant, everything else will fall into place. Just as Christians committed to the single new testament commandment to love others as thy self, do not need to be told not to steal, and not to murder, so organizations committed to their customers and to innovation, do not need to be told that productivity comes through people or that they must be close to the customer, since these sentiments and ideas are subsumed within *PFE*, and its two commandments.

However, while *PFE* clearly exists as an attempt to extend, and to promote, the excellence project, it adopts a rather different mode of presentation and persuasion. Whereas *ISOE* was based upon empirical research (however poorly conceived and executed), *PFE* adopts a different tack, which all but rejects the idea that managers will require empirical proof to persuade them of the vitality, and validity, of the excellence project. In common with a range of business and management books written during the 1980s, therefore *PFE* eschews theoretical reflection and methodological rigour, in favour of the logic of common-sense (Collins, 1998, 1996).

Apparently oblivious to the sociological problems of placing one's faith in simple facts (since this assumes that *my* simple facts are *your* simple facts), Peters and Austin take their inspiration from Thomas Paine. Applauding Paine's commitment to common-sense, and to plain talk, they imply that their book will offer the same: simple facts, plain arguments and common-sense. They admonish us, too, that this should be enough to persuade anyone with the courage to drop their defences and their prejudices, of the eloquence and validity of their business mission and the command-ments therein. With an amazing sociological sleight of hand, therefore, Peters and Austin, simultaneously, excuse the fact that their book lacks the methodological and theoretical basis required to substantiate their claims, while disempowering those who might wish to dispute their ideas and claims.

While we gather the strength necessary to deal with the blackguarding, which Peters and Austin would visit upon anyone with the (cynical and prejudiced) temcrity to challenge *PFE*, let us examine their ideas and their analysis in a little more detail.

### The Two Faces of Passion

Published in 1985, *PFE* looked out on an altogether more buoyant and more optimistic economy than was visible from *ISOE* in 1982. However, memories of the recession of 1981–83, and the desire not to live through another recession, still loomed large in the text. Introducing *PFE*, Peters and Austin note: 'The battering American business took in the seventies and during the 1981–83 recession (is there anyone who thinks recovery means we're permanently out of the wood?) has humbled virtually every American manager' (Peters and Austin, 1985, p. xviii).

In an attempt to extricate American managers from these metaphorical woods, *PFE* advocates 'leadership'. Thus Peters and Austin argue that leadership is to be regarded as the central, and key, component in achieving excellence. To ensure that customers receive exceptional care, and to ensure that organizations innovate constantly, leadership is required. Indeed, and according to their sub-title it is leadership which makes *the* difference.

So what does leadership do? What do leaders do? Frankly, and from a reading of Peters and Austin it would be easier to state what leaders cannot do – because it seems that there is nothing that leaders cannot do; there is nothing that leadership cannot achieve. One problem, as we shall see, is that Peters and Austin do not pause to consider what leadership might be! But for the moment let us look at what 'leaders' do; let us examine *PFE's* prescription for leadership.

### The Practice of Leadership

For Peters and Austin the practice of leadership is based upon Management by Wandering Around (MBWA). This concept, of course, had been introduced to readers in Peters' first text, *ISOE*, where it had formed a component of the 'bias for action' attribute. However, in *PFE*, the concept of MBWA moves centre stage to become the key factor underpinning managerial leadership, which in turn is the foundation underpinning the two commandments of excellence.

The concept of MBWA states that managers cannot lead from the boardroom. While managers can lead from the front, they cannot lead at a distance. Thus Peters and Austin argue that managers will only come to be viewed as leaders (and so, will only develop the followers required in value/vision-driven organizations) when they are able to connect with their staff. For some members of the boardroom elite, this approach to leadership, Peters and Austin acknowledge, may be a difficult and trying process. There is the implication, therefore, that for some a passion for excellence may actually turn out to be a Christ-like passion.

Peters and Austin warn us, however, that there is no way to avoid the challenge, and no way to avoid the pain, which a passion for excellence may bring, because there is no means, aside from leadership, to solve the problems and paradoxes of modern management. Whereas *ISOE* argues that management needs to balance 'soft' and 'hard' analysis, *PFE* argues that 'soft' analysis is 'hard'! In fact, page after page of *PFE* celebrates 'soft' analysis. Thus managers are exhorted to follow their instincts; to do the obvious. Likewise they are encouraged to throw off the chains of statistical analysis, so that through naïve listening, they might see problems anew.

This, of course, does not mean that *PFE* is anti-analysis. What it does imply is that Peters and Austin are attempting to undermine the privileged position of 'hard', 'number-crunching', as *real* analysis in order to demonstrate that 'soft' forms of analysis are equally (often more) reliable than 'hard' analysis. As Peters would say – if the guys who built it, tell you it walks like a duck and quacks like a duck, why would you need focus groups in twenty-nine states to tell you that it is a duck?

So what do we do with all this information? Well it would be tempting to dismiss *PFE* as a technique-fixated (Hilmer and Donaldson, 1996) approach to management. But, in truth, such a claim will not stick easily to *PFE*. In fact there is much within the text of *PFE*, which, at one level, promotes careful, thoughtful and reflective management practice. Every few pages, in fact, Peters and Austin issue their readers with questions and topics for *analysis*. The question we must ask of our management 'gurus', however, is this: short of exhortation and distracting anecdotes what has been done to lighten the burden? What has been done to smooth the way; to soothe our problems? Unfortunately the answer is very little.

*PFE* is a 'galvanizing' book (Hamper, 1992). It exhorts action. It exhorts a customer focus. But it provides little in the way of material which might actually help managers to locate, and to analyse the problems they face. Indeed, it is difficult to escape the conclusion that Peters and Austin would have offered a greater lasting benefit to management had they published fifty pages of questions (rather than 400 pages of 'war stories') and, then, just left managers to sort things out themselves, because after ploughing through more than 400 pages of densely packed text, this is the end result anyway!

After all what does *PFE* actually teach us about the nature of management? It teaches us that managing is difficult – well we knew that thank you (although many managers do not seem properly to comprehend why managing is so fraught and problematic, since, as we saw in chapter 2, most analyses of managing obscure questions concerning the nature of management). *PFE*, of course, teaches us that western economies are open to foreign competition – but this is old hat! *PFE*, its supporters claim, teaches us that leadership is the key to business success, and so, teaches us how to lead – well, no it doesn't do this at all.

In fact *PFE* does much to obscure and to make opaque what is, anyway, a complex topic for analysis. Leadership, Peters and Austin tell us, is the key to excellence. Yet, as we plough through *PFE* we move from a position where leadership is the key; to a position where leadership and trust are required; then to a position where leadership, trust and integrity are all required. From here, *PFE's* position becomes one where leadership, trust, integrity and listening are all central to management, before moving to advocate leadership, trust, integrity, listening, coaching, empowerment (and as Bert Moorhouse my tutor at the University of Glasgow would say when confronted with such lists from dim under-graduates) 'Uncle Tom Cobley and all and all, Uncle Tom Cobley and all . . .' will be required.

Rather than present a clear and useful statement on leadership and excellence, therefore, Peters and Austin, in fact, could be argued to have produced an approach to this complex question, which denies the very real problems of conceptualizing leadership, while obscuring and mystifying its practice. However, we should acknowledge that *PFE's* mystification of leadership does perform one analytical function. It prevents readers from unpacking the concept and practice of leadership, and so, prevents readers from unpicking the gossamer threads, which hold *PFE* together. Thus Peters' and Austin's common-sense approach to business might well be thought of as an attempt to stop readers recognising that the central analytical component of *PFE*, leadership, is no simple and self-evident 'fact'.

### Leader Ship (or Fleet)

Quite contrary to the intention of its authors, *PFE* is an intensely theoretical work. Indeed as we noted in earlier chapters, discussions of organizations and management cannot help but be theoretical discussions; no matter how much authors may protest that they are dealing with straightforward and common-sense matters. Grint (1997a) notes, in fact, that those who argue that 'theory' is irrelevant to their mission and project have (often unwittingly) adopted a theoretical position. Since to argue that theoretical analysis and reflection is irrelevant is to argue that 'facts' stand for themselves, that 'reality' is objective and self-evident to all (see Burrell and Morgan, 1980) and this is, itself, a theoretical stance.

Thus when Peters and Austin assert that a passion for excellence is required, and when they assert that leadership is the difference between excellence and mediocrity (and mediocrity means failure), they invite the following inquiry: which model of leadership do you have in mind? Yet in response *PFE* offers only a range of proverbial responses. Leaders listen; non-leaders talk. Leaders are humble; non-leaders are arrogant (see Peters and Austin, 1985, pp. 354–361). Yet these aphorisms actually do little to answer our question; and we do need an answer because leadership is a theoretical construct, interpreted differently by various schools and scholars. Any attempt to analyse leadership, therefore, reveals a fleet of diverse accounts and models. As Grint (1997a) notes:

> despite an enormous outpouring of material in the second half of the twentieth century, we appear to be little closer to understanding leadership than either Plato or Sun Tzu, who began the written debate several thousand years ago; certainly Chester Barnard's (1946) concerns that we should stop focusing upon the formal leader seem to have gone un-noticed. Since the post-war period we appear to have gone full circle: from assurances that personality traits were the key, through equally valid counter-arguments that the situation was critical, to a

controversy over whether the leader was person – or task-oriented, and back to hunting out the charismatics whose visions and transformational style would explain all.

(Grint, 1997a, p. 116)

Grint demonstrates, therefore, that when Peters and Austin assert that leadership is *the* difference, they are making a range of theoretical judgements. Indeed through Grint's analysis, it becomes clear that Peters and Austin cannot argue for leadership in the abstract, since there is no general consensus as to the nature, or performative function of leadership. Thus when Peters and Austin advocate leadership they are, in fact, arguing for a particular model of leadership.

Peters' and Austin's preferred template for leadership has its roots in 'contingency' thinking. Their preferred model of leadership, as we shall see below, asserts that business requires a cabal of leaders to help it to deal with a particular set of structural and historical contingencies.

## A Contingency Model

For Peters and Austin, leadership is *the* difference between excellence and mediocrity, because in turbulent times when competition is fierce, when technologies change rapidly, and when innovation in customer service is the key to survival, organizations need the vision of a leader to maintain energy and direction. This, in a nutshell, is the message of *PFE*.

A leader for Peters and Austin, therefore, has two over-arching duties to perform. The leader must:

1 diagnose the key contingencies facing the organization
2 fit the organization to these contingencies.

However as Grint (1997a) has observed this implies:

1 We know something about leadership; that we know what to look for in a leader.
2 We can actually make sense of the situation confronting the organization; we actually know which contingent variables to respond to.

In spite of Peters' and Austin's commitment to plain facts, to fun and to flexible and adaptive responses, therefore, it becomes clear that their flexible and adaptive account of management is, in fact, both theoretical and deterministic. Indeed, in spite of Peters' and Austin's faith in the capacity of leaders to shape, and to manage change, it appears that the situation determines the leader.

There is a paradox, therefore, in that the leader using the elusive (difficult to analyse, problematic to grasp) qualities of vision and experience is supposed to shape and to deliver lesser mortals from ruin, yet the leader is, in essence, a victim.

Summarizing *PFE*, therefore, we should note that in spite of the text's avowedly anti-theoretical stance, *PFE* is clearly a theoretically-rooted piece of work. However, the text does not offer a well-developed theoretical analysis. In its attempt to dismiss the need for theoretical reflection and theoretically based analysis, *PFE* acts to privilege certain forms of discussion, and to silence competing forms of analysis. Rather than examine leadership and the breadth, and depth, of scholarship on leadership, therefore, Peters and Austin construct leadership as a collection of aphorisms, which have little practical value or import for managers. Little surprise, then, that in his next major work Peters (this time working alone) was encouraging his devotees to embrace 'chaos'.

## Thriving on Chaos

*Thriving on Chaos* (1988), first published in 1987, presents a picture of the world as 'chaotic', and offers a dualistic vision of organizations and management which divides the world into two camps: those who thrive and those who fail. Indeed Peters warns us, in *Thriving on Chaos*, that many organizations will fail because they are unaware of the revolution in management which the 'chaotic' nature of our times call forth.

To save these organizations from failure and to allow organizations to 'thrive on chaos', Peters offers a 'handbook for a management revolution'. Introducing his text, Peters warns us that we should not think that we can escape the chaos that threatens to envelope each one of us. Thus, as Peters begins his text he quotes from Barbara Tuchman in order to warn of the dangers of self-deception. This quotation, presumably, is intended to humble readers in preparation for the revolution to come. Thus we are warned that folly has three persistent aspects – obliviousness, self-aggrandizement and the illusion of invulnerability.

Given this concern over the folly of self-aggrandizement, it may come as a surprise to find that within the first few pages of *Thriving on Chaos* (*TOC* for short), Peters bestows upon himself the elusive qualities of leadership and vision, which in *PFE* he was happy to celebrate in others.

In *TOC*, therefore, Peters seem to elevate himself above the in-house managerial leader to the position of paramount leader, as he conveys his stark message; that there are no longer any 'excellent' companies. In this Peters implies that companies which consider themselves to be 'excellent' have embraced the three persistent aspects of folly, and so, will surely fail. Other, more aware, organizations, he warns, will take advantage of what we might term the complacent folly of excellence, to undermine what, in less chaotic times, might have been a sustainable market advantage.

Why are there no longer any excellent companies? We might suggest three forms of explanation.

1   There were never any in the first place. Peters and Waterman (1982) using superficial and unsystematic research had manufactured a category of organizations entirely lacking in explanatory appeal.

2   Peters' disavowal of 'excellence' allows him to explain away a key critique made of *ISOE*: that a range of the excellent companies had subsequently failed (Guest, 1992).

Or the explanation preferred by Peters in *TOC*:

3   The chaotic nature of the modern business environment makes excellence a moving target. Thus one cannot *be* excellent. However, the chaotic nature of the business environment requires that organizations must always strive towards this unattainable state.

In an attempt to help organizations in this never-ending journey, Peters offers a new basket of prescriptions designed to ensure that managers commit to change being the only constant. However, as we shall see, there is something rather hollow about a prescription for chaos.

## Striving in Chaos

In the late 1980s a body of rather complex mathematical thinking known as 'chaos theory' became a 'hot topic' in many forms of academic and popular discourse. Chaos theory, if you will, became a fad. In lecture theatres and in bars people discussed chaos theory. Some spoke knowledgeably, most did not. Peters unfortunately falls into this latter camp when he discusses the need to thrive on chaos.

Grint (1997a) argues that chaos theory implies six conditions critical to organizational analysis.

1   *Organization is both predictable and unpredictable*: This is the now familiar butterfly effect, which argues that, not only is the nature of events in complex systems unpredictable, but there is a tendency for effects to multiply and to become increasingly unpredictable. Small events, therefore, may have a tendency to produce massive, yet unpredictable outcomes. Thus chaos theory suggests the potential that a butterfly beating its wings in Peking today may transform storm systems next month in New York. Or as Grint puts it: 'I had thought about chasing a dog sauntering past my window, but the thought of starting a hurricane in Tokyo on Thursday has worried me a lot' (Grint, 1997a, p. 63).

2   *Causal analysis is nigh on impossible*: The analysis of links and causation within complex systems is virtually impossible. Since initial conditions generate large and unpredictable outcomes, it is too difficult to trace the relationship between events and outcomes. In the realm of

organizational analysis this might imply some elements of what Peters advocates, since it suggests the abandonment of the notion of long-term, grand strategy, to embrace the idea that organizations should develop systems to cope with change and unpredictability.

3　*Diversity offers a productive base*: Quite contrary to the arguments and prescriptions of many of the management 'gurus', Peters included, chaos theory implies that organizations which seek to unify, say through the development of 'strong' cultures (Deal and Kennedy, 1982), will be prone to catastrophic errors since they will be unlikely to react promptly to change.

4　*Self-organization*: Chaos theory implies that management will be unsuccessful in their attempts to tinker with, and to re-equilibrate systems. Indeed chaos theory implies that failing systems must disintegrate. Applying these ideas to organizational analysis, Grint argues that chaos theory suggests that management's impotence and incompetence in managing complex and chaotic systems, must imply that organizations should be allowed to self-adjust, from the bottom up. This, of course, runs contrary to Peters' support for the glories of leadership.

5　*Individual discretion*: The known tendency towards chaos and disintegration may be offset to some degree by enhancing individual discretion. In this sense individual discretion may counter organizational tendencies towards ossification, and so, may allow systems to change and to adjust without disintegrating.

6　*Irreversibility*: Minute variations will cause changes across time. This suggests that all decisions are irreversible since, given the knock-on effects of change, organizations will be unable to revert to prior states or conditions.

Based upon this analysis of 'chaos', Grint suggests that managers would be well advised to adopt a more cautious and reflexive (a critical-practical?) approach to managing. Thus Grint's analysis of chaos suggest that managers may need to suspend their commitment to the grand strategies of cultural management and leadership, to allow self-organization and worker representation in the workplace. What, then, of Peters' approach to 'chaos'?

In comparison to Grint, Peters (1988) offers a far less rigorous account of chaos. In fact key elements of Peters' model seem to run counter to chaos theorizing. Whereas Grint argues that chaos is the more-or-less inevitable outcome of system complexity, Peters seems to imply that 'chaos' is the result of foreign competition and management complacency. So where Grint studies 'chaos' as a complex theory designed to grasp, and to grapple with complexity, Peters seems to deploy 'chaos' as a marketing device, designed to 'unfreeze' (Lewin, 1958; Burnes, 1996) his readers in preparation for the acceptance of his (now unavoidable) prescriptions. This allows Peters a few liberties in the exposition of his analysis.

In comparison to Peters' previous texts where suggestions were made and where, in *PFE*, managers were asked to reflect upon issues, *TOC* represents, apparently, a decision to 'get tough' with managers. Thus in *TOC*, Peters no longer offers suggestions and advice on constructing visions. Indeed he seems frustrated by his two previous attempts to encourage managers to develop new visions of business practice; so frustrated in fact, that in *TOC* it is *his* vision which American management is to follow.

This vision is spelled out in forty-five prescriptions. Each of these forty-five prescriptions turns upon leadership and each contains such indispensable advice as the need to attend to the 'intangibles', to set 'conservative' financial targets and about being service 'fanatics'. But is this useful? Does this reflect an analysis rooted in chaos theory?

Elements of Peters' account do carry resonances (Grint, 1994) of the arguments of chaos theory. Thus Peters' commitment, at least in rhetoric, to empowerment does resonate with notions of self-organization. Similarly Peters' mistrust of 'hard' data analysis carries echoes of the idea that organization is both predictable and unpredictable. Yet aside from these resonances, Peters actually offers a remarkably anti-chaotic view of the world since he:

- assumes systems may be controlled, culturally, through the elusive qualities of some amorphous thing he calls leadership (which Grint suggests leads only to disaster within chaotic systems)
- assumes that organizations, in spite of unpredictability, and in spite of the multiplier effect, will react to his forty-five prescriptions in a useful and predictable fashion.

These assumptions as Grint's analysis shows are highly unchaotic and are unlikely to improve the management of organizations in a chaotic system, or any other kind of system for that matter!

In his next offering, first published in 1992, soon after the gulf war (hence the taste for phrasing such as 'become a corporate scud missile'!) Peters, again, promises a revolution in management. It is to this revolution that we now turn our attention.

## Liberating Management?

Peters begins *Liberation Management* (Peters, 1993), *Liberation* for short, by noting that his earlier books on management and organizing had been flawed. These earlier works, he tells us, had failed to comprehend, and so, had failed to embrace the forms of thinking required to engender a revolution in management. Notably, Peters argues that each of his earlier works had a tendency to 'put the cart before the horse'. Thus he argues that while *ISOE* and *PFE* urged managers to get close to the customer, the tendency to study action and to ignore structure, evident in both of these works, actually prevented managers from understanding that in spite of a commitment to customers, and in spite of a bias for action, it tends to be organizational structures which prevent the achievement of total customer satisfaction.

In a fairly neat reversal of his previous work, and of his intellectual up-bringing, therefore, Peters advocates a more structural form of analysis. Thus he argues that it is a commitment to demolishing organizational structures, and a commitment to 'necessary disorganization' which holds the key to the revolution required. Yet we should note that in keeping with *PFE* and *TOC*, Peters actually offers no systematic analysis of organizational structures, nor does he study the impact of structures on service. Instead we are treated to a range of anecdotes and reminiscences concerning 'necessary disorganization'. So what is necessary disorganization?

In a sense Peters' commitment to 'necessary disorganization' might be viewed as a further elaboration of the 'chaos' metaphor adopted for his 1987 text, *TOC*. Thus in *Liberation* Peters argues that individual discretion and *ad hoc* co-operation (underpinned by strong cultures) hold the key to delighting customers. This, of course, is the central theme running through all of Peters' work. However, in *Liberation*, Peters claims to offer a new structural form of analysis, geared to releasing this talent and potential. Indeed harking backing to *ISOE* and to *TOC*, Peters notes that his earlier work had, in an almost unconscious fashion, focused upon large manufacturing concerns as the key sites of management, industry and excellence. Thus he observes that his earlier works had a tendency to look east, which, given America's tendency to look, and to go west, might be considered as 'looking back'.

In *Liberation*, however, Peters argues that we need to 'look west' to California (and elsewhere) to grasp the structures required for 'necessary disorganization'. In *Liberation Management* therefore, Peters distances himself from his old exemplars, from the likes of IBM, in order to tell stories of Cable News Network (CNN) and McKinsey and Co., which are all designed to illustrate his new aphorisms of management: that management should shred (not just shed) hierarchy; and that management must destroy the organization – before a competitor does!

Despite Peters' apparent disavowal of the canon of social scientific research, and in spite of the fact that Peters offers no systematic analysis to support his 'liberation' thesis, his homage to fashion and to ephemera takes over 800 pages. Do we (could we) learn anything of value from this?

### Royal Flush / Royal Flop?

In spite of Peters' claim to be concerned to revolutionize management, it is difficult to discern in *Liberation* anything that is truly new or truly revolutionary. Indeed far from representing 'the epistemological break' in

'Petersian' thought, *Liberation* seems to rehash all of the key foibles and preoccupations we have come to expect in the work of Tom Peters.

In *Liberation* managers are encouraged to get/go a little crazy. They are encouraged to mess around; to experiment; to make mistakes and to take risks. Managers are encouraged to engage in radical delayering; to reduce office staff; to trim overheads and to slash through hierarchy.

Yet all this activity serves one purpose alone; to facilitate the action of that elusive creature, the managerial leader. But why is this leader required? Because the pace of change, and the demands of consumers in the 1990s, require leaders within organizations; leaders who can delight; leaders with what it takes to make customers say 'wow'. But was this not the message of *PFE*? Indeed it was.

So what of Peters' revolution? Can a model of management which builds on an under-theorized and rather deterministic account of leadership really liberate? Could a model of management which celebrates the activity of a social elite, without ever pausing to consider the nature of management really hope to over-turn, to revolutionize thinking? I doubt it. Indeed as Peters makes *the pursuit of wow*, first published in 1994 (Peters, 1995), the central theme of his next guide to management (and a key theme of his seminar presentations (Peters, 1994)), this author finds himself more likely to mouth 'huh?', than to shriek 'wow!'.

## The Pursuit of What?

*The Pursuit of Wow* (Peters, 1995), *Wow* for short, reads like a secular cate-chism (see figure 5.1). Eschewing a normal narrative structure *Wow* offers, instead, a set of questions and answers (of course) designed to offer guid-ance for the converted and pure of spirit. The book, of course, also offers hope for the lost and dispossessed. Like the catholic catechism, *Wow* demon-strates a concern with the beatitudes, the beatitudes of business and commerce in the 1990s.

The road to business beatification, it seems, requires that we must under-stand and commit to combining a large and diverse range of elements. *Wow*, in fact, offers 210 elements which we, as followers of Peters, are encouraged to take onboard. For example, Peters celebrates the impor-tance of 'design'; of 'values'; of 'empowerment' and of respecting the skills and talents of employees. In a similar vein Peters also preaches on the value of leadership and on the importance of managing culture. Each of these elements is listed and discussed, we are told, with just one aim in mind, to allow readers the opportunity to stand out; to make others say 'wow'. But how are we to put all these elements together? How are we to make sense of these potentially competitive imperatives?

In common with each of Peters' texts since *ISOE*, *Wow* is a work unfet-tered by the normal concerns of social scientific theorizing and research. No methodology underpins its 'analysis'; no (explicit or rigorous) abstract

*What is the key to business success?*
Striving constantly to satisfy customers is the key to business success.

*How are we to satisfy customers?*
Orienting the whole organization to reflect the needs of customers is the key to ensuring customer satisfaction.

*How is this transformation to be achieved?*
Leadership is the key to organizational transformation.

*Will leadership deliver business success?*
Yes, leadership and vision will deliver business success.

*Is anything else required?*
Leadership, vision and integrity are necessary.

*Will these deliver business success?*
Yes, leadership, vision, integrity and trust are the necessary components of business success.

*Anything else?*
Leadership, vision, integrity, trust and empowerment will be required.

*Anything else?*
Leadership, vision, integrity, trust, empowerment and skunkworks will be required.

*Anything else?*
Leadership, vision, integrity, trust, empowerment, skunkworks and commitment will be required.

*Will these be sufficient to deliver business success?*
Yes, leadership, vision, integrity, trust, empowerment, skunkworks, commitment and a sense of fun will be required.

*Are you having a laugh?*

*Figure 5.1* The Peters modern catechism of business?

theorizing supports its key postulates. Instead *Wow* is conceived of as an attempt to offer, and to generate, 'yeasty responses' (Peters, 1995, p. vii) to deal with 'these very yeasty, and frequently frightening times' (Peters, 1995, p. vii).

In common with *PFE, TOC* and *Liberation*, therefore, *Wow* is a book which celebrates common-sense as the only thing, for sure, that we can depend upon during times of change. Common-sense, then, and common-sense attitudes to leadership and cultural management are viewed as the keys to long-term survival. Yet somewhat paradoxically this commitment to 'common-sense' actually makes for mystique. Thus while celebrating 'common-sense' as the basis for change management, Peters makes management, simultaneously, common-sensical and theoretical, structural and processual, tragic and comic, everything and yet nothing. This would be disturbing enough, were it not for the fact that in one grand gesture Peters attempts to silence all his critics, since the key to Peters' managerial leadership is that it is not confined by traditional and out-moded forms of thinking; it is crazy; it is 'frizzy'. It is, above all else, anti-cynical.

Those who would seek to disagree with or take issue with Peters, therefore, must reject his business beatitudes. Yet anyone who would reject the Peters catechism of modern business commits the mortal 'sins' of cynicism and staidness as these are defined by Peters.

Yet as we shall see it is a small step from beatitude to platitude. Or in terms that Peters might relate to, we might note that a typical yeasty response is inherently self-destructive since yeast is an organism which, in essence, consumes its own environment until life in that environment (even for the yeast) becomes unsustainable (Vonnegut, 1973). But let us not trade analogies; let us move on to tackle the latest word from Peters.

## Grateness

In *The Circle of Innovation* (Peters, 1997), *Innovation* for short, Peters tells us that he has gathered together the slides, some explanatory text, and the combined knowledge acquired from the 400 seminars he has offered since the publication of *Liberation*. The sub-title of *Innovation*, which, like *Wow*, eschews a normal narrative structure, is *You Can't Shrink Your Way to Greatness*. This, however, seems to contradict Peters' support in *Liberation* for those organizations that had pursued a strategy of downsizing their corporate staffs. Furthermore, this sub-title also seems to cause tensions with *Innovation's* support for radical decentralization. But we are not allowed to mention this.

In a typically grand and dismissive gesture, Peters tells us that all bets are off! His work *is* inconsistent, he tells us, because the world is! Only a cynic would ask for anything more. Only a 'sinner' would have the temerity to venture that inconsistency is the product of flabby modelling, populist thinking and ready-made science (Chia, 1996). Only a cynic would venture that a tendency to reinvent the world, and to reverse your preferred pattern of thinking, is the product of the three persistent aspects of folly: the tendency to obliviousness, self-aggrandizement and the illusion of invulnerability. So at least Peters is not entirely inconsistent, these three aspects, at least, remain consistent within his pronouncements on management, even when 'excellence' is supplanted by 'innovation'.

In *The Circle of Innovation*, Peters' commitment to 'excellence' is finally abandoned. Innovation, it seems, is the key to future success. However, it would probably be more appropriate to say that 'excellence' (striving to satisfy customers), becomes subsumed by 'innovation', since those factors central to excellence – skunkworks, leadership, cultural management, change, leadership, leadership and leadership – form the core of Peters' discussion of design and innovation. This time, however, Peters' business beatitudes are packaged differently. This time, they are surrounded by photographs; by bold type; by bold phrasing (*yikes!*) and by what, apparently, is to be regarded as bold, profound and innovative thinking: to 'think revolution not evolution'; to work on your own ideal and not the ideal of someone else; to make mistakes; to bloody your nose; to innovate; I-N-N-O-V-A-T-E.

All this (and less) is conveyed by Peters' eponymous 'circle of innovation'. To call this a diagram would be unfair. Diagrams convey information. This is just a circle; a circle with fifteen spikes attached. Each of these spikes is labelled with a different beatitude; praising erasers as a management tool; exalting women as a market and as a resource; praising love and so on.

But Peter's praise for such things as love must be viewed with suspicion, since if inconsistency is the order of the day, then might it not be the case that management may well have to be faithless and loveless by design! Like Peters' earlier discussion of leadership, therefore, this faith in innovation and his commitment to women and to bloody handkerchiefs, is actually little more than a contingent response to environmental needs. And with this point in mind, we would do well to note that a contingent approach to management suggests that it may, indeed, be possible (and if we accept the logic of the market as our only metric, it may even be desirable) to shrink your way to business greatness?

So what are we to make of Peters' offerings? What would I have you do with my frustrations? Let us examine the changes and the stabilities in Peters' work before we attempt a, critical-practical, summary.

## Change

Our analysis of Peters' main texts (his offerings of 1982, 1985, 1988, 1993, 1994, 1995 and 1997) has revealed a number of important changes in Peters' thinking and in his preferred mode of presentation.

*ISOE* represents the most traditional and, for all its faults, the most rigorous and analytical of Peters' works. In spite of the errors and omissions evident in this text, therefore, we should acknowledge that *ISOE*:

1    was based upon a testable hypothesis; that successful companies have something in common which distinguishes them from the mass of less successful companies
2    used a sampling mechanism in an attempt to establish this.

Unfortunately 1982 represents the analytical high point of Peters' published work and leads us to the first clearly identifiable change in his work:

- The abandonment of the canon of social scientific research (whether qualitatively or quantitatively conceived) with the publication of *PFE* in 1985.

By 1988, and with the publication of *TOC*, we have the next key change in Peters' work. Peters as we have seen had, by 1985, already abandoned any pretence to conducting research and instead had taken to publishing 'war stories' and other forms of personal endorsement concerned with 'excellence'. However in 1987, with the publication of *TOC*, Peters disavows his 'excellent' companies. Thus in his second key change Peters announces:

- That there are no longer 'excellent' companies.

In 1992 this claim is matched to a further disavowal of the excellence phenomenon. Thus in 1993, with the publication of *Liberation*, Peters announces his third key change and the reversal of his previous analytical focus. Thus in 1992:

- 'Analysis' of structure, not action, becomes the key means of getting close to customers.

All of which is slightly ironic, because in 1995 with the publication of *Wow*, Peters makes a fourth key change and abandons the normal restrictions and conventions of narrative structure in his own published work!
   Within and between these changes, however, key points of stability are evident.

### *Stability*

In spite of Peters' mistrust of, and impatience with theorizing, it is at the conceptual-theoretical level that Peters' work demonstrates its essential stability. Readers will recall that in our discussion of management theory (see chapter 1) we noted that all forms of discussion (even those that profess themselves to be non-theoretical), are inextricably and inescapably theoretical at root. Readers will recall, too, that in developing a theoretically rooted account of action within the context of work organizations we observed the need to examine and to account for:

- the nature of human action and interaction
- the nature of work organization
- the nature of the wider society.

Let us unpick Peters' approach to these three elements as a means of uncovering the stability in his work.

### Human Action and Interaction

A clear and apparently humanistic interest in employees underscores all of Peters' work on management. Indeed in *Wow,* Peters' liberal sentiments are clear to see in his rejection of mandatory drug tests at work. Yet together with this notion of the essential wonder of humanity, Peters has tacked on a concern with perfectibility which, in many ways, leads him to analyse humanity as a plastic for him to mould. Thus Peters' dual concern with leadership and with cultural management, which underscores his commitment to excellence (whether excellence is to be regarded as a thing, as an unattainable goal, or as 'innovation'), can only be possible where humanity is regarded as being of a plastic character; 'corrigible' (Ackroyd and Thompson, 1999) and prone to managerial manipulation.

### Work Organizations

Peters' commitment to changing employees, and his commitment to getting close to the customer is facilitated by a unitary (Fox, 1985) modelling of work organizations. As we saw in our earlier discussion (see chapter 1) a unitary account of work organizations asserts that the relationship between management and workers is characterized by harmony and by goodwill. This understanding underpins all of Peters' work on management. Indeed it is the (theoretical) understanding that organizations are unitarist in nature which holds all of Peters' so-called common-sense assertions together. For example, Peters' account of 'excellence', his research methods and his initial praise for 'excellent' organizations in *ISOE,* only makes sense within a unitary framework which takes 'the organization' as the unit of analysis.

In a similar way we should note that Peters' anti-theoretical works (a long list including *PFE, TOC, Liberation, Wow* and *Innovation*) are actually facilitated by a unitarist abstraction concerning the nature of organization. Indeed Peters' conviction that the problems and pitfalls of managing can be explained by recourse to common-sense and plain facts, actually, represents an extreme version of unitarist theory. Thus 'plain facts' can only be plain, and can only be 'facts' where no sensible form of competitive understanding is possible. Only within the realm of unitarist theory (Collins, 1998) is this argument plausible!

### Wider Society

All of Peters' works on management are notable for their limited and truncated treatment of the wider society. In part, this limited treatment of the wider society is explicable in terms of Peters' focus upon action, and his belief that managerial leaders can make a difference. Indeed facing down criticisms made of the internally focused account of management and organization which he offers in *ISOE*, Peters tells us in *PFE*, that it is his intention to maintain this internal focus since while: 'businesses can be temporarily or permanently set back by external forces . . . these *other* factors are seldom, if ever, the basis for lasting distinction' (Peters and Austin, 1985, p. 4, emphasis added).

Leaving to one side the fact that this is an assertion which Peters never tests, nor validates by empirical means, it is worth observing that Peters' commitment to the existence of a capricious business environment actually provides his model with an in-built stabilizing mechanism. Quite paradoxically, in fact, Peters' (limited and acontextual) account of the wider society (which tends to portray the competitive environment as turbulent and capricious) is the key point of stability in Peters' account of management. We should note, therefore, that as opposed to the contextual account of management developed in chapter 1, Peters offers an account of the environment of business. This, it seems, is an environment charged by imperatives. These imperatives for Peters are, by definition, inescapable. In this way the imperatives he identifies – globalization, technological change and so on – actually facilitate the prescriptions (for leadership, excellence and innovation) which have remained stable in all of Peters' works. From 'change', therefore, Peters conjures stability. Or perhaps, reflecting the basic appeal of Peters' ideas, we should say that from change Peters conjures prescriptions which promise future stability for management actors.

What are we to make of these prescriptions? Having unpicked Peters' ideas and assumptions, let us conclude by asking the question posed by Burnes (1998). Is Tom Peters mad? Bad? Or dangerous to know?

## *Mad?*

As we noted in our earlier discussion, when we accuse those who disagree with us of madness we do little to advance the cause of reasoned debate. We can, therefore, dispense with the charge of madness on two counts. First, silencing disagreement by refusing to accept that dissenting opinion can have any foundation is, in fact, the key tool deployed by unitarist theorists (yes, theorists) such as Peters.

Critical-practical accounts of management, conversely, build from and celebrate more fully developed, and properly pluralistic, accounts of organization; these are accounts which give credence to the 'plain facts' of others while recognizing these to be different from our own 'plain facts'. Second, I feel sure that Peters would now argue that the charge of madness is a compliment since it is irrational to be rational – and in this he is to some degree correct (Tsoukas, 1995).

## Bad?

Peters may not be mad. However his work is, plainly, bad. The work of Peters exhibits two key problems:

*   All his texts, barring *ISOE*, are based squarely upon a disavowal of theoretical analysis and reflection. This as we saw in our introductory discussion is a flawed self-deception. We cannot help but make use of theoretical models and constructs in any discussion, no matter how 'practical' our intentions.
*   Peters' faith in the power of simple facts represents the promotion of a particular theoretical position. However, Peters' conviction that plain facts exist, and that *his* plain facts are commonly held, means that competitive theoretical modellings of work and organizations, competitive versions of common-sense and plain facts to those preferred by Peters, are not allowed the privilege of a hearing. So, it seems that there are two world views possible in the sight of Peters, his and the wrong one!

## Dangerous?

Peters' analyses and prescriptions might be considered dangerous for a number of reasons. Reflecting the concerns of business management we might note that Peters' accounts of management and organization have become increasingly crude and simplistic. Yet over and above this the *bricolage* of ideas, which he passes off in the name of analysis, has become increasingly inconsistent and self-contradictory. Contrast, for example, his praise for radical downsizing and delayering in *TOC* with the central message of his latest work: 'you can't shrink your way to greatness'.

Yet rather than revisit his core ideas; rather than re-examine the self-important, yet anorexic body of theorizing which (implicitly) forms the emaciated rump of his work, Peters simply shakes off this challenge. Inconsistency is apparently 'a badge of honour' (Peters, 1997, p. xv). Yet all through *ISOE*, *PFE* and *TOC* when Peters was piling attributes upon, and heaping plaudits around, his managerial leaders, he was telling us that 'trust' and 'integrity' were paramount (or pretty close to paramount) concerns for leadership.

In addition to this line of criticism we might note that while Peters has increasingly encouraged organizations to chop and change between core ideas; downsizing *then* building, delayering *then* growing, pursuing excellence *then*, whoops, no more excellence, perhaps the only useful and reliable finding to emerge from *ISOE* was that the successful organizations of the early 1980s had ignored the consultancy advice of the previous decades (Guest, 1992) Thus Peters might be considered 'dangerous' because like the other 'gurus' of business he is more closely associated with business failure than with consistent business success.

Turning our attention from the narrow concerns of business to examine, briefly, more socialized and social concerns, we might allow ourselves to wonder what Peters' discussions of commitment, and of the need to love your organization and your job, may have done to the home lives of employees. Indeed, aside from the odd throwaway line, and the odd nod in the direction of female employees, Peters' texts seem to revolve around a male-oriented management hierarchy – a macho world of risk-taking and endeavour, a boys-only dorm where lunch is for wimps and family life is for pansies.

From this perspective Peters might be considered 'dangerous' since, at one level, his model of management appears to attempt to reclaim the world of work, or at least its important jobs, for men.

Yet perhaps above all this, Peters is dangerous because in the name of liberty, energy and creativity he has developed a totalitarian and total-izing argument which will allow no credible form of dissent; no competing world view. This form of spiritual guidance, we can all do without!

## Summary

This chapter has analysed the 'excellence' buzzword through an analysis of the main works of Tom Peters. Subjecting Peters' works to a critical analysis, which has sought to unpack Peters' analytical schema, this chapter has argued that Peters supplies little in the way of insight or advice which might be employed, usefully, by managers.

Indeed as a 'guru' selling advice and services to students and managers, our 'critical-practical' analysis of Peters suggests that he over-estimates his product and misunderstands his potential. Peters fails to model either management or the world of work in a sensible or defensible way. He misunderstands chaos theory and he has, repeatedly, failed to revolutionize management. As soon as I have the opportunity I intend to examine my rights under the Sale of Goods Act. I suggest you should do likewise!

# 6  Total Quality Management

## Introduction

The concepts of quality and quality management now figure prominently in management courses, in management textbooks and on the agendas of management conferences. *Prufrock* (the name adopted by the columnist Rupert Steiner, when acting as a diarist for the UK newspaper, *The Sunday Times*) gives us a feeling for the lengths some actors will go to just to forge an association with the concept of 'quality'. Writing in late 1998, the *Prufrock* diary, an ever reliable means of deflating egos, observed that:

> THE government in Budapest has come up with a marvellous way to get journalists to – 'help the national cause' – it is giving them huge quantities of cash for writing positive stories. It is willing to pay a £550 reward under the guise of a competition called 'Quality 98' which offers prizes for articles promoting excellence in industry. The economics ministry says it has a million other ideas about how to reward journalists helping this national cause.
>
> (*The Sunday Times*, 29/11/98)

This academic, practitioner, governmental and journalistic interest in quality, and in systems of quality management, in Britain and America, at least, is recent, and is indicative of a key change in management thinking. Indeed, the current focus upon quality, and quality management, represents, at one level, a break from the attitudes to quality predominant in the USA and Europe throughout the 1950s, 1960s and 1970s.

Until the 1980s, attempts to manage quality at work, if considered at all seriously, tended to focus upon reworking and rectifying production defects (Blauner, 1973). However, since the 1980s, quality improvement has come to focus more upon attempts to build quality into products (rather than checking for it later). In this sense, the approach to quality management, and quality improvement, which has been developed in Britain and the US (largely to meet the challenge of Japanese manufacturing), might be summarized as focusing attention on the need to build products 'right first time'. Collectively these policies, processes and tools designed to ensure that products (and, more recently, services) are 'built right first time', have become subsumed within the catch-all title Total Quality Management (TQM). This chapter will offer a 'critical-practical' analysis of TQM.

Total Quality Management has attracted many devotees. Many commentaries have been written that, in various ways, have sought to encourage managers to change their organizational policies, and their organizational infrastructures, in the pursuit of TQM. Yet, much of this advice/exhortation is glib because it has been couched in a 'grammar' of imperatives. The grammatical formulation of these commentaries has done much to give force and immediacy to the buzzword of quality. However, the commentaries themselves do little to inform action because they tend to obscure questions of a social and political nature. Arguably, then, the 'guru' discussions of quality fail to analyse those aspects of organization which should be central to the analysis of change management (Collins, 1998).

With this point in mind, we will attempt to demonstrate that the 'guru' account of TQM is limited and limiting. It is limited because it fails to analyse the political complexity of organizations. It is limiting because it fails to acknowledge the ambiguity, which surrounds the concept of 'quality', and the pursuit of management. Recognizing these omissions and oversights, we will seek to overthrow this 'guru' advice and the 'grammar' which underpins it.

The 'gurus' of management, as we have seen (see chapter 1), are keen to offer practical advice and guidance. They offer practical advice, which locates such things as quality and empowerment as practical and unavoid-able necessities. However, this advice is often unhelpful and ultimately proves to be impractical because its grammatical construction over-simplifies processes, which are inherently complex (Chia, 1996).

In an attempt to break free from the limitations of this form of practical guidance, this chapter will offer a 'critical-practical' analysis, designed to show the ways in which the political nature of (Total Quality) management makes the 'grammar' of managing 'imperfect'. It is hoped that this more political account will offer readers a more useful representation (De Cock and Hipkin, 1997) of the problems of managing quality at work.

The analysis offered by this chapter, therefore, is designed to look into, and to look through, the models of management and TQM which have been developed by the 'gurus' of management. In this sense the chapter is designed to allow readers to:

• *Locate quality management.* This chapter will ask: how should we define quality? It will ask: how and why did organizations come to embrace TQM?

- *Understand TQM.* We will ask: what ideas underpin quality management? We will ask: is quality really a transparent concept, commonly understood by all?
- *Critique TQM.* We will ask: is TQM deserving of its grandiose title, is it, in practice, 'total'? Furthermore we will ask: should we celebrate the changes in our lives and in our methods of working which have been advocated in the name of TQM?

Before we embark upon our 'critical-practical' analysis of TQM, however, it is worth observing that quality management does not begin and end with TQM, lest we fall into the trap of assuming that earlier eras of production were notable for their total disregard of customers' needs.

## Systems of Quality Management

In spite of the current and populist fixation with TQM, in spite of exhortations to 'build it right first time' and to 'build it like you own it' (Hamper, 1992), Wilkinson and his co-authors (Wilkinson *et al.*, 1998; Hill and Wilkinson, 1995) remind us that there are, in fact, any number of different policies and procedures associated with 'quality management'. De Lorean's (Wright, 1980) biographer, for example, shows us the approach to quality management favoured by John De Lorean during his years at General Motors.

Discussing the life and career of one of the automobile industry's more colourful characters, Wright recounts De Lorean's attempts to manage quality at work. Wright tells us that De Lorean instituted an important quality improvement programme while he was in charge of Pontiac (a division of General Motors). This programme, which cost $400,000 and was instigated as an attempt to improve the image of GM's cars, called for a factory dedicated, solely, to the tasks of checking and repairing the Pontiacs recently produced by General Motors' main factories. Thus De Lorean's quality improvement programme invested $400,000 in a factory which made nothing, and had one purpose alone, to repair new cars so that Pontiac's management could be assured that the products shipped to GM's dealers were of the appropriate quality standard, demanded by the customer. Of course, General Motors was not alone among US car manufacturers in facing significant quality and image problems during the 1960s and 1970s. Halberstam (1987) shows us, for example, that Lee Iacocca, during his time at Ford faced similar problems. Halberstam notes, however, that while Ford and General Motors faced similar quality problems, Iacocca chose a slightly different path to quality management than that chosen by De Lorean.

De Lorean, as we have seen, elected to bear the costs of quality directly. He set up a dedicated plant to rework Pontiacs so that they might achieve an appropriate quality standard. Iacocca, however, seems to have been of the opinion that a plant dedicated to rework activities alone would be a waste of resources. Iacocca, therefore, chose a different approach to quality management. While De Lorean chose to deal with quality matters 'in-house', Iacocca chose to push Ford's quality problem on to the dealer network. Thus, Iacocca decided that Ford's dealer network should shoulder the responsibility (and the cost) of reworking the cars built so shoddily by Ford's production plants.

Both of these approaches to quality management paid dividends, to some degree. Ford's customers welcomed the cars, which had been reworked by the dealer network. Likewise, the rechecked Pontiacs were welcomed by GM's customers. Indeed, GM's reworked cars did much to improve the reputation of Pontiac with dealers and with the general public. However, we should note that no aspirant or career-minded manager in the 1990s would dare to admit (let alone, proudly proclaim) that they had implemented a programme to rework their product. Why would managers choose to disguise this activity as a source of embarrassment?

An extensive repair and recheck programme would be an embarrassment to today's managers because the preferred approach to quality management, in Britain and in America, has changed quite fundamentally since the mid-1980s. Today, the preferred approach to quality management has swung from an earlier concern with correction, in order to embrace, rather more fully, a range of policies and procedures designed to ensure that products will not require reworking, since management's aim, now, must be to build products and services 'right first time'.

Reflecting this concern to build products 'right first time', Wilkinson *et al.* (1998) note that while organizations may attempt to manage quality in a variety of different ways, Total Quality Management (TQM), has become the most celebrated approach to prevention (as opposed to correction) oriented quality management. Indeed Wilkinson and his co-authors, observe that TQM, in Britain, has now spread from its roots in the manufacturing industry, to encompass a wide range of industries and organizations, including the financial services industry and the public sector.

The advocates of TQM use the term 'quality' in a special sense. To make sense of TQM we must make some attempt to comprehend the nature of 'quality', as this is understood, by the proponents of TQM. In the section that follows, therefore, we will consider the nature of quality as this has been spelled out in the core principles of Total Quality Management.

## The Nature of Quality

Three core principles are said to underpin 'quality' as this is defined by the advocates of TQM (Wilkinson *et al.*, 1997):

- *Customer orientation*: While common-sense and everyday definitions of 'quality' encourage us to think of 'quality articles' as representing the very best which the market has to offer – BMW, for example supplies the 'quality end' of the car market, while Ford and General Motors target the 'fleet' market – TQM defines quality slightly differently. Within TQM, the customer for any particular product is placed as the sole arbiter of quality. Thus the cars produced by BMW, by Ford and by General Motors, might all be considered to be quality products so long as each car conforms to its design specification, and meets the standard required by its consumer. In this sense, Ford's cars (and the cars made by Lada, Skoda, Seat and all other car manufacturers) are quality products, so long as these conform to the specifications and design standard required by those purchasing the vehicle. The Ford, the Skoda and the Lada may all be cheaper than the BMW, and may, in the eyes of such connoisseurs as *Top Gear's* Jeremy Clarkson, be inferior products to the BMW, yet, so long as these other cars conform to their customers' requirements they will be, within the lexicon of TQM, quality cars.
- *Process orientation*: Customer orientation is, clearly, central to TQM. But how can we ensure that organizational activities reflect customer needs? In an attempt to ensure that products conform to customer requirements, the advocates of TQM (see Beckford, 1998) argue that production processes should be arranged so that all employees are keenly aware that, no matter where they work within the organization, they are, above all other considerations, serving the customer. To foster such a view, the advocates of TQM argue that the activities within an organization should be broken down into basic tasks, or processes, and then linked together into 'quality chains', to form extended processes (Tuckman, 1998). These quality chains are designed to link producers and consumers together, in order to emphasize that all employees, ultimately, must direct their efforts to meet the needs of the customer. Indeed, we might note that within TQM, the logic of the marketplace is drawn back into the arena of production. TQM practices, therefore, encourage employees to think of their workmates, or the next stage of the production process as the 'customer' for their contribution to the overall production process. As Wilkinson *et al.* (1998) note, this tendency to draw the logic of a consumerist marketplace into the process of production might, usefully, be thought of as 'a means of unifying processes as well as determining the objective of organizational activities' (Wilkinson *et al.*, 1998 p. 13). In this sense, as we shall see, TQM might be regarded as a system designed to discipline and control workers, as well as (or because of?) having a concern with the quality of output which these employees produce (see Du Gay and Salaman, 1992; Drummond, 2000).
- *Continuous improvement*: How does BMW ensure that it is not displaced by other organizations as a producer of quality (that is, luxury) cars?

How does Ford stay ahead of General Motors in the UK 'fleet' market? How should Ford work to ensure that Lada does not encroach on its market share? Superficially the answer to these questions is quite simple. Organizations, self-evidently, develop and prosper by working to satisfy customers. But this begs another question: how is customer satisfaction to be achieved?

In response to this follow-up question, the advocates of TQM argue that committing to continuous improvement represents the key means of ensuring continued, customer satisfaction. Anticipating the follow-up question, which, again, suggests itself here, the advocates of TQM inform us that continuous improvement is a central component of TQM. Indeed the advocates of TQM argue that quality is delivered by continuous improvement, and is a design outcome.

Quality goods, as we have seen, are goods that conform to customer requirements. Quality, then, for the advocates of TQM, does not occur by accident, and cannot be delivered by good intentions alone. To meet customer preferences, and to ensure continuing customer satisfaction, therefore, quality must be 'designed-in', both to the product, and to the process of production. At one level, therefore, quality, which is a product of customer orientation, process orientation and continuous improvement, is a managerial responsibility. Yet, if managers are to design quality goods, services and processes, they must find some means to encourage employees to collaborate with them. A collaborative approach to process and product design, therefore, allows managers to tap into the sources of insight and information necessary to improve quality-by-design. Clearly, those involved directly with products, and/or those who interact directly with customers will often have the experience, and so, the necessary insights and information required to improve products and services so that these reflect, better, the orientations of customers. Recognizing this, advocates of TQM suggest that, while quality is a design-led activity and a top-level responsibility, managers, in the pursuit of continuous improvement must find ways to tap the skills and insights of those workers directly involved in the process of production (see chapter 7).

To assist managers in this, the proponents of TQM offer a range of tools and techniques that are designed to promote the key principles of TQM. Thus managers and workers have been urged to make use of:

*   '*Improvement tools*': designed to simplify and to improve processes.
*   '*Measurement systems*': designed to expose to management, for example, the financial cost of inspecting for quality, as opposed to ensuring that quality is 'built in'.
*   '*Organizational approaches*': including initiatives such as self-inspection of work, teamworking and, of course, quality circles which are all designed to reorient the organization towards 'quality' and customer satisfaction.

Overall, then, it should be apparent that the current focus upon quality as an organizational goal, and the focus upon TQM as the primary means of delivering quality, implies a distinctive approach to management, which, in turn, requires a new organizational infrastructure designed to support this approach. Reflecting this understanding Wilkinson *et al.* (1998) note, that the: 'new organizational infrastructure is seen as a necessary condition for TQM: it both enables the operation of total quality management and ensures [its persistence as an organizational initiative]' (Wilkinson *et al.*, 1998, p. 14).

How long might customers expect to wait for TQM to become the dominant approach to management? A long time! In spite of the 'gurus' and their 'grammar' of imperatives, the British and American experience of 'quality' suggests that Total Quality Management has been facilitated by a less-than-perfect mode of persuasion.

## The Long Gestation of TQM?

Introducing this chapter we suggested that quality considerations had been, until quite recently, a low-grade concern for management. Indeed, we suggested that, until recently, the preferred approach to quality management in Britain and the US had centred upon reworking and repairing products, which proved to be defective when subject to post-construction inspection. From the 1980s, however, this rework and repair based approach to quality management has been, increasingly, called into question by the concept of TQM.

Wilkinson (Wilkinson *et al.*, 1991) perhaps one of the foremost 'critical' commentators on quality management, writing in 1991, predicted that TQM would be one of the key topics of the decade for British and European managers. He observed: 'Total Quality Management (TQM) looks like being one of the management fashions of the 1990s' (Wilkinson *et al.*, 1991, p. 24).

Of course, we might say that as a tipster, Wilkinson shows a taste for safe bets. Nevertheless, it must have pleased Wilkinson, writing in 1995 (Wilkinson and Wilmott, 1995) to be able to look back on his earlier prediction, to report that his judgement had been vindicated. TQM had, indeed, risen to become one of the key management fashions of the 1990s. Indeed, writing in 1995, Wilkinson and Wilmott could look back on the elapsed half-decade to observe that: 'In recent years there has been an explosion of books and articles that champion the cause of "quality management"' (Wilkinson and Wilmott, 1995, p. 789).

Yet, management's commitment to TQM is not just confined to rhetoric and to the reading of 'galvanizing' literature. Writing in 1995 (this time with Hill), Wilkinson was able to report that the 'galvanic' literature (Hamper, 1992) on TQM had in fact led to changes in management practice. Thus, writing with Hill, he observed: 'Total quality management practices have spread widely over the last half decade, while in the US and Britain pioneers have now been involved in TQM for more than a decade' (Hill and Wilkinson, 1995, p. 8).

Attempting to contextualize the development of TQM, Wilkinson and his co-authors (Wilkinson *et al.*, 1991) observe that TQM has close links with three major themes of the 1980s: Japanization (the push to learn from/ mimic Japanese managerial practices), human resource management (HRM) and 'excellence' (see chapter 5). However, they warn us that we should not imagine that quality, and quality management are simply products of the 1980s; nor they warn us, should we imagine that 'quality management' in this form is entirely a recent theme for British management.

Indeed Wilkinson and his co-authors remind us that as long ago as the early 1960s, the, state sponsored, British Productivity Council was running campaigns which exhorted Britain's management and workers to get it 'right first time'. However, Wilkinson *et al.* (1998) note that it took some time to move from exhortation to experimentation. Indeed, in spite of the activity and the exhortations of the 1960s, the earliest phase of TQM experimentation in Britain actually dates from the 1970s (see also Cole, 1999, for a discussion of America and its response to TQM). This protracted gestation period suggests, as we shall see, that the imperatives of TQM (so-called) have been mediated and/or deflected by actors, forces and movements, which have been overlooked (or disguised) by management's 'gurus'.

Of course, it is true that during the 1970s, and especially during the 1980s, British and American managers apparently converted in droves to the message of TQM. However, Wilkinson and Wilmott doubt both the value and the sincerity of this conversion process. Indeed, they suggest that managers have adopted the rhetoric but (1) have failed to live up to the changes implied by this rhetoric and (2) have failed to consider the wider, social issues, which shape, and in turn are shaped by the discourse of management. They note: 'In recent years there has been an explosion of books and articles that champion the cause of "quality management" . . . few champions of quality management have reflected upon its meaning, its practical implementation, or its wider social significance' (Wilkinson and Wilmott, 1995, p. 789).

In an attempt to overcome this lack of reflection and the absence of what might be termed a larger, more 'critical-practical' and reflexive concern with quality management, Wilkinson and Wilmott have put forward an alternative (research) agenda for TQM. This alternative agenda, they tell us, is representative of an attempt: 'to open up quality management to questions and perspectives that are absent from the received wisdom of the quality literature and textbook [it is an attempt to] facilitate a more balanced assessment and holistic understanding of TQM' (Wilkinson and Wilmott, 1995, p. 790). It is this alternative agenda for TQM, which underpins our 'critical-practical' account of quality management.

Reflecting this larger agenda, our 'critical-practical' account recognizes that Total Quality Management, in common with other movements in management has been criticized as a 'fad'. However, our 'critical-practical' reading of TQM, and other recent developments in management, suggests that this dismissive account is flawed and misleading. Indeed, our reading of TQM suggests that there are at least two good reasons to reject the analysis of TQM as a fad. The first reason is this: while we should acknowledge that the advocates of TQM invoke a model of organizing which is flawed and misleading, we must also recognize that these 'guru' models and exhortations are being used to encourage managers and governments to embark upon changes which could be far-reaching in their effects. For this reason we should be sceptical of forms of analysis which would seek to dismiss TQM as empty rhetoric, unworthy of serious analysis. Second, TQM, as we shall see in a moment, occurs in a variety of shapes and formats, and so, cannot be regarded as *a* fad.

Reflecting the first of these two points, a concern that TQM may have important, far-reaching effects, we will take TQM very seriously indeed. Rather than dismiss TQM as a silly fad, we will examine it carefully. It is hoped that this more careful form of analysis might help us to understand both the limitations of 'guru' grammar, and the appeal of their vocabulary. In the next section, therefore, we will examine the rise of TQM as a management tool/philosophy. Following this, we will then move on to analyse the varieties of TQM which are subsumed within this catch-all title. Having accomplished this, we will then move on to examine aspects of the alternative agenda suggested by Wilkinson and Wilmott (1995). It is hoped that this 'critical-practical' analysis will offer ideas, arguments and questions, which might encourage readers in their own attempts to develop 'a more balanced assessment and holistic understanding of TQM' (Wilkinson and Wilmott, 1995, p. 790).

## Quality Sells!

Many of the fads and buzzwords selected for analysis in this text rose to prominence in Britain and the US during the 1980s, and reflect the political and economic features of that turbulent decade (see Gilmour, 1992, for a critical, insider's account of the Thatcher years of government). Indeed, many of our fads and buzzwords might be argued to have common origins in the economic, political and social changes of the 1980s. Given the limitations of space and budget, however, it seems wasteful and repetitious to attempt to offer a fully developed socio-political account of the development of each and every one of our fads and buzzwords. In order to avoid unnecessary repetition, therefore, we will offer an account of the development of TQM, designed to facilitate a critical awareness of the arguments, which have been used to justify/market the practices, and infrastructural changes, which follow in its wake. Those interested in a more socio-political account of the development of management ideas might wish to refer to the account of the development of 'cultural management' offered in chapter 4. Alternately, readers may wish to consult Huczynski's (1993) account of management's 'gurus', or Grint's (1997) account of management thought and practice.

We begin our analysis of the formation of 'quality management' with an account of Beckford's discussion of the rise of TQM. Beckford (1998) in his *Quality: A Critical Introduction* offers two different accounts of the rise of 'quality management'. The first account focuses upon the 'imperatives' of TQM, while the second discusses a 'quality crisis'. We will delay analysis of Beckford's 'quality crisis' for a moment, to allow us to examine the 'imperatives' of quality argument.

## The Imperatives of Quality

As he begins his exposition of quality management, Beckford argues that management's concern with quality, and with TQM more specifically, has been driven by imperatives. There are three imperatives of quality for Beckford. These imperatives are driven by economic factors, by social factors and by environmental factors. Let us examine each of these in turn.

### *The Economic Imperative*

Beckford's account of the 'economic imperative' of quality is based upon a rather caricatured set of ideas and assumptions. Harking back to the 1950s, Beckford observes that in the immediate post-war period the market for consumer goods far out-stripped the available supply in Britain, and in a range of other war-ravaged states (see Halberstam, 1987, for a discussion of Japan in this period). Given these shortages, consumers, we are told, were inclined to accept products, which by today's standards would be considered shoddy. However, Beckford notes that by the 1970s the production potential of a range of economies (thanks, in part, to maturing markets and growth stabilization), had caught up with, and in key areas, had overtaken consumer demand. These changed market circumstances (excess supply, where there had been excess demand), together with the increasing costs of energy and raw materials, Beckford argues, led managers to focus upon policies designed to control the costs of production, so that their goods might remain competitive in the marketplace.

In Britain, these attempts to achieve cost-savings led managers (and unions), to develop productivity bargains and demarcation agreements. In Japan, Beckford notes, the desire to stem rising costs led some managers to relocate production facilities from economies with high wage levels, or high social costs of employment, to economies such as Cambodia, Indonesia, Korea and Vietnam, where low-cost labour might be secured.

Beckford argues, however, that before too long the Japanese were forced to pursue a different competitive strategy, because their neighbours in Korea, and elsewhere, had developed indigenous industries with the capability to engage in price competition with Japan. Thus Beckford argues that, over time, the strategy of relocating production to underdeveloped economies proved to be double-edged for Japan, since it helped economies, such as Korea to develop their own, indigenous production facilities capable of challenging Japan's.

Recognizing, both the new, tighter, market conditions and the threat from newly industrializing countries such as Korea and Indonesia, Beckford argues that, in advance of their western competitors, the Japanese (see Halberstam, 1987) modified their approach to market competition. Thus, rather than attempting to compete on cost alone, which is a competitive strategy easily mimicked by rivals, Beckford argues that the Japanese developed a competitive strategy built around a concern for quality and customer service.

For Japan, this strategy has been very successful. Indeed, Beckford argues that this quality strategy has been so successful that producers in the developed economies of Britain and America, have, over the last few decades, been forced to change their approach to production and competition in an attempt to woo the now more selective and discerning consumer.

Reflecting this account of changing economic circumstances, Beckford's economic imperative argument is based on the understanding that, while consumers in the 1950s would have been only too pleased to accept shoddy goods and services, today's consumers are different. Today's consumers are more sophisticated, and have more alternatives available to them. Accordingly, they tend to reject goods and services which do not entirely satisfy them. Beckford argues, therefore, that organizational growth and survival in the 1990s, and beyond, reflects an economic imperative, and is predicated upon the ability of organizations to supply 'quality' goods and services in a crowded market. In this sense quality is to be regarded as an economic imperative; a fact of economic life which cannot be ignored or avoided.

To be fair to Beckford, we must concede that certain aspects of his, economic imperative, argument are appealing and seem to make sense. Indeed it is vital to locate the rise of TQM (as well as other fads and buzzwords such as culture – see chapter 4) within a discussion of economic factors. Yet, it would be wrong to state that quality has been driven by an economic imperative, since, as we shall see, this presents an overly-simplistic and deterministic account of the rise of TQM, which fails to take account of the difficulties associated with adopting and implementing this approach to quality management (see Cole, 1999; Clegg, 1993; and chapter 1).

Let us examine this notion of an imperative for change.

### *Imperatives for Change?*

*The Concise Oxford Dictionary* defines an imperative as reflecting a command, or as an urgency. Let us look, first, at the notion of imperative as a command.

If we define an imperative to be 'a command', Beckford's economic imperative of quality argument seems to suggest that a change in economic circumstances has forced the development and implementation of TQM upon organizations. This change in economic realities, it seems, forces TQM upon organizations since it robs managers of the luxury of choosing any alternative and viable approach to competition. Thus, Beckford's command-based analysis of quality management seems to suggest that economic changes have forced organizations to change, and to develop a new approach to competition.

While at an intuitive level this economic imperative argument is appealing – after all, a range of US and British organizations have, indeed, modified their structures and strategies to take account of Japanese policies and practices (see Cole, 1999; Iacocca, 1986; Hamper, 1992; Starkey and McKinlay, 1993) – we must note that it is, surely, a strange imperative *command* which *allows* certain British managers to *choose* one form of response (productivity agreements) while *allowing* certain Japanese managers to *choose* another (capital migration and quality management).

What then of our second definitional choice? What if, when Beckford considers the economic imperative of quality he means to imply that managers face a need for urgent action and change? Does this improve or refine the imperative argument? Perhaps, but only a little. Indeed, we must note that it is a strange form of urgency which allows the British pioneers of TQM to *delay* the adoption of TQM until the mid-1980s (Hill and Wilkinson, 1995), in spite of the British Productivity Council's concern with 'right first time' quality since the 1960s.

This criticism of Beckford's economic imperative of quality does not mean, of course, that economic factors have played no role in the development of TQM   clearly economic factors do play a role in the sense-making and choice-making activities of managers. However, the implication of economic factors in an argument does not imply that we should assume that change management initiatives actually turn upon an economic imperative. Instead, as we shall see, our reservations regarding Beckford's economic analysis suggest that we require a qualitatively different form of analysis with which to explore TQM. Our criticism of Beckford suggests, therefore, that rather than accepting an argument based upon the notion of 'imperatives for change', we would do well to develop a more political approach to the analysis of TQM and change. This form of approach, unlike one which accepts imperatives as an empirical 'fact', would be able to analyse the 'guru' discussion in ideological terms. Thus a political account of 'imperatives for change' would tend to view this mode of argument as an attempt to create an ideologically laden representation of organizational change, designed to 'unfreeze' (Lewin, 1958) structures and customs in the workplace and in the larger society more generally. For the moment, however, we will concentrate our attention on the analysis of Beckford's second imperative.

### The Social Imperative

Summarizing the social imperative of quality Beckford argues that it is: 'the responsibility of all managers to minimise waste of costly human resources and maximise satisfaction through work for their subordinates in order to support social cohesion within their own sphere of influence' (Beckford, 1998, p. 8). All of which makes me wonder if Beckford has a 'day-job' as a 'spin-doctor', since this is exactly the sort of 'spin' I have come to expect from our political representatives and their media officers.

Beckford's idea that managers have a duty to structure human resources to support social cohesion, it must be said, seems rather trite. This argument implies that TQM has the capacity to liberate talent and human capability, which may, of course, be true. However, Beckford implies that the liberation of human talent is possible only under TQM. Furthermore, he implies that the progress of human emancipation has been postponed by a particular form of scholarship. Thus Beckford suggests that out-moded ideas, proffered by out-dated scholars have held back the development of TQM. In this, Beckford bemoans the out-dated academics and practitioners who have failed to keep abreast of the new developments in organization and management, which, he argues, are key to understanding the significance of TQM. So who are these scholars that the academic community has ignored to the detriment of all concerned?

Three key names figure on Beckford's list of the up-to-date, yet overlooked: Mayo (who died in 1949!), Herzberg (who published in the 1950s!) and McGregor (who died in 1964!). So much, then, for Beckford's attack on the out-moded approach of his contemporaries. However, a key question remains within this rebuttal of the social imperative: why should the social engineering advocated by the likes of Mayo and Herzberg, be required within systems of (quality) production?

Analysing Beckford's work, it becomes apparent that social engineering is required within systems of quality management to deal with two issues (so now we have two social imperatives, a dual imperative, competing imperatives!?). The first of these imperatives takes place at the organizational level, and reflects the requirement that managers should respond to worker demands for learning, and for the freedom to pursue growth and self-expression while at work. Thus, the first of Beckford's two (?) social imperatives implies that TQM is driven by workers, and reflects worker demands for growth and development at work. Through this line of argument, Beckford seems to imply that TQM is predicated upon the release of talent. Furthermore, Beckford implies that TQM turns upon the existence of some form of democratic decision-making within the workplace. However, these implications are difficult to establish as fact (Wilkinson *et al.*, 1997).

Indeed, based upon research conducted in the UK, some have argued (Garrahan and Stewart, 1992; Beale, 1994) that TQM is actually designed not to liberate, but to control and to discipline workers (see also Drummond, 2000; Hart, 1993). Furthermore, we should note that Beckford's social imperative(s) makes certain assumptions about the operation of the state, which do not bear empirical scrutiny. Notably, his 'social imperative' implies that TQM is called forth, and grows up to reflect the social democratic aspirations of the population as a whole. Thus the push for TQM within organizations is said to mirror the democratic ideals and aspirations of the wider society. Yet, this would seem to rule out, altogether, the possibility that TQM might develop and take root in more authoritarian states such as China, Korea and Indonesia. These states, however, are already employing TQM systems. Indeed China, which has an appalling record on human rights, has had an active TQM society for some years now (see www.wwdir.com/quality/index.html).

The second imperative, implicit within Beckford's social imperative, relates to the adjustments and social dislocation associated with TQM, and with economic globalization (see chapter 11) more generally. Thus Beckford seems to imply (although he is very vague on this) that 'downsizing' policies (see chapter 9) associated with TQM, cause unemployment and the social problems associated with exclusion (see Hutton, 1996; Burnes, 1998; Gray, 1999; Moore, 1997). In this respect, management seems to be the cause and the solution to the social imperative of TQM. Thus out-dated management, implicitly, is the cause of social dislocation, while updated management (built upon the works of Mayo and Herzberg!) seems to be the, all too glib, solution to the social imperative of TQM.

What, then, of Beckford's third imperative?

### The Environmental Imperative

In his discussion of the social imperative, Beckford implies that 'modern' management has a responsibility to ensure the even, and socially responsible development of employees, both at work and at home (see Rose, 1990; Gramsci, 1976, for a more critical account of this). This places a huge onus upon management: the responsibility to manage the workplace for competitive advantage (Porter, 1985), while securing social stability in the surrounding community. Yet, it seems that managers have extra responsibilities over and above these, since alongside this duty to shareholders, and the duty to the wider community, it appears that managers must, simultaneously, and through TQM, work to save the planet! Thus Beckford implies that TQM is environmentally responsible since its policies (to 'design in' quality so that workers might build products 'right first time') save precious resources, through minimizing rework and the necessity for remedial action. Beckford implies, therefore, that TQM is 'green' because it addresses: 'the rising desire for reductions in environmental damage, helping to ensure the survival of all species' (Beckford, 1998, p. 9).

The desire to protect the environment is, of course, a noble idea, and reflects a noble sentiment. But, surely the nobility of TQM's environmentalism rings hollow when we examine the processes of management under TQM, and the products which TQM is employed to develop and to build (see Hart, 1993).

Can TQM be quintessentially 'green' when it is invoked to ensure the built-in obsolescence of products? Can TQM be quintessentially green, when it is, so easily, harnessed to the end of developing 'family' cars which can travel from 0–60 mph in a handful of seconds, which have a top speed in excess of 150 mph and can be delivered in any one of, say, 215 paint and trim variations? So much, then, for the imperative of the environment!

Thankfully, Beckford is on firmer ground when he attempts his second take on the rise of quality management. This second take which builds more from the analysis of a complex of politico-social factors, Beckford refers to as the 'quality crisis'.

## The Quality Crisis

In this analysis of TQM, Beckford suggests that a 'quality crisis' precipitated managerial interest in quality management. This crisis, he tells us, was formed of three factors:

- the 'guru' influence
- the influence of cost pressures
- the influence of consumer pressure and preferences.

### *'Guru' Influences*

Reflecting our earlier discussions of 'gurus' (see chapter 1), Beckford's notion of the 'quality crisis' acknowledges that a range of influential commentators and consultants have invoked a particular form of 'grammar' to create the idea that quality *must* be a key consideration for management. The 'gurus' have managed this 'unfreezing' (Lewin, 1958) process, as we noted earlier, by generating a sense of crisis at the organizational level (Pattison, 1997), and in the manager's sense of self (Jackson, 1996; Clark and Salaman, 1998).

## Cost Pressures

In generating a dual sense of crisis, the 'gurus' have been aided by the pressures on cost, and competitiveness, which have encouraged managers to seek savings, both in manpower (eliminating quality inspectors and layers of middle-management), and in resources (eliminating the costs associated with warehousing and with remedial work). In spite of our earlier attack on Beckford's economic imperative, therefore, it does seem clear that pressures to save on costs have done much to suggest and promote the TQM practices which the 'gurus' have promoted (Halberstam, 1987).

## Consumer Preferences

Together with the pressures to reduce costs, Beckford also reminds us that consumer demand, and consumer preferences, have done much to focus the minds of managers on quality matters. Indeed, we saw in our discussion of 'culture' (see chapter 4), how the ability of Japanese organizations to supply high quality, low cost goods to eager consumers, in Europe and the USA (see Iacocca, 1986; Halberstam, 1987), led to a decline in the market for home-produced goods, and so led US and European managers to focus upon the practices of 'Japanese' management, in an attempt to reflect consumer preferences for cheap, yet high quality, goods and services.

Taken together, it should be clear that Beckford's three-piece 'quality crisis' offers a more useful and more valid account of the genesis and spread of TQM in Britain than the imperative argument. This argument is preferable to one based upon 'imperatives', because it draws attention to political factors, and to the role which the 'gurus' of quality have played in shaping the contours of the quality debate.

In the section that follows, we will look more carefully at the works of those 'gurus' who have promoted TQM as the solution to the crisis, they, themselves, have helped to initiate. This analysis is important to our 'critical-practical' account of quality management, since it reveals TQM to be a complex, contestable and contested concept, even among the 'guru' fraternity!

# The Varieties of TQM

Critical, academic accounts of quality management and TQM often have a tendency to be rather dismissive of management's 'gurus'. Indeed Jackson (1996) has observed that 'guru' models and ideas, concerned with the management of enterprise, are: 'generally considered to be too philosophically impoverished, theoretically underdeveloped and empirically emaciated to warrant serious academic scrutiny' (Jackson, 1996, p. 572).

Thus Jackson notes that, often, critical, academic scholarship has tended to ignore, or to dismiss, the contributions of management's 'gurus'. It is true, of course, that not all critical academic scholarship has chosen to ignore the 'gurus'. Indeed some scholars have chosen to challenge the 'gurus' head-on. Yet, often, the critical, academic commentaries, which have embarked upon a critical engagement with 'guru' ideas and formulations, tend to treat the 'guru' commentaries in an off-hand and dismissive manner.

Critical, academic commentary on that sub-set of 'guru' theorizing concerned with TQM, for example, has a tendency to set the TQM 'gurus' up as all too convenient 'Aunt Sally' figures. Thus critical accounts of TQM have, often, tended to bunch TQM's 'gurus' together, so that they might all be knocked over with a single projectile.

For example, Snape and his co-authors offer the following introduction to TQM and its 'gurus':

> The proponents of total quality management (TQM) define quality in terms of the customer requirements or 'fitness for use' and the 'TQM organization' as being committed to continuously improving customer satisfaction. Those employees without direct contact with external customers are encouraged to view their colleagues as customers, linked via a chain of internal customer relationships to the final (external) customer. Organizations are urged to move away from supervisory approaches to quality control, and all employees, from top management to the shop or office floor, are to develop a commitment to continuous improvement as an integral part of their daily work. There is a need to develop a 'quality culture' .
>
> The problem is that the prescriptive literature on TQM says little about how we are to achieve this.
>
> (Snape *et al.*, 1995, p. 42)

I have been guilty of this myself. Working with another I have written: 'There can be little doubt that quality and total quality management are the hot topics for the 1990s. From a rapid expansion in the 1980s born of the work of Deming and what we might call the quality gurus such as Crosby and Juran, everyone is getting into quality' (Sinclair and Collins, 1994, p. 19).

This form of presentation has features that recommend it, of course. Notably, it affords an economical and critical analysis of TQM *in situ*. However this mode of presentation does have a tendency to disguise, or to gloss over some of the subtleties of TQM. It obscures the fact that the 'gurus', while acting as 'proponents of TQM', tend to promote quality management in a variety of different guises. Indeed, this tendency to lump all the 'gurus' together, disguises the fact that some of the quality 'gurus' have produced conflicting accounts of TQM.

Thus, in spite of the fact that, previously, I felt it useful and appropriate to name Deming, Crosby and Juran in one breath, and without qualification, Beckford reminds us that these 'gurus', these proponents of TQM, do not speak with one voice. In an attempt to reveal, properly and fully, the richness and variety of TQM, therefore, Beckford draws our attention, in particular, to the dispute over the form and meaning of TQM, which exists between Deming and Crosby. Quoting Bank (1992), Beckford reports that: 'Dr Juran seems to think that [Crosby is] a charlatan and hasn't missed many opportunities to say that over the years' (Beckford, 1998, p. 61).

Through an analysis of the works of the quality 'gurus', we will attempt to make sense of the varieties of TQM, as we reveal the divisions (and the name calling) evident in the ranks of the quality 'gurus'.

## A Framework for Analysis

The precise origins of TQM are difficult to pin down satisfactorily. Discussing the origins of TQM, Wilkinson and his co-authors (1998) observe that Peters and Waterman (1982) should be acknowledged as offering an early statement on the importance of quality. Others, however, (see Halberstam, 1987) would be more inclined to trace the origins of TQM back to the work of Shewhart who, in the 1940s, mentored Deming – now a recognized quality 'guru' – while they were both employed to service the US Defense Department's need for reliable statistical analysis. These works of Peters' and Waterman's, and Shewhart aside, there are generally acknowledged to be seven, or eight, quality 'gurus'. Wilkinson (1994, Wilkinson *et al.*, 1992), for example, tends to list seven quality 'gurus': Juran, Taguchi, Deming, Ishikawa, Feigenbaum, Crosby and Oakland, while Beckford (1998) adds the name of Shingo to this listing, to discuss the works of eight quality 'gurus'.

In attempting to discuss the various contributions made by these quality 'gurus', any number of frameworks for analysis might be invoked. For example, had our aim been to analyse the emergence, development and refinement of TQM, we might have adopted a chronological form of analysis, comparing Deming's early and late works on TQM (Drummond, 2000), or analysing the early discussions of TQM, such as Shewhart's, prior to analysing later contributions. Equally, had our aim been to offer an introductory exposition of TQM, we might (see Beckford, 1998) have offered a discussion framework which, simply, listed the 'gurus' (and their contributions) alphabetically. However, since our aim, here, is to highlight the varieties of TQM, and to highlight the divisions which exist between the quality 'gurus', we will offer a different framework for analysis. This framework attempts to analyse the extent to which the work of each 'guru' might be considered to be either 'hard' (focused mainly upon statistical measures of performance and conformance), or 'soft' in orientation (focused more upon methods and systems of persuasion designed to encourage managers and employees to 'commit' to new

'Hard' TQM                                                                    'Soft' TQM

<--------------------------------------------------------------------------->

Emphasis upon 'improvement tools'          Emphasis upon 'organizational approaches'
and 'measurement systems' to highlight     to facilitate TQM
deviations from conformance to standards

*Figure 6.1* A continuum of TQM

ways of working). This framework, suggested in the work of Storey (1991)
for the analysis of human resource management (HRM), and by Wilkinson
*et al.* (1991) for the analysis of TQM, might be represented as a continuum
(see Figure 6.1).

Those quality 'gurus' demonstrating a concern with 'hard' TQM, a
concern with measurement and with statistical analysis over and above a
concern for, say, people management matters, appear towards the left-
hand side of our continuum. Meanwhile, those quality 'gurus'
demonstrating more of a concern with the 'soft' side of TQM, with issues
such as customer awareness and internal marketing (Wilkinson *et al.*, 1991)
are, by the same token, grouped towards the right-hand side of our
continuum. All things are relative, however, and so it is worth drawing
attention to the fact that 'soft' TQM might tend to appear as 'hard' and
as statistically oriented, when compared to, say, the 'soft' side of HRM as
this is proposed in Storey's (1991) discussion of HRM.

### *'Hard' TQM*

On the 'hard' side of our continuum of TQM, we might list the works of
such quality 'gurus' as Shingo (1987), Taguchi (1987) and Juran (1988).
These authors have been placed on the 'hard' end of our continuum, since
each places a stress on 'improvement tools' and 'measurement systems'
above 'organizational approaches' (such as teamworking and empowerment) in the pursuit of TQM. For example, Shingo's analysis, which is
clearly influenced by Taylor's (1911) 'scientific management', demonstrates
a mechanistic concern with production and with organizational matters.
Thus, in his pursuit of total quality and 'zero-defect' production, Shingo
argues that human workers, and the human assessment of quality, are
both error prone and inconsistent. For Shingo, TQM is rooted in error-
prevention through design conformance, and is said to hinge upon good
engineering. Indeed, as distinct from 'soft' analyses of quality management, Shingo argues that it is senseless to exhort workers to strive to limit
defects. Instead, Shingo argues that defects can be prevented only through
the development of engineering and material technology. These 'hard'
forms of material technology, he warns us, are far less prone to error and

to inconsistency, and so, represent a preferable basis for TQM than one which is reliant upon worker vigilance. Viewed in these terms, therefore, Shingo's account of TQM is 'hard'. It has little to say about human motivation and, in fact, envisages no real role for the 'soft' aspects of TQM – workers – in the development of TQM.

Like Shingo's account of TQM, Taguchi's model might also be considered 'hard'. Taguchi's (1987) account of TQM, like Shingo's, argues that 'hard' statistical measures of performance and conformance are central to quality management, and are required to identify (and ultimately), to eradicate quality problems. Also in common with Shingo, Taguchi argues that the attainment of TQM rests with good design. Thus, Taguchi argues that good design builds quality in from the earliest stages of the production process. Indeed Taguchi argues that, where design is inadequate, quality will be sub-standard. For Taguchi, therefore, inadequate design is to be regarded as the root cause of sub-standard quality and customer dissatisfaction.

To be fair to Taguchi, we should acknowledge that he does envisage some role for workers in the engineering design process. Thus he argues that operators, together with managers, have a role to play in improving design. He argues, therefore, that once management has identified (through statistical analysis), a quality problem, both management and workers should engage in brainstorming sessions to work towards the eradication of the problem. Yet, aside from this (deviation), Taguchi conceives of the workplace in an almost entirely mechanistic fashion. Thus, for Taguchi, workers tend to play a role in the production process, not as the creative mediators of some socio-technological potential (McLoughlin and Clark, 1994), but only as ciphers for statistical information. In his focus upon improvement tools, in his commitment to statistical analysis, and in his relative disregard for human activity within the production system, therefore, Taguchi must be considered to offer a 'hard' account of TQM.

In comparison to the accounts of TQM offered by Shingo and by Taguchi, Juran's (1988) account of TQM is, perhaps, just a little 'softer'. For example, Juran, more explicitly than either Shingo or Taguchi, discusses the need for management 'involvement' in, and 'commitment' to 'quality'. Indeed, Juran's discussion of change management, his counsel to encourage participation, and his counsel to allow those affected by change some time to adjust to new realities, all seem to indicate a 'softer' approach to TQM. However, when we look beneath this advice and exhortation, it becomes apparent that Juran's is a rather mechanistic approach to management and organization. In fact, Juran's conviction that most quality management problems – 80 per cent (Juran, 1988) – are managerial at root, and his conviction that management must 'own' problems, both tend to rule out the scope for greater worker discretion, and for wider organizational changes such as might be expected in a, properly, 'soft' approach to TQM.

### 'Soft' TQM

Towards the 'soft' side of our continuum we might list the works of Ishikawa (1985), Feigenbaum (1986) and Oakland (1993). In common with the quality 'gurus' listed on the 'hard' side of our continuum, each of these authors demonstrates a concern with 'improvement tools' and 'measurement systems'. However, what sets the accounts of Ishikawa, Feigenbaum and Oakland apart from their 'hard' counterparts is their willingness to document 'organizational approaches' designed to facilitate both measurement and improvement. In this sense, the advocates of 'soft' TQM operate with a qualitatively different model of humanity, a model which expresses the idea that humans are, to some degree, the creative mediators of technological potential (McLoughlin and Clark, 1994) and so must be regarded as central to the processes of production and improvement.

Ishikawa, for example, while advocating 'hard' tools and processes such as 'fishbone diagrams' and 'control charts', is also a keen supporter of quality circles and other forms of participation designed to foster collaboration and worker satisfaction. Indeed Ishikawa argues that to maintain motivation, management should reward not only achievement but also worker effort. Thus as compared to the mechanistic accounts of organization offered by the 'hard' accounts of TQM, Ishikawa seems to offer a more sensitive and more organic account of work motivation and management. In this respect, the work of Ishikawa is similar to that of Feigenbaum.

Feigenbaum (1986) places great stress on the 'soft' aspects of organization. He argues that worker participation and commitment, together with organizational approaches designed to 'sell' TQM to workers must be allied with measurement and statistical analysis. Thus, while perhaps pushing the 'softer' aspects of analysis, Feigenbaum stresses that both the 'hard' and the 'soft' aspects of organizational analysis must be considered to be core elements of quality management. This is a point echoed by Oakland (1993) – a British 'guru', and so something of a rarity – who argues that while statistical measures are a key component of quality management, it is management commitment which must be considered to be central to TQM. However, unlike the 'hard' accounts of TQM which argue that managers are central to TQM – since management is at the root of most quality failures – Oakland's concern with management commitment is based upon the understanding that, until management is committed to the organizational changes designed to facilitate quality, workers will not commit to quality management, and so, will not participate actively in the organizational changes necessary to TQM.

Taken together, the two extremes of our continuum account for six of the eight quality 'gurus' discussed by Beckford (1998). We have delayed the discussion of our two remaining 'gurus', Deming (1986) and Crosby (1979), because they are, perhaps, more problematic to place on our continuum. We will now look to the works of Deming and Crosby.

### Deming versus Crosby?

Deming (1986), as we have already seen, has little time for the work of Crosby (1979). As distinct from Crosby, who offers a somewhat evangelical account of quality management, Deming has argued that exhortations and slogans have no role to play in TQM. Indeed, Deming argues that quality slogans designed to encourage workers to alter their work patterns and behaviours in a positive fashion have precisely the opposite effect (see Hamper, 1992). Observing, as he sees it, an approach to TQM based upon slogans, and upon imprecise and non-measurable characteristics, such as managerial leadership, in the work of Crosby, Deming has tended to dismiss Crosby's account of TQM as so much 'soft' nonsense. We might, therefore, be tempted to locate Crosby with the other 'soft' advocates of TQM, towards the right-hand extreme of our continuum. Yet, this location would not give an accurate reflection of Crosby's approach to TQM. In spite of his advocacy of managerial leadership and worker participation, Crosby, actually, envisages a rather passive role for workers within the initiatives and work processes designed to improve product quality. In this sense, Crosby's work might, equally, be thought of as displaying a 'hard' orientation. Recognizing these difficulties and inconsistencies in Crosby's analysis, therefore, it seems inappropriate to give Crosby a fixed location on the continuum. In an attempt to capture the inconsistencies in Crosby's work, therefore, readers might like to visualize Crosby as being 'in motion' on the continuum; opportunistically scuttling back and forth between the 'hard' and 'soft' polar extremes!

Like Crosby's, Deming's work is also difficult to pin down to one solid location. For example, in common with the 'hard' analyses of TQM, Deming's work is predicated upon measurement and upon statistical analysis. Indeed, Deming argues that these hard techniques are vital to TQM, since they allow management to eliminate from the analysis special causes of failure. This elimination of the special causes of failure, Deming argues, frees managers to pursue the regular and predictable problems, which diminish quality. Thus Deming argues that the elimination of less predictable forms of error, through the 'hard' techniques of statistical analysis, allows management to regain control of the production process by highlighting the key areas where management intervention will bear fruit. Yet, in other ways, Deming's work is 'soft'. For example, Deming draws attention to the need for leadership, and the need to drive blame, and so, fear from the analysis of quality problems, so that teamworking and communication might be improved.

Overall, then, and perhaps, untypically, among the quality 'gurus', Deming's analysis seems balanced between a concern for 'hard' and 'soft' matters. Indeed, in comparison to the extremes of our continuum, Deming's work seems neither definitively 'hard' nor 'soft'. It seems sensible to suggest, therefore, that Deming might be allocated a position in the

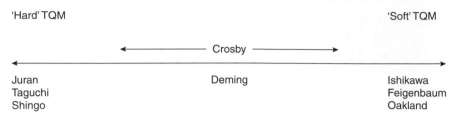

*Figure 6.2* A continuum of TQM highlighting the different approaches adopted
by the quality 'gurus'

middle of our continuum, and at some distance between our two extreme
camps. This discussion is summarized in Figure 6.2.

This analysis of 'hard' and 'soft' TQM is helpful for our 'critical-
practical' analysis. It illustrates that at the conceptual level, TQM presents
in a number of different formats, each of which implies a different approach
to management, and to the design of organizational infrastructures. Having
established this conceptual variety, however, we must now move beyond
the vanity of abstract accounts, as we attempt to offer a, properly,
'critical-practical' analysis of quality management. Our 'critical-practical'
account of TQM, therefore, attempts to transcend the limiting accounts
of the 'gurus', and is based upon an attempt to embed TQM (Granovetter,
1985). Until we have embedded TQM within a social and organizational
context, we cannot hope to understand the push-pull of political factors
which, will, variously, constrain and facilitate the organizational infrastructure required for the success and persistence of TQM. In the section
that follows, therefore, we will attempt to move from an abstract account
of TQM, towards a more embedded analysis of TQM in practice and
*in situ*.

### Good Thing Going?

Total Quality Management, it should now be apparent, is not a mono-
lithic doctrine. Given the varieties of TQM which we have encountered
so far, it seems sensible to suggest that we might expect to find variation
in the organizational practices associated with TQM, both between, and
within, national boundaries. In the discussion that follows, therefore, we
will attempt to locate TQM, not as an abstract imperative, but as a set
of organizational and political practices, which will be shaped by organizational contexts while acting to shape the context of the organization. In
this regard we should expect the experience of TQM, as a set of organizational policies and practices, to depart from the idealized and apolitical
account of quality management offered by the 'gurus' (see De Cock and
Hipkin, 1997).

This attempt to offer an embedded, 'critical-practical' framework for the analysis of TQM harks back to our introductory comments, and takes its cue from Wilkinson's and Wilmott's (1995) attempt to entreat American academia to think more carefully, and more socially, about TQM. You will recall that in discussing the need for a more critical account of TQM, Wilkinson and Wilmott (1995) have argued that the proponents of TQM, the 'gurus', tend not to reflect critically upon:

- the meaning of TQM
- the 'practical' problems of implementing TQM
- the wider social significance of TQM.

Let us examine these concerns in a little more detail.

## The Meaning of TQM

'Guru' discussions of business and management, as we have seen, tend to operate with a unitary (Fox, 1985) model of organization and management. 'Excellence' in production (see chapter 5), therefore, is a construct developed and defined to meet the needs of customers, and reflects an assumption that what is required by the customer is good for the organization and, in turn, good for each individual employed by the organization. Likewise the 'guru' discussion of culture and cultural management (see chapter 4) is underpinned by a unitary, or integrationist (Martin, 1992) account of organizational culture, which assumes that organizations are bound together as harmonious wholes, by a unifying code of cultural norms and values. It should not be a surprise to find, therefore, that in common with 'guru' accounts generally, the 'guru' discussions of quality and TQM (in spite of the divisions we have observed), are underpinned by a simplistic and unitary account of management and organization. When the 'gurus' discuss TQM, therefore, there is a tendency to present it as a 'good'. Indeed for the 'gurus' active at the 'soft' end of our TQM continuum, quality management becomes a socio-political project, synonymous with empowerment (see chapter 7), and associated with policies, ostensibly, designed to release worker talent and skill from the shackles of scientific management. In this way TQM tends to be treated as the antithesis of Taylorism, and so, attracts bouquets, effusive support from the 'gurus' (Wilkinson *et al.*, 1997).

Yet, not all commentators accept this account of TQM. Basing their arguments upon a more political account of the workplace, a number of commentators have argued that the meaning and effect of TQM is quite different to that which is depicted by the 'gurus'. Garrahan and Stewart (1992), for example, have argued that innovations in management, such as TQM, are disempowering. They argue that TQM is, essentially, a Taylorist approach to management which seeks to capture the tacit skills and knowledge of workers, so that these might be turned to address issues which have been defined, solely, by management as problematic and in need of attention. Thus, Garrahan and Stewart suggest that the bouquets of TQM are a rhetorical device designed to disguise the reality of TQM. They argue, therefore, that, in spite of the rhetoric, which portrays TQM as a liberating and empowering alternative to Taylorism, the actual experience of working under TQM is exhausting and degrading. Parker and Slaughter (1988) offer a similar line of analysis. They argue that TQM actually extends the Tayloristic requirement for control, since management's need to secure control over standards, and the need to minimize variance, which is central to both 'hard' and 'soft' TQM, leads to more direct control over employees, not less. Similarly Delbridge *et al.* (1992) have observed that, while TQM may, indeed, lead to an increase in the delegation and devolution of responsibility for production (what Hales (1993) would term the limited de-separation of management), these changes lead not to the release of talent, but to the intensification of effort. Reflecting a similar form of analysis, and a similar concern with management control, Tuckman (1998) argues that TQM represents not the negation but the culmination of Taylorism (see also Collins, 1995). Where the 'gurus' of TQM see 'bouquets', therefore, others are inclined to hurl 'brickbats', uncomplimentary remarks.

This contest between the 'guru' bouquets and the, critically intentioned, brickbats of a wider community of scholars, uncovers an important area for analysis which the 'gurus' of TQM have failed to address. This contest reveals that, in spite of the common-sense pronouncements of the 'gurus', the central elements of TQM – quality and management – do not have singular and stable meanings. At one level, then, the contest between the 'gurus' and this wider community of scholars, reveals that, in practice, the key elements of TQM, and the initiatives developed to promote and to facilitate quality management, will be contested, contestable and potentially controversial (Chia, 1996). This must imply, therefore, that the process of managing and implementing TQM is likely to be complex, difficult and, like earlier innovations in management, subject to contest and reversals (Hales, 1993).

In spite of the willingness of the 'gurus' of quality management to portray TQM, uncritically, as a 'good thing', therefore, we should, properly, regard TQM as a political attempt to deal with complexity and ambiguity. Viewed in these terms, TQM is political because it reflects an attempt made by certain powerful groups to animate and orientate people towards processes or goals (Weick, 1995). In this sense, the 'guru' accounts of TQM might be regarded as an attempt to privilege, and to maintain a particular account of management, and a particular construction of Total Quality Management as an imperative which is, fortuitously, a 'good thing'. Yet, the ideological appeals made by managers, and their 'gurus', as we have seen, are seldom completely successful (see chapter 1).

*Table 6.1* Bouquets and brickbats

| Bouquets | Brickbats |
|---|---|
| Education | Indoctrination |
| Empowerment | Emasculation |
| Liberating | Controlling |
| Delayering | Intensification |
| Teamwork | Peer group pressure |
| Responsibility | Surveillance |
| Post-Fordism | Neo-Fordism |
| Blame free culture | Identification of errors |
| Commitment | Compliance |

*Source*: Wilkinson *et al.*, 1997, p. 800.

As an ideological construct, Total Quality Management is powerful, yet flawed (Collins, 1999). It is powerful because it has the capacity to develop a persuasive account of the nature of competition and organization, which resonates with contemporary events and fears (Grint, 1994), in order to prepare, orientate and animate (Weick, 1995) workers towards a new, and changed agenda. However, this ideological construct is flawed. It is continually pierced by other forms of human experience which, rather inconveniently, encourage orientations and actions which conflict with the account of life and work preferred by the advocates of TQM. Thus, TQM is powerful, yet flawed because, while it seeks to develop a single, authoritative account of TQM, it is forced to attempt to encapsulate, simultaneously, contradictory perspectives; different sets of meaning. Wilkinson *et al.* (1997), for example, list two sets of meaning; the 'bouquets' and 'brickbats', which, they argue, are associated with 'quality management', and with the scholarship which surrounds it (see table 6.1).

This contrast between the 'brickbats' and 'bouquets' of TQM reveals, to some extent, the political nature of TQM which has been ignored by the 'gurus'. However, this stark contrast does not quite capture the complexities and ambiguities which surround the social organization of production. Thus Wilkinson and his co-authors (1997) argue that the extreme positions adopted by the 'gurus' and their critical detractors fail to recognize the fragmentary (Martin, 1992; see chapter 4) nature of human experience, and so fail to recognize that actors have the ability to recognize, and to endorse, contradictory ideas and opinions. Thus Wilkinson and his co-authors suggest that both the bouquets and the brickbats of TQM are 'blinkered' because they fail to capture the complexities of managing in a multi-faceted political arena. This is a point echoed by McArdle *et al.* (1998).

## Removing the Blinkers?

In an attempt to examine the contests, the complexities and the ambiguities which *suffuse* (what we should now label) the meanings and effects of TQM, McArdle *et al.* attempt to analyse TQM *in situ*. They argue that contrary to the 'guru' accounts of quality management, which focus upon the empowering and liberating potential of TQM, worker experience indicates an increase in the intensity of labouring. Yet far from hurling brickbats, McArdle *et al.* observe that the employees of PCB Electronics (a pseudonym selected by the authors) reported a, qualified, satisfaction with the changes in work tasks and processes which had ensued. Thus McArdle *et al.* offer the following testimony from a PCB employee: 'I'm forty-six and I've been doing this new job for nearly two years and I've been completely turned around. It has given me a new lease of life. I'd rather work this way. *It's hard work with more responsibility and more worry, but there is a lot more job satisfaction*' (McArdle *et al.*, 1998, p. 164, emphasis added).

Similar forms of testimony, and analysis, have also been offered by Waddington and Whitson (1996). However, it is important to note that these forms of analysis should not be taken as implying that employees, naturally and uncritically, welcome the changes to working practices associated with TQM – this, after all, is the message pinned to the bouquets of TQM. Instead, if we are to make sense of worker attitudes to TQM, it is important to examine the context of changes in work, and in work design, which quality management endeavours call forth. As McArdle *et al.* suggest, it should not surprise us if workers seem to welcome changes at work, where the alternative to such change is closure and redundancy. Similarly Munro (1998) and Tuckman (1998) both suggest that attitudes towards TQM are shaped by the attempts of managers to commodify labour, and labour relations, by drawing the ideology of market relations into the sphere of production. In this way, both Tuckman and Munro show the power of TQM as an ideological construct. Thus, the authors suggest that workers have become orientated and animated towards TQM, and have been unable to mount a challenge to the policies which have increased the intensity of their labour because the logic of the marketplace, and the lexicon of consumption, which is used to justify TQM at work serve to limit critical commentary and dissent. Thus both Munro and Tuckman suggest that worker ambivalence as regards TQM – the positioning of workers between the brickbats and the bouquets of TQM – is, to some degree, a product of the ambiguity and the ideology of quality management. In this, Munro and Tuckman seem to suggest that workers would be inclined to dispute TQM, yet find the 'grammar' and ideology of this managerial initiative – that customer satisfaction is imperative, that quality is 'good' – has constructed a political order which makes it problematic to articulate a legitimate line of dissent.

This more political account of management and TQM has implications for our second issue which is concerned with the (study of the) take-up and implementation of TQM.

## Implementing TQM

The 'gurus' of TQM say a lot about what managers should achieve via the implementation of TQM. Similarly the 'gurus' of TQM also have a lot to say about the deficiencies of traditional approaches to management and quality, *less than* TQM. The 'gurus', then, offer prescription and, in a superficial sense, offer description. What they do not offer, in any meaningful sense, is research that analyses the actual spread and depth of TQM practices (De Cock and Hipkin, 1997).

This is a key oversight, since the empirical experience of TQM, in Britain, conflicts with the descriptions and the prescriptions offered by the 'gurus'. Indeed, Webb (1998) suggests that the 'guru' accounts of quality management are an active deceit of the empirical reality of TQM in Britain. Thus, Webb suggests that the 'gurus' of TQM ignore or obscure the empirical reality of TQM because they fail to acknowledge the complexities and ambiguities of organizational life.

Typically, the 'gurus' of TQM argue that changes designed to deliver quality management represent reciprocal win-win agreements where producers secure their future by dedicating themselves to the needs of the customer. Reflecting this consensus-oriented, win-win account, Crosby (1979) argues that quality is 'free'. TQM, he argues, meets the individual's needs for job satisfaction and self-actualization and, as a result, organizations benefit from increased individual commitment to organizational goals. However, Hill (1991, 1998) argues that such forms of analysis and explanation understate the problems of gaining workforce commitment to TQM because they misunderstand the political nature of the workplace, and so, overstate the efficacy of the levers designed to facilitate and to deliver changes in (and at) work.

Reflecting this concern with the levers designed to deliver TQM, and with the relative disregard of questions relating to the implementation of TQM systems in British workplaces, Wilkinson *et al.* (1998) have attempted to investigate the take-up and implementation of TQM. Their analysis suggests that, in spite of the 'guru' prescriptions and exhortations, British workers and managers have been unable to commit themselves to TQM as an imperative force (see Figure 6.3).

Why the 'gap' between the experience of TQM and the 'guru' rhetoric?

Our 'critical-practical' approach to this issue suggests that the gap is caused by the failure of the 'gurus' to analyse TQM as an aspect of management's incomplete and self-defeating quest for control over the processes of work (see chapter 1). In this sense, the gap between the rhetoric and practice of TQM, perhaps surprisingly, might be regarded as a product of the

| Authors | Approach | Results |
|---|---|---|
| Kearney (1992) | Survey | 80% failure rate reported for TQM |
| Cruise O'Brien and Voss (1992) | Self-assessment against Baldridge quality award criteria | Most firms rated poor, would not qualify for consideration |
| Witcher and Whyte (1992) | Survey | Too early to judge success |
| Economist Intelligence Unit (1992) | Case studies | Cynicism widely reported regarding TQM |
| Zairi *et al.* (1994) | Analysis of publicly available information | TQM contributing to bottom-line success |
| Wilkinson *et al.* (1993) | Survey and case studies | Minority responding that TQM is very successful |

*Figure 6.3* The implementation of TQM. *Source*: Adapted from Wilkinson *et al.* (1998).

'guru' advice and exhortation, which encourages managers to view TQM in a particularly limited and limiting way. Reflecting upon the nature of this 'guru' advice, De Cock and Hipkin (1997) argue that the 'gurus' have encouraged managers to view TQM as a prescriptive set of techniques. However, they argue that this account of TQM has discouraged managers from committing to the process of reflection and self-development, incumbent upon those who would seek to manage the social processes of change (Chia, 1996). Viewed in these terms, therefore, the gap between the prescription and the practice of TQM, turns upon the existence of an account of management and change which obscures the political ambiguities of the workplace. To analyse the take-up and implementation of TQM, therefore, we will require a form of analysis that recognizes management as an amorphous and ambiguous project. This call for a more political analysis of TQM, however, does not mean that this form of analysis is easy to undertake.

Reflecting upon the practices and politics of TQM, Hill (1998) and Wilkinson *et al.* (1998) encounter a key problem. The authors note that while it is important to move beyond the 'guru' prescriptions for TQM, so that we might assess the take-up and implementation of Total Quality Management, it can be difficult to offer a coherent and rigorous analysis of TQM *in situ*. Hill suggests that this difficulty has at least two root causes. First, and perhaps most importantly, Hill notes that, since TQM appears in a variety of guises, we cannot be sure that when we analyse the take-up of TQM systems across organizations, we are actually comparing like with like. Second, Hill notes that a range of the studies undertaken, ostensibly, to gauge the processes and pitfalls associated with the implementation of TQM, have been undertaken by organizations – such as consultancy firms – which have an interest in exaggerating the spread and depth of TQM practices. Hence Hill argues that all analyses of TQM – 'guru' exhortation as well as empirical observation – must be treated cautiously and must be taken with a generous pinch of salt.

Accepting these caveats and limitations, Hill argues that to analyse the take-up of TQM we must, first, have a model of TQM. Hill's construction of TQM, which, in a sense, is a distillation of 'guru' advocacy and Japanese managerial practice, delineates a number of defining characteristics (see also Tuckman, 1998). Summarizing these characteristics we might say that TQM reflects an approach to management and organization where:

1   Quality is a strategic issue driven by top management, where senior management 'determines quality priorities, establishes the systems of quality management and the processes to be followed, provides resources and leads by example' (Hill, 1998, p. 36).
2   Organizational structures and policies are redesigned to facilitate quality improvement, both within existing departmental structures (vertical improvement) and across departments and functions (horizontal improvement).
3   Managers, both at senior and middle-management levels, take responsibility for the management systems so that rank-and-file organizational members are encouraged to contribute and to commit to quality.
4   Rigorous and systematic techniques are used by all employees to identify and to resolve quality problems.
5   TQM both creates yet depends upon culture change.

Hill's (1998, 1991) research activity is based around an attempt to ascertain the extent to which British managers have implemented TQM, as defined by these five key characteristics. Hill reports, as we would expect, some degree of variation in the experience of quality management in Britain. In addition, he reports a gap between the promise/rhetoric of TQM and the empirical reality of the organizational practices which managers have been keen to label as Total Quality Management. Indeed, he notes that, in Britain TQM is seldom total. He argues:

> it looks as if many British companies which claim to have introduced TQM have done so on the cheap and in the hope of a quick fix, ignoring the principles of best practice and the substantial investments required, and proceeding in a half-hearted, unsystematic and partial way, with the result that they have got it wrong.
>
> (Hill, 1998, p. 48)

Wilkinson *et al.* (1998) concur with Hill on this account of TQM. Indeed, they offer a range of case examples (see Figure 6.3) which suggest that, often, managers fail to understand that effective TQM, as this had been sold by the 'gurus', requires a fundamental transformation in both policy and action. Hill suggests, therefore, that managers have often failed to implement *Total* Quality Management because (1) they lack commitment, and because (2) they have been misled by the 'guru' advice. Reflecting this understanding, Hill suggests that managers have been disappointed by their attempts to implement a new and distinctive approach to quality management because they have 'ignored the realities of organizational power and inertia' (Hill, 1998, p. 52). Hill argues, therefore, that the managerial converts to TQM have failed to realize the investment in time, in materials and in intellectual resources (Chia, 1996) necessary for the successful implementation of TQM. This is a point echoed by De Cock and Hipkin (1997) who have argued that TQM might be regarded as a technical attempt to manage ambiguity.

De Cock and Hipkin argue that TQM, as it is articulated by management's 'gurus', is a technical attempt to cope with the ambiguity of managing others. Indeed, they argue that TQM should be regarded as a concept portrayed as a procedure. Sold to management as a procedure, this conceptualization of TQM, they argue, claims to have the capacity to transform the recurrent and persistent micro-political problems of managing into technical matters which may be resolved. However, De Cock and Hipkin warn us that this attempt at transformation fails. Indeed they argue that while the concept of TQM promises to reduce ambiguity, the technical-technicist account of TQM offered by the 'gurus', has a tendency to increase confusion, because it denies managers a means of navigating the politics of quality management. Somewhat paradoxically, therefore, De Cock and Hipkin suggest that the 'guru' discussion of TQM animates organizational politicking through its attempts to develop an apolitical account of working and managing. As distinct from the 'guru' accounts, which are glib about management's power to bring about change at work, therefore, it seems clear that models of control and inertia should be made central to the 'critical-practical' analysis of TQM.

## Inertia and Change

Discussing the development of TQM in Britain, Tuckman (1998) identifies four key periods or phases of development. These phases reflect a process of organizational learning in British business, and signal, too, the increased willingness of governmental actors to become involved in quality matters. These phases cover the period from the late 1970s until the late 1980s and reveal, in a number of ways, the political nature of organizational change.

### Phase One (late 1970s–early 1980s)

Tuckman argues that the early experimentation which took place in Britain during the late 1970s was confined to those firms who faced direct competition from Japanese competitors. Thus Tuckman suggests that the early converts to quality management, in Britain, turned to these initiatives in an attempt to regain ground lost to Japanese competitors who had stolen a competitive advantage due to the quality of their products.

Hill (1998) and Tuckman (1998) warn us, however, that it would be a mistake to think of this early experimentation with quality in terms of TQM. Indeed, Hill and Tuckman argue that, if anything, this initial phase of interest is remarkable because of the difference between the organizational processes and policies implemented in Britain, when compared to those common in Japan. Thus, Hill notes that, while Japanese managers had attempted to develop a rigorous, coherent and systematic model of quality management, British managers chose a more *ad hoc* approach, in part, one suspects, because they lacked the mathematical and technical ability to comprehend the 'hard' aspects of TQM (see Whittington, 1993). During the 1970s, therefore, UK managers seem to have viewed Total Quality Management as a technique to boost motivation and commitment. Consequently, UK managers borrowed only aspects of the Japanese system – mainly simple structural interventions such as 'quality circles' – and either failed to commit to the larger changes required for TQM, or failed to realize that quality circles were but one aspect of *Total* Quality Management.

Perhaps unsurprisingly this limited experimentation with QM (it seems wholly inappropriate to call it TQM) led to disappointing results. Hill (1991), for example, notes that, most often, quality circles failed due to a lack of management support. Senior managers, he argues, tended to instigate quality circles, yet offered middle management little reason to commit to, or to see through quality management in the face of obstacles and problems. And there were problems. Hill's (1991) analysis of thirteen organizations, for example, shows how employees    both managerial and rank-and-file – were, typically, doubtful of management's motivation for implementing quality circles, and so, tended to remain unconvinced about the virtues of quality circle activity. As Hill (1998) notes: 'it was rare for more than 10 per cent of the eligible employees to join, and non-members disparaged circle programmes, despite a widely held belief among employees that more participation in managerial decisions was highly desirable' (Hill, 1998, pp. 34–35).

### Phase Two (1980s)

The second phase of quality management identified by Tuckman, again, stems from the attempts made by British managers to match the production innovations made by competitors. These production innovations became grouped under the umbrella term JIT (just-in-time) production. The concept of JIT production describes an approach to manufacturing where organizations make considerable cost savings because they produce goods as and when they are needed by the market, rather than producing these for inventory – just-in-case they are required. A key component of JIT production, therefore, is the absence of buffer-stocks.

Yet, while JIT production clearly conveys certain business benefits, this low inventory approach to manufacture also brings with it certain problems for the management of production and for quality assurance. Under JIT production systems there is very little slack in production. Inventories are kept low, and so managers must be assured that the components and sub-assemblies delivered just-in-time by suppliers are always of the appropriate quality standard, since any problem with suppliers will soon halt production. Thus the need to ensure continuity of production *and* product quality has encouraged managers to develop a closely managed and controlled relationship with suppliers. Reflecting this need for quality and control, therefore, the second phase of quality management in Britain reflects, in part, the need to control suppliers and sub-contractors within a system of production which depends upon close co-ordination and co-operation throughout an extended chain of production.

However, this second phase of quality management was also given increased impetus by the development of quality standards – such as BS 5750 and ISO 9000 – which were awarded by state-trained external assessors to those organizations which could demonstrate their commitment to the documentation of quality systems and procedures. Taken as a whole, therefore, this second phase of quality management saw the extension and development of inter-firm quality chains, and the growing involvement of the state in the shaping of industrial conduct.

### Phase Three (from mid-1980s)

The third phase of quality management in Britain represents an attempt to push quality management into the service sector, and in comparison to earlier phases, represents an attempt to develop a more coherent and cohesive approach to management via attempts to manage organizational culture. This phase represents, at one level, a move from 'hard' quality management techniques, towards a 'softer' account of quality. However, Tuckman seems to suggest that, in spite of the appearance of coherence, the culture-led model of TQM was always destined to lead to a less than total approach to TQM. Thus Tuckman argues that the metaphor of culture encouraged a disregard of statistically based analyses of variance and quality, which, of course, are central to TQM. He notes that in the mid-1980s: 'The emphasis in the training programmes that accompanied the introduction of total quality management moved from the tools of quality assurance – essentially statistical process control – to discussion of the internal customer' (Tuckman, 1998, p. 73).

Yet, while the cultural metaphor of quality may have hampered the development of *Total* Quality Management, the new market-oriented focus, prompted by the concept of cultural management seems to have encouraged quality management to take root in a range of nationalized and de-nationalizing industries.

### Phase Four (from late 1980s)

The fourth phase of development clearly builds from, and seeks to extend the cultural approach developed in the third phase of quality management. Thus the fourth phase of quality management in Britain represents an attempt to develop systems and procedures designed to improve quality within public sector services.

We have already seen how, from the earliest stages of the development of TQM, various governments and state agencies in Britain have played a role in the development of quality management. However, Tuckman's account of TQM shows us how, from the late 1980s (and especially in the early 1990s), politicians in the UK have intervened more directly in the management of public services, in an attempt to ensure the implementation and maintenance of quality standards. At root, many of these changes have been aimed at improving financial accountability in the public services. However, for most of us, these changes have been experienced as a range of Citizens' Charters, which carry promises concerning such things as waiting times, and standards of courtesy and service, in a whole host of public service environments (*The Economist*, 22/06/91, 27/07/91, 27/06/92, 19/09/92).

The churlish amongst us, may of course, find the advent of a Citizens' Charters within a society where we are, formally, subjects of the crown, just a little paradoxical. Likewise those schooled in history might, equally, point out that a Citizens' Charter which grants us rights as consumers, serves only to vindicate Napoleon's judgement of the English – it seems the English, are, after all, a nation of shop-keepers. So let us not be churlish. Let us, instead consider the impact and social significance of the discourse of TQM, which now attempts to shape, and to manage, key aspects of our lives. Let us ask two key questions which are suggested by our desire to go beyond the ideas of the 'gurus', so that we might offer a more social form of analysis:

* Can/should TQM be used to deliver quality in public services?
* How might we make room for an account of 'quality' which commits to the study of politics and inertia?

## A Social Account of TQM?

Discussing the development of quality management in local government, and the problems associated with constructing customers for public services, Bennington and Taylor (1992) highlight the problems of defining and delivering quality which have been glossed over by the 'gurus' and their 'customer knows best' approach to management. Examining the problem of defining quality, and quality management in the public sector, they highlight a contest between a 'new right approach', and a 'new left approach' to quality management in the public sector.

The 'new right approach' to the management of the public sector offers an account of quality and management couched in the terms of liberal, free-market economics (see Gray, 1999; and chapters 10 and 11). Thus, the new right approach to quality management in the public sector reflects the assumption that: 'private markets offer the best way of pursuing quality, through competition between producers and choice for consumers' (Bennington and Taylor, 1992, p. 168).

In public services this understanding of markets has led to the construction of customers and to the development of service standards designed to promote responsiveness and accountability (Tuckman, 1998). Thus quality management in public services has taken physical forms such as, compulsory competitive tendering (CCT), the division of 'purchasers' and 'providers' within an internal market for health services, and, of course, the development of performance tables which are now used to rank such things as schools, hospitals and universities (Walsh, 1998).

Some (see Paddon, 1992) have argued, however, that it is difficult to perceive improvements in quality as the outcomes of such initiatives. Indeed Wilkinson *et al.* (1998) have argued that detailed studies of compulsory competitive tendering reveal that, while significant changes are often made in service delivery following the introduction of CCT, these changes are not always beneficial to the consumer, and are seldom beneficial to the employees providing the service (Walsh, 1998). This is a point echoed by Tsoukas (1995). Indeed, Tsoukas discusses the case of local authority where the implementation of quality management and performance indicators actually led to a reduction in the quality of service provided.

Discussing the provision of 'home-help' services such as 'meals on wheels', Tsoukas argues that performance measures designed to control the provision of public services may, in fact, lead to a deterioration in service quality. Examining the operation of performance tables within the management of a local council, Tsoukas notes that performance measures designed to focus attention on quality and improvement actually inhibited innovation in the provision of local services. Thus Tsoukas observes that, thanks to performance tables and performance indicators, the system of meal provision preferred by those receiving the 'meals on wheels' service (the sole arbiters of quality within TQM!) – periodic deliveries of frozen prepared meals designed to be reheated by microwave – could not be supplied, since the council providing the meals was ranked for quality on a range of indicators, including the number of home helps per thousand of population. Since the system of meal delivery preferred by the recipients of the service would have led to a reduction in the number of home helps, and so, to a reduction in one of the indicators used to measure the council's performance, the council could not risk providing the form of service preferred by the consumer!

Tsoukas shows us, therefore, how a disregard of organizational politics scuppers both the analysis and the management of TQM. His discussion shows how the imposition of an inflexible metric for the analysis of quality – based upon the assumption that quality standards are self-evident and are held in common – actually led to a reduction in the quality of service as this was judged both by consumer and by provider. Indeed Tsoukas argues that, quite against the intentions of those developing the system of performance measurement and accountability, the performance measures in this case had themselves become a key source of quality failure. In short, Tsoukas warns us of the problems which arise within the new right's agenda for quality. Indeed, he shows how attempts to separate management from (party) political forms of decision-making in the public sector (Walsh, 1998) may actually reduce service quality. Thus Tsoukas reveals the mechanism whereby management by indicators may be redefined, tacitly, as the management of indicators!

The 'new left' approach to quality in public services, by way of contrast, is an attempt to acknowledge the political nature of decision-making, and the ambiguous nature of quality. Thus, where the approach advocated by the new right is either silent on the existence of conflicting accounts of quality or assumes that such conflicts will be taken care of by market competition, the new left agenda accepts such forms of difference as legitimate and positive. Rather than look to a market (or quasi-market) system, such as the purchaser–provider split in the UK health service, to squeeze out such differences, the new left approach to quality is an approach much more clearly based upon politico-economic considerations. Thus the new left approach to quality (and the new left quality audit) acknowledges that definitions of quality will be contested. Consider for a moment how many definitions of quality might exist in a hospital. Would the concept of 'quality of care' mean the same thing in an emergency operating theatre as in a geriatric ward? Would a 'quality' police service have the same meaning for a police sergeant, a chief inspector, a magistrate, a civilian clerk and a female police officer? Would any of these individuals concur with the definition of quality policing as defined by, say, a single parent on a housing estate?

Recognizing the importance of these sorts of issues, in any system designed to deliver and to manage quality improvement, the 'new left' approach to quality is more concerned with democratic considerations

such as the inclusion of disadvantaged groups, and the breadth of participation in decision-making, than with simple consumerist accounts of
quality which assume that common definitions of 'quality' are easy to
develop and to maintain.

This brief analysis of the division between the 'new right' and 'new left'
account of quality, therefore, seems to suggest the need for a more social-
political form of analysis. This is a concern echoed by some commentators
(Tuckman, 1998), and by sections of the British trade union movement,
who, recognizing problems with TQM, have attempted to make space for
a more radical account of quality.

## Room to Roam?

In attempting to make space for a more radical (a more socialized and
less consumerist) account of quality, the new left discussion of quality
suggests that if we think of ourselves solely as the economic consumers of
quality goods and services, we may suffer disappointment and disillusion-
ment as customers. Furthermore, in its commitment to notions of
democracy, and to democratic decision-making, the new left account of
quality reminds us that, if TQM is to be truly total it must say something
about the quality of our lives, and our rights as producers. As Fisher (1991)
observes: 'Unions have been pressing for quality for years – more
employees, safer working, more investment, better quality raw materials,
opposition to built-in obsolescence, and so on. However, "quality" in TQM
does not really mean this, it really means *complete flexibility and absence of
opposition to management's goals*' (Fisher, 1991 quoted in Tuckman, 1998,
emphasis in original).

A similar concern over the impact of TQM on producers may be found
in the work of Fucini and Fucini (1990). Discussing the development of
Mazda's first US plant, the Fucinis note that Mazda's success in producing
zero-defect cars, with beautifully aligned body panels, is not free. Indeed,
quite contrary to Beckford's (1998) account of TQM and its environ-
mentalist credentials, the Fucinis' account of Mazda's total quality system
reveals it to be resource-hungry.

However, the resources expended in the production of Mazda cars do
not tend to figure on balance sheets, and do not conform to normal
accounting conventions. Instead the real costs of quality and the tariff
consequent upon Mazda's intensified system of working is more properly
measured in human terms: chronic lower back pain and repetitive stress
injuries – painful and, ultimately disabling forms of ailment – which reached
epidemic proportions under Mazda's, apparently post-Taylorist production system.

As we work towards the conclusion of our 'critical-practical' account of
TQM, therefore, it seems sensible to suggest that if we are to challenge
the limitations and the abuses, which our analysis suggests are built into

TQM, we will require a wider and more socialized account of the meanings and effects of TQM. At its most prosaic, such an argument reflects a concern that the TQM policies and procedures used to develop, say, acoustically superior hi-fi systems, will do little to improve our enjoyment of life, if we have suffered treble-deafness or worse, tinnitus, thanks to the roles which we perform as producers within a TQM environment.

Yet our social and more holistic concern need not be confined to such a managerialist dialogue. We might, for example, widen the analysis to ask about social exclusion (Burnes, 1998) and stakeholding (Hutton, 1996). Can quality be 'free' where its policies intensify worker effort? Can TQM be 'good' when its outcomes include 'downsizing' (Walsh, 1998)? Should we celebrate the consumerist benefits of quality management, when the policies associated with TQM at the organizational level (flexibility) lead to increasing polarization, between affluent and poor, between the overworked and the work-poor (Gray, 1999) in the wider society?

Here there are no easy answers. Unlike the 'gurus' I cannot pretend to provide a ready solution to such problematic and intractable issues. I am convinced of one thing, however, that as students (of management) we should work to ensure that the more socialized arguments and concerns of our 'critical-practical' account of TQM greet a wider readership.

## Summary

This chapter has attempted to offer a critical account of the orientation and operation of TQM. However, while keen to provide a critical-practical analysis of TQM, the chapter attempts to avoid the dismissive tone which critical, academic commentary on the 'gurus' has, at times, tended to adopt. Thus, rather than lump the 'gurus' together (so that we might mock, efficiently, the flaws in their thinking on TQM), this chapter has attempted to explore the varieties of TQM evident in the various accounts offered by the 'gurus'. This treatment, of course, does not imply an endorsement of these 'guru' accounts of TQM.

Indeed, in an attempt to explore, and to expose, the limitations of TQM, in theory and in practice, this chapter has adopted the larger and more socialized concerns voiced by Wilkinson and Wilmott (1995) as its vehicle for analysis. Accordingly, the chapter has attempted to look critically at the meanings of quality and management within TQM.

Rejecting the 'imperatives of quality' argument as (1) an inadequate conceptualization of TQM which (2) has a political function designed to facilitate change by limiting opposition (Collins, 1998) and dissent, we have attempted a 'critical-practical' analysis designed to show that critical insight may, usefully, inform practice by offering a more truthful representation of managing and organizing.

Recognizing that the 'gurus' of TQM portray quality as a transparent concept, conceived and understood in a common fashion by all, this chapter has, by way of contrast, attempted to highlight the plurality of meaning which will tend to surround any attempt to manage 'quality'. Building upon this more political form of analysis, the chapter has attempted to highlight the practical problems of implementing TQM. Indeed, our analysis suggests that the accounts of TQM which have been developed as templates for/exhortations to change, actually limit managers' ability to comprehend Total Quality Management as an ambiguous and amorphous project. Thus we have argued that the 'gurus' of quality offer an inadequate representation of the problems of organizing and managing which serves to deform rather than inform action because it fails to model the political realities of organization.

Finally, the chapter concluded by offering a brief discussion designed to remind readers of the limitations of the consumerist account of quality. This analysis was designed to show that the quality benefits, pursued in the name of 'consumers', may not seem so beneficial, nor as advantageous from the position of the 'producer'. Recognizing that a majority of us are, both, producers and consumers of goods, an attempt has been made to set the consumer benefits of TQM against the, potential, producer costs – work intensification and injury – borne by those who work under systems of quality management.

# 7 Empowerment

## Introduction

Ricardo Semler claims to have the world's most unusual workplace. According to the title of his second book he is a *Maverick* (Semler, 1994). He claims that he is, in keeping with the origins of this term, 'unbranded' in the world of business, because of his preferred approach to management, which is based upon a commitment to 'empowerment'.

If you are reading this as a practising manager you will, no doubt, already be familiar with 'empowerment', since the term has been one of the central motifs of popular management discourse for more than a decade. Hopfl (1994) for example, notes that by the time Block's (1986) work on empowerment was published in 1986: 'the term was already in use in large-scale organisations committed to large-scale culture change and was actively promoted by evangelical management gurus as a *sine qua non* of change' (Hopfl, 1994, p. 39)

If you are involved in a managerial role within an organization, perhaps within a bank; within an automobile company; within a school; within a hospital, indeed within almost any form of work organization you could imagine, there is a high probability that at some point in time, since the 1990s, you experienced 'empowerment' directly and personally.

If you are a middle manager, you may have experienced empowerment as part of a downsizing programme (see chapter 9) designed by senior management to enhance shareholder value by 'doing more with less'. If you hold a more senior position in your organization, perhaps you, on the advice of a consulting organization, decided to empower your colleagues by instigating a change programme, designed to re-engineer the organization (see chapter 8), and to release the talents of your subordinates, with the goal of achieving total customer satisfaction.

Whatever your personal experience of empowerment, whether positive or negative, foul or fair, there is no escaping the fact that empowerment has been one of the key business buzzwords of the 1990s. Perhaps unsurprisingly, the popularity of this buzzword has led to the publication of numerous books and articles geared to explaining to managers how, and why, they should empower their workers (see Bowen and Lawler, 1992).

The majority of those who have offered counsel on empowerment at work have been keen to emphasize the benefits of an empowered system of working for organizations, and for the individuals who make up these organizations (see for examples of prescriptive accounts, Block, 1986; Clutterbuck and Kernaghan, 1994; Foy, 1994; Mitchell-Stewart, 1994). Others, however, even while supportive of the concept of empowerment at work, have been more reserved in their praise for the merits of empowerment as a management philosophy and technique. For example, early in his discussion of Semco's empowered system of working, Semler acknowledges that his organization is: 'not the only company to experiment with participative management. *It's become a fad.* But so many efforts at workplace democracy are just so much hot air. Not that the intentions are bad, it's just that it's much easier to talk about worker involvement than to implement it' (Semler, 1994, p. 7, emphasis added).

A similar, guarded, endorsement of empowerment (within a more general prescription for its achievement) can be found in the work of Malone (1997). Writing for *Sloan Management Review*, Malone outlines his key concerns by addressing his managerial audience as follows:

> Are you stifling innovation and creativity by trying to micromanage? Or are you operating your organization as many autonomous fiefdoms and missing the benefits of being one company? Should you give more autonomy to the people who work for you? Or perhaps you feel you should take more control and show 'real' leadership?
>
> Nagging questions like these indicate that some of the most difficult problems for managers are those of exercising control. A central issue for organizations in the twenty-first century will be how to balance top–down control with bottom–up empowerment. For example, recent business rhetoric has focused so much on the importance of 'empowering' workers that the term has become an almost meaningless cliché. *Is the talk of empowerment just a fad?*
>
> (Malone, 1997, p. 23, emphasis added)

In this chapter we will attempt to unpack and unpick the 'guru' advice on empowerment, so that we might offer a 'critical-practical' analysis of what Malone and Semler fear may be just a(nother) management fad. Countering this notion of fads and faddishness, we will offer a qualitatively different form of argument. We will argue that the managerialist discussion of empowerment, in common with other recent developments in management, such as Total Quality Management (see chapter 6) and Business Process Re-engineering (see chapter 8), represents an attempt to give shape and form to a process, which is, essentially, amorphous and ambiguous (De Cock and Hipkin, 1997). Thus, we will argue that the managerial discourse of empowerment should be regarded as an attempt to convert the social processes of labour (which resist control and direction) into technical processes, which are amenable to managerial intervention. This attempt to convert/divert the social processes of labour into a form amenable to technical/technique-based approaches to managing, as we shall see, is given force and immediacy by a 'grammar' of imperatives, which attempts to shape worker consciousness and identity (Ramsay, 1997) so that employees might be oriented and animated (Weick, 1995) towards managerial goals. However, we will also argue that this attempt to shape worker identity and subjectivity, like all other managerial tools and techniques, is subject to contest and reversal (Hales, 1993). This contest and reversal, however, is seldom acknowledged by managerialist authors. In this chapter, therefore, we will direct our attention towards the contests, which exist within, and take place over, empowerment at work. Basing our analysis upon the experience of conflict and contest, we will argue that the discourse of empowerment is flawed by omission and over-statement. Indeed, we will argue that the discourse of empowerment overstates managerial capability, because it misrepresents the nature of workplace relations.

In keeping with the mode of presentation offered in earlier chapters, therefore, this chapter might be regarded as an attempt to allow readers to:

- *Locate management's concern with empowerment*: This attempt to locate empowerment hinges upon a larger discussion of power. Offering a historical analysis of the nature of the employment relationship we will argue that empowerment is one aspect of a set of practices designed to reflect and to maintain an asymmetry of power in the workplace.
- *Understand the concept of empowerment and the controversies often disguised within the managerial discussion of empowerment*: Having located empowerment contextually, as a historically situated and maintained set of practices which reflect the nature of the employment relationship, we will turn our gaze to the 'guru' discussions of management, in an attempt to ascertain the extent to which the 'gurus' understand the concept of power. Perhaps unsurprisingly, given the limited accounts of working and managing which have been offered by the 'gurus', we will argue that, for the most part, managerialist discussions misrepresent the realities of managing and working. Thus we will argue that the 'gurus' invoke a 'grammar' of imperatives to facilitate an insensible account of work and power, designed to orientate workers towards managerial goals. However, we will argue that this technical-prescriptive approach to empowerment fails to deliver the changes sought at work, because it is based upon a denial of the lived-experience of working (Chia, 1996; Burrell, 1997).
- *Critique the managerialist literature on empowerment*: Building from our account of power, we will offer a framework for action and analysis

designed to illustrate, practically, the omissions and misunderstand-ings which characterize the 'guru' accounts of the workplace, and the managerialist tales of empowerment. Having outlined these failings, we will, then, offer a framework for analysis, which seeks to present a more sensible account of empowerment (one which does not deny experience, and so, makes use of our five senses), which has the poten-tial to allow us to be actors, rather than spectators in our lives (Wright-Mills, 1973).

This attempt to locate, understand and critique empowerment does not mean, however, that we will seek to dismiss empowerment as a simple fad. Indeed, quite unlike the analyses offered by Semler and by Malone, we will argue that it is unhelpful to think of empowerment as a fad.

Reflecting our concern with language and power, more generally, we will argue that the dismissal of empowerment as a fad, is based upon a limited understanding of the nature of power. Thus we will argue that empowerment should be taken very seriously. In fact, we will suggest that empowerment is deserving of serious analysis for three key reasons.

First, empowerment is reflective of a larger historical concern with power and decision-making at work, which remains central to the contemporary discourse of management. As Ramsay has observed: 'The search for effec-tive means by which employees might exert equitable influence over matter affecting their working lives is as old as capitalism' (Ramsay, 1997, p. 314).

Second, we should take empowerment seriously, because in the name of empowerment, managers are manufacturing real, physical changes at work. The 'gurus', perhaps unsurprisingly, have argued that we should be supportive of these changes. However, other scholars (see Ramsay, 1997) have argued that attempts to restructure workplace relations on a more individualized basis may lead to anti-democratic outcomes. Thus we will take empowerment seriously, since the controversies revealed by careful analysis draw our attention to the need to unpack and unpick this concept.

Third, and reflecting a concern with democracy, we might argue that we should take empowerment seriously, because if we do not we trivialize democracy. As we shall see, the advocates of empowerment (see Semler, 1994; Malone, 1997) tend to invoke a range of synonyms to convey their analysis. Malone's casual approach to semantics, for example, suggests that empowerment is synonymous with democracy. Yet Malone also suggests that empowerment is a fad. This places a rather distasteful tension at the heart of Malone's discussion of empowerment. Thus Malone's conflation of empowerment initiatives, with democratic decision-making more gener-ally, seems to suggest that questions concerning the 'means by which employees [and others] might exert equitable influence over matters affecting their working lives' (Ramsay, 1997, p. 314) are trivial matters.

Rejecting this concern with fads and triviality, this chapter will seek to recast the analysis of empowerment in the hope that readers will be encouraged to reflect more critically upon the practice of management. In this sense our analysis is 'critical-practical'. It is critical insofar as it seeks to show the limited nature of 'guru' advice. Yet it is also practical inasmuch as it seeks to show the ways in which the 'grammatical' construction of 'guru' advice and exhortation encourages change, yet hamstrings purposive action.

Accordingly, this chapter is structured as follows. We begin by attempting to locate the concept of empowerment within a larger discussion of management and organization. No one would dare to call civil democracy a fad. However, a number of authors have argued that policies which seek to overhaul the processes of workplace decision-making, to allow for empowerment, are *just* fads. To understand the contours of this empowerment debate, therefore, we must locate our concern with empowerment as a workplace phenomenon, facilitated, and yet constrained by management, and by the context of managing.

For the most part, however, 'guru' accounts of management (see chapter 2), tend not to reflect, critically, on the management process. This is unfortunate, since, as we have seen, accounts of management, which accept managing as a natural, and self-evident phenomenon, lack a dynamic to explain changes in management thought and action (Hales, 1993). In an attempt to develop a more dynamic account of management, to explore how and why empowerment rises to become a key motif in contemporary management, we must go beyond the 'guru' account to embrace a more dynamic and historical mode of analysis.

To accomplish this more dynamic form of analysis we shall seek to locate management's conversion to empowerment within a more general discussion of management and the incomplete nature of managerial control. As we shall see, this form of analysis helps us to understand management's concern with empowerment, and with the processes of workplace decision-making more generally. Indeed, our willingness to go beyond the 'guru' account of management, to adopt a historical form of analysis, allows us to offer a counterpoint to much of what has become the received wisdom concerning the empowerment of workers.

Quite unlike the model of management employed by the 'gurus', therefore, our historical account of management is focused upon the managerial struggle to secure, and to maintain control over work rhythms within a social context which makes control problematic. Where the 'gurus' see/assume harmony and consensus, our more dynamic account of managing reveals a conflict potential, which, in many ways, would argue for a reversal of the standard managerial account of empowerment. Thus, while managerial, and other common-sense accounts of organizing argue that empowerment is the necessary ingredient for quality, for re-engineering and for cultural management such that 'empowerment' is to be regarded as *the cause* of subordinate action, our more historical form of analysis argues that empowerment, and management's 'need' to empower workers, is more usefully thought of as *a consequence* of subordinate action (Wilmott and Wray-Bliss, 1996). Building from this dynamic, historical discussion, we will, then, return to the works identified at the head of this chapter, as we attempt to gauge the extent to which empowerment is, properly, just a(nother) fad.

Having dealt with this issue of fads and faddishness, we will attempt to understand, and to make sense of the models of empowerment, which have been drafted by management's 'gurus' and would-be 'gurus'. These 'guru' discussions, as we shall see, are intended to encourage managers to empower their organizations, yet beyond offering exhortation, they do little, in fact, to facilitate change because they fail to understand/concede the complexity of workplace decision-making. Following our analysis of the 'gurus' and their exhortations to empower, therefore, we will widen our analytical ambit to examine, in more depth, the criticisms which have been made of these managerialist accounts of empowerment. We will, then, conclude by spelling out the implications for practice and for analysis of this, our preferred, 'critical-practical' form of analysis.

Let us begin with our account of management and control.

## Empowerment and Control

The 'gurus' of management discuss their central analytical concerns, management and managing, in a highly limited manner. As part of their attempts to give shape and meaning to the nature and conduct of management, the 'gurus' often invoke metaphorical forms of expression. Metaphorically, these 'guru' accounts often compare management to science and/or art, and assume that management takes its effect through the medium of communication. However, no attempt is made within these accounts of management to contextualize 'communication', nor is any sensible attempt made to explore the power structures which shape, and are shaped by language and communication (C. Collins, 1999). This is a key failing since, without some means of contextualizing the meaning and effect of management, we cannot offer critical analysis, nor could we hope to offer practical advice.

Any properly, critical account of empowerment at work must make some attempt to examine power and authority in the workplace. Since, to a greater or lesser degree, the managerial discussions/exhortations to empower represent calls to restructure the forms and processes of decision-making at work, we must, if we are to understand both the potential and the problems of empowerment, make some effort to comprehend the nature of managerial power, which allows decisions to be made. To understand the processes of decision-making, as these are currently discussed, however, we must also make some attempt to understand those processes which cause managers to celebrate empowerment as the key to effective decision-making at work.

Empowerment, in common with the so-called fads and buzzwords of management, more generally, is a human construct. Its meanings and effects are the outcomes of human action, and human representation. We should not, therefore, assume that empowerment either exists concretely or springs forth spontaneously as a set of policies and practices discovered by the 'gurus' (Kennedy, 1996, 1998). Instead, we should make some attempt to map, and to understand the creation of empowerment as a representation of the processes of working and managing. To achieve this, we must make some attempt to comprehend the nature of management power; its limits and the attempts, both contemporary and historical, which have been made to extend/maintain managerial prerogative.

However, few commentators on workplace decision-making have offered a properly historical form of analysis. Within a larger discussion of pan-European attempts to harmonize labour–management practices and structures, for example, Ramsay suggests that we should adopt a historical approach to the analysis of workplace decision-making, because the specific origins of workplace schemes continue to shape the form and content of contemporary workplace decision-making. Thus Ramsay argues that we must make some attempt to trace the history of workplace decision-making if we are to make sense of contemporary movements. Yet, he warns us that 'in most analyses history has done a bunk' (Ramsay, 1997, p. 315).

Let us attempt a brief historical analysis.

## A Brief History

Commentators, as we saw in our earlier discussion of the nature of management (see chapter 2), differ over the specific chronological origins of management. Some, for example, would claim the existence of management as early as 6000 BC (see Collins, 1996a). Others, such as Child (1981) and Anthony (1977), while acknowledging the long history of management-type activity, would argue that management, as we now understand it and experience it, within capitalist economies, is a distinctly modern phenomenon.

While there is room for debate over the origins of management, most critical commentators would tend to agree that, no matter when management, as a concept, as a grouping, and as a set of practices (Child, 1981) emerged, it is clear that from the outset, those concerned with management, and with the managerial activities of planning, allocating, motivating, controlling and co-ordinating the efforts of others (Hales, 1993), have been engaged in an ongoing struggle to secure control over output levels, and to secure labour discipline more generally. Today, discussions of management are often couched in terms of culture and empowerment. Within these, contemporary discussions, the facets which constitute modern management (Child, 1981; Collins, 1998) are justified as reflecting the need to satisfy organizational goals, which it is assumed, are held in common throughout the organization. Historical forms of analysis reveal, however, that this representation of managing and working is mocked by empirical inquiry. Historical forms of analysis, therefore, demonstrate that it is seldom safe to assume that organizations have goals, which are held in common. Indeed, discussing the origins and construction of the English working class, Thompson (1972) has observed that during the early period of industrialization in Britain, managers had such great difficulty in establishing, and promoting the, so-called, 'goals of the organization', that, often, employers and overseers, had great difficulty persuading employees to attend work at all (see also Marglin, 1976).

Discussing a lost 'golden age' of working – a period before the development of factory production, a period before factory forms of discipline, 'the factory bell or hooter, the time-keeping which overrode ill-health, domestic arrangements, or the choice of more varied occupations' (Thompson, 1972, p. 337), E. P. Thompson notes that: 'it had been a frequent complaint with employers that the weavers kept "Saint Monday" – and sometimes made a holiday of Tuesday – making up the work on Friday and Saturday nights' (Thompson, 1972, p. 338).

Of course, it was not only weavers who were active in the Saint Monday Observance Society. Many other groups, including colliers and shipwrights, shared the weavers' dislike of the systems of workplace discipline which were developing during England's industrial revolution, and, like the weavers, adopted the habit of awarding themselves extra time off, in an attempt to resist the efforts made by factory owners and 'gang masters', to disrupt the organic rhythms of working which had characterized earlier periods in English history. Reflecting on the extent of the change in working lives in England, the first industrial nation, Thompson notes: 'Only a minority of weavers in the nineteenth century would have had as varied a life as the smallholder weaver whose diary, in the 1780s shows him weaving on wet days, jobbing – carting ditching and draining, mowing and churning – on fine' (Thompson, 1972, p. 338).

However, the casual absenteeism noted by Thompson, annoying and troublesome as it must have been for the new managers in this period, was not the only problem faced by the owners and controllers of the new factories. Indeed, historical analysis reveals that those managers lucky enough to have workers present on Monday, on Tuesday, or on any other day of the working week, often found that the workers who had, that day, chosen to attend work, demonstrated an alarming tendency to abandon the workplace in order to pursue any one of a range of more agreeable forms of activity (see Zuboff, 1989).

Thompson (1972) notes, for example, that:

> The weaver-smallholder was notorious for dropping his work in the
> event of any farming emergency; most eighteenth-century workers

gladly exchanged their employments for a month of harvesting; many of the adult operatives in the early cotton mills were 'of loose and wandering habits, and seldom remained long in the establishment'.

(Thompson, 1972, p. 394)

Yet even a continued presence at one's place of work carried no guarantee that work would be performed carefully and with due diligence, as this extract from the list of punishments and fines at the Wedgewood Etruria works demonstrates:

Any workman striking or likewise abusing an overlooker to lose his place.

Any workman conveying ale or liquor into the manufactory in working hours, forfeit 2/-.

Any person playing at fives against any of the walls where there are windows, forfeit 2/-.

(Thompson, 1972, p. 394)

Reflecting these problems of managing and controlling often intransigent employees, a complex of techniques and ideologies (Anthony, 1977) has grown up with, and within, management (see also Ackroyd and Thompson, 1999). Thus, within the context of our discussions of workplace decision-making, authority and change, we should note that, over time, in their attempts to ensure labour discipline, and to control output levels, managers have experimented, and have attempted to implement a range of tools and techniques designed to ensure that employees would present themselves for work, would remain at work, and would toil with due diligence and self-discipline, for the full duration of the contracted period.

Many of these early attempts to secure labour discipline rested on compulsion, and, as the example above shows, were backed by a range of fines and punishments (some physical) invoked at the place of work (see for example Cockburn (1983) for an account of the corporal punishment of apprentices in the printing industry). However, forms of workplace control which rest solely on compulsion, seldom deliver the co-operation necessary for most forms of labour. It should not be surprising to learn, therefore, that attempts to secure working discipline by punishing workers for their weaknesses and transgressions, at work, in time, came to be reinforced by more wide-ranging attempts to moderate the cultural life of England's nascent working class. Indeed Thompson draws our attention to some early attempts at cultural management (see chapter 4). He notes, for example, that legislation designed to control, and to suppress, the amusements of the poor – their fairs, sports and festivals – was enacted in England, in the hope that the manufacture of key changes in the lives and rhythms of working-class life might encourage a more sober approach to life, and a lifestyle which might discourage casual absenteeism from work (Thompson, 1972). In a more up-to-date example, it is worth noting that Gramsci (1976) has argued that America's prohibition era (when the trafficking and consumption of alcoholic beverages was made illegal in America), performed an important role in facilitating the success of Ford's production line system, since it served to discipline and moderate the cultural life of America's emerging working class.

This account of management and its attempts to secure, and to extend control does not, of course, imply that managers and the wider agencies of the state have enjoyed great success in their attempts to shape and to control our lives. However, this historical analysis of power relations does help us to understand why managers, so readily, embrace movements and techniques such as Total Quality Management (see De Cock and Hipkin, 1997) and empowerment. Our account of management's faltering attempts to control, cajole and discipline workers, therefore, suggests that managers fall prey to the prescriptive-technical solutions promoted by the consulting industry, because the job of the manager is inherently complex and problematic. Thus our historical analysis of management suggests that managers are keen to seek out, and keen to implement new techniques and new prescriptions, because the social processes of work are inherently difficult to control. Our historical account of working and managing suggests, therefore, that a ready market exists for technical (rather than social) accounts of empowerment because managers find it intensely problematic to control the co-operation of others.

Our discussion of management's attempts to control and to co-ordinate the efforts of others, therefore, suggests that the key problems which managers confront on a day-to-day basis – how to control co-operation in a manner that does not damage motivation – are amorphous and often ambiguous (De Cock and Hipkin, 1997). However, the approaches commonly touted by management's 'gurus' do not fully reflect this. Indeed we could argue that the schemes and movements currently popular with management have attracted an audience, precisely because of this social-scientific weakness. We could argue, therefore, that empowerment, in common with the fads and buzzwords of management, more generally, is an appealing concept for managers, because in neglecting the realities of managing, it appears to give shape and meaning to the problems which have frustrated management throughout its history.

Of course, these tools and techniques carry only the promise of managerial salvation. They do not, and could not resolve the ambiguities of managing. In spite of their promise to give shape and meaning to management, therefore, the fads and buzzwords of management are unable to deliver, in a sustained fashion, the controlled co-operation, which managers desire. Indeed, we saw in our earlier discussion of management, and management control (see chapter 2), that all attempts to secure labour discipline (even those modern initiatives which wrap an iron-fist within a velvet glove) are fraught affairs; problematic to implement, difficult to maintain, and subject to reversal (Hales, 1993).

It is worth examining this tension between control and co-operation in a little more depth.

## Conflict and Regulation

When analysing the nature of management, and the character of the employment relationship, scholars of work and management confront an essential paradox. By and large, the British school of industrial relations (taking a broad view on the school with which I have greatest familiarity) would tend to view humanity as being basically 'good'. Human decency and human co-operation would be, I suppose, just a few of the attributes associated with this, essential, 'goodness'. Yet, in spite of this commitment to a view of human nature as good and co-operative, scholars in the field of industrial relations regularly confront situations where they must explain conflict and a general absence of co-operation in the workplace.

In attempting to explain such occurrences and events, industrial relations scholars have been keen to stress the importance of context. Thus they have argued that while humanity is essentially good, and while human nature is, essentially, co-operative, certain contexts, and certain forms of relationship, tend to divide actors and communities, and so, dampen the co-operative spirit.

When examining the experience of working, therefore, industrial relations scholars tend to argue that conflict is the result, not of human nature, but of a certain form of socio-economic relationship commonly known as the contract of employment (Edwards, 1986; Keenoy, 1993). Thus, when industrial relations scholars come to analyse work, and the problems of controlling co-operation, they are primarily concerned to investigate the nature of the employment relationship. In this regard, industrial relations scholars argue that when managers and workers enter into a contract of employment they agree to a form of relationship which separates, divides and polarizes their interests.

Managers, as we saw in chapter 2, are employed to secure the profitability of work organizations. In today's parlance, managers are employed to enhance shareholder value. In order to maintain their employment, therefore, managers must extract a certain (often an increasing) level of productivity from workers. It is in the interest of managers, therefore to attempt to raise worker output and productivity, since this will help to improve profit levels (see for example the discussion of re-engineering in Hammer and Champy, 1993). Historically, managers have attempted to increase profitability in a variety of ways. Managers might, for example, choose to boost productivity by the simple expedient of requiring their employees to remain longer at work each day – perhaps turning the factory clocks back to confuse employees (Noon and Blyton, 1997). Alternately, managers could choose to reduce wage levels and/or increase the pace of working in order to improve profit levels.

But what of the other half of this contractual relationship? What of the workers and their interests?

While managers have an interest in extracting more production from workers (for any given wage), the interests of employees, unsurprisingly, tend to run counter to this. Thus, while managers have an interest in attempting to ensure that their employees work far harder, and for longer, it is in the employee's interest (given any rate of reward) to resist such demands. Thus employees, over time, have tended to develop strategies designed to oppose, or to cope with management's attempts to extend working time, or to intensify working effort. For example, Blauner (1973) reports that in US car firms, workers tended to adopt the practice of 'working up the line' so that they could enjoy an unscheduled break from the pacing and monotony of production-line working. In a similar fashion Roy (1960; see also Ott, 1989) in his study of work and monotony, discusses how employees had developed a means of coping with boredom at work, by dividing the day into a number of chunks of time. Yet, perhaps the most widespread and most visible means of coping with management control (Ackroyd and Thompson, 1999) has been for employees to band together as a collective to form a guild, or trade union designed to secure, for workers, a voice in/to the processes of workplace decision-making.

So, how does this analysis help to explain conflict at work? How does this help us to resolve the paradox whereby decent men and women become locked in conflict?

The answer is quite simple really. This analysis of the nature of the employment relationship helps us to understand how, and why, employees and managers become drawn into conflict situations. Thus the parties to the contract of employment become drawn into conflict situations because the employment contract divides their interests. To secure profitability, managers must extract effort and output from their employees, yet working under the same calculus – attempting to maximize gain within the terms of the contract – the day-to-day interests of workers are best served by limiting their work rate and performance. Thus, scholars of industrial relations argue that much of the conflict evident at work is to be regarded as the product of a particular form of contractual relationship. In this sense, conflict is to be regarded as being built into the employment relationship.

Reflecting upon the contract of employment, and the experience of work, Edwards (1986) argues that the employment relationship should be regarded as antagonistic. Indeed, since workplace conflict is built *into* the contractual relationship, Edwards (1986) argues that employee relations should be conceptualised in terms of a 'structured antagonism'. Thus, for scholars of industrial relations, the conflicts we often experience at work are to be regarded, not as epiphenomena, nor as strange and, unusual episodes, but as part-and-parcel of the employment relationship. This suggests that conflict at work is an ever-present possibility, which cannot be *solved*, nor eradicated by managers so long as work is arranged under capitalist social relations. It is worth noting, however, that while the interested parties in the employment relationship cannot sweep away the antagonism built into the employment relationship, steps may be taken to ameliorate and/or *regulate* these problems. Reflecting this understanding, Burawoy (1982) has suggested that analyses of the labour process should examine the ways in which 'both conflict and consent are organized on the shopfloor' (Burawoy, 1982, p. 4).

This analysis of conflict at (and in) work has clear implications for the analysis of empowerment.

## *Implications for Empowerment*

Our analysis of management and managerial control suggests that when we study empowerment (or indeed, any of the latest and hottest of management's concerns), we should keep in mind that, at root, we are analysing but one particular articulation of management's ongoing struggle to maintain control over the effort and manners of the workforce. Furthermore, our analysis of the employment relationship suggests that to comprehend the problems and ambiguities of managing empowerment, we must engage in a particular form of analysis. Thus our historical inquiries into working and managing suggest that the analysis of empowerment should be built upon a dynamic and dialectical (perhaps even a dialogical (C. Collins, 1999)) form of analysis, which is able to show the contexts (Clark, 2000) which shape what Goodrich (1975) termed the 'frontier of control'.

Goodrich's notion of the frontier of control represents an important contribution to the study of workplace relations. While 'guru' analyses and certain forms of Marxist writing (Braverman, 1974) have tended to develop an 'Olympian' model of management (Whittington, 1993), which portrays managers as the sole architects of corporate strategy and policy (Collins, 1998), Goodrich's analysis reminds us that: 'workers can play an active part in shaping their own labour process' (Wilkinson, 1983, p. 15).

Thus Goodrich suggests that workers attempt to shape and to control the processes of their own labour. However, we should not imagine that managers simply sit on their hands while this process takes place. While workers are attempting to shape the labour process for their own ends, managers are doing precisely the same thing. Thus Goodrich argues that a frontier of control develops as workers and managers dispute prerogatives, rights and responsibilities. Over time workers have sought to police the frontier of control in a number of different ways. They have, of course, developed bodies, such as guilds and trade unions, which represent the rights and interests of workers *vis-à-vis* management. Yet, workers' attempts to shape the processes of their own labour are by no means restricted to trade union activity. Indeed, there is a rich body of literature (see

Burawoy, 1982; Ackroyd and Thompson, 1999) dedicated to showing the range and the variety of informal mechanisms which have developed as attempts to advance, or to protect the frontier of control. In this sense, staffing agreements, demarcation agreements, and the willingness of groups to indulge patterns of behaviour (such as pilfering or shrinkage) formally proscribed in other agreements, may be regarded as the outcomes of a dynamic relationship which is built upon control, but dependent upon co-operation.

Viewed in terms of the frontier of control, the empowerment of workers ceases to be a fashion item, and ceases to be an initiative discovered by the consulting industry. Instead the concept of empowerment, together with its associated practices, is revealed as part of a larger historical attempt to manage the politics and ambiguities, which are built into the relationship of employment. Thus, empowerment may be analysed as a managerial attempt to maintain, or to move the frontier of control in a fashion that suits the interests of certain sections of management. Sadly, however, the 'gurus' of management seem unaware of Goodrich's work, and so, offer us an Olympian account of management, and an apolitical view of the workplace, which culminates in the development of glib prescriptions for change. For example, managers experiencing 'quality' problems (see chapter 6) are advised to empower their employees so that the full range of the organization's talents might be brought to bear on the improvement of products and services. Similarly, managers experiencing problems due to a lack of innovation are encouraged to empower their employees to experiment with new products, or with new forms of service. Yet, while this argument, that empowerment is the key to most forms of management, and a lack of appropriate empowerment, the root cause of most managerial problems, has an intuitive appeal, for some (see Collins, 1994; Sewell and Wilkinson, 1992) our analysis of the frontier of control suggests that the account of managing, which underpins this initiative makes empowerment a rather flimsy concept within a glib line of argument. Thus our analysis of the labour process suggests that the 'gurus' misunderstand, or fail to concede the social dynamics of workplace relations, and so, misrepresent the social problems of managing as technical difficulties.

There is a paradox in this, however. If our analysis is correct, it seems that, to appear useful to managers, 'guru' prescriptions must, at some level, misrepresent the problems of managing. If 'guru' prescriptions are to attract an audience, they must claim to be able to resolve the problems of managing (Huczynski, 1993). Indeed, Huczynski (1993) suggests that 'guru' ideas, if they are to attain a viable standing in the market for management advice must claim that they have the capacity to give form and meaning to a process which is notable for being amorphous and ambiguous.

This suggests a key question. If 'guru' works misrepresent the processes of managing, and if 'guru' works disappoint managers because workers use their experience to question, and to subvert the techniques and the technical solutions which the 'gurus' have developed, why do experienced managers buy the analysis?

Perhaps surprisingly, our analysis of the frontier of control suggests that the social-scientific weaknesses of the managerialist prescriptions of/for empowerment work to promote 'guru' ideas to managers. 'Guru' models of management and 'guru' models of empowerment, in short, may be attractive to hard-pressed, busy and ambitious practitioners, because they invoke a grammar, which gives tremendous force and meaning to a vocabulary which resonates with popular ideas (Grint, 1994) and representations. 'Guru' ideas are attractive, therefore, not because dim managers are duped by slickly marketed representations of their own work (see chapter 3), but because the 'grammar' and the vocabulary invoked by the consulting industries promises to deliver solutions to the inherent problems of managing by transforming the very nature of the labour process. The discourse of empowerment is persuasive, therefore, in spite of experience, because it promises technical mastery of a transformed system of working.

However, we must note that while the 'guru' spin on empowerment seems to have an appeal on the managerial side of Goodrich's frontier of control, this spin does not translate into a useful and purposive approach to managing the effort of others, because this representation of managing and working, brazenly, overstates the ability of managers, unilaterally, to (1) cause change at work and (2) to resolve the tensions and conflicts which are central to the employment relationship. Small wonder then, that Malone (1997) and Semler (1994) have voiced the fear that empowerment might be just a(nother) fad.

## *Just a Fad?*

As we saw at the beginning of this chapter, both Malone (1997) and Semler (1994), while acting as advocates of empowerment, have voiced the concern that empowerment may be a 'fad'. In an attempt to examine the validity of this concern, we will analyse the work of Malone, since between these two contributions Malone's offers the most developed account of empowerment as 'fad'.

Malone's discussion is built around a number of key and related concerns:

- that empowerment may be a fad
- that the developing information technology (IT) systems will only be used to their full potential where empowered forms of decision-making are developed and are in place
- that the promise of empowerment is not being realized.

The main focal point for Malone's analysis is his concern that managers remain unconvinced about the need for empowerment. Indeed, within

Malone's discussion there is the suggestion that previous initiatives which promised much, but delivered little (as we now understand, because of the inherent tensions in the employment relationship) have encouraged managers to treat empowerment as a fad; not really deserving of time, effort or commitment.

At one level, this concern that managers might lack the necessary commitment to empower their workers is perfectly understandable. If managers are indeed faddish in their treatment of empowerment, addressing themselves to the problem of empowerment only until some new (and less thorny) solution to the problem of managing the efforts of others emerges, Malone's analysis suggests that the productive opportunities of a range of information technologies will be squandered (or worse, reaped by foreign competitors).

However, while Malone's argument does have an intuitive appeal, we should note that social-historical accounts of work and management reveal that these fears over management's so-called faddish concern with empowerment represent little more than an analytical cul-de-sac.

To be fair to Malone, however, we should note that a cursory analysis of the historical contours of workplace relations, and worker participation in decision-making, does seem to suggest that managers might be prey to the whim of fashion. For example, Ramsay (1977) in his studies of worker input to the processes of decision-making at work, has shown the alternate waxing and waning of management's interest in securing the participation of workers. At one level, therefore, Ramsay's work does seem to suggest that managers might, indeed, have only a whimsical and faddish concern with empowerment. Yet, this would be a simplistic reading of the history of workplace decision-making, since, as we now know, it is based on a rather limited and simplistic account of workplace relations.

At one level, Ramsay's analysis does, of course, demonstrate that managers have shown variable levels of commitment in the pursuit of worker participation. However, we cannot answer the charge of 'faddism' until we have some understanding of the motives which have led managers to institute participative forms of management in one period, only to scrap, or diminish them in the next. Or more succinctly; we cannot accuse managers of being the victims of fashion until we can establish that their choice-making behaviour is guided by the strictly arbitrary decree of fashion.

Analysing the changing contours of participation at work, Ramsay suggests that variations in the context and forms of decision-making reflect the dynamic and dialectical nature of workplace control. Thus Ramsay demonstrates that, in certain periods of history, managers have made strenuous efforts to solicit, and to secure, the participation of subordinates in workplace decision-making. Asking a variant of 'the Roman question' – *who benefits from these changes?* – Ramsay's explanation for the waves of participation, which he discloses, is rooted in an analysis of managerial control.

Ramsay argues, therefore, that managers tend to become interested in worker participation schemes when the achievement of controlled co-operation is especially problematic. Thus Ramsay argues that managers take an interest in soliciting worker inputs to the process of decision-making when their organizations suffer a profits crisis, or when a challenge to managerial control is experienced. In this sense, Ramsay argues that managers attempt to cope with crises, and with challenges to managerial prerogative by offering workers a different range of inputs to the processes of decision-making – the question of outputs remains a moot point!

Through allowing such changes to the processes of decision-making, Ramsay argues, managers seek to advance, or to maintain the frontier of control. In this way, Ramsay suggests that managers have been inclined to advance or to institute systems of workplace decision-making when they perceive that the control of co-operation is becoming problematic. In this sense, workplace participation schemes represent attempts to maintain, or to re-establish the legitimacy of management action in the eyes of workers. Thus Ramsay's analysis suggests that policies designed to secure worker input to the processes of decision-making – what we now term empowerment – are *outcomes* of subordinate action and power.

Contrary to Malone's fears, therefore, Ramsay's analysis suggests that material considerations, over and above the whim of fashion, condition management's choice-making behaviour. Indeed, Ramsay's analysis of the waves of participation experienced by British industry over the last hundred years highlights at least two key issues, important in the discussion of management 'fads'. Thus, Ramsay shows:

1    That managerial, choice-making behaviour is rooted within an ongoing struggle to secure, and to maintain co-operation and consent within a relationship, which, systematically, makes this state of affairs problematic to achieve. Viewed in these terms, management's movement within and between ideas and technologies is explained not as the senseless pursuit of fashion, but as the relentless, yet forced, pursuit of adequate control measures, within a relationship which makes control both incomplete and self-defeating. This, of course, should not be taken to imply that managers operate as independent decision-makers, free from mimetic influences. Clearly, managers are influenced by 'fashion setters' (Abrahamson, 1996). However, Ramsay's analysis does ask us to consider the real, material concerns which condition the willingness of managers to seek out and to try 'guru' ideas (Grint, 1997).

2    That the waxing and waning of participation schemes demonstrates, not a faddish absence of commitment on the part of management, but the regular and periodic renewal of management's interest in the processes of decision-making. This argument is supported by Grint, (1997,1997a). Mapping changes in management practice, Grint argues that these changing techniques share, in common, a concern to secure

and to maintain management control, which may be articulated in a variety of different ways, dependent upon political and economic circumstances. For example, comparing changes in management technique against Kondratieff waves – phases of economic development spurred by periods of capital accumulation or technological change – Grint suggests that the up-swing of a Kondratieff wave is associated with more normative or participative approaches to managerial control (Barley and Kunda, 1992).

What, then, are the 'critical-practical' outcomes of our academic and historical inquiry into the employment relationship? Thus far, our outputs are two-fold. Our historical analysis of management, and of the technology of management, has constructed a perspective where the activities of managers constitute a system of control. However, this system of control is incomplete and self-defeating, such that, 'on the hoof', managers must take steps designed as attempts to recalibrate, and to re-equilibrate management as a system of control. Placing this analysis of management within the context of our discussions of empowerment suggests that empowerment is (1) a consequence of subordinate action; not its cause, and (2) is no simple fad.

Yet, the outputs of our historical form of analysis may be used more extensively, to inform a more critical position on empowerment. Let us attempt this. Let us use this historical analysis to probe, in more depth, the 'gurus', their ideas and their promises regarding empowerment. Let us use our historically situated analysis to lance the boil on management which is the 'guru' literature on empowerment.

### How To Empower?

'Guru' commentators on empowerment tend to argue that the empowerment of workers should be a key goal for management (see Block, 1986; Peters and Waterman, 1982; Kanter, 1989). Even those writers such as Semler (1994) and Malone (1997) who have expressed reservations about management's commitment to empowerment, base their argument upon the concern that managers are failing to 'do' empowerment properly. In this sense, authors such as Malone share the conviction of the 'gurus' that the empowerment of the workforce should be management's key goal. But, why should empowerment be a key goal for management?

### Truth or Truism?

At root, the current managerial interest in empowerment conveys, if not a universal truth, then certainly a universal truism: that those who work directly on any production process, or directly with any client or customer, will tend to understand the requirements of the job better than those who operate at some distance from the immediate task.

It follows, therefore, that those on the 'front line' should be allowed some scope to make changes to their work practices as they deem appropriate. In addition, the 'empowering' literature tends to voice the universal truism that 'involved' workers are happier and so, more productive in their labours (Perrow, 1979).

Leaving aside these truisms, it is probably more accurate and, indeed more succinct to say that the interest in empowerment represents an acknowledgement that, in certain circumstances, managers may be inclined to restructure control initiatives so that larger business goals may be attained (Collins, 1995a).

In these terms, we can see that the dynamic which drives the interest in empowerment has driven all other forms of innovation in labour–management relations. This dynamic, as we have seen, revolves around management's need to secure control while simultaneously ensuring co-operation (Anthony, 1977; Bendix, 1956). We can see, for example, that in wrestling with this dynamic Fordist and Tayloristic production methods, methods often assumed to be the antithesis of worker empowerment, both acknowledge, yet simultaneously deny a role for the free-thinking, inquiring workers evident in the empowerment literature. Thus in timing and analysing workers as they work, Tayloristic and Fordist methods of production and management imply that work-study operatives must first learn from workers how to perform a particular task. Yet, having learned from workers, the processes of work-study then lead managers to look for ways to negate these skills, to control and progressively to restrict the opportunities which workers have to exercise discretion.

Taken together with our historical analysis, this account of Taylorism suggests that, when analysing the interest in empowerment which grew up within management circles throughout the 1980s, we do not have to explain management's interest in workers' skills and capability, nor do we have to explain the interest in empowerment *per se* (Wilkinson *et al.*, 1982; Burawoy, 1982). Instead, reflecting the variety of ways in which management may attempt to control workers, what we have to explain is the nature of the current interest in empowerment, and so, the particular conception of empowerment which has become popular in recent years. For the moment, however, we will remain with the 'guru' analysis of empowerment so that we might understand the concept, and the route to empowerment preferred by the 'gurus'.

## The 'Gurus' on Empowerment

Management-oriented, or managerialist accounts of empowerment (see Clutterbuck and Kernaghan, 1994; Foy, 1994; Mitchell-Stewart, 1994) in common with 'guru' accounts of management, more generally (Huczynski, 1993) tend to be driven by a particular reading of the nature of the business environment. While we do not have the space here to offer a full account and exegesis of managerialism (see chapter 2), it is worth making the observation that managerialist accounts of the workplace tend to portray organizations in a particular manner. Managerialist accounts of the workplace portray organizations in a top–down fashion, and represent an anti-conflict ethos (Collins, 1998). Here organizations are viewed as goal seeking, rational entities where managers work, guided by the principles of organization science to ensure mutuality and collaboration (Thompson and McHugh, 1995)

Noting a discontinuous change in the environment of business (Kanter, 1989) and changes in the nature of the working population (Bell, 1987; Drucker, 1991), a number of commentators have deployed goal-seeking, rationalist models of organization to argue that managers, in responding to these challenges, *must* work to release the talent of individual employees, so that these employees might simultaneously become more productive, more value-generating, and more satisfied in their work (Crosby, 1992; Plunkett and Fournier, 1991; Clutterbuck and Kernaghan, 1994; Block, 1986). In short, a range of managerialist commentators have advocated 'empowerment' as the solution to the problem of managing in these turbulent times.

Empowerment from this reading is a managerial challenge. Indeed given the changes which the empowerment of the workforce is said to call forth, it would probably be more appropriate to say that, within the managerial literature, empowerment represents a *leadership* challenge. Thus managers are advised that, if they are serious about empowering their workers, they will have to pay attention to a few key issues.

Indeed, managers are informed, therefore, that they will have to 'commit' to empowerment. They are warned that they will have to take steps to ensure that workers understand management's 'commitment' to empowerment so that the workers, in turn, might be able to commit to what their empowerment will require of them. For the 'gurus', therefore, empowerment is *the cause* of subordinate action.

According to the managerialist literature, the first step in the managerial journey to empowerment is said to be 'vision'. A vision of/for empowerment may be developed from a series of questions. Amongst other issues, the 'gurus' encourage managers to focus upon a series of key questions.

By reflecting upon: *what we do well; what customers say about us; what our competitors do better than us*, managers are encouraged to reflect upon processes and practices, and so, are encouraged to seek out opportunities for change and development. Yet, because competitive imperatives demand the release of talent, and because the challenge of empowerment is a challenge of leadership, managers are told that they must take steps to secure workforce commitment to their plans for change. This is the purpose of 'vision'. Thus the development and communication of a management 'vision' is said to smooth and facilitate the difficult process of transforming strategy

Management crafts vision of empowerment

Managers share vision

Vision is cascaded throughout organization

Organizational participants work to alter their priorities, their working rhythms and their reporting relationships in order to reap the benefits of an empowered system of working

*Figure 7.1* The vision and cascade of empowerment

into action. Crudely the journey to 'empowerment' might be represented as in Figure 7.1.

Not all commentators, however, are persuaded by this account of empowerment. Some scholars, for example, have argued that the 'guru' discussions of empowerment misrepresent the dynamics of the employment relationship, since they attempt to portray subordinates in a highly passive way (Wilmott and Wray-Bliss, 1996; Collins, 1995a). Meanwhile other scholars (see Garrahan and Stewart, 1992) have taken exception to the 'guru' discussion of empowerment, arguing that it is little more than a rhetorical device, designed to emasculate and/or incorporate those who might, in different circumstances, challenge the contemporary developments in workplace practices which are ushered in by the 'guru' construction of empowerment.

Wilkinson (1998) offers a useful, four-part summary and critique of the 'guru' account of empowerment which does much to facilitate a 'critical-practical' analysis. Accordingly, we will examine Wilkinson's contribution in the following sections.

## Empowerment Re-visited

Wilkinson's (1998) critical comment on empowerment articulates a concern with four key problems. These problems, he argues, limit the efficacy of the 'guru' discussion of empowerment. These criticisms reflect a concern with:

## The Meaning of Empowerment

As a concept, empowerment has clear affinities with a range of other concepts often invoked in the discussion of decision-making. Bowen and Lawler (1992), for example, in their discussion of the empowerment of service workers, clearly view the terms 'involvement' and 'empowerment' as synonymous. Building from this analysis of Bowen and Lawler (1992), Clutterbuck and Kernaghan (1994) 'define three types of empowerment' (Clutterbuck and Kernaghan, 1994, p. 16). These three types of empowerment, we are told, revolve around involvement and are, namely, suggestion involvement, job involvement, and high involvement. Malone (1997), likewise, shows a similarly cavalier approach to the terminology of workplace decision-making. Thus, in his discussion of the need to make changes in workplace decision-making, Malone seems to regard the terms 'empowerment', 'delegation' and 'decentralized control' as synonyms since he uses these terms interchangeably. Yet these terms are not synonymous. They are, at best, 'near synonyms', whose pretence of equivalence obscures complexity by disguising the different implications for the conduct and structuring of workplace decision-making, which each of these different terms implies.

Does this semantic problem imply that our first step when attempting to manage empowerment should be to clear up this minor definitional issue? Does this problem of meaning imply that academics and consultants should seek to develop a single, authoritative, definition of empowerment so that everyone involved might, as management consultants say, 'sing from the same hymn sheet'? No it does not, since as we shall see, it is difficult and, probably, impossible to develop a single, authoritative definition of/for empowerment, since the terms – empowerment, involvement, democracy, participation and consultation (to name just some of the terms invoked to describe the processes of decision-making) – are ambiguous, and so defy definition (De Burgundy, 1995).

### The Ambiguity of Empowerment

A key problem is encountered as soon as we seek to analyse empowerment at work. The problem is basically one of conceptual elasticity. Or, as Cressey and MacInnes (1980) might put it, a problem of semantics intertwined with and, in part, expressions of a range of political and academic viewpoints. Seen in terms of semantics, empowerment is a problematic concept since it carries different implications for those subject to the innovation at work. Indeed, as we shall see, the term empowerment also carries widely different connotations for a range of academic commentators and business 'gurus'. Thus the fact that all parties in industry may agree on the worth of employee involvement, or empowerment, or participation, may do little more than prove the semantic elasticity of the term under discussion. For example, Wickens (1987) claims, in his account of Nissan's management system: 'We seek to delegate and involve staff in discussion and decision making, particularly in those areas in which they can effectively contribute so that all may participate in the effective running of NMUK [Nissan Motors UK]' (Wickens, 1987, p. 82).

Yet, within the context of our discussions of empowerment as an ambiguous concept we have to wonder if Wicken's statement actually conveys the authoritative account of Nissan, which he had hoped to develop. The terms, which Wickens uses to describe the Nissan Way – delegation, involvement, participation and effective contribution – are ambiguous. Each of these terms might, therefore, carry different meanings for different actors. Thus, while Wickens may have assumed he was offering a clear statement on 'the Nissan Way', our account of semantics and elasticity reveals scope for a qualitatively different message and mode of expression, to that intended by Wickens. For example, Wickens statement might be interpreted as follows:

> Using an approach to the management of workers which was pioneered by Henry Ford (see Thompson and McHugh, 1995) we seek to make production more efficient. We achieve this aim by intensifying the pace of work, and by extending the boundaries of semi-skilled labour. These policies are part and parcel of our ongoing attempts to secure the full flexibility of labour.

Alternatively we might choose to interpret 'the Nissan Way' as: 'An attempt to secure managerial legitimacy through the use of behavioural science technology (Baritz, 1965) designed to push back the frontier of control (Goodrich, 1975)'. Equally, we might interpret the ambiguous terms invoked by Wickens as implying: 'The systematic disempowerment of employees (Garrahan and Stewart, 1992) through the use of a set of linguistic codes and symbols (C. Collins, 1999) designed to incorporate workers to a management-oriented agenda.'

As an attempt to pierce the semantic confusion revealed here, it is useful to try to distinguish, analytically, between different types of employee input into the decision-making process. At a basic level then, it might be useful to distinguish direct versus indirect forms of worker input to the processes of work, and workplace decision-making.

*Direct Involvement*

What we have termed direct employee involvement in workplace decision-making would include those initiatives which focus explicitly on the
individual worker and the immediate work group. Thus direct forms of
employee involvement include a limited delegation of areas of responsibility, previously guarded as managerial, through the redesign of the
organization of work. This type of involvement would also include an
increase in certain worker responsibilities as these relate to production.
Thus the creation of semi-autonomous work groups and the devolution
of responsibility for tasks such as quality management, previously claimed
as the responsibility of management, would be included here as examples
of direct forms of involvement.

*Indirect Involvement*

Those initiatives we have labelled as indirect forms of employee involvement in workplace decision-making have, in comparison to direct forms
of involvement, more of a policy character. Ostensibly the function of
indirect involvement is more concerned with worker representation than
with the development of functional motivation alone, although there are
argued to be links between these two. Indirect forms of involvement would
include worker representation on management boards, consultative
committees and of course trade union collective bargaining.

This analytical distinction between indirect and direct forms of employee
involvement helps us to grasp the variety of inputs to the process of workplace decision-making often disguised within terms such as employee
involvement and participation. However, the dichotomy presented here
still fails to illuminate, properly, the fluidity of the terms involvement,
consultation empowerment and participation.

As our analysis of Wickens reveals, terms such as collective bargaining,
quality circles, task forces, autonomous work groups and worker participation are all forms of shorthand expressions, which are deployed by
actors, in their attempts to describe/prescribe the processes of decision-
making. The problem both analytically and practically, however, is that
while each might be reduced to a generic term such as involvement, and
while each might be labelled as a direct, or indirect form of involvement,

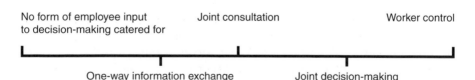

*Figure 7.2* A range of the potential meanings of empowerment expressed as a
continuum of decision-making policies and structures at work

these interventions cover a wide range of ideas, to promote a variety of potentials for the outcomes of employee involvement. A continuum may be used to express the fluidity of the concept as a whole (see Figure 7.2).

## A Continuum of Empowerment

Generally speaking, continua are drawn to encompass a full range of non-discrete possibilities, say from 'zero' to a positive sum. Alternatively, as in the case of the continuum of human resource management, detailed by Storey (1991), a continuum may envisage a contrast between a world of 'hard', and a world of 'soft' policies and procedures. In this regard, our continuum of workplace decision-making is distinctive in the sense that its lower limit is not, properly speaking, the polar opposite of our upper extreme. Thus our continuum of workplace decision-making begins, not at 'zero', but at a positive sum.

It is worth examining this feature of our continuum of empowerment.

When discussing management, and the incomplete nature of managerial control, we were at pains to point out that throughout history managers have (not always with great success) sought to control worker effort in a fashion designed to retain the initiative and co-operation which managers require in order to secure output. Thus we argued that empowerment – management's willingness to cede control over aspects of the production process – is a consequence of subordinate action, and not its cause (Wilmott and Wray Bliss, 1996).

This idea is neatly summarized in Bendix's account of the limited, and self-defeating, nature of managerial control. As Bendix (1956) notes:

> beyond what commands can effect and supervision can control, beyond what incentives can induce and penalties prevent, there exists an exercise of discretion important even in relatively menial jobs, which managers of economic enterprises seek to enlist for the achievement of managerial ends.
>
> (Bendix, 1956, p. 256)

In this quotation, Bendix shows that under all systems of managerial control, no matter how draconian, there is always the need for some form of involvement on the part of employees. Without some feeling of involvement, whether it be based on professionalism, emotional attachment, or some other set of factors, the plain fact is that work would simply not be done on time, or to the requisite standard. Indeed, without some base level of involvement there might be no work done at all. As MacInnes notes: 'Management no matter how expert cannot set out in advance what exactly must be done under all circumstances and how, but must rely to some extent on the workers' co-operation, initiative and experience' (MacInnes, 1989, p. 130).

Our continuum is designed to reflect this analysis. Thus, we have at one polar extreme, a position concerned with worker control, while at the other extreme we have, not 'zero', but 'some' worker involvement/engagement. At this lower extremity, we have no *formal* employee involvement. Yet our continuum recognizes the need for some form of *ad hoc* informal engagement, necessary to achieve some basic level of output (Bendix, 1956).

In essence, the continuum, as a whole, turns upon the extent to which the balance of power in the enterprise is altered by the type of employee involvement in the operation. To illustrate this we might postulate that at the low employee involvement pole of the continuum we would find forms of management such as Taylor's scientific management. In Taylorist management systems, employee involvement is systematically removed from production systems as attempts are made to design work scientifically. Here workers are not so much involved in the production and management systems, as engaged through the carrot of high wage rewards. This, of course, does not imply an absence of involvement on the part of workers. For managers this would be unworkable as a viable system of production, since as Kusterer (1978) notes, even under Taylorist systems of working, 'unskilled workers must acquire a substantial body of knowledge to survive and succeed on their jobs – despite mechanization and automation, and despite bureaucratization and the ever narrower division of labour' (Kusterer, 1978, preface).

The other end of our continuum is perhaps more of a logical extreme than the low involvement pole. Thus the high involvement pole of our continuum implies some fully developed form of industrial democracy or workers' soviet.

Whether or not the high involvement pole is only a logical possibility remains, of course, a moot point. What our continuum does show, however, is that employee involvement, in common with other terms deployed in the analysis of decision-making is a broad term which covers an extremely broad range of concepts. Any developed analysis of involvement/empowerment/participation would have to take note of this. Unfortunately, few accounts of decision-making within 'guru' analyses of management exhibit this reflective quality. Instead, a small range of rather under-theorized viewpoints dominate.

'Guru'-inspired, or managerialist discussions on empowerment tend to operate from an implicit ideological perspective which is never made explicit. With this point in mind, it is worth noting that the choice of the term; employee involvement in the accounts of empowerment proffered by Clutterbuck and Kernaghan (1994) and by Bowen and Lawler (1992) could be viewed as the implicit betrayal of a particular type of thinking, which has implications for practice and analysis. It is true, of course, that different subject disciplines tend to adopt different terms to discuss related concepts. However, the choice of these terms is not random. Instead the terms chosen by actors, and by the disciplines they work within, denote different agendas and point towards different problematics.

Industrial relations for example, is predominantly a pluralistic or radical (Collins, 1998) field of inquiry. Industrial relations scholars have, at some level, (Kelly, 1998) a concern with power, and tend to be attracted to forms of scholarship which seek to offset asymmetries of power. As a field of study, therefore, industrial relations would tend to view employee involvement as a sub-set of the larger discussion of worker participation. Within the boundaries of industrial relations, therefore, many writers would be dismissive of the term 'involvement' (Brannen *et al.*, 1976). Indeed, this term would be viewed as an unnecessarily restrictive term whose usage leads to unpalatable practical outcomes. Thus industrial relations scholars have argued that the term 'involvement' encourages a form of analysis (and action) designed to give only the illusion of some more extensive form of participation, and some more far-reaching form of change at work. Within the boundaries of industrial relations scholarship, therefore, the term employee involvement would probably be viewed as an attempt to restrict debate in order to forestall discussion of more extensive forms of worker decision-making, such as collective bargaining. For scholars of industrial relations, therefore, the willingness of the 'gurus' to invoke the term, involvement, might be viewed as an attempt to erase the rightward extreme of our continuum. Thus scholars educated in the traditions of industrial relations would be sceptical of the term involvement, since, for them, this term seems to deny the possibility, the viability and the validity of any more extensive input from workers to decision-making processes. On this basis, employee involvement, as this is conceived by Bowen and Lawler (1992) and by Malone (1997), fails Pateman's (1970) test for 'genuine participation', as offering participation in the formulation of strategy and decisions rather than being involved only in the execution of decisions made by others.

Reflecting our concerns regarding the terminology used to describe workplace decision-making, it is interesting to note the manner in which the vocabulary of decision-making has changed. Thus we would do well to note that the discussion of workplace decision-making which is predominant today, is unlike that in earlier periods. Indeed, we would do well to note that today's discussion has drifted from an earlier concern with social justice and democracy and has been redefined as a business issue. This change process has taken place during a period in which successive governments in Britain have sought to deregulate the economy (MacInnes, 1989) so that management prerogative might be unfettered.

In the late 1970s, for example, the debate over power and authority at work was conducted in terms of democracy and social representation, with effective worker participation, and so, effective worker involvement in production-related decisions, assumed to take place through trade union representation of worker interests. Over time, however, with the advent of Human Resource Management (HRM) and the more individualized approaches to excellence which HRM promotes (Beaumont, 1993; Legge, 1995), the debate on workplace decision-making has been recast, moving from the discussion of collective representation towards a focus on individuals. Thus, whereas earlier accounts of participation and involvement centred around notions of democratic representation, the contemporary discussion of involvement-as-empowerment, is focused upon the transfer or cascade, of information, and includes a range of related initiatives such as financial participation. Increasingly, therefore, the discussion of workplace decision-making has come to mean some restricted form of information exchange, such that the term empowerment is now often used to describe situations where managers simply inform workers of their intention to change some aspect of the system of working.

As the following sections will demonstrate, such changes in the terms of the debate are illuminating and deserve discussion. Indeed, rather than present this current articulation of the discussion of workplace decision-making as part of the natural order of things, as the 'gurus' tend to do, we should investigate why such changes and adaptations have come about. Thus we should attempt to analyse how and why empowerment (in the guise of involvement/communication) has supplanted the pre-existing vocabulary (and 'grammar') of workplace decision-making. This, as we shall see, must imply an analysis of the context of empowerment.

## *The Context of Empowerment*

There is a saying that 'they do it differently in France'. This is true for many things. It is, undoubtedly, true of the structuring of decision-making at work. Indeed when it comes to 'empowering' – implementing changes designed to change and/or legitimate structures and processes of decision-making at work – not only do they do it differently in France, they also do it differently in Germany, in Sweden and in America. Indeed almost everyone does this differently from Britain (Bean, 1986; Poole, 1986) since Britain has a unique system of industrial relations (Wedderburn, 1986). However, few of the analyses prepared by the 'gurus' of management betray any awareness of this. For 'guru' forms of analysis, management is timeless and stateless. It is scientific. Its practices, therefore, are principles. And the principles are to be regarded as global in their importance and global in their application. Yet this, of course, is mistaken.

Any discussion of empowerment if it is to be of significance either academically or practically (since these issues are, of course, inseparable) must begin from the understanding that empowerment, as a concept, and as a set of practices, finds its expression in particular institutional forms which vary according to context. As such the 'empowerment' of German steelworkers is likely to represent changes in processes and practices quite different from those associated with the 'empowerment' of workers in the car components industry in Japan (see Bean, 1986). Thus any account of empowerment, if it is to be useful and sensible, must build its analysis with due reference to the impact of the wider society on workplace policies and processes. In this regard, it is worth observing that the meaning of empowerment seems to vary both contextually and historically. Viewed in these terms, the construction of empowerment, currently preferred by management's 'gurus' – empowerment as information for business success – is symptomatic of a change in the wider context of business and government. Thus, the restrictive account of empowerment preferred by the 'gurus' has grown up, and has taken root under a series of right-wing administrations which held power during the 1980s and early 1990s (MacInnes, 1987; Beale, 1994), and used their position of power to attempt to engineer cultural change (Keat and Abercrombie, 1991). In contrast, the earlier and more extensive discussion of empowerment at work (as part-and-parcel of a wider concern with social democracy) grew up under a centre-left form of governmental control.

### A Universal Appeal?

'Guru' discussions of empowerment, as we have seen, tend not to analyse empowerment in context. This failure to analyse empowerment contextually means that the managerialist discussion of decision-making at work fails to understand or fails to concede the complexity of workplace decision-making. The managerialist discussion assumes that the term 'empowerment' has one stable and transparent meaning. In practice, however, the term 'empowerment' may have a range of meanings and a variety of effects (Cunningham *et al.*, 1996). As we saw in our discussion of the context of empowerment, the parcel of institutions, and the processes of decision-making which underpin the empowerment of workers in any particular locale may be entirely different to those experienced by workers in an adjacent locale. Thus we should note that the empowerment of, say, General Motors' employees in Detroit will tend to be underpinned by quite different institutions and processes of decision-making, as compared to those which underpin the empowerment of General Motors' employees in the southern United States, or in Mexico. Were this not the case American corporations would have few incentives to relocate their production facilities!

So what does this imply for the analysis of empowerment?

In contrast to our academic and analytic discussion of the legitimate varieties of involvement and empowerment, 'guru' discussions of empowerment have often agonized over the search for a definition of empowerment (Foy, 1994; Block, 1986; Baruch, 1998). Based upon the calculation that empowerment represents the primary means of coping with the globalizing imperatives of modern business (Baruch, 1998) managerialist discussions of empowerment have often been at great pains to develop a single, definitive and categorical understanding of the term, empowerment. But this search for a singular, stable meaning for empowerment has proved elusive.

Baruch (1998), for example has argued that empowerment is not, and should not be confused with delegation. Yet, Pastor (1996) in her discussion of what empowerment 'is' (and 'is not'), argues that empowerment *is* delegation (where delegation grants autonomy). So, which of these positions is wrong? They cannot both be correct; so which misunderstands empowerment? Perhaps surprisingly, neither of these positions is incorrect. Yet, neither definition is, nor could be, categorically correct.

Empowerment, as we have seen, is an essentially ambiguous term. It is a term characterized by semantic elasticity. It is illusory to imagine, therefore, that managers or academics will be able to define empowerment in an unproblematic way. Indeed it is quite brazen to state, categorically, that delegation is not empowerment when history reveals that the concepts used to describe, and to analyse workplace decision-making, and managerial control, have been remarkable for their definitional fluidity. Of course, commentators are perfectly entitled to say delegation is not empowerment. But this negation of empowerment *as* delegation, carries weight only when we are able to locate this argument within a specific context. Thus, we may say that delegation *does not* equal empowerment, only where we can show this to be a conflation, which conflicts with the historically rooted, and developed understanding of empowerment in the particular system of industrial decision-making we are studying.

If we want to attempt to define empowerment (and our analysis of ambiguity suggests that we should not), we must be prepared to qualify our definition to reflect the potential definitions of empowerment which, in turn, are reflective of empowerment's essential ambiguity. Thus if we find circumstances where an academic, or a particular management group attempts to portray empowerment *as* delegation, it is much more useful, academically and practically, to avoid becoming bogged down in a fruitless definitional battle where we bicker, in categorical terms, about what empowerment 'is' and 'is not'. Instead, we would do better to remind the manager, or the commentator in question, that any attempt to define empowerment *as* delegation in Britain, for example, is likely to lead to conflict since this would represent an attempt to enforce a view of empowerment, which conflicts with a historically entrenched understanding of the appropriate forms of workplace decision-making, and managerial authority, in a British context.

This analysis has implications for our fourth concern; the treatment of power within the discussions of empowerment prepared for managerial audience.

### (Em)Power(Ment)

Discussions of the concept of empowerment, and indeed the process of empowering must revolve around some discussion of power. This is demonstrated quite clearly when commentators (see for example Malone, 1997) observe that, instead of actually empowering their employees, managers often engage only in more limited forms of power-sharing, such as delegation. Most 'gurus' are clear, however, that 'empowerment' must go beyond delegation, and must imply some, more significant, transfer of control and responsibility from management to workers. However, the modelling of the workplace used by managerialist authors fails to capture the subtleties and complexities of the process of empowering, since it is based upon a limited account of power and authority and offers what might be termed a one-dimensional model of power (Lukes, 1974), or a 'quantity model' of authority relations (Collins, 1998a, 1998c).

Quantity models of power relations, as these describe workplace decision-making, tend to assume that power is an observable, behavioural phenomenon. Thus, a quantity account of power assumes that managers *have* power, and that to empower, managers must relinquish some of their power. Yet while this is intuitively plausible, the quantity view of power relations does not really explain situations in which subordinate groupings empower themselves by wresting control (Collins, 1995a). Thus, the quantity model of power relations fails to analyse, and fails to explain (1) why groups would wish to usurp what the 'gurus' take to be management's legitimate authority and (2) how apparently powerless groups (*groupings in need of empowerment*) are able to alter the conduct of power relations.

In order to explain the dynamic social contests which characterize attempts to manage workers, we must abandon simple quantity models of power, to move towards a position where management, as a group and as a set of practices, is no longer considered to be unconditionally legitimate. In short, we must be able to adopt a position where power (as distinct from authority) is analysed as a product of social relations, since it is only by adopting such a view that we will be able to explain (1) why managers are now keen on a particular construction of empowerment and (2) the ability of managers to persuade other groups to accept this construction.

Lukes (1974) offers a useful account of the concept of power which illuminates the limitations inherent in the modelling of power which is used, implicitly, by the 'gurus' of management. Indeed Lukes argues for a three-dimensional account of management, which, he argues, is necessary for a full account of social dynamics.

Countering the limitations of behavioural accounts of power Lukes argues that the simplest, one-dimensional account of power, views power as an observable, behavioural phenomenon. Thus a one-dimensional view of power argues that we may say someone is powerful, or has power over another, where they are able to make people do things they might other-wise choose not to do. Lukes, however, is dissatisfied with this account of power. An account of power, which is focused only on the visible mani-festations of power, he warns us, misunderstands the nature of power relations. Thus he warns us that we should not focus upon power as a behavioural and observable phenomenon since this fails to understand that a defining characteristic of power can be the ability it gives individuals (and groups) to choose not to act.

Lukes argues, therefore, that a second dimension of power relates to non-decisions and non-action – which, of course, cannot be observed as behavioural phenomenon. Steven Spielberg, the film-maker, offers us a frightening illustration of the power of non-decisions. In his film *Schindler's List*, Spielberg offers us insights into the nature and conduct of the Nazi holocaust. During the film a relationship develops between the eponymous Schindler (an entrepreneur) and the commandant of a German concen-tration camp. This camp commandant has, literally, the power of life and death over the inmates. Indeed, the commandant has total power over his charges, and exercises his control over human mortality in an arbi-trary fashion. On the basis of a whim, or when provoked to anger, he subjects his prisoners to summary execution.

Schindler, perhaps unsurprisingly, is horrified by the killings. However, he cannot confront the commandant about this, and he cannot *make* the commandant stop. The simple behavioural account of power, therefore, would tend to present Schindler as impotent when compared to the camp commandant. Yet, in the film Schindler proceeds to exercise some degree of power over the commandant.

In an attempt to stop the killings, Schindler has to adopt a different tactic, which does not require a head-on challenge to the commandant's power. The approach adopted by Schindler, as we shall see, is illustrative of the second and third dimensions of Lukes' preferred approach to the analysis of power.

In an attempt to stop, or even reduce the killings, Schindler suggests to the camp commandant that the power to kill is surpassed by power in another form. He suggests that truly powerful, and truly regal personages, have the power to choose not to act. Thus, Schindler suggests to the commandant that he can appear truly awesome to his prisoners by choosing not to kill them. In this way he encourages the commandant not to act on a whim. Instead of killing on a whim, Schindler encourages the commandant to forgive his prisoners on an arbitrary basis. Thus Schindler, through Spielberg, shows an awareness of the second dimension of power.

Spielberg's camp commandant is powerful because he can kill. However, Schindler suggests to the commandant that he will be even more powerful, and will show his power more fully, when he chooses not to engage in the behaviour expected of a camp commandant. Thus Schindler encour-ages the camp commandant to wield his power in a fashion not properly

revealed by the analysis of observable behaviour. Spielberg's film, therefore, demonstrates the need to analyse the second dimension of power.
We should note, however that Spielberg's feel for the reality of power is
not limited to two dimensions. In his account of Schindler's dealings with
the camp commandant, Spielberg also illustrates the third dimension
of power.

The third of Lukes' three dimensions of power relates to the construction of identity. Lukes argues that the operation of power need not always
work to force us to do things against our will. Instead the power of social
actors may work to influence our will and our drives. Thus Lukes' third
dimension of power achieves its effect by acting to shape the construction
of subjective understanding. In this sense, Lukes argues that power may
influence human action, not by an act of force, but by shaping our beliefs,
and our subjective understanding of events and circumstances, such that
our felt-need to dissent is reduced. Returning to our cinematic example
its should be apparent that, in encouraging the commandant to embrace
the second dimension of power, Schindler makes use of the third dimension to affect the commandant's subjective understanding of his role in
history. Thus we see how Schindler chooses to encourage the commandant to see himself as a sovereign, in the hope that the commandant might
come to think of himself as an all-powerful life-giver, rather than as a
powerful executioner.

Taken together, our discussion of the frontier of control, and this discussion of the three views of power offer us important insights into the nature
and processes of empowerment at work. Indeed our account of Lukes
allows us to see why the concept of empowerment is so powerful.

Scott (1994) tells us that the most powerful groups in society are those
which have the capacity to shape our subjective understanding. Groups
are truly powerful, he tells us, when they have the capacity to define a
cauliflower to be a rose, and can make others share this judgement. Viewed
in these terms, the concept of empowerment is powerful since it builds
upon contextual changes in the wider society, and in the discourse of
management, to shape our understanding of events. Thus the 'guru' discussion of management, which is shaped by the notion of competitive
imperatives (see chapter 1) has used concepts such as empowerment to
create an agenda for change at work, so that we become animated and
oriented to particular forms of action (Weick, 1995), which we might otherwise reject.

The concept of empowerment is truly powerful, therefore, because it
(1) appeals to the managerial need for control by promising to transform
the labour process and (2) because its resonant quality (Grint, 1994) and
its semantic elasticity reduce dissent by incorporating worker interests
(MacInnes, 1989; Collins, 1994). Management's preferred construction
of empowerment (as an individualized relationship built upon flexibility
to reflect the needs of the customer), therefore, draws workers into a

relationship where, paradoxically, they enjoy few of the democratic rights achieved in earlier periods. Indeed, we should note that the discourse of empowerment has been invoked during a period, which has witnessed the dismantling of forms of democratic decision-making at work (Beale, 1994). In this sense, we could argue that managers have used the third dimension of power to disempower (Collins, 1994) workers. Using Lukes' work, then, we might argue that managers have manipulated worker subjectivity to promote particular forms of change at work. Or more succintly we might say that in the name of empowerment, workers have been disempowered (Collins, 1996a).

But it is not all bad news.

Our analysis of subjectivity, and of the disempowering logic of empowerment, shows, more fully than the 'guru' account, the power of empowerment. However, our analysis of Lukes' radical view of power does not imply that worker subjectivity is a blank canvas for managers to inscribe as they please. Instead our discussion of the frontier of control serves to remind us of the dialectical nature of power relations at work, and the mediated nature of worker identity and subjectivity. Despite managerial attempts to shape worker identity, therefore, workers retain the ability to question, and to challenge their roles in the labour process (Collins, 1999).

For example, Graham (1994) reports that among the (empowered) female employees she studied, the experience of short-notice overtime working, and the problems of juggling this pattern of working alongside other domestic responsibilities, led employees to confront management. Indeed, Graham notes how demands for labour flexibility led workers to challenge the construction of empowerment enforced by management. Thus, Graham notes that in spite of managerial attempts to shape employee subjectivity, workers came to question, and so, came to attack their 'empowerment' as restrictive and illegitimate. In short, workers came to challenge the construction of empowerment and the framework of managerial power, because the managers of the organization in question failed to ensure that worker experience would continue to endorse the managerial representation of the workplace. The workers studied by Graham, therefore, came to challenge their empowerment because managers sought to maintain a form of working which demanded flexibility from workers yet refused to offer a reciprocal form of exchange by offering a flexible approach on the part of management (Collins, 1999).

Taken together, this four-part critique of empowerment suggests a radically different agenda, both practically and academically, for the analysis of innovations in workplace decision-making.

## Towards a New Agenda

Our critique of the 'gurus' and their preferred approach to empowerment shows the managerialist representation of empowerment to be weak in application. However, while our critique is driven by academic concerns, it is not of academic interest alone.

With our 'critical-practical' aims in mind, our critique demonstrates, at one level, that in order to achieve significant changes in workplace decision-making, (which live up to the social-democratic marketing) a more pluralistic form of action and analysis may be necessary. Thus our analysis highlights an understanding that actors committed to empowerment would do well to focus upon institutions and forms of decision-making, which meet the demands and expectations of organizational participants both at, and below, managerial level. This must imply, therefore, that if we are to work towards addressing the important issues which the (ambiguous and contested) concept of empowerment raises, concerning power and decision-making at work, we will require a framework for the analysis of empowerment which can allow for a basic plurality of interest. In turn, this must also imply a model of power conceived not in terms of parcels and lumps, but in terms of social relations. This, as we have seen, calls for a more critical and socio-historical account of work, power and empowerment.

In attempting to develop this more socio-historical account of empowerment, management research should be redirected to analyse empowerment in a qualitatively different fashion. Hijacking an approach summarized in terms of mnemonics, in order to reclaim a useful mode of expression now, peculiarly (and pejoratively) associated with the 'gurus' of management (see Hammer and Champy, 1993; Kanter, 1989), this project/programme of work might be summarized as an attempt to analyse the *4 Cs* of empowerment. Thus our 'critical-practical' call to analyse the *4 Cs* of empowerment represents a call to analyse the following.

### *The Context of Empowerment*

Recognizing the acontextual, and the ahistorical nature of managerialist accounts of empowerment, research should be directed to analyse the context (Pettigrew, 1985) of empowerment. Through this redirection, actors might be able to locate and to understand management's concern with empowerment as a technique, which claims to manage ambiguity, yet achieves its effect via the manipulation of worker identity and subjectivity.

### *The Construction of Empowerment*

Building from a more historical and contextual analysis, it is apparent that a key aspect of any thoughtful research on empowerment must relate to the attempt to understand the meanings and effects (Cunningham *et al.*, 1996) of empowerment. Since empowerment is an ambiguous concept, it seems appropriate to suggest that research on empowerment should make strenuous attempts to make sense of the various possibilities for the construction of empowerment. An understanding that empowerment is a construction and a human representation, it is hoped will encourage more of us to become actors rather than spectators (Wright-Mills, 1973) in these matters, since when/where we are able to recognize that hands and minds construct imperatives, we should be in a better position to decide whether and to what extent we would wish to celebrate, accept or reject the vocabulary of management's 'gurus'.

### The Cascade of Empowerment

Managerialist accounts of empowerment, as we have seen, suggest that managers should 'cascade' their vision of/for empowerment throughout the organization. At face value this is an apparently sensible suggestion. However, in describing/prescribing a cascade mechanism, commentators tend to discuss social action in a fashion which fails to recognize the complex problems associated with the management of meaning (Keenoy and Anthony, 1992).

The 'cascade' of empowerment begins with an attempt to construct and to privilege particular notions of an essentially ambiguous concept. Recognizing this, future research on empowerment should be careful to analyse the management of empowerment in a fashion which acknowledges the complexities of power (Lukes, 1974), and the limited nature of managerial control. Thus research on empowerment should be directed away from a simple-minded concern with communication and with leadership (see chapter 5) to examine the cascade of empowerment in terms of power and subjectivity. Again, it is hoped that this form of understanding might lead to a more active approach to empowerment at work (Collins, 1995a)

### The Contests Within Empowerment

Managerialist accounts operate with a unitary (Fox, 1985) conception of organization and with a truncated understanding of 'power'. Managerialist accounts, therefore, tend not to acknowledge the conflict potential within attempts to construct, and then to cascade, particular invocations/ incantations of power. Recognizing this conflict potential, research into empowerment should be careful to investigate opportunities for the articulation of dissent and contest within the process of empowerment (see C. Collins, 1999; Collins, 1999).

As an approach to the analysis of empowerment, this framework, of course, carries no promise of success in the management of empowerment. In fact, the *4Cs* of empowerment, outlined here, demonstrate why there can be no guarantee of success when attempting to manage the ambiguities of empowerment. However, in attempting to offer a 'critical-practical' analysis of empowerment, this chapter has highlighted the oversights and omissions associated with the managerialist account of empowerment. Through this analysis the chapter has attempted to provide a more useful basis for reflexive action.

## Summary

This chapter has attempted a 'critical-practical' account of empowerment, and through this analysis attempts to provide a useful counterpoint to that proffered by the 'gurus'.

Unlike the analytical approach preferred by the 'gurus', which examines management in a limited way, this chapter has attempted to look critically at the processes of managing. Locating management as a system of control, which is incomplete and self-defeating, the chapter has argued that managers 'empower', not because they choose to, but because material changes and mimetic influences oblige them to do so. Thus the chapter has argued that empowerment should be regarded as a control innovation invoked and refined to ensure the fulfilment of the goals defined, designed and pursued by management. With this in mind, the chapter, then, turned to examine the 'guru' account of empowerment. Articulating a dissatisfaction with the 'guru' account of empowerment the chapter argued for an alternative account of empowerment, which places the concept of power at the centre of the analysis in an attempt to encourage readers to become actors in rather than spectators of change.

# 8  Business Process Re-engineering

## Introduction

I do not often eat breakfast. I do enjoy breakfast, but nowadays I am normally too busy, and too tired to make time for it (see chapter 9). However, when I do find time for this meal I demonstrate a childish taste for certain types of foodstuff. Currently, my preferred form of breakfast food is a particular type of cereal. When I have time for breakfast, therefore – normally on Saturday mornings – I like to feast on a delicious combination of toasted, chocolate-coated rice, which I drench in ice-cold milk. In pursuit of this delicacy I am able to select from a range of brands. Kellogg's, probably the key brand in this market, for example, offers Coco Pops. Tesco and Sainsbury's, meanwhile, offer, what marketing experts would term, an 'own-brand' substitute called, Choco Snaps.

But, to be honest I do not care which of the many available brands I consume. I am, as economists would say, indifferent between Coco Pops and Choco Snaps. I am, however rather finicky about the milk; it must be ice-cold and, where possible, it should be from an Ayrshire cow – the milk from this breed being rich and creamy.

But what have my domestic concerns to do with business and management? What has all this talk of brand names, of breakfasts, and of milk, to do with 'business process re-engineering' (Hammer and Champy, 1993)? More than you might think.

Our small diversion into the domestic world of breakfast cereals offers a useful starting point for a discussion of business process re-engineering for four key reasons as follows.

First, and perhaps most importantly, our brief examination of my life-style and the manner in which my work encroaches on my home life is intended as a self-conscious attempt to contrast my experience of life, as I live it, with the deathly pale simulation of life which is presented by text-books (Burrell, 1997) and by the ready-made 'guru' theories of management (Chia, 1996). Wright-Mills (1973) captures this tension well. He argues that, often, men and women find their lives to be 'a series of traps' (Wright-Mills, 1973) because their visions, powers and orbits have been confined by a form of theorizing, which denies the validity of personal experience, and so fails to locate private difficulties as part of larger social movements. In an attempt to (re)locate private concerns and difficulties within the context of these social movements, movements which shape, and are shaped by the discourse of management, this chapter begins with an account of the most mundane aspects of domesticity, in an attempt to show how a different and more imaginative (Wright-Mills, 1973; Chia, 1996) approach to theorizing allows us to locate the problems experienced within our private orbits, as part of a larger, more generalized social trend. Thus, the discussion of my domestic concerns – the time pressures and hunger pangs which punctuate all of my life, because of the stress of my working life – is designed to encourage readers to forge linkages between their private difficulties, and our public concerns. In making this linkage, between the private, and the public, I hope that together we might become social actors in change, rather than spectators (Wright-Mills, 1973) of change.

Second, if we are to be actors in change, rather than spectators of change, we must be able to make sense of the public world. In the context of this chapter, we must be able to make sense of the concept of re-engineering, and the terms used to convey its arguments. Here a discussion rooted in domestic affectations is, again, useful, since it helps to uncover the nature of 'guru' theorizing, as well as the contours of re-engineering. For example, Tesco and Sainsbury's offer an excellent breakfast cereal which, to my tastes, is little different from the Coco Pops offered by Kellogg's. Yet, in spite of the essential similarities of Coco Pops to the own-brand equivalent offered by Tesco and Sainsbury's, it is illegal for these supermarkets to sell, or to market, their own products as Coco Pops, since Kellogg's claims exclusive ownership over this term. Reflecting a similar concern with ownership and with 'passing off' this chapter will not analyse 'reengineering', because Mr Champy claims exclusive rights to this word and has attempted to file a copyright claim on the term (Kennedy, 1996). Our discussion of brands, and of the legal restrictions which surround branding, therefore, offers us important insights into the nature of 'guru' theorizing. Indeed, our account of my taste for Coco Pops suggests that management's venerable business commentators (Jackson and Carter, 1998) are, above all else, businessmen, and not philosophers. In fact our analysis of brands and branding suggests that the 'gurus' are worthy of note, not because of their analyses, rather, they are worthy of note because they would make a cash charge applicable to free speech. To avoid the legal difficulties of licensing agreements and copyright law, therefore, this chapter will analyse, 're-engineering', the own-brand or *generic* product equivalent to the buzzword, now, apparently owned by Mister Champy.

My third reason for mentioning breakfasts cereals is to draw attention to the nature of markets, and to the role which marketing plays in creating product demand. As we shall see, Hammer and Champy (1993) assume the existence of an autonomous body of customers who enforce their demands upon organizations. However, my indifference as regards brands of toasted, chocolate-coated rice cereals, and my strong preference for particular types of cow's milk draws our attention to the ways and means of marketing, and its attempts to create consumer demand and customer loyalty. Thus, our analysis of breakfast foods, and of the attempts made by companies, such as Kellogg's, to create, and to sustain consumer demand, suggests that it would be wrong to consider demand to be an autonomous, self-generative variable. Yet, our analysis of brands and branding also reminds us that we are not bound to accept the products which the processes of marketing would seek to create a demand for. This understanding of the nature of customer demand, as we shall see later, offers a powerful critique of re-engineering (however this is spelled).

Our brief discussion of my preferred breakfast food offers a different and, I hope, a distinctive introduction to the topic of re-engineering. Thus, the fourth reason for introducing the topic of 're-engineering' via a discussion of Coco Pops and Choco Snaps, is based upon a calculation that readers quickly tire of academic analyses which employ the following linguistic device as their introductory comment:

> Business Process Reengineering (BPR) is set to become the most influential management idea, or fad, of the 1990s.
> (Wilmott and Wray-Bliss, 1996, p. 62)

> Business Process re-engineering (BPR) is the latest business panacea to emerge from the American academic-consultancy complex.
> (Grey and Mitev, 1996, p. 6)

To facilitate our 'critical-practical' discussion of re-engineering, this chapter is structured as follows:

If we are to unpack and unpick the concept of re-engineering we must, first, be able to locate, and to understand re-engineering as a concept, and as a set of practices. Clearly, then, our 'critical-practical' account of re-engineering must begin with an analysis of those writers who have toiled to make re-engineering a central part of the discourse of management. Yet, if our analysis is to be, truly, critical, it must go beyond the account offered by Hammer (1990) and his co-authors (Hammer and Champy, 1993; Hammer and Stanton, 1995) to embrace a larger range of discussions (some revisionist, yet supportive; others hostile and damning) which, in a variety of ways, seek to question re-engineering, its intellectual underpinnings, its practices, and its outcomes.

To offer the balance between exposition and critique, which is vital for a 'critical-practical' account, we begin by offering an account of 're-engineering' as this has been presented by Hammer (1990) and his co-authors (Hammer and Champy, 1993; Hammer and Stanton, 1995). Employing a framework which acknowledges the homiliary nature of these texts, we will then contrast the work of Hammer, as the 'prophet' of re-engineering, with the works of another two, key groupings, which have grown up around the re-engineering phenomenon. These two groupings, a group we will call 'non-conformist preachers', and a group we will refer to as 'secular dissenters', offer us two forms of critique.

Our, 'non-conformist preachers' offer, what might be termed, an instrumental critique of re-engineering (Grint *et al.*, 1996). In this sense, the account of re-engineering offered by our 'non-conformist preachers' is distinctive, in that it is designed to improve, and to refine the implementation of 're-engineering' (see Bryant, 1998; Bryant and Chan, 1996a, 1996b; Oram, 1998). Through this attempt to extend and to refine the discussion of re-engineering, the 'non-conformist preachers' offer us a useful analysis, which goes beyond the assertion and hyperbole which is, unfortunately, the stock-in-trade of our 'guru-prophets'. Indeed, as we shall see, our 'non-conformist preachers' offer us a lever which may be used to open 're-engineering' to more critical comment.

Making use of the 'critical jemmy' supplied by our analysis of the 'non-conformist preachers', we will then attempt to pursue the form of critical analysis undertaken by our 'secular dissenters'. This form of analysis which, as we shall see, eschews the managerial concerns of the 'prophets', and the concerns of the 'non-conformist preachers', in favour of an analysis 'helpful in formulating responses and resistances to BPR' (Grey and Mitev, 1996, p. 7). We will outline key aspects of this 'critical-practical' account before offering a, brief, concluding discussion.

Let us begin, then, with an account of the 'prophets' of re-engineering.

## Prophets Who Profit

Hammer's discussions of re-engineering mark him out as a prophet of business. In common with the religious prophets identified by Pattison (1997), Hammer (1990) and his co-authors (Hammer and Champy, 1993; Hammer and Stanton, 1995) offer an all-encompassing account of life and faith. In Hammer's work we are offered an account of a future state of being, which focuses upon corporate success as the barometer of our futures. However, Hammer's work is no dispassionate business commentary. His work is, in fact, a passionate account (see chapter 5) of business and management, whose effect, immediacy and claims to authority hinge upon a mode of argument remarkably similar to those invoked in religious teaching. Viewed in these terms, re-engineering is similar to a religious doctrine, and Hammer is a prophet (rather than an analyst) because of the mode of argument which is invoked to facilitate the discourse. In common with the old testament prophets, therefore, Hammer's version of life and work offers a blunt and simplistic account 'of corporate consumer, competitive capitalism' (Pattison, 1997, p. 137) designed to show the risk of (competitive) damnation and the promise of (corporate) salvation.

In secular terms, Hammer's account of American corporate capitalism is underpinned by a call to establish a new means of organizing and a new mode of competition. This new means of organizing, we are told, stems from the need to abandon 'old ways', a concern with efficiency and control, to embrace the 'new way' (note the move from plural to singular, from polytheism to monotheism!), which is built around a concern for innovation, speed and quality. However, in presenting this (secular) argument Hammer adopts a mode of presentation at some remove from that traditionally adopted by the orthodox business press. Indeed, as we shall see, Hammer's is a prophetic (but not a forward-looking) account of modern, secular, business concerns, which is theological in its mode of expression and worshipful in its approach to the concept of management.

But how can re-engineering be theological? How is it possible for management, a secular activity, to represent a new religion? How can Hammer be a prophet when his account of business and management is, by any calculation, godless?

## Not Science, Not Art: Religion?

Analysing the writings of a range of commentators, influential in the field of management, Pattison (1997) notes that management's 'gurus' offer a form of analysis and exposition more commonly associated with works of theology. Based upon this observation, Pattison suggests that we would do well to regard management's 'gurus' as the representatives of a form of belief system which is religious, both in its mode of expression, and in its claims to truth and truthfulness.

Perhaps surprisingly, Pattison (1997) argues that a work might be considered theological (and its author a prophet), even where the work makes no reference to a recognisable deity, so long as the concepts articulated by the text form 'an overarching moral order'. Indeed he argues: 'To depersonify the transcendent by getting rid of any kind of overt deity . . . is not to dispose of its transcendent nature, though it may make it less obvious.' (Pattison, 1997, p. 137).

Viewed in these terms it seems clear that Hammer is a (business) prophet. In common with the 'gurus' of management more generally, he has constructed an account of business, which seeks legitimacy by cloaking itself in a theological-ideological mode of expression. In this sense Hammer is a prophet because he has attempted to construct an over-arching moral order. Hammer's works, therefore, might be considered theological, not because they speak of a recognizable deity, but because they seek to provide a means to situate, and to explain America's corporate slippage (*the fall*) whilst, simultaneously, spelling out the steps which must be taken to ensure corporate America's salvation. Hammer's arguments might be considered religious in spite of the absence of a recognizable deity, therefore, because his work, his mission – if you will – is clearly built around an attempt to construct for managers, and for others: 'An overarching moral order within which all events, meanings and experiences can be situated and explained' (Pattison, 1997, p. 137).

Let us bow our heads to receive the word of Hammer.

## In the Beginning

Hammer launched what he was later to term 'the reengineering revolution' (Hammer and Stanton, 1995) with an article in the *Harvard Business Review* (Hammer, 1990). This article entitled 'Don't Automate: Obliterate' began with an examination of the state of corporate America.

In this survey of corporate America Hammer was not impressed with what met his gaze. Indeed, he argued that in spite of the attempts, which had been made during the 1980s, to automate and rationalize the conduct of business in the pursuit of improved business performance, American companies remained unprepared for the competitive challenges of the 1990s.

*And Hammer saw mechanization and automation and saw that they were bad.*

Hammer argued that the, admittedly, strenuous attempts made by American managers to automate business activities during the 1980s had been misguided and short sighted, since the competitive challenges of the 1990s would not be focused upon mechanization and rationalization. Mechanization and other, similar, attempts at rationalization, he informed his readers, were methods which had been developed by managers as attempts to secure control, and to improve efficiency. Yet, in the 1990s control and efficiency would be insufficient for business success. Instead Hammer argued that the watchwords of the 1990s would be: 'innovation and speed, service and quality' (Hammer, 1990, p. 104).

But why would the 1990s be so different from the preceding decades? In response to this issue, Hammer argued that key changes in demography and technology, which later became the 'three Cs of a competitive crisis' (Hammer and Champy, 1993), would force fundamental changes in the nature of business competition.

Let us look more closely at this motor of social and economic change.

## The Three Cs

Articulating a vision of the competitive crisis, imminent in America, Hammer and Champy (1993) argued that three, main, competitive forces 'have created a new world for business' (Hammer and Champy, 1993, p. 24). Customers, competition and change, they argued, demanded 'flexibility and quick response' (Hammer and Champy, 1993, p. 24) from companies designed to operate in an entirely different business environment.

Thus, Hammer, and his co-author, argued that organizations would have to be changed, redesigned in a root-and-branch manner, to meet these new demands. In short, they argued that organizations would have to be, in the now familiar parlance, re-engineered.

We can learn much about re-engineering; its aims and orientations from an analysis of these, 'three Cs':

- customers
- competition
- change.

*Customers*

Hammer and Champy (1993) offer an account of consumers which will be familiar to those who have studied Total Quality Management (TQM) (see chapter 6; and Beckford, 1998). Discussing a change in the balance of power between producers and consumers in America, Hammer and Champy imply that, until recently, the relationship between these two groupings has been dysfunctional and abusive. Thus Hammer and Champy argue that American corporations indulged themselves in the belief that there was a mass market for their goods and services, and so, produced for this market using the convenient fiction that 'one size would fit all'.

Of course one size did not fit all. However, Hammer and Champy argue that in earlier eras consumers, either (1) did not comprehend the depth of their dissatisfaction with what the market had to offer, or (2) could find no real alternatives to the unsatisfactory products made available to them, and so settled for the mass-market products produced by the large corporations.

Yet this picture of producer arrogance, we are told, has changed quite fundamentally. Indeed, Hammer and Champy argue that consumer expectations, thanks, in part, to the skills of Japanese managers and engineers, have soared such that consumers will no longer accept shoddy goods and corporate complacency:

> In short, in place of the expanding mass market of the 1950s, 1960s and 1970s, companies today have customers . . . who know what they want, what they want to pay for it, and how to get it on the terms they demand. Customers such as these don't need to deal with companies that don't understand and appreciate this startling change in the customer-buyer relationships.
>
> (Hammer and Champy, 1993, p. 21)

This, of course, carries with it a number of implications for the second C, competition.

## Competition

Hammer and Champy argue that because consumers are now more sophisticated, the rules of competition have become more complex. Presenting an account of business practice in the decades before the 1990s, (which often descends into caricature) Hammer and Champy argue that corporate success is, no longer, guaranteed by the production of 'adequate' mass-market products, because effective niche competitors have taken advantage of declining trade and tariff barriers to change the nature of competition.

Technology, in the form of information and communications technologies, plays a pivotal role in this. Indeed, as we shall see, information technologies play a key role in re-engineering, both facilitating changes in competition, while, simultaneously, working to meet the challenges thrown up by changes within, and between, the '3Cs'. Thus, Hammer and Champy argue that information technologies make new products and new forms of service viable, because they 'expand the limits of the possible' (Hammer and Champy, 1993, p. 22).

*And Hammer saw information technology and saw that it was good.*

## Change

Employing a linguistic device favoured by 'gurus' and by managerialist commentators alike, Hammer and Champy argue that: 'change has become both pervasive and persistent. It *is* normality' (Hammer and Champy, 1995, p. 23, original emphasis). This understanding of change-as-normality, Hammer and Champy tell us, carries a range of implications for management and for organizations. In short, and in common with 'gurus' such as Kanter (1989) and Peters (Peters and Austin, 1985), Hammer and Champy argue that there has been a discontinuous change in the nature of the business environment.

Where, once upon a time, organizations could 'tool-up' for long production runs, safe in the knowledge that product life cycles would last for years, Hammer and Champy argue that the life cycle of many products is now measured in months. Yet, they warn us, it is not only the product life cycle which is collapsing. Due to changes in the other Cs, due to changes in competition, and in customers, the product development process is also collapsing. Taken together these changes amount to a revolution in management since, we are told, they will force organizations to find new ways of working and new ways to get close to the customer (Peters and Waterman, 1982).

Perhaps unsurprisingly, Hammer and Champy claim to have the answer to this revolutionary turn in human history. Thus they inform us that re-engineering offers organizations the new ways of working, and the new ways of getting close to the customer which the 3Cs demand. Let us examine this, re-engineering, solution to the problems of management.

## Hammer Time

Making a case for the importance of re-engineering as a concept, dedicated to changing the essence of management and work organization, Hammer and Champy launch a broadside against their contemporaries. Demonstrating both the variety of management's fads and buzzwords, as well as the problem of defining the term, fad, they argue:

> none of the management fads of the last twenty years – not management by objectives, diversification, Theory Z, zero-based budgeting, value chain analysis, decentralization, quality circles, 'excellence', re-structuring, portfolio management, management by walking around, matrix management, intrapreneuring, or one-minute managing – has reversed the deterioration of America's corporate competitive performance. They have only distracted managers from the real task at hand.
>
> (Hammer and Champy, 1993, p. 25)

The implication of this attack is clear. Unlike all the earlier approaches to management (which have been tried and have been found wanting), re-engineering is different. Indeed, we are warned that re-engineering is no fad. Accordingly, we are assured that re-engineering will not distract managers from the 'real' problems of management, as the 'fads' listed above, have. In fact, by offering a new way of working, and a new means of organizing, re-engineering, it is argued, will arrest and reverse the decline of corporate America. But what is re-engineering?

Hammer and Champy define re-engineering boldly and immodestly. Re-engineering we are told: 'is the fundamental rethinking and radical redesign of business processes to achieve dramatic improvements in critical contemporary measures of performance, such as cost, quality, service and speed' (Hammer and Champy, 1993, p. 32).

This definition, we are told, contains four key terms.

* *Fundamental*: Re-engineering begins by asking basic questions about managing and organizing. It encourages managers to ask: *Why do we do this? Why do we do the things we do?* Re-engineering, it is argued, asks these questions in order to reveal the tacit rules and assumptions – the 'givens' built into the design processes of organization and management. In this way Hammer and Champy argue that re-engineering helps managers to throw out the 'rules' of business, which in the current environment are 'obsolete, erroneous, or inappropriate' (Hammer and Champy, 1993, p. 33). Re-engineering, therefore, is said to allow

organizations to overcome taken-for-granted assumptions about managing and organizing which limit change and competitiveness. Indeed, Hammer and Champy argue that 're-engineering begins with no assumptions and no givens' (Hammer and Champy, 1993, p. 33).

- *Radical*: Re-engineering is radical, we are told, because it seeks root changes in the design of organizations. Unlike other (faddish) approaches to management, such as TQM and *kaizen*, which seek improvements in current approaches to managing and organizing, re-engineering, it is claimed, is built around a radical concern to re-invent organizational structures, processes and policies.

- *Dramatic*: Since re-engineering throws out the old assumptions of organizing, and seeks radically different solutions to the problems thrown up by the 3Cs, it is free to pursue dramatic improvements. Both the dramatic improvements of re-engineering and the drama-tism of Hammer's prose style are clear to see in the initial discussion of re-engineering published by *the Harvard Business Review*. In this, the initial exegesis of his credo, Hammer warned of the requirements, which the re-engineering revolution would make of its adherents. He warned: 'We must have the boldness to imagine taking 78 days out of an 80-day turnaround of time, cutting 75%, of overhead, and elim-inating 80% of errors' (Hammer, 1990, p. 112).

- *Process*: This term, we are told, is the key to re-engineering. Most busi-nesses, we are told, are focused upon structures and functions. In order to control large-scale, 'm-form' organizations, such as Ford, IBM and General Motors, management, over time, has developed mechanisms to divide activities and responsibilities so that business functions might be made more efficient and more amenable to control. On the shopfloor, for example, work tends to be sub-divided among workers such that no, single, worker is now able to perform the full range of tasks required to produce the product or service supplied by the organization. Higher up the organization, this complex division-of-labour is mirrored by the development of specialist functions – administration, personnel, research, design, maintenance, marketing and so on – each staffed by individuals dedicated to ensuring that their individual efforts contribute to smooth administration, bureaucratic personnel management, valid research, appealing designs, timely maintenance, and cost-effective marketing. Hammer (1990) warns us, however, that while each of these specialisms is vital to the effective functioning of organizations – managers, consultants and business-minded academics – have lost sight of one essential and inescapable fact: that each of these functions exists to facilitate one process, and one process only. Within the business world of the 1990s, each and every unit, and each and every staff member, no matter the nature of their functional specialism, has only one organizational purpose – to ensure customer satisfaction. However, Hammer warns us that the functional division of labour and the bureaucratic practices of working which are employed by modern organizations, actually serve to institutionalize (if not to guarantee) customer disappointment and dis-satisfaction.

For example, discussing Mutual Benefit Life, an American insurance firm, Hammer (1990) notes that BR (before re-engineering) it took between five and twenty-five days to process a customer's application. He warns us, however, that this delay occurred, not because the process of dealing with customer applications itself is complex, but because the organization's detailed division of labour was focused upon function rather than process. Thus, Hammer argues that delays in work occur because actors focus upon the needs of the organization rather than upon the needs of the customer. Reflecting upon this costly and wasteful division of labour, he notes that at Mutual Benefit Life: 'an application would have to go through as many as 30 discrete steps, spanning 5 departments and involving 19 people' (Hammer, 1990, p. 106). Yet he warns us that application processing is really quite simple; so simple, in fact, that: 'another insurer estimated that while an application spent 22 days in process, it was actually worked on for just 17 minutes' (Hammer, 1990, p. 106).

Re-engineering organizations to focus upon process rather than function, and upon the possible rather than the traditional, Hammer argues, offers dramatic potential for improvement. In the case of the insurance example, a reduction in processing time from 22 days to 17 minutes! However, we are warned that we should not allow the elegance of re-engineering as a concept to make us complacent. Indeed, Hammer warns us that we should not allow the prospect of dramatic improvements in performance to foster the illusion that re-engineering endeavours may be accomplished with ease. Accordingly, Hammer and his co-authors spend some considerable time explaining how re-engineering might be achieved.

## Managing Re-engineering

On the question of managing re-engineering, Hammer and his co-authors (Hammer, 1990; Hammer and Champy, 1993; Hammer and Stanton, 1995) are keen to point out that it takes courage and determination to achieve process-focused organization. At face-value, this 'warning' seems like a poor marketing tactic. After all, car manufacturers do not produce advertising copy which reads – *don't buy this car, it's expensive to run, difficult to maintain . . . and will lead people to make stereotyping judgements about your mores and manners.* Instead they produce copy which highlights the more attractive aspects of their products – *buy me, I'm fast, I'm expensive . . . If you buy me men will envy you and women, in droves, will seek you out for sexual services.* So why is Hammer generating negative copy for his product?

The short answer is that Hammer is not, truly, developing copy designed to dissuade us from buying re-engineering. Instead, his protestations regarding the need for courage and determination should be regarded as a cunning feat of marketing prestidigitation.

You see, if re-engineering is, truly, a bold undertaking, then the boldness required of its adherents should serve not to dissuade, but to attract managers to re-engineering. The courage and endeavour implied in the discourse (if not the practice) of re-engineering, therefore, acts as a positive marketing platform. In short, the supposed difficulty of re-engineering acts as a recommendation for management, since there can be no surer way to mark one's self as an attractive, risk-taking individual with 'the right stuff' (Wolfe, 1979) for advancement, than to accept the challenge of business process re-engineering (see Grint, 1997, 1997a).

While extolling the virtues of risk-taking, however, Hammer is also keen to warn us against the perils of fads and sloppy thinking. Countering the sloppiness of mind which might, otherwise, mar re-engineering efforts, Hammer warns us that we cannot re-engineer departments. We can, he tells us, only re-engineer processes. Anything else, we are warned, is just structural tinkering (structural tinkering being something which occurs in the crawl spaces of conservative-minded managers) which, of course, will fail to deliver the dramatic improvements that await the committed and determined 're-engineer'.

In an attempt to counter the conservatism and sloppiness of mind, normally associated with management's fads and buzzwords, therefore, Hammer tells us that the first steps in the process of re-engineering, properly so-called, begin with (1) a blank sheet of paper, and (2) a team drawn from the various functions who currently 'contribute' to a business process. On this blank sheet of paper the team is invited to re-invent the business. Throwing off the traditions of organizational design, throwing off the normal design conventions which underpin our assumptions about who should do a task, where and when, 're-engineers', Hammer tells us, look beneath what is taken for granted to focus upon the actual processes which constitute what we call 'work'. From an understanding of these processes, 're-engineers', we are told, work to restructure the organization, its tasks, its management and its value system (Hammer and Champy, 1993, p. 80) to ensure that all 'work' undertaken is geared to satisfying customers. At this point, however, re-engineering becomes problematic.

Re-engineering, as we have seen is a fraught and difficult undertaking. Indeed, Hammer warns us that all re-engineering endeavours confront a key problem. Re-engineering's key problem is this; aside from the customer, it has no natural allies for its radical agenda. Re-engineering activities, of necessity, must span the functional boundaries of organizations. This raises a vital concern for Hammer and Champy, since their experience of management and organizations suggests that attempts to develop, or to implement re-engineering programmes may falter or fail due to a lack of sponsorship within the organization. After all, it is one thing to crave the image of an attractive, risk-taker, quite another to preside over a risky programme, such as the one undertaken by Ford, which affected many areas of the business and which, ultimately, reduced the number of staff involved in the business process by 75 per cent (Hammer, 1990).

To overcome the problems of resistance and boundary-politicking, Hammer and Champy (1993) advocate the development of specialist roles, and the formation of re-engineering teams. Thus we are advised that re-engineering will require:

- A *leader*: a senior person to authorize the project.
- A *process owner*: a manager given responsibility for a process.
- A *re-engineering team*: dedicated to diagnosing the existing process and redesigning it.
- A *steering committee*: responsible for re-engineering at a company-wide level.
- A *czar*: who, although Hammer and Champy are coy on this, can *kick ass*, and overcome resistance and blockages.

At root, all of these roles and processes turn upon one key issue: leadership. Indeed, it would not be an over-statement to say that, for its 'prophets', re-engineering is a dramatic and radical change programme, which can only be delivered by leadership. At this point, sadly, re-engineering, which has never been modest, becomes aphoristic, and so, unconvincing.

As we saw in chapter 5, leadership is a complex and contested concept (Grint, 1997a). Accordingly any discussion of the benefits and merits of leadership as a strategy to facilitate change, must be qualified by a discussion of the *specific* account of leadership which underpins the strategy. This, Hammer and his co-authors fail to supply.

Thus, it is a disappointment to have to report that Hammer tends to deal with the topic of leadership in a proverbial and aphoristic fashion, in spite of the centrality of this concept to the project of re-engineering as a whole. So, when discussing the importance of the leader and the role of re-engineering's czar, Hammer does not turn to the many available and scholarly accounts of leadership. Instead, as befits a 'prophet' of re-engineering, he retreats into a biblical example.

Leaders are like Moses, Hammer tells us, which, of course, is perfectly true – of some leaders. But not all leaders derive their authority from a charismatic base! Some leaders derive their authority from the possession of a special skill; some from the possession of physical strength (Homans, 1968). Only a very few leaders derive their authority directly from God – so we must ask, does this illustration, Moses as leader, do much to illuminate the fraught problems of managing and leading re-engineering in a modern business organization?

Recognizing fragilities in the analysis of leadership, and in the 'prophetic' account of re-engineering, more generally, a number of commentators have sought to modify, or to attack re-engineering. Let us examine, first, those who would modify re-engineering. Let us examine the commentators I have labelled 'non-conformist preachers'.

## Non-conformist Preachers

In religious circles non-conformist preachers have a strange and some-times, precarious existence. They accept many aspects of mainstream religious teaching, yet find themselves driven to dissent. For example, the Jesuit order of catholic priests accepts, fully, man's fall from grace; the coming of Christ; the resurrection and the promise of eternal life; to name just a little of what I can remember of my religious indoctrination. Yet the Jesuit order tends to find itself in conflict with other orders, and with the Vatican, when it comes to questions concerning how one might live one's life in a holy fashion.

The Vatican, you see, is a wealthy organization; rich in material things. In the Vatican these riches perform, I suppose a variety of functions. Key among these functions is the glorification of God. Thus, in the eyes of the Vatican it is, it seems, important to worship the Kingdom of Heaven in a rich and regal setting. Yet, not all agree with the Vatican on this matter. Indeed the Jesuit order has argued, strongly, that the appropriate image for Christian worship is the image of Christ, the poor man (see Eco, 1983, for a dramatized account of this form of religious debate and division). Thus in comparison to services in the Vatican, Jesuit services are simple and modest, reflecting the Jesuit belief that one will only achieve life after death if one is willing to dispense with material distractions. In this sense, the Jesuits offer a non-conformist account of Catholicism; they accept the key principles of catholic religious instruction yet demand the right to dissent.

Extending this understanding of religious dissent into the (quasi) secular world of management, it is possible to identify writers who, while accepting the value of Hammer's re-engineering project, would prefer to modify and/or refine the methods and techniques of re-engineering. In this sense it is possible to identify 'non-conformist preachers' within the re-engineering project. These 'non-conformists', as we shall see, offer an instrumental critique of re-engineering.

## An Instrumental Critique

Those who demonstrate an instrumental orientation to work and the bene-fits of working exhibit a calculating approach to work. Thus a person with an instrumental orientation to work will have a tendency to measure their effort and output. Indeed the work effort of someone with an instrumental orientation to work will be conditional upon the rewards accruing from their toil, and will vary with those rewards. Recognizing a concern with measurement and with benefit as the defining characteristic of an instrumental orientation, those I have labelled as 'non-conformist preachers' within the re-engineering movement should be regarded as offering a revisionist account of management and work organization, rooted in a calculative account of the instruments deployed in pursuit of business process re-engineering. Yet, in comparison to the accounts offered by our secular dissenters this is a positive critique. It is a line of analysis which, while critical of Hammer's account of re-engineering, seeks to modify the instruments and techniques he employs so that the promise of re-engineering might be secured.

Notable among these 'non-conformist preachers' is Bryant (1998, see also Oram, 1998; Harrington *et al.*, 1998), who with a number of co-authors (Bryant and Chan 1996a, 1996b; Bryant and Vanhoenacker, 1999), has attempted to refine and improve re-engineering. This non-conformist account of re-engineering is informed by a few key concerns.

- That the terminology of re-engineering is imprecise and ambiguous. Notably Bryant and Chan (1996a) argue that the notion of a business process is ill-defined.
- That the mechanisms for initiating and managing re-engineering are ill-defined.
- That evidence for the use, and for the success of re-engineering, is anecdotal and sweeping in its generalizations.
- That re-engineering is a euphemism for large-scale redundancies (see chapter 9).

In an attempt to engage with these problems, Bryant (1998) and his co-author (Bryant and Chan, 1996a) have promoted the concept of Goal Directed Development (GDD) which, it is argued, may have the capacity to overcome the shortcomings identified in re-engineering.

## Goal Directed Development

The notion of Goal Directed Development as articulated by Bryant (1998) should be regarded as an attempt to overcome the deficiencies of Hammer's account of re-engineering. In this sense Goal Directed Development (GDD – the authors had originally toyed with the concept of Goal Oriented Development, but became wary of the acronym!) is, squarely, an attempt to harness 'the power of BPR' (Bryant, 1998, p. 25).

Summarizing this, powerful, potential Bryant argues that, in spite of the fact that BPR has been reported as having an 80 per cent failure rate, re-engineering remains a useful, and powerful approach to managing and organizing, because it:

- encourages organizations to reassess, fundamentally, their objectives
- encourages the identification and location of core business processes
- encourages organizations to clarify goals and objectives
- uses process analysis to drive IT implementation/incorporation.

However, Bryant is concerned that these gains might not be achieved because, he tells us, re-engineering lacks a valid and reliable methodology for the analysis of business processes in context. Thus, in his attempt to develop a more reliable methodology for re-engineering, Bryant argues that we must make a greater attempt to locate organizations in their business environments.

Analysing the 'three Cs' promoting re-engineering, we noted that Hammer's key motivation in constructing BPR, as a managerial concept, was to help modern organizations deal with rapid change, and with the uncertainties which follow from such turbulence. Bryant argues, however, that Hammer is wrong when he asserts that all organizations face such a turbulent environment. He argues: 'It would be incorrect to assume that all organizations have to contend with similar levels of uncertainty' (Bryant, 1998, p. 27). In an attempt to overthrow Hammer's, overly simplistic and singular, account of the environment of business, Bryant employs Emery's and Trist's (1969) four-fold classification of business environments.

## The Environment(s) of Business

Emery and Trist identify four types of business environment:

- *Placid*: Placid environments, as you might imagine, are remarkable for their stability and predictability. In a placid environment, therefore, there is no real difference between tactics (day-to-day concerns) and strategies (long-term aims). Organizations adapted to placid environments optimize performance by ensuring their continued adaptation to the environment.
- *Clustered*: In a clustered environment the prevailing procedures and principles of the environment do not strike all businesses with equal force. Instead clusters of businesses, divided according to their roles and norms, exist within the environment. Under these conditions, Bryant (1998) argues, a more strategic approach to management is necessary. Thus, Bryant contends that, in a clustered environment, organizations must make efforts to match the environmental contingencies which each faces, to allow 'the organization to move towards opportunities and withdraw from threats' (Bryant, 1998, p. 27).
- *Reactive*: In comparison to the first two environments classified, the reactive business environment is more complex. In this environment power and dependence play an important role in business dealings. Indeed, we are warned that the complex interactions between parties

of unequal strength make predictions difficult and management a more problematic undertaking.

- *Turbulent*: Turbulent environments, (the singular environment assumed by Hammer), defy prediction. In these settings, change is constant and discontinuous. The turbulent business environment, therefore, is chaotic (see Grint, 1997a). Accordingly, prediction of outcomes is, essentially, impossible.

Bryant argues that as we move from predictable to less-predictable business environments we will tend to find that organizations, of necessity, develop a range of coping mechanisms. Notably, Bryant states that as organizations come to operate in less predictable environments they have a tendency to implement policies designed to enhance flexibility. However, as organizations adjust to cope with complexity, Bryant argues they confront a paradox that is not easily resolved. Thus Bryant notes that while organizations need to invest in change, and in developmental systems, key operational systems must also be maintained if the organization is to remain in business. Yet Bryant argues that Hammer (1990) fails to give attention to this fundamental issue.

Thus, while Hammer has encouraged managers to 're-invent' (Hammer and Champy, 1993) the business and to 'obliterate' (Hammer, 1990) existing business processes, Bryant argues that a policy of obliteration would serve only to alienate customers. He notes: 'You cannot simply obliterate existing processes – some form of operationality must be maintained' (Bryant, 1998, p. 28). In an attempt to develop a means of managing this paradox, thrown up by the need to manage stability within change, Bryant urges the adoption of his Goal Directed Development approach to re-engineering. This orientation is preferable, we are told, since it displays greater sensitivity to the environmental and social issues which will surround any attempt at change management.

Arguing that re-engineering adopts an aggressively mechanistic approach to managing and organizing, Bryant contends that Emery's and Trist's (1969) classification of business environments reveals that in the 'turbulent' environment (where re-engineering promises most), the key problem for management will be goal maintenance under conditions of uncertainty where: 'there will always be processes to consider alternative processes for reaching the same goal and, if circumstances necessitate it, the goal itself can be reformulated or even replaced, with the process starting over' (Bryant, 1998, p. 28).

Thus Bryant's promotion of GDD represents an attempt to offer a less mechanistic, and so, a more socialized (Clegg, 1993) account of managing and organizing. This account of change, and of the problems of managing change, he assures us, is better able to comprehend, and to appreciate the complex and often conflicting ideas and agendas which will tend to collide during periods of change (see Collins, 1998).

Yet, while recognizing the benefits of a more socialized account of change, GDD is, I fear, a flawed attempt to develop a more rounded and embedded (Granovetter, 1985) account of managing and organizing, since, as we shall see, its concern to refine, and to contribute to re-engineering, via an instrumental critique, ultimately, hamstrings its pursuit of complexity and contradiction.

## Managing Complexity?

Those who would seek to manage complexity confront a key problem. To make sense of complexity one must, in a sense, celebrate it (Reed, 1992). Yet to celebrate complexity one must pursue it without wishing either to catch it or to tame it. So when Bryant argues that he would push re-engineering to one side, to allow a richer and more complex account of change management to emerge, we must consider his final end.

For example, in our analysis of the 'guru' industry (see chapter 3), we observed that what distinguished the commentaries offered by the 'redemptive' texts, from those offered by the 'atheists' of the 'guru' industry, was a willingness to serve managerial ends. Indeed, we argued that it was a desire to operate at some distance from the normal concerns of management, which made the contributions of the 'atheists' both incisive and critical. Thus, in discussing the contribution made by the 'atheists' of the 'guru' industry, we stressed that Burrell's (1997) account of *Pandemonium* offered a useful and distinctive analysis of the 'gurus', precisely because it aimed to critique, rather than to refine the current preoccupations of management. Conversely, we argued that the accounts of the 'guru' industry drafted by Shapiro (1998) and by Hilmer and Donaldson (1996), remained limited and partial, since they tended to side with management as an elite, and as a result, displayed a tendency to treat the goals of management *as if*, these represented the needs of the organization as a whole.

As we look over the modified account of re-engineering prepared by Bryant (1998) and his co-authors (Bryant and Chan, 1996a, 1996b; Bryant and Vanhoenacker, 1999), therefore, we must wonder how Bryant hopes to forge a methodological compromise between managing, directing and controlling complexity while celebrating complexity as a primary outcome of human interaction. Indeed, the concern voiced by the 'secular dissenters' of re-engineering is that, in these matters, no balanced compromise can be forged. Thus the 'secular dissenters' of re-engineering would tend to argue that, while Bryant has begun to develop a useful critique of re-engineering, his analysis remains limited, partial and compromised by an unwillingness to disavow the key tenets of re-engineering, so that a more radical and fundamental critique might be offered. Let us pursue this matter through an analysis of a group I have termed, the 'secular dissenters'.

## Secular Dissenters

While the work of those I have labelled as the 'non-conformist preachers' of re-engineering, offers an account of business process re-engineering, which is designed to improve its take-up, implementation and success rate; those I have labelled as 'secular dissenters' offer a more fundamental critique, designed to supply practitioners with the tools necessary to allow them to resist, and to overcome re-engineering (Grey and Mitev, 1996; Wilmott, 1994). In this sense, the secular dissenters of re-engineering go beyond the instrumental critique offered by Bryant (1998), to offer a form of analysis which rejects the more moral order crafted by Hammer.

Viewed in these terms, the 'secular dissenters' go beyond the critique offered by the 'non-conformist preachers', as they attempt to question, and to undermine the assumptions, assertions and outcomes promoted by Hammer (1990) as the 'prophet' of re-engineering.

To facilitate an analysis of this line of secular dissent we will offer a three-pronged attack on re-engineering. In this critique we will examine, first, the assumptions of re-engineering. We will, then, move on to examine re-engineering's assertions, before moving on to examine the outcomes of the re-engineering movement as these have been summarized by a range of critical thinkers, whom I have chosen to label as 'secular dissenters'.

## Re-engineering's Assumptions

We saw in our discussion of Hammer that re-engineering was said to be driven by movements and developments in the 3Cs: customers, competition and change. Those I have labelled as 'secular dissenters' of re-engineering, however, view the discussion of these 3Cs with suspicion, and would seek to unpack this 'ready-made' account of management. Thus the 'secular dissenters' of re-engineering display a willingness to explore, and to expose re-engineering's assumptions. Let us revisit the '3Cs' of re-engineering with a more critical eye.

### Customers

Re-engineering is driven, fundamentally, by the idea that organizations must be redesigned so that structures, policies and processes are geared to satisfying the demands of customers. The demands of customers, therefore, are said to shape organizational processes. So, where customers demand higher quality, organizations, if they wish to remain in existence, must find ways to improve the quality of their goods and services. Likewise, where customers demand a more speedy response from organizations, managers must find ways to streamline structures and processes. A key message which emerges from the prophets of re-engineering, therefore, is this: organizations should attempt to understand their customers, since success in business requires that organizations must allow consumer preferences to shape business processes. What, then, does re-engineering have to say about customer demand and consumer preference?

If customers shape, and reshape, organizations; what shapes customer demand? Hammer's response to this is rather confused.

At one level, an image of the independent consumer/customer drives re-engineering. Indeed movements in customer demand, and in consumer expectations, are said to cause imperatives for change, which, in turn, call forth re-engineering solutions. Yet, at other times, Hammer, when writing with Champy (Hammer and Champy, 1993), has suggested that customer demand and consumer preferences do not exist separately and autonomously, divorced from the sphere of production. Thus Hammer, when writing with Champy suggests, quite contrary to the vision of consumer demand as an autonomous variable, that Say's Law (supply creates its own demand) must be acknowledged as a factor *shaping* customer demands.

When offering a dissenting account of re-engineering, authors such as Grey and Mitev (1996) and Grint (1994) have tended to argue that re-engineering is flawed, since it fails to consider, in a non-reductive fashion, the myriad of factors which shape customer demand and consumer preferences. As Grey and Mitev note: 'BPR starts with the untenable assumption of the autonomous nature of the customer' (Grey and Mitev, 1996, p. 9).

While agreeing with Grey and Mitev that the assumption of an autonomous customer is, indeed, untenable, it is important to note, I think, that Hammer and Champy do not, quite, make this assumption. Thus rather than damn Hammer and the minor prophets around him, on the charge that they view consumer demand as autonomous, which is a charge which cannot be made to stick, it is perhaps more useful and fruitful to point out that Hammer offers a dualistic and contradictory account of 'customers', which swings from a view of customer demand as autonomous and independent, to a point where customer demand is actively created.

Similar problems have been observed by 'secular dissenters' in the analysis of the second 'C': competition.

### Competition

Re-engineering is driven by a view of the competitive environment and by concerns over the place of corporate America within this new environment. Indeed, re-engineering is said to build upon the strengths of American character and ingenuity, in order to see off the challenge posed by 'Japanese' pedestrian-incrementalist approaches to organizational change.

Grint *et al.* (1996), however, have been mocking of this rhetorical account of re-engineering. Thus they note that re-engineering could hardly be said to build upon American character/cultural traits, since, while US society is supposed to be individualistic, re-engineering is clearly a team endeavour. Similarly, Grint and his co-authors also note that re-engineering could hardly be said to embody American values, since while re-engineering is said to depend upon the development and maintenance of supportive social networks, American society is said to be based upon self-reliance.

Yet, while it is relatively easy to demonstrate that re-engineering could hardly be said to be a distinctively American approach to business we have not yet addressed the central feature of Hammer's account of re-engineering – that the forces of competition which are currently being unleashed make re-engineering unavoidable.

Analysing the competitive environment, the 'prophets' of re-engineering tend to employ a rather simplistic model of competition, one normally, employed in introductory courses on economics, and then quietly discarded as an unhelpful abstraction from reality (for a humorous account, see O'Rourke, 1998). Thus, in Hammer's model of competition, all companies are driven by competitive changes and must, continually, adapt so that they do not fall prey to the vagaries of the increasingly turbulent environment.

However, this model of competition is built upon a range of assumptions which seem limited and distorting in the light of analyses of industrial competition. For example, Hammer seems to imply, in part, thanks to information technologies, that all markets are under threat and that all organizations face threats from, both actual and potential, market entrants. Yet, for this threat to exist in reality, all markets would have to be free of barriers to entry, and exit, so that good competitors would be able to drive out those market incumbents who were under-performing (Porter, 1985). This assumption, however, is untenable since, as Grey and Mitev note: 'good does not necessarily drive out bad, for example, where resources are available to block new entrants or where there is not perfect knowledge' (Grey and Mitev, 1996, p. 9). The notion that re-engineering will be driven, inexorably, by forces of competition, which will impact upon all organizations, equally and savagely, therefore, does not bear close scrutiny.

This analysis of 'competition' has implications, of course, for the third C of re-engineering: change.

### Change

The discussion of re-engineering put forward by the 'prophets' we have analysed is facilitated by a discussion of 'change', which portrays corporate America as being in a state of flux. Change, we are told, again and again, is the only constant. However, this discussion of change and upheaval only holds water if we accept that markets are, always and everywhere, subject to the free-play of market forces. Where barriers to perfect and free market competition exist, which is almost everywhere, there will be forms of 'constants' other than change.

Closer analysis of the factors which are said to drive re-engineering (the 3Cs), reveals, therefore, that there is no clear and direct link between these factors and re-engineering. Customers, for example, cannot drive re-engineering unless customer demand is separate and autonomous. Likewise, the forces of competition could hardly be said to drive re-engineering where companies can evade, or even change these 'forces'. At root, then, the assumptions which, simultaneously, are said to underpin and to call forth re-engineering are falsely conceived and poorly articulated.

It should not surprise us, therefore, to discover that the assertions, which the 'prophets' employ to 'sell' their ideas also lack substance.

## Re-engineering's Assertions

Hammer, in common with the other 'gurus' discussed in this text makes a number of assertions regarding the nature, and form, of his concept of re-engineering. We do not have the space here, systematically, to document and refute each of these assertions. We will confine ourselves, therefore, to an analysis of, perhaps, the two key and fundamental claims which Hammer makes for re-engineering.

When discussing re-engineering Hammer (Hammer, 1990; Hammer and Champy, 1993; Hammer and Stanton, 1995), claims that it offers a new way of managing and working. In an attempt to analyse, and to qualify re-engineering's assertions, we will therefore attempt to gauge the novelty of re-engineering. Yet, before turning our attention to the question of re-engineering's novelty (or otherwise), we will examine a, perhaps, more fundamental assertion – that BPR is free from assumptions, and so, offers managers *carte blanche*.

### All Things Are Possible?

Re-engineering, Hammer (1990) argues, represents a radical approach to the redesign of organization. Indeed, Hammer claims that re-engineering amounts to the reinvention of the corporation. It is, we are told, an attempt to reverse the industrial revolution, inasmuch as it seeks to break down the narrow functional division-of-labour, and the separation of management from working (Hales, 1993) which has characterized the development of large-scale work organizations (Thompson and McHugh, 1995). In this sense, re-engineering, through its attack on features of organization design which have become taken for granted, seems to offer a form of analysis which throws out many of the, deep-seated, assumptions of management and managing. As Hammer, in his seminal introduction to re-engineering, argues:

> Every company operates according to a great many unarticulated roles. 'Credit decisions are made by the credit department.' 'Local inventory is needed for good customer service.' 'Forms must be filled in completely and in order.' Reengineering strives to break away from the old rules about how we organize and conduct business. It involves recognizing and rejecting some of them and then finding imaginative new ways to accomplish work.
>
> (Hammer, 1990, pp. 104–105)

Perhaps, more succinctly, Du Gay and Salaman (1992) have observed that Hammer's account of re-engineering mixes a range of influences and ideas to offer 'a powerful critique of contemporary institutional reality' (Du Gay and Salaman, 1992, p. 630).

At one level, then, re-engineering is an attempt to overcome those assumptions, which, for something approaching a century at least, have underpinned organizational design. But does this mean that re-engineering is, itself, without assumptions? Does re-engineering, truly, begin with a blank sheet of paper? Are all things possible within re-engineering?

The short answer to this question is that re-engineering is not free from the limiting confines of unspoken assumptions. Re-engineering is, in fact, riddled with assumptions which, in a variety of ways, shape it as a concept and lead its operation and implementation.

Detailing a catalogue of assumptions which underscore re-engineering, Grey and Mitev (1996) note that in spite of the fact that Hammer has claimed to offer a reversal of the industrial revolution and the obliteration of accepted practices and principles, it would, in fact, be more accurate to suggest that re-engineering chips at the edges of the edifice which has grown up since the industrial revolution. Thus, Grey and Mitev note that re-engineering accepts and celebrates certain facts of life. It assumes, for example, that competition is a 'good'. Furthermore, as we saw in our discussion of the '3Cs', re-engineering assumes that competition is free and unfettered. We should note, too, that while re-engineering is said to obliterate all that we hold true, and all that management holds dear, it accepts the ownership structure of modern organizations as a given. It *assumes* and accepts the existing pattern of organizational ownership and, because of this, it *assumes* and accepts managerial prerogative. Finally, in this regard, we would do well to note that, in common with Peters (see chapter 5), Hammer assumes rather than investigates the potency of 'leadership' as a strategy for securing re-engineering.

The assertion that re-engineering is free from assumptions, therefore, is false and without foundations. What, then, of the assertion of novelty?

## A Novel Idea?

Never one, modestly, to sell his wares, Hammer (1990) claims that re-engineering represents a novel solution to the problem of managing in a turbulent, fast-changing environment. Grint (1994) is unconvinced, however. Indeed Grint argues that re-engineering is, entirely, lacking in novelty. Furthermore, and echoing Huczynski's (1993) analysis of management's 'gurus', Grint suggests that re-engineering has attracted a following precisely because its ideas and orientations are already familiar to its intended managerial audience. Thus, Grint argues that re-engineering's success lies, not in its novelty, but in its capacity to do two, key things. Re-engineering, he tells us, is popular because (1) it resonates with the existing fears and concerns of corporate America, and because (2) it has the capacity to provide a persuasive, yet familiar, rendering of these fears.

Detailing this rendering of ideas and fears, Grint outlines ten features of re-engineering which Hammer and Champy (1993) have claimed contribute to the appeal of re-engineering as a path-breaking approach to management. We have already touched upon some of these ideas in our discussion of the three 'Cs' of re-engineering. We will, therefore, discuss a selection of Grint's ten points, selecting those that are most salient to our current discussion.

(1) Hammer and Champy claim that re-engineering offers an attack upon the functional division-of-labour, to promote instead, a team-based approach to working which, it is claimed, represents a novel departure from historical and contemporary practices. However, Grint notes that not all organizations adopted, fully and wholeheartedly, the complex and functional division-of-labour which Hammer *assumes* to be the norm (see also Thompson and McHugh, 1995). Indeed, we would do well to remember that Volvo, the car and truck manufacturer, instituted a team-based form of production some thirty years ago. These and other familiar counter-examples to the functional division-of-labour, so derided by Hammer, suggest that on the question of team-based working, re-engineering offers little that is new.

(2) Hammer and Champy claim that re-engineering, through its attack on functional approaches to management, leads to the development of multi-skilling. There are two points worthy of note here. First, Hammer seems to suggest that until 1990, deskilling was the order of the day in all modern organizations. While we might wish to concede that deskilling may be a major dynamic within capitalism, it would be wrong to suggest, 'given the degree of technical and organizational change that has occurred over the last two centuries . . . that new skills have not been developed' (Grint, 1994, p. 124). Thus, Grint reveals that Hammer has, once again, sought to caricature history in his attempt to present, vainly, an image of re-engineering as novel.

On the second of our two points, we should note that re-engineering carries with it the *assumption* that 'deskilled' workers who are offered 'multi-skilling' by re-engineers, will become happier in their work, and so, will become more productive. Yet, while this assumption has an intuitive appeal, it does not bear empirical analysis. Looking back to the job enrichment schemes of the late 1960s and early 1970s (Goldthorpe *et al.*, 1968;

Kelly 1982) we may say one thing with certainty on this matter: that no strong connection has been made between worker happiness and productivity (Perrow, 1979). In spite of Hammer's attempts to claim novelty for re-engineering, therefore, it is worth observing that the multi-skilling promoted by re-engineering is familiar to the world of business. Indeed we could go further to state that the multi-skilling favoured by Hammer, and portrayed by him as novel, is, in fact, familiar, yet questionable in its worth to business.

(3)  Hammer and Champy claim that re-engineering attempts to make all workers and work processes customer focused. To become, fully and properly, customer focused, organizations must tap all the available skills of their employees. Hence, Hammer and Champy claim that re-engineering promises 'empowerment' to employees (see chapter 7). Empowerment, however, is hardly a new idea. Indeed we could say that empowerment is as old as the doctrine of sovereignty (see Clegg, 1975). In the sphere of management studies, empowerment is perhaps a more recent phenomenon. However, the concept certainly pre-dates Hammer's rendering of re-engineering, having been analysed for a managerial audience, notably, by Kanter in her discussion of male and female experiences of work and careers (Kanter, 1977). In addition to this criticism, we should note that, while Hammer and Champy (1993) portray empowerment as the voluntary reversal of managerial prerogative where empowerment is a consequence of management action, Grint (1994) argues that empowerment is in fact the consequence, not the cause of subordinate action. Thus, drawing our attention to strategies of subordinate opposition such as 'working to rule' (see chapter 7), Grint reminds us that managers engage in 'empowering' strategies in an attempt to remain powerful! Let us examine this, apparently counter-intuitive, line of analysis.

In the workplace superordinates are powerful because they have the ability to issue commands and orders. Yet, contrary to what we think we know about management, the formal right to issue orders tends to overstate the power of managers. Managers, you see, are powerful only so long as subordinates accept their subordination. When/where subordinates choose to reject their subordination, the power of managers evaporates. Thus managers are, perhaps surprisingly, weakest at the very moment they use their power to issue commands. At the moment when the superordinate issues a command, it is subordinates who, in fact, occupy the more powerful position in the relationship, since, at this very moment the subordinate has been given an opportunity to challenge, or to refute the superior's legitimacy by refusing to obey the command. Managers facing this turn of events may, of course, invoke sanctions in an attempt to force employees to conform. However, these sanctions are, for managers, double-edged, since attempts to control by compulsion, alone, tend to pierce and to disrupt the co-operation necessary within work organizations.

Confronted with this shifting balance of power, managers, in recent years, have tended to invoke the vocabulary of empowerment. Thus managers have sought to invoke empowerment in an attempt to make (claims to) managerial prerogative legitimate in the eyes of the subordinate. As Grint has observed: 'The upshot of this [shifting balance of power] is that, contrary to the reengineering assumption, subordinates *already* hold the key to power while the superordinate must persuade them that they do not, if she or he is to remain in power' (Grint, 1994, p. 186 emphasis in original). It seems clear, therefore that Hammer as the main prophet of re-engineering both misrepresents and misunderstands 'empowerment'.

(4) As part of its larger concern with organizational restructuring, the doctrine of re-engineering argues that systems of payment and reward will have to be redesigned to ensure a focus upon customer-oriented processes. Thus, Hammer and Champy argue that while organizations, typically, reward people according to their position in the hierarchy, or according to the length of time they spend at work, re-engineered organizations will reward people with bonus payments, according to their contributions. A few points are worth making with regard to this *assertion*.

First, few workers are paid for their attendance alone. Indeed recent years have seen a proliferation of payment systems, over and above traditional piece rate systems, which have been designed to forge closer linkages between performance and reward (Kessler and Purcell, 1995).

Second, as with the problem of defining and analysing business processes, this speculative 'analysis' attempts to side-step the thorny problem of measuring performance and value-added. For example, how should/would we measure the value-added of a firefighter's work? How would we judge the performance of a fire prevention officer? Or a doctor? Or a copy-writer?

Third, and in a related fashion, we might wonder that if we are to measure performance, over what timeframe should value-added be measured? Weekly? Monthly? Yearly? Over five years perhaps?

On the question of pay, as in much else, therefore, Hammer and his acolytes offer little that is new – and much that is open to question. Let us examine the third concern we highlighted, the (potential) outcomes of re-engineering.

## Re-Engineering's Outcomes

The prophets of re-engineering present us with two contrasting visions of the future which awaits us – here, 'us', might, more properly, be rendered in capitals, since in common with the majority of management's 'gurus', Hammer and his acolytes are addressing the American economy and polity.

Making a case for re-engineering, Hammer and Champy turn their gaze to our imminent futures to see more clearly, the scenarios fate has painted for us. Examining what fate has in store for us, they argue that we can choose between two potential futures. We can disregard re-engineering, and so, confine ourselves to no future at all, or we can embrace re-engineering and secure a future in the new competitive environment. Let us ignore the notion of imperatives built into this statement to ask: what sort of a future would this be? What are the outcomes of re-engineering?

To embrace re-engineering we must commit ourselves to certain pre-conditions. If we accept the work of Hammer and Champy, it seems clear that these pre-conditions will work to shape our futures under re-engineering. In this regard, the outcomes of re-engineering must be considered worthy of further analysis. To embrace re-engineering, we must commit ourselves to total customer satisfaction; we must accept empowerment, and we must rethink management. However, since these commitments will shape our futures at work and at home we have the right to ask:

- Should the customer be king?
- Does re-engineering empower?
- Does re-engineering's rethink of managing inform, or deform our view of management?

### Customer as King?

Articulating their vision of re-engineering, Hammer and Champy argue that organizations must ensure that they are dedicated to serving the needs of customers. They warn us that 'companies today have customers . . . Who know what they want, what they want to pay for it, and how to get it on the terms they want' (Hammer and Champy, 1993, p. 21). We have already scorned the idea that customer demand is autonomous, that customers do, in fact, know what they want. There is, however, another means of criticizing this notion that customers should get just whatever they want. This line of criticism turns upon a consideration of the outcome of such a policy.

If the customer is king, and purchasing power is the order of the day, does this mean that, as a society, we are bound to supply whatever the market asks for? Hammer's answer to this question is, it seems, yes – most emphatically.

But what if the customer wants child pornography; what then? What if the customer wants to buy an automatic weapon? What if the customer wishes to smoke in the presence of non-smokers? What if the customer wants chemical nerve agents?

Would we supply the customer with these 'goods'? No, we would not, since we would find the outcome of such a policy to be distasteful in the extreme. As a society we demand the right to regulate customer demand, to deny 'customers' certain of their demands, to define 'goods' as 'bads'.

The suggestion that the customer is and should be 'king', always and everywhere, therefore, misunderstands those things – those statutes, customs and moral judgements which delimit and regulate customer behaviour. The celebration of 'customer as king', therefore, is at best, an amoral notion and is not, I believe, an outcome that should be pursued with vigour.

## Empowering?

While celebrating the benefits to the consumer of re-engineering, Hammer and his co-authors also argue that re-engineering carries with it beneficial outcomes for producers. Key among these benefits is worker empowerment. Thus, Hammer and his colleagues argue that re-engineering leads to empowerment. We have already noted that empowerment is a consequence, not the cause of subordinate action. In this section, however, we will place this argument to one side to consider the extent to which re-engineering, through 'empowerment' leads to changes at work which adjust managerial prerogative in favour of subordinates. This is no simple task, however. Empowerment (see chapter 7) is an essentially ambiguous concept. As such, it is a concept open to a variety of interpretations. In an attempt to gauge the empowering outcomes (or otherwise) of re-engineering, therefore, it is important to note that empowerment may be defined and interpreted in different ways.

Addressing this definitional ambiguity, Wilmott and Wray-Bliss (1996) remind us of the need to separate the two, distinctive, approaches to organizing which may be subsumed within the concept of empowerment. Thus Wilmott and Wray-Bliss remind us of the need to separate and to distinguish between two systems of accountability; hierarchical accountability and socializing accountability. They note:

> Within a system of hierarchical accountability, each employee is encouraged to show their value as a productive force; to engage in a competition for recognition and reward; and to compare and differentiate him/herself from others on the strength of productive ability or use value.
>
> (Wilmott and Wray-Bliss, 1996, p. 73)

This hierarchical form of accountability, they tell us, contrasts with socialized accountability, which is:

> Distinguished by a strong sense of interdependence between employees – a sense that is fostered where accounts of events and actions are collectively *interpreted* rather than hierarchically imposed.
>
> (Wilmott and Wray-Bliss, 1996, p. 73)

When analysing the outcomes of re-engineering, therefore, we can, perhaps surprisingly, agree with Hammer (1990; Hammer and Champy, 1993; Hammer and Stanton, 1995) that re-engineering does, indeed, lead to the empowerment – with empowerment defined as an essentially ambiguous concept we could hardly do anything less! Yet, we can part company with the prophets of re-engineering when it comes to weighing the benefits, and so, the desirability of the 'empowerment' pursued within re-engineering, since while Hammer and his acolytes would sell us a collegiate, a humanistic and socialized view of worker accountability within re-engineering, the actual experience of re-engineering suggests a competitive, Darwinian model of empowerment.

Indeed, reflecting a 'critical-practical' orientation, Wilmott and Wray-Bliss make the nature of empowerment under re-engineering, both 'transparent and accessible' (Wilmott and Wray-Bliss, 1996, p. 72) in a passage which is worth quoting at length. They note:

> BPR purports to advance a shift away from hierarchical toward more horizontal and egalitarian forms of accountability, where managers are 'coaches' not bosses. But, . . . for all its shimmering humanistic rhetoric of empowerment, Hammer's formulation of BPR is founded upon an authoritarian negation of any shift in which employees are identified and treated as factors of production who must simply accede to the 'obliteration' of established practices . . . including their jobs. Even for those remaining in employment, there is the prospect of an intensification of effort as elements of supervisory activity are (re)integrated into their work and the (relative) security provided by contracts tied to specific jobs is eroded by pressures to work more flexibly and cooperatively. Indeed . . . the BPR call to obliterate established practices includes the obliteration of regulations that provided employees with valued measures of security and predictability.
>
> (Wilmott and Wray-Bliss, 1996, p. 72)

This leads us to our final concern; a concern over another outcome of re-engineering. If, as Wilmott and Wray-Bliss (see also Wilmott, 1994; Grey and Mitev, 1996) note, re-engineering must be made 'transparent and accessible' (Wilmott and Wray-Bliss, 1996, p. 72) we must wonder if, by some mix of accident and design, re-engineering serves, not to inform, but to deform management.

This matter we will address, briefly, in our final section.

### Don't Automate: Deform!

Arguably the key role of any (non-fiction) text should be to inform, especially when that text has been written, co-written, (or even ghost-written) by someone celebrated as a 'guru'. When we examine the work of Hammer and his acolytes, therefore, we have a right to ask: has this text served to inform our understanding of management? Sadly, and on a number of counts, the response to this question is no!

Taking an instrumental line of analysis, such as that adopted by our 'non-conformist preachers', it is apparent that, for all the talk of redesigning organizations to reflect business processes, Hammer's account of re-engineering misinforms, since it lacks a reliable methodology for the analysis of process and, furthermore, lacks a sensible methodology for managing the implementation of re-engineering (Bryant, 1998).

When we throw off the managerialist confines (see chapter 3) of instrumental criticism to embrace the more critical accounts of those I have termed 'secular dissenters', re-engineering appears, not so much as a misinformed account of management, but as a deformed account of management. We may elaborate on this deformation in a couple of ways.

First, we could observe that the account of management, skill and the division-of-labour (Grint, 1994) developed by the prophets of re-engineering represents a grossly deformed history of management and organization which caricatures the problems of managing.

Second, we could observe that the prophets of re-engineering offer a deformed account of the process of management. Thus the violent rhetoric of re-engineering (Grint *et al.*, 1996), the advice to smash and to obliterate organizational structures, policies and procedures, flies in the face of any sensible account of the process of management. We should note, therefore, that in spite of the violent rhetoric of re-engineering, managers seldom have the ability to force through change, and in any case would be fearful of adopting such a 'violent' approach for fear of what this might do to workflow, to quality and to customer service.

Finally, and on a more positive note, we might observe that re-engineering as a persuasive and violent rhetoric holds sway only so long as it is allowed to deform our view of management. Accordingly, this chapter has attempted to open avenues for criticism, so that those concerned to manage in a more responsible and sustainable fashion might be able to find and/or make room for a more 'critical-practical' approach to the very real problems of managing.

## Summary

This chapter has offered a 'critical-practical' account of re-engineering. It began with an account of domesticity and domestic affectation. Discussing breakfasts and branding, we argued that 'guru' accounts of management limit and confine our understanding of larger social movements. Using the work of C. Wright-Mills (1973) we argued that the 'gurus' offer a 'ready-made' (Chia, 1996) approach to managing and organizing which limits our understanding of social movements (Wright-Mills, 1973) because it refuses to take our own, personal experience seriously. Thus, we argued that the 'ready-made' science of management tends to dismiss those things that are important to us – our lived experience – as an idiosyncratic distraction from the rigour of science (Burrell, 1997). In an attempt to unpack, and to unpick this ready-made science, this chapter has attempted to show how we can use our own 'domestic' experience to locate larger social problems. To this end, we have offered a brief account of breakfast and branding, which has been designed as an attempt to break the traps of ready-made science, which might, otherwise, confine us within private orbits built upon self-denial.

Surveying a range of contributions on re-engineering, this chapter has adopted a mode of expression which should be familiar to readers who are, perhaps, not so familiar with managerial matters, or who might be inclined to see managerial matters as issues divorced from their own private concerns. Recognizing that some form of religious education forms a key part of each of our own, personal biographies, this chapter moves quickly from an account of breakfasts and branding to offer an account of re-engineering, which is based upon a reading of Christian theology. This religious account of re-engineering is designed (1) to mimic and to parody the approach adopted by management's 'gurus' and (2) to encourage readers to forge linkages between private matters, and larger public concerns, in the hope that a 'critical-practical' review might be forthcoming.

Accordingly, this chapter has sub-divided the discussion of re-engineering into three orders, or chapters: a group of 'prophets; a grouping labelled as 'non-conformist preachers'; and a final grouping labelled as 'secular dissenters'. The chapter has offered an account of these three groupings, their ideas and preoccupations, before presenting a concluding discussion designed to raise questions in respect of re-engineering's assumptions, assertions and outcomes.

# 9 Downsizing

## Introduction

In the spring of 1981 the senior management of Glenfield and Kennedy Ltd (acting on the instructions of its parent corporation, located in North America) dismissed my father, and most of his friends.

No, that is not how we talk of such things now. Let's begin again.

In the spring of 1981, Glenfield and Kennedy Ltd, specialists in hydraulic engineering, 'downsized' its operations in Kilmarnock.

*   My father was 'dehired'.
*   Alec Dunn was 'involuntarily separated' from the company.
*   Jimmy Alexander was 'de-recruited'.
*   Sam Alexander was 'de-selected'.
*   Jimmy Craig was 'displaced'.
*   Jimmy Lightbody was 'rightsized'.
*   Davy Kerr was selected for involvement in a 'workforce imbalance correction' programme.
*   Jimmy White was 'transitioned'.

Yet, however you choose to name this event, the following Monday morning, these eight men (and many more like them) reported at Kilmarnock benefit office to claim the payments, which in 1981, were made available to the unemployed in Britain.

A number of things happened quite quickly following my father's brush with downsizing:

*   I no longer had to walk the family's dog each morning; in fact, that old dog soon clocked up more miles than Ranulph Fiennes
*   the council reduced our rent to the princely sum of fifty pence per week
*   and I became eligible for 'free' school meals.

Always keen to handle such issues and transitions with sensitivity, my school ensured that those receiving 'free' school meals received a dinner ticket which was quite unlike that issued to its paying customers. Short of having uniformed men, sporting blue berets and driving white Land Rovers handing out the free meals in the school grounds, I could not think of a better way of stigmatizing those receiving this benefit-in-kind!

This change in my domestic/scholastic circumstances could have been quite traumatic had it not been for the fact that almost all of my school friends were now receiving free school meals. Kev's dad was a cooper and had been out of work for some time. Joak's dad (English people always get it wrong when they call us 'Jocks') was an engineer of some sort, but he too had been 'given his jotters'. And Paul's dad . . . well no one really knew anything about Paul's dad. He had walked out on Paul's mum when Paul was just a baby, so Paul had been picking up the dodgy dinner ticket for as long as anyone could remember.

This is what 'downsizing' means to me. But here the biography tails off to some extent. I am no Alan Bleasdale, and to be honest, I do not have a particularly grim tale to tell of my experience of downsizing. After a period of unemployment my father worked away from home, for a time, before finally buying into a small business. Similarly, my father's long-time friend, Jimmy Craig, soon found alternative employment as the janitor for a 'special school', and so, traded the noise and grime of the machine shop for the unconditional love of forty, 'special' children.

But, I do not think that we should treat 'downsizing' glibly. Instead, I believe that we should look critically at the 'downsizing' buzzword to investigate its origins, its extent, and its wider implications for individuals, for their families, and for the communities they inhabit. Accordingly this chapter is structured as follows.

In the next section we will spend some time analysing the etymology of 'downsizing'. We will attempt to analyse the origins of the downsizing buzzword, and through this we will try to understand (via an analysis of the meaning and effects of downsizing) why managers have adopted this as their preferred term when discussing large-scale organizational restructuring. Reflecting upon the nature and process of large-scale organizational restructuring, we will argue that downsizing is a euphemistic form of phraseology. Thus we will argue that term downsizing is a convenient, shorthand form of phrasing deployed (1) to disguise the meaning and effects of recent organizational restructuring activities, which (2) acts to distance (Grint, 1997) management from responsibility for the mass dismissals associated with organizational restructuring since the 1980s.

Having analysed the meaning of downsizing, we will, then, attempt to examine more closely its impacts and outcomes. Accordingly, we will try to explore the extent and the experience of downsizing in the deregulated labour markets of Britain, the home of the author, and in the deregulated labour markets of America, the physical and spiritual home of management's 'gurus'. It is worth noting, however, that our reasons for studying the US and UK experience of downsizing self-consciously transcend the prosaic affiliations of nationalism and domesticity. Our account of downsizing, for sure, commences with an extract from my personal biography. However, this extract has been reproduced in an attempt to encourage readers to locate their own experiences and their own private difficulties, as part of the larger social movements which have shaped and reshaped the contours of our societies. Viewed in these terms, the extract from my biography is not simply a personal and idiosyncratic account of growing up in Scotland. Instead, the extracts from my biography have been reproduced as an attempt to encourage others (1) to recognize the value in their own (not-so-idiosyncratic) experiences, so that they might (2) break out of the personal orbits which confine them (Wright-Mills, 1973). Our comparison of America and Britain, therefore, is designed to encourage others to locate their experiences of life, as it is lived, within a larger and more dynamic, analytical framework.

Analysing a range of issues and concerns associated with globalization (see chapter 11), Gray (1999) suggests that Britain and America might fruitfully be paired for the purpose of a cross-national comparison, designed to reveal the social impacts of economic policies. Discussing the political, economic and social changes of the 1980s and 1990s, Gray has argued that, during these decades, the policy-makers of both America and Britain were avid in their pursuit of a particular brand of free-market economics (see also, Gilmour, 1993). Arguing that market policies and free-market strategies must be viewed as being embedded in wider social frameworks, Gray's analysis of these changing times offers us the means to trace, and to examine:

- Those factors common in British and American economic policies; policies which, in the name of free-market economics have allowed, or more properly, have indulged a range of management 'fads' and buzzwords, not least of which has been downsizing.
- The impact of social institutions and wider social frameworks on downsizing in Britain and in America.
- The meaning and effects of downsizing; the impact of downsizing on social life and on the social institutions of Britain and America.

Through this analysis, Gray offers us a useful counterpoint to the 'gurus' and their commitment to downsizing policies as a useful strategy for organizational change and economic redevelopment.

Following our cross-national comparison of Britain and America, we then offer a third, concluding, section which will consider the experience of downsizing, and the response of management academia to mass terminations of employment. Reflecting upon the response of management academia to downsizing, we will highlight the concern with 'survivors' (those who, with some mixture of fear, resentment and anger, maintain their employment during periods of downsizing), evident within management academia. Noting the minimally, palliative, concerns of the 'survivor' discussion, we will conclude by arguing that management academia has offered only a muted response to downsizing, which has failed to challenge, and so, has failed to stem both the rhetoric, and the practice of organizational restructuring, in spite of the damage which downsizing through its impacts upon individuals, on families, and on the community more generally, has had upon the larger social fabric of America and Britain.

Let us begin by analysing the etymology of downsizing.

## The Lexicon of 'Downsizing'

In our brief introduction to this chapter we alluded to the fact that the lexicon of employment and unemployment, the words and terms used to discuss, describe and to explain the experience of work, careers and unemployment, has changed in a variety of ways. While in employment, for example, workers are now expected to work *proactively* as *team members* within a *high powered*, or *empowered work team* (see Graham, 1994; Garrahan and Stewart, 1992; Fucini and Fucini, 1990). It is, therefore, no longer enough to be an engineer, or to be a welder, a technician, or a turner, as my father was, since one is now expected to work *flexibly*, as a *committed* member of a *multi-skilled team*, in pursuit of *total quality management* and *customer satisfaction*.

This vocabulary of markets, and of customer satisfaction which now characterizes the sphere of employment (see Munro, 1998) is also invoked in attempts to rationalize and to justify unemployment. Or, perhaps more properly, we should note that a new vocabulary has been invoked to justify the transition from employment into unemployment. Thus when my father received notice that his contract of employment was to be terminated unilaterally by his employer, he had not been 'sacked', he had not been 'laid off', he had, in today's parlance, been 'downsized'. It is worth examining this (euphemistic) form of phraseology in some detail, since as we shall see, the term and the practice of 'downsizing' runs contrary to the preferred UK terminology, 'redundancy', and to the normal policies and conventions associated with (mass) employee termination in a UK context.

### A Redundant Term?

The term 'downsizing', when applied to the radical restructuring of organizations is now a familiar one in widespread usage. As it has become common parlance, however, downsizing seems to have supplanted the term previously in use, 'redundancy'. This substitution of terms, as we shall see, has altered the contours of British discussions of industrial and economic restructuring in a subtle, yet far reaching manner.

In Britain, the word 'redundancy' is used to refer to special form of dismissal. Within the framework established by common law and by statutory provision it is, normally, only reasonable to terminate a person's contract of employment under certain circumstances. Listing just a few of the examples which would give legal grounds for dismissal; it would be legal to dismiss an employee if it could be demonstrated that the person:

* was incompetent
* had failed to execute their contractual duties
* had committed an offence (such as an assault at work, an act of theft, or an act of industrial sabotage), amounting to gross misconduct (Wedderburn, 1986).

In special cases, however, it is perfectly legal to dismiss competent and diligent employees who have fulfilled, completely, their duties under the contract of employment (Mukherjee, 1973). This special form of dismissal is known as a 'redundancy' and, in Britain, is governed by certain statutory measures.

Under British law, to dismiss an employee, or employees, for reason of redundancy an employer must, first, establish certain preconditions. Thus, under the Redundancy Payments Act (1965), an employee may be dismissed, legally, for reasons of redundancy where (Wedderburn, 1986):

* The employer ceases to carry out that form of business which the employee is employed to perform.
* The employer intends to relocate.
* The employer experiences a reduction in that form of work which the employee was contracted to perform.

In Britain workers who experience redundancy may, subject to certain qualifications (Wedderburn, 1986; Daniel, 1985), receive a payment which may be part financed by the state. When first instituted these payments were offered (see Cross 1985; Daniel, 1985; Mukherjee, 1973) in an attempt to:

* Improve the mobility of labour and to facilitate industrial restructuring.
* Relieve hardship during the period of transition.
* Avoid industrial conflict.

In addition, the Redundancy Payments Act (1965) also carried with it the understanding that employees, over time, accumulated 'property rights' in their employment. Thus, when first instituted under the Redundancy Payments Act (1965), the payments made to redundant employees were, in part, regarded as a form of compensation to employees who had lost the 'ownership' of their job. However, few commentators now think of employment and employment rights in property terms. This change of heart is, to a large degree, the result of the British experience of widespread and large-scale redundancy from the 1970s onwards. Indeed, given the widespread experience of redundancy and non-standard (that is part-time and temporary) employment, few, if any, commentators now conceive of jobs in 'property' terms, or as conveying ongoing rights to the post-holder that are considered as analogous to property rights (Wedderburn, 1986),

As understood today, therefore, the Redundancy Payments Act should be considered as an attempt to facilitate labour mobility and industrial restructuring in a manner designed to maintain, and to improve industrial harmony. In this sense, redundancy situations (the case of industry relocation aside) normally refer to situations where for reasons of industrial restructuring, technological change or recession, fewer workers are required to perform a reduced quantity of work. It is this which sets the terms 'redundancy' and 'downsizing' apart.

## The Etymology of Downsizing

In common speech 'downsizing' and 'redundancy' now tend to be invoked as synonyms; as linguistic alternatives which convey the same meaning. Yet, this is not quite accurate, since where redundancy situations are associated with a decline in both employment and work, downsizing is associated with a reduction only in the former. As Cappelli notes: 'Downsizing refers to reductions in employment that are not accompanied by a reduction in output' (Cappelli, 1995, p. 577). To allow us to locate and to understand this subtle, yet important shift, disguised within the assumption that 'downsizing' and 'redundancy' are synonyms (albeit euphemistic synonyms), we must make some attempt to locate the term, downsizing.

Chik Collins (1999) observes that while the term downsizing is, typically, used to describe factors associated with the radical restructuring of organizations, the etymological origins of the term suggest a qualitatively different sort of concern with 'structures' and with their 'restructuring' (see also Ayto, 1999). He notes: 'The term downsizing has its origins in the US automobile industry – particularly in Detroit – where it was used to encapsulate the drive to reduce car size and engine capacity in response to the oil crisis and the growth of environmental concerns during the early 1970s' (C. Collins, 1999, p. 73).

This leads us to an important issue. Why, given the rich argot of the workplace, and the existence of any number of terms which are, already, available for the discussion and analysis of termination and dismissal, should managers and their 'gurus' feel the need to borrow, and to adapt, a term more commonly associated with automotive design? In pursuit of this issue, Chik Collins argues we would do well to consider the benefits of 'downsizing' as a euphemistic form of phrasing.

## *The Power of Euphemism*

Scott (1990) argues that we tend to invoke euphemisms, and are encouraged by others to invoke euphemistic forms of phrasing, as a means of skirting around issues and ideas which, otherwise, would be problematic and/or discomfiting to address by more direct means. Thus, when discussing death, and the deceased, we have a tendency to avoid mentioning the word, death. Instead, we use euphemisms to convey sympathies to the bereaved, and to express our own thoughts about death and dying.

When we discuss death (or perhaps more truthfully, we should say – when we attempt not to discuss death), we speak of those who have 'passed away', or less politely we might speak of 'kicking the bucket', of 'curling up your toes', or of 'going to see the great beautician in the sky'. In Scotland, the deceased may be said to have gone 'up the crow road' (see Banks, 1995). Both the variety of these euphemisms and the extensive use of such euphemistic forms of phrasing are suggestive of our attitudes to human mortality.

Since euphemisms work to distance life from death, to distance the living from the dead, and work to distance speakers from the realities of human mortality, the widespread use of euphemistic forms of phrasing, in this instance, suggests that, as a species, we find death to be a problematic and discomfiting concept. For fear of our own reaction to the concept of death, and for fear of the reaction of others (especially the recently bereaved), therefore, we have developed methods to avoid the discussion of, potentially, painful and embarrassing concepts – even while we are, of course discussing these!

Reflecting the ability of euphemistic forms of phrasing to head off embarrassment and discomfiture, Scott (1990) notes that euphemistic phrasing is 'a nearly infallible sign that one has stumbled on a delicate subject' (Scott, 1990, p. 53). He continues: 'It is used to obscure something that is negatively valued or would prove to be an embarrassment if declared more forthrightly . . . [as a consequence] more graphic, ordinary language descriptions are frowned upon and often driven from the realm of official discourse' (Scott, 1990, p. 53).

Based upon this analysis of euphemism, Chik Collins argues that management's 'gurus' have borrowed, and have adapted, a term more at home in the field of automotive engineering, because this term assists the attempts made by managers and their 'gurus' to recast the meaning and the impacts of radical organizational restructuring. Thus he argues: 'the selection of the term "downsizing" as the public title for this policy [of radical restructuring and mass termination] sought to mask and euphemise the harsh consequences which flowed from it' (C. Collins, 1999, p. 74).

In this sense, the term 'downsizing' – with a root definition which refers to the attempts made to restructure American cars in response to the oil crises and environmental movements of the 1970s (Ayto, 1999) – might be considered as an effort, facilitated by euphemism, to accentuate key moments of downsizing, moments of planning, strategy and the *inevitable* business outcomes of competitive imperatives, while downplaying other negative moments, months of uncertainty, hardship and enforced mobility within a changing system of work (Cappelli, 1995; Moore, 1997).

In the section that follows we will attempt to examine the extent, and the experience of this phenomenon which we have been encouraged to discuss in euphemistic terms. Let us, first, examine the US situation.

## Downsizing in Context

As the spiritual home of the management 'guru', as the originator of the term, downsizing, and as the exemplar of a free market economy, often viewed as a template for the economics of globalization (Gray, 1999), America's experience of large-scale, organizational restructuring represents a useful starting point for a more detailed discussion of downsizing, its extent and its impact upon the lives of the American citizenry.

Often, when discussing key 'management' issues, when pondering important questions such as:

- how to improve quality?
- how to build commitment?
- how to empower workers?

there is a tendency to treat 'management' and working in isolation. Indeed, it would not over-state this problem to say that, most often, discussions of work and working tend to be presented in an overly formalized manner (Sims *et al.*, 1993; Ackroyd and Thompson, 1999), and in a fashion which seems to suggest that work, and working, may be considered without reference to the wider context of society, wherein management and organizations are embedded (Collins, 1998; Noon and Blyton, 1997; Clegg, 1993). Rejecting this form of analysis, Gray (1999) has argued that market institutions must be regarded as being embedded within a larger social context, such that changes in market regulation (notably the economic deregulation experienced in America and Britain) have consequences for those social institutions (the church family and community) which are required to facilitate, and to support market economies.

Acknowledging the importance of this contextual form of analysis, we will offer an analysis of the downsizing of America which seeks to embed the American experience of downsizing within an account of American institutions and systems of regulation.

### *The Silent Depression*

In contrast to the tendency towards acontextualism, evident in management studies, Peterson (1995), in his discussion of America's 'Silent
Depression', is keen to ground his analysis of the American economy
within a discussion of the lives and dreams of ordinary citizens. Reflecting
upon economic change, Peterson argues that America's recent experimentation with downsizing is but one symptom of a longer-term,
twenty-five year decline, which has afflicted the American economy and
its wider society.

Addressing his comments at fellow members of the middle class, Peterson
begins his discussion of economic and organizational change in America,
with the following statement:

> If you feel you are making and spending more money than you did
> ten or twenty years ago but are losing ground, if it appears that your
> children will do less well than you have done, if your job is less secure
> than it used to be, you are not alone. Millions of other Americans are
> equally perplexed. Many millions are angry to find that they have to
> run faster to stay in the same place.
>
> (Peterson, 1995, p. 9)

At the root of this instability and change, Peterson argues, is a decline,
which has forced a twenty-five year squeeze on the American middle class.
Indeed, Peterson argues that over the last quarter century, America's socio-
economic compromise, which traded effort and loyalty for prosperity,
security, and a career management system, facilitated by internal labour
markets (Cappelli, 1995), has been squeezed, diminished and downgraded.
Thus, he argues that the tri-partite contract between American workers,
their government, and their corporations has been breached.

The tendency to downsize organizations evident in the US economy
since the early 1980s (Cappelli *et al.*, 1997) represents, perhaps, the clearest
and deepest rupture in this historic compromise.

## Downsizing in the US

Reporting on a range of surveys (those of Harris and Associates, 1991;
Wyatt, 1993; American Management Association, 1994), Cappelli and his
co-authors observe that downsizing has been practised as a strategy of
reorganization by a huge range of organizations. Noting that a variety of
blue-chip organizations – 'IBM, Xerox, Procter & Gamble, Kodak and
Citicorp' (Cappelli *et al.*, 1997, p. 66) as well as 'Du Pont, McDonnell
Douglas, Pratt & Whitney, Sears . . . Grumman, Boeing, General Motors,
American Airlines, American Express, ITT . . . and many more' (Peterson,
1995, p. 23) – have embarked upon, and in some cases, intend to continue

to downsize their organizations, Cappelli *et al.* note that: 'Everyone, worker and manager alike, appears vulnerable to the risk of downsizing, regardless of industrial sector or the size of the company' (Cappelli *et al.*, 1997, p. 66).

However, while the analyses of Peterson and Cappelli *et al.* capture the extent to which large-scale American corporations have practised downsizing, their listings seem just a little strange. In their inventory of blue-chip organizations who have embraced downsizing as a strategy for large-scale organizational restructuring, neither Cappelli *et al.* (1997), nor Peterson (1995) make mention of General Electric. This is a curiosity since as Chik Collins notes:

> General Electric is credited with being the first of the western multinationals to see the need for a radical restructuring of their operation during the 1980s in order to meet the threat of international competition and retain a leading position in the developing global marketplace. Under the stewardship of Jack Welch a massive restructuring operation was undertaken.
>
> (C. Collins, 1999, p. 73)

Having recognized the role of (Neutron)[1] Jack Welch, and the influence of General Electric on America's downsizing endeavours, let us turn to look, more closely, at the meaning and effect of downsizing.

In an attempt to offer a framework designed to allow us to capture the scale and impact of this form of organizational restructuring, Cappelli and his co-authors distinguish between the 'depth' and 'breadth' of downsizing. Let us look, first, at the depth of downsizing in the US.

### The Depth of Downsizing

When we consider the 'depth' of downsizing, we offer an estimate of the number, the head-count, of workers affected by restructuring. In America, with its free-market policies (Gray, 1999; Sennett, 1998) and its 'employment at will' doctrine, which, under common law, and in the absence of special circumstances, allows management to dismiss employees at any time, and without notice (Sweet, 1985), downsizing has bitten deeply.

Cappelli *et al.* note (1997) that during the 1980s, approximately one in every five American workers suffered a permanent separation from their employer. In this, Cappelli and his co-authors alert us to a key change in the management of US industry. Cappelli and his co-authors remind us that, whereas American managers have, by tradition, made extensive use of temporary lay-offs to accommodate fluctuations in demand (see Hamper, 1992, for a first-hand account), a range of surveys undertaken in the 1990s highlight a greater tendency towards permanent job-cutting in America.

Sweet (1985), for example, notes that while close to 1.3 million American workers endured a separation from work in 1982, only 1 million of these workers could hold out much hope of being recalled to work by their employer. Using more up-to-date figures *The Economist* (30/01/99) notes that, thanks to a merger boom in 1998 – the ten largest mergers in US history took place in this year – 677,795 American employees lost their jobs in 1998.

In America, separation and displacement from employment has, in the post-World War II era, been a predominantly blue-collar experience. Thus, clerical and professional workers have not tended to be subject to lay-offs, nor have they been asked to endure the other, palliative approaches geared to addressing fluctuations in demand, such as short-time working. An analysis of the 'breadth' of downsizing in America, however, suggests that white-collar employees may no longer enjoy their traditional safeguards and protections from economic fluctuation.

## The Breadth of Downsizing

Calculations of the breadth of downsizing represent an attempt to gauge which types of industry, and which types of employee, have been subject to downsizing initiatives. Writing in 1985, Sweet observed that of the nearly 1.3 million instances of separation and displacement reported in America in 1982, 68.5 per cent occurred in the manufacturing sector. Looking a little more closely at these figures, Sweet reports that almost one-third (32.3 per cent) of these, permanent and temporary, lay-offs took place in the transportation industry and may have contributed to a severe decline in the US auto-industry (see Iacocca, 1986). Indeed, reflecting upon the complex and inter-connected nature of modern economies, Sweet (1985) notes that the severity of the decline in the auto-industry led to knock-on problems in the iron and steel industries such that the primary metal industry, alone, accounted for more than 10 per cent of the lay-offs in that year.

In the years following the early 1980s, however, the experience of permanent lay-offs in the US has spread out from the manufacturing sector to impact more upon employment in the service and retail trade sectors. Cappelli and his co-authors do point out, however, that: 'even in the face of this broadening, jobs displacement [downsizing remains] disproportionately concentrated in manufacturing and goods-producing industries' (Cappelli *et al.*, 1997, p. 68). Yet, while noting this sectoral stability/continuity in the experience of downsizing, Cappelli and his co-authors report another aspect of the broadening of downsizing. Thus the work of Cappelli *et al.* highlights the fact that the spread of downsizing is not confined to a move from manufacturing to the retail and service sectors. Indeed the sectoral figures for downsizing portray a false stability in the experience of large-scale organizational restructuring, since during the

1980s downsizing in America has moved along the occupational axis. Quite unlike earlier eras, therefore, downsizing in America, today, is no longer a predominantly blue-collar phenomenon. Now, large-scale restructuring initiatives finger white as well as blue collars.

The American Management Association (AMA, 1994), for example, notes that while salaried employees held 40 per cent of all jobs in America in the year 1993–1994, salaried employees had held more than 62 per cent of all jobs eliminated in that year. Indeed, in contrast to the historical experience of lay-offs in the US as a phenomenon of hourly paid, blue-collar work, contemporary statistical analysis reveals that, by the middle 1980s, downsizing had become sufficiently broadly based to make managers more likely to lose their jobs than their blue-collar subordinates (Cappelli *et al.*, 1997).

For managerialist analyses (the form of analysis performed and proffered by management's 'gurus') downsizing policies represent an end-point, if not an end of management policy (C. Collins, 1999; Slater, 1998). Yet, where one story ends, another (or perhaps that should be another's) begins.

In the following section, therefore, we will pick up the trail of down-sizing at the very point where managerialist forms of analysis lose their way. Thus, we will attempt to examine the impacts and effects of down-sizing, not on the corporation, but upon the wider society which supports and reflects economic activity. Thus, despite the normal focus upon downsizing as a corporate/business matter, we will analyse the impact of large-scale corporate restructuring upon individuals, families and communities in America. Later, in a discussion of 'survivor syndrome' (Sennett, 1998; Gray, 1999; Brockner, 1992; Baruch and Hind, 1997) we will turn to look, critically, at some of the unanticipated, and unintended, organizational consequences of downsizing. For the moment, however, we will attempt a more social analysis of the impacts of downsizing.

## The Wake of Downsizing

As Gray's (1999) discussion of the social underpinnings of the market economy reminds us, any analysis of the social impacts of downsizing in America must be firmly rooted in an understanding that downsizing occurs, takes on meaning and exercises its effect (and affects) within a particular socio-economic context. Thus, where we argue that, in America, downsizing tends to lead to a decline in living standards, and to a problematic, and costly, period of adjustment, it must be borne in mind that this outcome is not natural, nor necessarily universal. Instead, we must note that this outcome, in America, is the result of a particular system of tax and benefits, which tends to deny support to those who have been downsized, until their meagre resources decline sufficiently for them to be reclassified as unemployed and suffering hardship (Sweet, 1985; see also

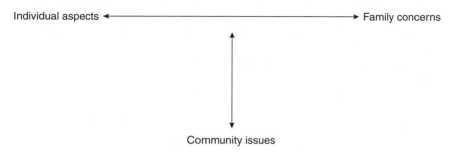

*Figure 9.1* Analysing the outcomes and impacts of downsizing

*The Economist*, 20/03/99, for an account of America's recent attempts to reform welfare expenditure).

To facilitate our analysis of those things which follow in the wake of downsizing, we will employ a framework designed to tease out the implications of downsizing for the social fabric of the US. Accordingly, we will examine the consequences of downsizing for individuals, for families, and for communities more generally, given America's free-market, individualistic politico-economic policies (Gray, 1999; Sennett, 1998; Peterson, 1995). These three aspects of our analysis are represented in Figure 9.1.

### 'Individual' Impacts

The experience of downsizing, indeed the general experience of widespread corporate reorganization in America, even where this does not lead immediately to downsizing, carries with it a number of implications for individuals. These changes do not, of course, strike all individuals equally. In comparison to other groupings, for example, certain groups of employees seem to suffer disproportionately the consequences of large-scale organizational restructuring initiatives. In this regard it is worth observing that older, male, blue-collar and black workers seem to recover poorly from downsizing. Nonetheless, it makes sense, I believe, to highlight individual outcomes, in relation to the problems which downsizing causes for US families, and for the communities these families live in.

At the individual level, it is worth highlighting a few issues associated with downsizing in America. The first issue, we will address, briefly, relates to the concepts of age and value-added at work.

### Prime Age Workers

Aside from the loss of income and the consequent hardship associated with downsizing, which we have alluded to already, it is also worth observing that, in America, the 'prime age' of employees (that age at which employees are said to offer the greatest 'added value' to their organizations) is being redefined. In spite of the fact that, on average, the life-span of Americans is increasing, the actual working lifetime of individuals is being redefined to reflect a smaller section of this, increasing, life-span. Thus, we should note that in spite of the fact that Americans, on average, may expect to live into their seventh decade, and can expect to continue to play an active role in civil society in their advanced years (Freedland, 1998; O'Rourke, 1998), the span of their, useful, working lives is being redefined to refer to the thirty years of life between the ages of twenty-four and fifty-four, as employers choose to downsize older workers, and as commentators choose to celebrate this 'ageism' (see Newman, 1988).

Reflecting this change in the 'prime age' calculation of employees, Sennett (1998) notes that, in spite of an ageing population base, the number of men aged between fifty-five and sixty-four declined from 80 per cent of the total number of US employees in 1970, to represent only 65 per cent of US employees in 1990.

## The End of the Career

If our analysis of 'prime-age' workers is correct, many employees will be 'washed up', at the latest, by their early fifties. Yet, the changes associated with downsizing, at the individual level, do not only limit US expectations of continuing employment, they also work to reduce career prospects. Indeed, Sennett (1998) argues that the concept of the career – a model of working life and work expectations, where employees could look forward to periodic (and meritocratic?) advance within an internal labour market (Cappelli, 1995) – is under threat. Cappelli (1995) has noted, for example, how the tendency towards 'broadbanding' in America (the reduction in job titles and gradings associated with the restructuring of American work organizations as flexible, multi-skilled, team structures) is tending to: 'break down traditional job and promotion ladders where unskilled jobs were at the bottom, semi-skilled positions in the middle and supervisory jobs at the top' Cappelli, 1995, p. 575). This, we are told, should be a cause for concern at a social level, and at an economic-organizational level, because in this 'new' system (actually Cappelli suggests it is, in reality, a return to an older system) where work is externalized, or reallocated within team structures, 'it is not obvious how new workers will learn the work-based skills needed to get into these teams' (Cappelli, 1995, p. 595).

Taken together, changes to the management and structuring of employment suggest that 'insiders' (those who have secured employment within a large firm) may be denied access to a traditional career and promotion ladder, while an enlarging body of 'outsiders' may be denied access to secure, full-time employment altogether as they are pushed out to become contingent or 'externalized' workers.

## The 'Externalization' of Work

As part of a programme designed to 'externalize' employment, many large organizations in America have taken advantage of changing business conditions to increase their use of part-time, temporary and agency employees. Cappelli and his co-authors (Cappelli *et al.*, 1997) note that in America, no reliable measure of contingent employment is available, since government statistics are inadequate for the task of tracing contingent employment in all its many forms. Nonetheless, they argue that indicative data suggests that contingent employment in 1988 amounted to some 25 to 30 per cent of the civilian labour force (Belous, 1989).

Often, when figures such as these are uncovered, this acts as a cue for some commentator to suggest that such forms of temporary and contingent working are representative of changing employee preferences, that people choose to work part-time. Callaghan and Hartmann (1991), however, have argued that 90 per cent of the growth in part-time working, which they measured over the period 1970–1990 was involuntary and reflected employer, rather than employee, preferences for contingent and externalized forms of labour. Given the enlargement of contingent and 'externalized' forms of employment, it should not really be a surprise to find that, in America, the largest employer is not General Motors, nor Ford, nor Boeing. In fact, the Manpower Temporary Help Agency with in excess of 600,000 employees on its books is the largest 'employer' in America (Cappelli *et al.*, 1997).

This growth in contingent and externalized forms of employment, as we shall see, has implications for the rights which US employees enjoy at work.

## Rights at Work

In comparison to their European cousins, American workers enjoy little statutory protection while at work. Thus, while British employees are protected (subject to a qualification period) by statute from 'unfair dismissal' (Wedderburn, 1986), American employees 'can be dismissed at any time under the doctrine of "employment at will" without reason or notice' (Sweet, 1985, p. 13). This, of course, does not mean that US employees enjoy no forms of protection at work. Sweet (1985), for example, draws our attention to the attempts made by federal, and by state legislatures, to limit managerial prerogative particularly in regard to plant closure. However, it is worth observing that this federal and state legislation often does little to curtail management prerogative. For example, in the case of plant closure, the legislation enacted in the US seeks only to increase the notice period which employers are required to give, and so does little to bolster employee rights or management accountability. Furthermore, and with the issues of employee protection and management accountability in mind, it is worth pointing out that state level legislation on plant closure lacks stringency, is loosely enforced, and carries few real penalties for the defaulting employer party.

Fortunately (given the normally absent, and where present, the toothless nature of statutory protection), American workers have enjoyed more success in building certain forms of employment protection into their contracts by collective means. Thus, like their British cousins, American workers have had some success in curtailing managerial prerogative through the institutions of collective bargaining. Through the institutions and processes of collective bargaining, for example, a significant minority of American employees have been able to secure rights to severance payments as a compensation for lay-offs. In addition trade unionists have been able to secure collective agreements which commit managers to an open and equitable system of lay-off and recall, built upon 'seniority'.

Yet, in the context of the growth of contingent and 'externalized' labour, it is important to note that these collective agreements protect only 'insiders' and offer no protection to 'outsiders'. In this regard, Cappelli (1995) notes that, in spite of union agreements, and in spite of statutory measures designed to outlaw discrimination, organizations can avoid measures designed to protect employees by the simple expedient of making use of agency workers. As Cappelli notes: 'Dismissing an unsatisfactory worker, *for whatever reason*, is now as simple as calling up the agency and asking for a replacement' (Cappelli, 1995, p. 573, emphasis added). Summarizing this section on the 'individual' impacts of downsizing, it is worth observing that, in America today, US workers often enjoy little employment security. They are likely to be deemed surplus to organizational requirements at a comparatively young age. They are, in comparison to their parents' generation, less likely to enjoy a stable career. Indeed, thanks to the growing use of contingent and 'external' employment, American workers may find that, perhaps, like their grand-parents and their great grand-parents, they must settle for *a job*, since, increasingly they are being denied access to a career.

While retained in their job, it is also worth pointing out that many Americans may find themselves beyond the reach of both collective and statutory systems of protection. All of which would be bad enough, were it not for the fact that, within this new system of working, employees are expected to work harder, or at least for longer (*The Economist*, 30/01/99; *The Financial Times*, 18/01/95). Peterson (1995), for example, argues that compared to 1969, employees in 1989 had increased the time they spend at work by 8 per cent – the equivalent of working an extra month each year! Similarly, *The Financial Times* (18/01/95) reports that, as compared to 1975, Americans in 1995 worked, on average 164 more hours.

Let us examine the impact of these changes on the home and family life of these individuals.

## Family and Domestic Impacts

It should be obvious that when individuals lose their employment their level of income, and so, their standard of living tends to decline. What is less apparent, at first glance, however, is what the wider ramifications of such individual changes in employment and income *might* be for the domestic unit.

## Mobility in America

American citizens are geographically mobile; much more mobile than Britain's subjects, for example. This mobility is due, at least in part, to the willingness of American managers to relocate production facilities from the northern US to the cheaper southern US, where unions exert no mediating effects on managerial prerogative. Gray (1999), for example, notes that thanks to America's 'free' labour markets, US workers have been forced to become geographically mobile to maintain their employment. Indeed Gray notes that, compared to British workers, US workers are twenty-five times more likely to move to a new region in pursuit of employment. Reflecting on this, Michael Moore (1997) argues that downsizing should be considered as a form of social terrorism, because it destroys communities, and because it has forced millions of Americans to become modern-day 'Okies' (after the migrant labourers of the US depression in the 1920s: see Steinbeck, 1939, 1988).

Noting that Timothy McVeigh used a Ryder Truck (a self-drive, hire van) to deliver his terror bomb to Oklahoma City, Moore (1997) argues that the moving van has become a symbol of terrorism, since it has become the key means of transport, both for America's disaffected sociopaths, and for its increasingly itinerant workers. Arguing that Ryder trucks, whether filled with 'ammonium nitrate and fuel oil' (Moore, 1997, p. 15) or with 'the kids' bunk beds and the dining room set' (Moore, 1997, p. 15) have become a symbol for destruction and social dislocation in the 1990s he notes: '[The Ryder Truck], this symbol of . . . downsized lives, has become a means to an end' (Moore, 1997, p. 15). This end, as Moore sees it, is the destruction of a way of life which was built around stable and continuous employment, and the prospect of regular career progression. Its consequences, he notes, include not only the end of a way of life, but also, and too often, the destruction of family and community life itself. Often, he suggests (and as we shall see) this destruction occurs by means far less humane than the sudden detonation of explosives.

## Deregulation, Downsizing and Abuse

Loss of employment brings with it a range of economic and social penalties. For men, the loss of employment often amounts to a loss of social identity (Noon and Blyton, 1997). It should not be surprising, therefore, to find that downsizing seems to have a negative effect upon domestic harmony. Indeed, Peterson (1995) notes that US research suggests that for every 1 per cent increase in the unemployment rate, divorce rates jump by 10,000. Similarly, Peterson, while conceding that statistics on domestic matters are scanty, and often unreliable, argues that there is evidence to suggest that both spouse abuse and child abuse increase during periods of economic difficulty.

While all forms of abuse are to be deplored because they are terrible and frightening, it is worth pointing out that spouse and child abuse are, surely, more difficult to manage, and to control, in an economic system which destroys community-based systems of support, or which relocates sons and daughters thousands of miles from their (failing) communities.

Let us turn from a concentration on domestic matters, in isolation, to examine the impacts of downsizing on the community.

## Community Impacts

Widening the scope of our analysis to embed domestic units within a larger social and community framework, it becomes more and more difficult to find the economic and social benefits of downsizing which were once vaunted by America's business 'gurus' (see C. Collins, 1999).

Focusing his analysis at the level of the community, Sennett (1998) argues that the downsizing of America has damaged the fabric of community life as it has weakened the bonds which tie people together. Thus, Sennett (1998) and Gray (1999) argue that the downsizing of America since it has been set within a larger attempt to deregulate the economy and to deregulate labour markets, has tended to promote a number of important, yet deleterious, community outcomes. These social impacts Gray (1999) argues have economic consequences since, he tells us, they undermine the supports necessary for the functioning of a market economy.

## Inequality in America

Since the 1970s, and especially since the 1980s, when large-scale corporate restructuring, and the economics of the free market became the vogue, inequality has increased in America. For example, Gray (1999) notes that the real earnings of 80 per cent of rank-and-file working Americans fell by 18 per cent between 1973 and 1995. Yet, he notes, that while the rank-and-file suffered between 1973 and 1995, the earnings of American chief executives, thanks, in part to their share options schemes rose, in real terms, by 19 per cent. However, this is not the end of the story. Gray argues that when we factor in changes in the US taxation system, the earnings and wealth disparity becomes more pronounced.

Thanks to taxation changes and tax breaks, Gray tells us, the real earnings of American Chief Executives actually rose, not by 19 per cent, but by one-third, during the period 1973 to 1995. Putting a little more detail on these figures, Gray observes that American chief executives now earn, on average, 150 times the average worker's wage (Moore, 1997, estimates this at 212 times). This disparity of earnings suggests that American CEOs earn, by any definition of the term, fantastic sums. However, we should note this earnings disparity has widened, not just because 'fat cats' have awarded themselves huge pay rises and share options within a 'supportive' taxation regime. Instead, it is important to note that, in comparison to the poorer members of American society, the rich have become richer because those at the bottom of the pile have suffered a significant decline in their income. So, while CEOs have become rich on tax breaks, and on the increasing value of their share options (which in many ways might be considered the profits of downsizing, since share valuations often rocket on news of plans for downsizing), Peterson (1995) reminds us that in 1990, 14.4 million workers in America were in full-time employment, yet had earnings below the poverty threshold.

Adding these figures for the working poor, to a calculation of the level of unemployment in the US, Peterson suggests that in 1990, 45.9 million (or 18.5 per cent of the population) had income levels below the poverty threshold. Peterson reminds us, however, (see also Moore, 1997) that such calculations of averages (shocking as they are) disguise the poverty and exclusion suffered disproportionately by some regions and by some social groupings. Thus Peterson observes that American blacks (constituting close to 30 per cent of Americans in poverty) suffer disproportionately from unemployment and under-employment. Likewise Peterson observes that Negro infants, born to the unemployed and under-employed, have a mortality rate of almost 18 per thousand births. This is double the rate suffered by white Americans, and is higher than the infant mortality rate in Malaysia! Such high rates of poverty and social exclusion, when allied to tensions and breakdown in family life, have tended to lead to crime in America (and have led American policy-makers, via a range of moral panics and outrages to imprison vast swathes of the American adult population).

### The Incarceration of America

In its attempts to manage a free-market economic system where employment is hard to secure, and, often, poorly rewarded, America has become a carcereal community. Gray (1999) notes that by 1997 one in every 50 adult Americans was a prisoner – this compares with one in 193 in 1994. Reflecting, and endorsing this analysis *The Economist* (20/03/99) reports that by June 1998, the American prison population numbered 1.8 million. This, they inform us was 4.4 per cent more than in June 1997. However, in fairness, we should acknowledge that this figure does represent a dip in the trend, since the average growth rate of the US prison population has been running at 6.2 per cent per annum since 1990!

Taking the whole US population as its base figure (i.e. the figure including groups we might normally exclude, such as children) *The Economist* notes that in 1998 one in every 150 American residents was behind bars. This is an incarceration rate, we are told, of 668 per 100,000 residents. This is a rate of imprisonment, which runs at five to ten times European rates of incarceration, six times Canada's rate, and nearly twenty times that of Japan. As if all this were not bad enough, Gray notes that around one in every twenty Americans (5 per cent of the population) enjoys their liberty thanks only to a parole or probation order.

Such averages, of course, tend to disguise the true impact of these changes. In an attempt to show the extremes which averaging obscures, Gray uncovers (see also *The Economist*, 20/03/99) a divided, fragmented and deeply racist society. A society which includes: 'Some 28 million Americans (more than 10% of the population who) now live in privately guarded buildings or housing developments' (Gray, 1999, p. 116). And excludes whole groups and/or whole districts such as the more than '40% of all Black males between eighteen and thirty-five years of age living in the district of Columbia (who are) in prison, on probation, on parole awaiting trial, or on the run' (Gray, 1999, p. 117).

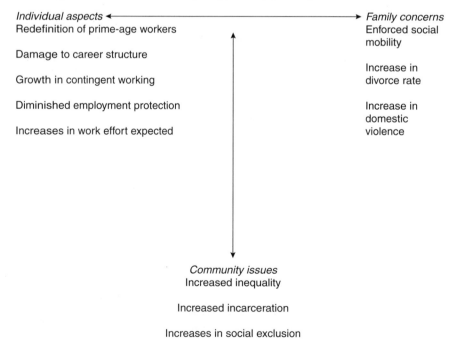

*Figure 9.2* Analysing the outcomes and impacts of downsizing in the US

Unlike the 'guru' analysis of downsizing which tends to 'tail-off' at the moment of downsizing, therefore, our attempt to forge linkages between the public and private affects of large-scale organizational restructuring suggests that recent changes in the management of the US economy, and in the management of US organizations must be viewed as having serious consequences for American workers, for American families, and for the fabric of American society more generally.

Figure 9.2 offers a summary of our discussion of the downsizing of the US as a prelude to our discussion of the British experience.

## Downsizing in Britain

In comparison to the accounts of American downsizing, which document well the scope of restructuring initiatives, their impact upon profitability, and on employee morale, British surveys of redundancy appear somewhat piecemeal. Recognizing this deficiency in the British accounts of down-sizing, we will, nonetheless, attempt to sketch the UK experience of downsizing. Thus, in keeping with our analysis of downsizing in America, we will analyse the impact of downsizing on British individuals, their fami-lies, and their communities, before moving on to look critically at management academia and its response to downsizing.

Before we attempt this, however, we must, in keeping with our analysis of American society, and in keeping with our discussion of Gray's (1999) embedded view of the economy, make some attempt to locate downsizing in a UK context. In this regard, it is worth drawing attention to the polit-ical and economic changes in Britain, which form the backdrop to the changing UK experience of large-scale organizational restructuring.

In common with our analysis of America, therefore, it is worth drawing attention to the fact that the downsizing of Britain has occurred during a period in which a range of economic reforms was introduced in an attempt to deregulate the economy. These changes have included a variety of industrial and statutory reforms (MacInnes, 1988; Millward, 1994; Blyton and Turnbull, 1994) and a series of reforms designed to alter, quite funda-mentally, the operation of the tax and benefit system in Britain (Walker and Walker, 1997).

Reflecting upon the changes in this tax and benefit system, Walker and Walker (1997) argue that the policies adopted by Britain's Conservative administrations during the 1980s and 1990s were shaped by three key beliefs:

1   That welfare payments debilitate recipients economically and morally.
2   That any form of non-governmental welfare assistance is preferable to state welfare provision.
3   That economic trickledown – a term used to describe an assumed process whereby spending by the wealthy, over time, works an effect

among the poor, by calling them into employment – should be the preferred basis for welfare reform.

As we analyse redundancy and downsizing in Britain, therefore, we should keep in mind the larger social and economic system which shapes and conditions the experience of downsizing for Britain's workers, and for Britain's communities.

## Redundancy and Decline

In Britain, rates of redundancy have, typically, been viewed as an indicator of recession. Writing in the mid-1980s, for example, Gordon introduced his discussion of redundancy in the UK by noting that: 'One of the clearest indictors of the recession in the United Kingdom has been the massive increase in redundancies that has occurred since the late 1970s' (Gordon, 1984 p. 1). For Gordon, therefore, redundancy – a special form of dismissal associated with business closure, with reductions in product demand, or with company relocation – is *prima facie* evidence of business failure and of an ailing economy. The new, and euphemistic term, downsizing, however, carries with it no such connotations in the 1990s. Indeed, we should note that downsizing in America is associated with both boom periods, and with periods of stagnation and decline. Thus Cappelli *et al.* 1997) note that, while America emerged from recession in 1993, it did not throw off its attachment to downsizing. They observe that survey data suggested: 'no letup in the pace of scale of downsizing, even in the midst of the strong national economic growth that occurred in 1993 and 1994' (Cappelli *et al.*, 1997, p. 68). Indeed Cappelli and his co-authors add: 'The percentage of companies planning to downsize actually rose slightly in 1994' (Cappelli *et al.*, 1997, p. 68). As we reflect upon the US experience of downsizing. As we reflect upon the costs downsizing imposes on the community as a whole, and as we work to uncover the UK experience of downsizing, it is worth reminding ourselves of this departure. From its origins as a symptom of economic crisis, therefore, large-scale organizational restructuring, in the guise of downsizing has been reinvented as part of the harvest of economic success.

## Redundancy Statistics in Britain

Reflecting the statutes which define and circumscribe 'redundancy' in Britain, the Department of Employment (now the Employment Department) has collected three sets of redundancy statistics (Gordon, 1994). These figures offer us calculations of:

- advance notification of redundancies
- redundancies confirmed as due to occur
- statutory redundancy payments.

None of these statistics, however, yields a fully comprehensive and accurate account of redundancy in Britain. For example, any calculation of the extent of redundancy based solely upon figures for 'advance notification' might tend to overstate the extent of redundancy dismissals, since ailing organizations sometimes manage to make adjustments in their operations which allow them to avoid a redundancy situation, or to make fewer workers redundant than had received notification. On the other hand, a calculation of the extent of redundancy in Britain based solely upon statistics concerning statutory redundancy payments would have a tendency to under-estimate redundancy, since this set of figures will not count those who have been made redundant, yet fail to qualify for statutory payments – perhaps because they have not been in-post for the necessary period of time.

In an attempt to overcome these statistical problems and to develop a more comprehensive account of redundancy in Britain, the *Labour Force Survey*, a survey based on UK households, has made attempts to analyse redundancy and, since 1989, 'has been the *principal source of statistics on redundancy*' (Casey, 1995, p. 1, original emphasis). Let us use these figures to examine the depth and breadth of downsizing/redundancy in Britain.

### The Depth of Downsizing

In spite of differences in data collection, and in spite of (declining) differences (see Gray, 1999) in the context and operation of labour markets in Britain and America, the UK *Labour Force Survey* figures for redundancy display similarities to those for the US. Field (1997; see also Cockerham, 1994), writing in *The Employment Gazette*, notes that the *Labour Force Surveys* show that redundancy rates in Britain (post-1989) peaked at 391,000 in 1991, declined to 324,000 and to 262,000 in the years 1992 and 1993, respectively, before settling to a more stable level at around 200,000 redundancies per annum in the years 1994, 1995 and 1996.

Like the American surveys, the UK figures also suggest an increase in the breadth of downsizing.

### The Breadth of Downsizing

In common with the US statistical surveys discussed earlier, the British figures for downsizing also show redundancy moving from the manufacturing sector to the service sector and, in common with US surveys, show an increase in the 'breadth' of downsizing, as redundancy has moved along the occupational axis. Thus Field (1997) notes that while we may be inclined to think of redundancy as a phenomenon of the manufacturing sector, it was, in fact, the 'services sector' which accounted for the majority of redundancies in 1995 and 1996 – 63 per cent in 1995 and 53 per cent in 1996.

Again, in common with the US experience, Field notes that during the 1990s, UK white-collar employees have become more prone to redundancy. Indeed, Field shows that clerical and secretarial employees, who accounted for 16 per cent of all redundancies, were the group most prone to downsizing, in Britain, during 1996. In suffering this relatively high rate of redundancy, however, clerical and secretarial employees are not, entirely, atypical. Indeed a range of other groups, traditionally regarded as being more insulated from the vagaries of the market have not been so far behind this figure. In this regard, it is worth noting that 'managers and administrators', as a group, accounted for 11 per cent of all redundancies in 1992, 9 per cent of redundancies in 1993, 15 per cent in the years 1994 and 1995 and 13 per cent of redundancies in 1996. However, Field does concede that those displaced from the service sector tended to recover more quickly from downsizing than those displaced from the manufacturing sector, who often had more trouble securing re-employment.

In the section that follows, we will attempt to pursue the outcomes, and the aftermath, of this deep and broad experience of redundancy in Britain. In keeping with our analysis of the US, we will analyse the impact of downsizing upon individuals, upon families and upon the community more generally.

### *'Individual' Impacts*

At the individual level, it is worth highlighting a few issues associated with redundancy in Britain. Thus, it is worth observing that, in Britain, the 'prime age' of employees (that age at which employees are said to offer their employing organizations the greatest 'value-added') is being redefined via downsizing. With this redefinition of 'prime age' workers in mind, it is worth pointing out that Field (1997) notes two groups of employees who seem particularly prone to redundancy in Britain; those aged 16–24 (one in five of those made redundant in 1996) and those aged over 50 (one in four of those made redundant in 1996).

However, perhaps a more significant indicator of the recalculation of prime working age relates not so much to the willingness of employees to make the over-50s redundant, as to the general unwillingness of employers to (re)hire these 'older' workers. As Field notes:

> The prospects of finding employment after redundancy are related to age – in spring 1996 26 per cent of those over 50 who were made redundant had found work when interviewed, but for the rest of the workforce the proportion was 39 per cent. Of those made redundant who were re-employed, 18 per cent were aged 50 or over, but of those who had not found a job 28 per cent were in this age group.
>
> (Field, 1997, pp. 136–137)

This willingness of employers to dispense with the services of workers aged over 50, and the mirror-like unwillingness of employers to (re)hire workers aged over 50 suggests that, as in America, British managers have been redefining their definition of 'prime age' workers.

Yet, this discussion of the depth and breadth of downsizing, and of the redefinition of prime age working, does not exhaust our catalogue of individual impacts. Along with these sectoral and age-related changes in the UK experience of redundancy, we should also highlight a raft of labour market changes. Notably, there has been a growth in part-time and temporary employment in Britain.

## Contingent Employment

The growth in contingent, and part-time, employment in Britain has affected both male and female employees. However, the growth in these forms of employment has been most marked for male workers. Sly *et al.* (1997) note that part-time employment in Britain has grown from a level of just over 4.6 million workers in 1986 to reach close to 5.9 million workers in 1996. Likewise Sly *et al.* note that temporary employment has grown from just over one million in 1986 to reach close to 1.5 million by 1996. However, Sly and her co-authors point out that while female part-time employment has grown relatively slowly from a high base figure (rising from 3.8 million in 1986 to almost 4.4 million in 1996), male part-time employment has more than doubled – rising from 343,000 in 1986 to 788,000 in 1996. Likewise, the figures offered by Sly *et al.* also show that while female, temporary employment rose from 666,000 in 1986 to 819,000 in 1996, male temporary employment also rose by a proportionately greater amount – from 388,000 in 1986 to 675,000 in 1996.

While Sly and her co-authors suggest that, for women at least, this growth in part-time and temporary employment may reflect employee preferences for this form of employment, it is less clear that men work part-time, or on temporary contracts, on a voluntary basis. Thus, the analysis offered by Sly and her co-workers suggests that male, contingent, employment might be better regarded as a form of involuntary under-employment.

Yet, in spite of these changes; in spite of the decline of the traditional, full-time contract; in spite of growing levels of under-employment, employees holding full-time posts seem to be expected to work harder, and to work far longer. As Seaton, writing for *The Independent* (10/12/95) notes: 'Restructuring, downsizing, de-layering: it's all taking its toll. Job insecurity is stressful in itself, but the knock-on effect is that people are working longer and longer hours in an attempt to prove how indispensable they are' (*The Independent*, 10/12/95).

This is a point echoed by Tooher, again writing for *The Independent* (16/09/96; see also *The Financial Times*, 18/01/95) who observes that a survey of managers revealed that they, just like their subordinates, felt stressed and demoralized because of downsizing. Thus Tooher notes that 60 per cent of the respondents to an Institute of Management Survey claimed that they *always* work more than their contracted hours, while 14 per cent claimed *always* to work at weekends. Perhaps, unsurprisingly, home and family life in Britain has endured some degree of restructuring in response to these changes.

## Downsizing and Domestic Life

It would, of course, be wrong to say that recent changes at work or that recent changes in the labour market cause a decline in domestic harmony. This would, I think, exaggerate the extent and the character of domestic bliss in earlier eras and, furthermore, would misrepresent an association between factors, as a causal relationship. However, since the 'gurus' of management have, for the most part, remained silent on the downside of downsizing, and since the 'gurus' often ignore social life and the world outwith work, it is worth pointing out a few associations between large-scale economic restructuring and the changing character of family life in Britain. Thus while the 'gurus' bleat that there are imperatives for downsizing, such that managers must lead the processes of downsizing within the organizations, we have a right to speak out, and have a duty to speak up, about the ramifications of such changes both within, and outwith, the workplace.

Reflecting upon the changing structure of the British economy, and upon the attempts of a series of Conservative administrations to deregulate industries and labour markets, Gray (1999) notes that this form of free-market, or *laissez-faire* economics, contains the seeds of its own destruction. Gray argues that markets build from, and depend upon, social institutions in order to maintain their vitality and their viability. Indeed, he argues that the family should be regarded as a key social and economic institution, since it both disciplines and supports workers, making them available for and amenable to systems of organizational discipline.

However, Gray argues that Britain's economic reforms have undermined the social institutions and the social networks vital to the functioning of the market economy. Thus Gray contends that Britain's recent economic reforms have undermined and have disabled the social institutions which make workers available for, and amenable to, systems of work organization. Discussing marriage and the family, Gray notes that the proportion of women aged 18–49 who were married fell from 74 per cent in 1979 to 61 per cent in 1990. While part of this change may be explained by a growth in co-habitation – (Gray seems to 'tut-tut' over a doubling in the rate of co-habitation from 11 per cent to 22 per cent in this period) – perhaps more significant within this discussion of the social underpinnings of the market economy is the marked increase in Britain's divorce rate.

Perhaps mindful of the fact that 'gurus' and policy-makers would disguise their complacency as a concern for statistical rigour, Gray offers us the following:

> By 1991 there was one divorce for every two marriages in Britain – the highest divorce rate of any country, and comparable only with that in the United States. Is it coincidental that no EU country apart from Britain has imposed American-style deregulation on its labour market? In those cities in which Thatcherite policies of labour market deregulation were most successful in lowering rates of unemployment, rates of divorce and family breakdown were correspondingly highest.
>
> (Gray, 1999, pp. 29–30)

What then of the community impacts of downsizing and deregulation? Let us widen our analysis of social institutions to embed the family impacts of downsizing within a larger socio-economic framework.

### Community Care?

Like America, Britain has become a carcereal society since the 1980s. Gray (1999) notes, for example, that between 1992 and 1995 Britain's prison population increased by one-third, to a level in excess of 50,000. Writing for *The Sunday Times* in 1998, Ungoed-Thomas (11/01/98) produces figures which suggest that Gray seriously under-estimates the size of Britain's penal population. Thus Ungoed-Thomas notes that 58,400 convicted criminals were imprisoned in Britain in 1993, with this figure rising to 79,100 by 1995.

While criminologists and social commentators are inclined to squabble over the root causes of crime – deprivation, prosperity, absence of deterrent mechanisms – the association seems clear. Crime in Britain has doubled since 1979. During a period in which individualism and entrepreneurship have been stressed (Keat and Abercrombie, 1991), it seems that key elements of the British population have, in a sense, made use of open windows of opportunity. Worryingly, however, these new entrepreneurs seem keen to adopt rather aggressive business tactics and strategies.

Thus while Britain has worked to effect *laissez-faire* economic policies, its rate of violent crime has increased, and has moved ahead of America's to reach a figure more than twice that of Austria's. Likewise, other indicators of crime and dysfunction have also increased in Britain during this period. Indeed, we should note that car crime in Britain is nearly twice the level experienced across the channel in France.

Within this experience of increasing crime and incarceration, indicators of social exclusion have also risen in Britain.

## Social Exclusion

Analysing social exclusion in Britain (a term used to describe situations where sections of the community find themselves excluded from the amenities, services and opportunities others take for granted) Gray (1999) notes that in 1994 close to 20 per cent of the households in Britain (excluding pensioner households) were entirely without employment. Indeed, in common with the US experience, Gray argues that increasing rates of income and wealth inequality, since the 1980s have seen a widening gap between 'haves' and 'have nots'.

Reflecting upon the experience of Britain's 'have nots', Walker and Walker (1997) note that in 1979, 5 million Britons (9 per cent of the population) had an income level below 50 per cent of the average income level, and so, were deemed to be 'in poverty'. By 1993–1994, however, the number of Britons living below this poverty line had jumped to 14 million. Walker and Walker remind us, and we would do well to note, that this figure amounts to 25 per cent of Britain's population living below the poverty line.

Investigating the lifestyles of Britain's 'haves', Leadbetter writing for *The Independent* on Sunday (03/11/96) notes that while the poorest 10 per cent of the population claimed 4.3 per cent of national income in 1979, by 1991 the share of this population had fallen to 2.9 per cent. Over this same period, however, he notes that the share of the richest 10 per cent of the population rose from 20.6 per cent to 26.1 per cent of national income. Reflecting a similar tale of growing inequality, Oppenheim (1997) notes that between 1979 and 1994, the poorest 10 per cent of Britain's population suffered a 13 per cent decline in income after housing costs were accounted for. However, Oppenheim notes that, based on a similar calculation, and thanks in part to the tax benefits associated with mortgage payments, the richest 10 per cent of Britain's population enjoyed a 65 per cent rise in income. Among OECD countries only New Zealand which itself had embarked upon an American-inspired programme of economic change and deregulation, suffered a greater rise in inequality during this period (Gray, 1999).

The foregoing analyses of Britain and America suggest, contrary to the 'guru' analysis, that large-scale corporate restructuring has damaged economic viability because it has served to undermine those family and community institutions which support the operation of both the economy and the polity. Thus, our embedded forms of analysis show the manner in which economic and political changes designed to regenerate economies in a 'virtuous circle' of change and development, have actually produced a 'vicious circle' of decline, decay and division. Taken as a whole, then, our analysis of downsizing has been designed to show that, in Britain and in America, policies designed to deregulate the economy, and its labour markets have facilitated management initiatives such as downsizing, which in contributing to increasing rates of inequality, dislocation and exclusion have damaged the vitality and viability of economic and social life.

What, then, has management academia done to intervene? What has management academia done to temper this? Did the academy fiddle whilst Rome burned?

## The Downsizing of Conscience?

Initially management academia and management's 'gurus' were up-beat about downsizing and about the prospects for corporate transformation via large-scale restructuring. Downsizing, it was argued, was a necessary part of the change required to transform organizations from moribund bureaucracies into fleet-of-foot, customer-focused enterprises (see C. Collins, 1999; Kanter, 1989; Peters and Waterman, 1982). However, as the depth and breadth of downsizing increased in America, commentators began to voice misgivings about the concept and practices of downsizing. By 1996, Roach, at one time a leading advocate of downsizing, was arguing that the practice of downsizing had gone too far (*The Financial Times*, 14/05/96; C. Collins, 1999). In a similar fashion Peters (1997), in his recent work, seems to recant his previous support for downsizing (see Peters and Waterman, 1982) when he protests, in his sub-title, that you 'can't shrink your way to greatness' (see chapter 5).

These revisionist accounts of downsizing offer us some food for thought. Indeed, within our larger discussion of euphemism, it should be interesting and illuminating to reflect upon the recent changes in the lexicon of organizational restructuring which have been facilitated by these revisions to the creed of downsizing.

Writing for *The Financial Times* (20/05/96; see also, C. Collins, 1999), Jackson notes that *The Wall Street Journal* has cast aspersions on the wisdom of downsizing. Thus *The Wall Street Journal* has suggested that open-ended organizational change initiatives which lead to large numbers of job losses should be renamed 'dumbsizing' in order to expose the limitations of downsizing as a force for positive change. In a similar, though perhaps less destructive fashion, other commentators have attempted to mount a (retreating) defence of downsizing. Thus St George, writing in *The Financial Times* (15/09/94) draws our attention to the computer industry term 'right-sizing' – the process of matching the solution to the task – and suggests that this term, and these practices, are preferable to downsizing (see also Ayto, 1999).

In the light of our earlier discussion of phrasing and euphemism, it is interesting to note the manner in which the advocates of organizational restructuring, sensitive to discomfiture and critique, have appropriated a new term, which has been designed to maintain the legitimacy of their activities. Thus, the standard-bearers of restructuring now argue that 'right-sizing' should be management's preferred concept and practice for large scale organizational restructuring. Indeed, they now argue that downsizing was flawed, in operation, because it was not executed strategically. Unlike the 'slash and burn' of downsizing (*The Financial Times*, 14/05/96), therefore, rightsizing is presented as an alternative *strategic* (as opposed to a knee-jerk) response to the *imperatives of change*, which restructures organizations in a fashion that it is claimed leaves business better able to meet competitive challenges. In this way, the concept of rightsizing, once again, makes use of the power of euphemism to direct our attention towards business and strategic concerns. Somewhat ironically, however, this term invokes the power of euphemism to undermine the downsizing euphemism itself, while seeking to deliver all the benefits originally promised by this, now compromised, approach to restructuring.

Yet this is not the only challenge to have arisen for downsizing. While practitioners and journalists have been revising their approach to change, and revising their allegiance to downsizing as a strategy of/for change, a range of management academics have also sought to voice their disquiet over the concept and practice of downsizing. In particular, concern has been voiced over the organizational legacy of downsizing. Indeed, noting a decline in morale and productivity post-downsizing (Cappelli *et al.*, 1997), a range of commentators and management academics have argued that managers need to consider the health and morale of those employees retained by the organization, as well as considering the welfare of those who have been downsized. Thus a range of academic commentators have identified downsizing's 'survivors' as a group requiring support, counselling, training and leadership. Never shy of opportunities to disseminate (i.e. to sell) ideas, management academia has argued that 'survivor syndrome' should be regarded as a key problem for modern organizations which requires urgent attention (Brockner, 1988, 1992; Baruch and Hind, 1997; Appelbaum *et al.*, 1999; Orr *et al.*, 1999).

### Survivor Syndrome

The term 'Survivor Syndrome' was borrowed by Brockner (1988, 1992) from studies of the Nazi holocaust, and was introduced to management academia to refer to the set of shared reactions common to those who experience downsizing as an adverse event, yet remain within the organization to tell the tale. In this sense, the survivors of downsizing are those individuals often overlooked in discussions of redundancy and change. They are those individuals who retain their employment following radical restructuring initiatives.

Making his case for the analysis of 'survivors', Brockner (1988, 1992) has argued that organizations have tended to lavish resources on those leaving the organization. Thus, Brockner notes that organizations tend to spend money on counselling and outplacement for those leaving the organization, yet neglect to consider the impact of radical change on those who will remain with the organization. This, Brockner argues, is a key over-sight, since survivors of downsizing, the organization's primary source of added-value, have been reported to suffer some mixture of demotivation, cynicism and demoralization as a result of their downsizing experiences. At one level, therefore, the 'survivor' discussion is a tacit acceptance of what history has taught us about the experience of 'insecure' work (Thompson, 1972), namely that workers experiencing employment inse-curity tend to develop responses, such as output restriction and sabotage (Taylor, 1911; Braverman, 1974), which are designed to offer some control over work rhythms and practices. Thus we should be little surprised by the links made between 'survivor syndrome' and declines in service quality, nor should we be surprised when 74 per cent of managers questioned, in organizations undertaking downsizing, state that their employees have become fearful of future changes, and had become mistrustful of manage-ment (Cascio, 1993).

Reflecting upon the problems of managing survivors, Brockner (1988) has argued that managers should take steps to minimize the dysfunctional impacts of downsizing. Reflecting this concern, Baruch and Hind (1997) argue that the adoption of what they term 'best practice' in the manage-ment of redundancy – a range of policies and proposals hinged around the need to ensure full consultation in the lead up to downsizing, together with steps to ensure open-ness and fairness in selection for redundancy – is vital.

The concept of a 'survivor syndrome' has attracted broad, popular support, in part, I suspect because the discussion resonates, both with historical accounts of working, and with our day-to-day, common-sense experience of work and commitment. However, there are reasons to be suspicious of, or at least guarded in our support of this, apparently attrac-tive concept. Baruch and Hind (1997), for example, note that while the notion of 'survivor syndrome' is attractive at an intuitive level, the concept of the 'survivor syndrome' is under-theorized and little investigated. Thus, they warn us that discussions of survivors have not been successful in unravelling organizational impacts from more general demographic concerns. In this way, Baruch and Hind argue that discussions of survivor syndrome, as an organizational phenomenon may, in truth, be reports of more general demographic indicators, which, in the absence of any notional syndrome, might be expected to have an impact upon work orientation and commitment. Accordingly, Baruch and Hind argue that more work is required at a conceptual level (to refine models of organizational commit-ment) and at an empirical level (for example, to analyse demographic influences and their mediating affects on survivors).

While accepting Baruch's and Hind's comments and critique as valid, and as sensitive to the dynamics of working and managing, we do not have to confine ourselves to this line of criticism alone. Earlier, we noted the tendency of management studies to demarcate its concerns. Thus we observed that management academics tend to focus upon corporate matters, and upon organizational 'needs', to the exclusion of wider, social concerns. In an attempt to go beyond these, limiting, concerns we have endeavoured to produce a more 'biographical' form of analysis, which has been informed by the work of C. Wright-Mills (1973). Eschewing the normal concerns of the downsizing literature, therefore, we have attempted to examine the social context, and the social impacts of downsizing. With this issue in mind, it is worth taking just a few moments to reflect upon this 'survivor' discussion, and its implications (both moral and ethical) for practice and analysis.

For example, we might, while acknowledging the importance of militaristic metaphors in discussions of management, allow ourselves a little shudder at the importation, into management studies, of a term coined to describe the aftermath of genocide. Thus, we might argue that discussing the aftermath of organizational downsizing in terms of 'survivors' has a tendency to trivialize the holocaust. In a similar way, we might also wish to consider the ends of the 'survivors of downsizing' discussion.

We noted, for example, the damage which *downsizing–rightsizing–dumbsizing*, has visited upon our lives and our communities. Indeed, discussing Moore's (1997) analysis of downsizing we noted a comparison between radical, organizational restructuring initiatives and terrorism, which was based upon a consideration of the devastating impacts each wreaks on the social fabric of society.

In the face of the widespread change and social devastation recorded in this chapter, we have, I think, the right to ask: what does the survivor discussion do to offset these tendencies? The answer it seems is not much, since, while evidence of the consequences of downsizing has mounted, and while we have been able to document a raft of outcomes which suggest that downsizing as a set of management practices has damaged both our businesses and (so) our communities, management academia has busied itself with the task of *refining* downsizing. Thus, management academia has busied itself with the analysis of 'survivors' for two main reasons. First, the analysis of survivors has been geared to assuring measures of stock-value and value-added, and, second, as a downstream concern, the survivor discussion has been designed as an attempt to limit the declines in organization commitment and morale, reported post-downsizing. Contrary to what we might have expected, therefore, the 'survivor' discussion cares little for the personal–family–community aspects of downsizing, since the whole analysis aims to ensure that organizations do not suffer adversely from large-scale restructuring!

Probably the best we can say on this project of work, is that it represents a limited agenda, which does management academia little credit because (1) it fails to locate management as a contested and contestable set of practices with consequences which extend beyond the workplace and (2) because it fails to understand or to care about the effect and affects of these practices. Accordingly, this chapter, in keeping with our 'critical-practical' agenda, has attempted to offer a more coherent and socially sensitive account of downsizing; its meaning; its extent and its impacts, which might be used to criticize and to oppose downsizing.

## Summary

This chapter has attempted to explore downsizing as a concept, and as a set of management practices which are representative of a more generalized attempt to deregulate labour markets. Noting the origins of downsizing, as a term developed by the automobile industry in Detroit, the chapter has examined the euphemistic potential of this phraseology. Building on the works of Scott (1990) and Chik Collins (1999) we noted that euphemisms are employed as an attempt to disguise, or to distance actors from outcomes. Thus we argued that the term downsizing represents an attempt to recast redundancy situations from the traditional picture where fewer workers are required to perform a diminished quantity of work to a position where fewer workers, (naturally), do more work, to respond to the competitive changes.

Keen to expose the realities, disguised by such euphemistic forms of discourse we have studied the outputs of 'downsizing' in the USA (as the home of the term) and in the UK (as the home of the author, albeit redesigned in ways to mimic the USA) in order to analyse the impacts on individuals, on families, and on communities of the 'gurus' and their models of/for change.

## Note

1   This epithet was attached to Jack Welch in recognition of his approach to organizational restructuring which, in common with the neutron bomb, wiped out people yet left buildings standing.

# 10  Knowledge Work

## Introduction

Over the last few years considerable attention has been devoted to the study of 'knowledge work', and to the analysis of knowledge intensive forms of organization (Coulson-Thomas, 1991; Drucker, 1991; Nomikos, 1989; Alvesson, 1993). By far the majority of those who use these terms seem to agree, broadly, that there is a form of work, different from other forms of toil, which we might, meaningfully, categorize as 'knowledge work'. In addition, these writers and commentators also tend to argue that as societies move into the (new) 'knowledge age', and develop 'knowledge intensive forms of organization', the 'knowledge workers' employed within these organizations will call forth new forms of management and, implicitly, new strategies for human resource management (HRM).

In this chapter we will look more closely at this notion of 'knowledge work' to offer a form of analysis, designed to look critically at the experience of work, generally, and at the concept of knowledge work, in particular. This chapter offers a much expanded version of a paper first published by the journal *Employee Relations* (Collins, 1997) which, in many ways, might be considered a rejoinder to an earlier paper penned by Despres and Hiltrop (1995). However, and in spite of my critical reading of this paper, it is worth drawing attention to the fact that Charles Despres was supportive of my discussion, and offered a constructive review, which did much to refine the paper. For this, I am grateful.

In common with the original discussion which was published by *Employee Relations*, and which, now, informs this analysis, our chapter on 'knowledge work' and the 'knowledge age' commences far from the rational world. Indeed, we start our analysis in the queer domain of metaphysics, since when analysing 'knowledge work', so-called, I am struck by an eerie feeling of *déjà vu*.

Somehow, a sense tells me that all the arguments marshalled with the aim of convincing managers and other policy-makers of the development of a new, knowledge age, and of the rise of a new professional elite, dubbed knowledge workers, have been rehearsed before. However, and in spite of all this activity, this chapter will argue that, when these new rehearsals are analysed critically, contextually (and rationally), it soon becomes apparent that each, subsequent, rehearsal of the knowledge work debate, has done little to add polish to the final performance.

In particular, this chapter articulates a concern that the current focus on knowledge work, on knowledge intensive forms of organization, and on the management practices and techniques which these call forth, represents, at an implicit level, a re-rehearsal of previous discussions of post-industrialism (Kumar, 1981) which like previous performances of this discussion are confusing, ambiguous and really not at all well directed.

In an attempt to share my misgivings regarding this (re-rehearsed) discussion of knowledge work and post-industrialism, this chapter is structured as follows: to offer a 'critical-practical' analysis of knowledge work we must, first, be able to locate this concept – only then can we hope to understand it; and only through understanding may we hope to offer a sensible, critical account of knowledge work. Accordingly, this chapter begins by attempting to locate the discussion of knowledge work, within the work of the economist, Machlup (1962), and within the framework of the larger debates on post-industrial society (Drucker, 1969, 1992, 1993; Bell, 1980, 1987; Handy, 1984; Sadler, 1993). Through this analysis we will attempt to outline the key contours of the discussion of knowledge work, and through this exploration we will attempt to show, both, the problems and the naiveté of much of the post-industrial literature.

Following our discussion of the knowledge or post-industrial society, we will, then shift our focus from the analysis of societal shifts and changes in order to examine, more closely, the concepts of knowledge and knowledge work, which it is assumed will be performed within these new societal formations. Accordingly, we will consider knowledge work as this is envisaged by those who have been keen to separate this form of toil as a meaningful category, deserving of the attention of senior managers and policy-makers. From this consideration, I hope to show that the advocates of knowledge work – as a specialist form of endeavour, performed by a skilled socio-economic elite – have developed a form of analysis, and a platform for management action, which remains unconvincing. Thus, our movement between levels of analysis is designed to allow us to locate the knowledge work discussion within the more general analysis of post-industrial society. Beyond this, however, our preferred analytical approach also represents an attempt to demonstrate that the confusion and ambiguity which surrounds the concept of knowledge work can be found within the general debate on post-industrial society and is, in fact, a product of this debate and its terms of reference. Through this discussion, we will attempt to show that the current run of the debate on knowledge work has done little to advance analysis, and has done little to promote our understanding of economic and social change, since its 'grammatical' construction of management and the need for change leaves it riddled with basic conceptual muddles and confusion.

Finally the chapter, in keeping with our 'critical-practical' agenda will suggest that this debate on the future of work organizations, and on the future of management and management control, should be refocused. Instead of attempting to define and analyse 'knowledge work' which, in spite of the muddle and confusion which surrounds it, tends to emerge as the privilege of a minority elite, this chapter will conclude by arguing that the debate should be refocused to analyse *working knowledge* across the population.

Let us begin, then, by analysing the origins and nature of the concepts of knowledge and knowledge work.

## Analysing Knowledge Work

Discussing the management 'gurus' and their contribution to the technology of management, Kennedy (1996) argues that the discussion of knowledge work, and of the managerial problems thrown up by the expansion of knowledge industries, may be traced back to the work of Fritz Machlup (1962). Indeed, she argues:

> The term 'knowledge industries', meaning those which produce and distribute ideas and information rather than goods and services, appears to have been invented in 1962 by Fritz Machlup, an economist working at Princeton University, in a book called *The Production and Distribution of Knowledge in the US.*
>
> (Kennedy, 1996, p. 75)

However, and in spite of noting Machlup as the progenitor of the knowledge work debate, Kennedy, in her discussion of the problems of managing and motivating knowledge workers, makes no further mention of Machlup or his analysis. Indeed in her next sentence she, quite neatly, side-steps the need to offer an analysis of Machlup and his work. Thus, in her very next sentence, Kennedy moves the focus of attention from the creator of the debate, to the follower and popularizer of the discussion, to argue that: 'As usual, however, it was the prescient Peter Drucker who picked the new coinage up and examined its implications in his remarkable book *The Age of Discontinuity* (1969), which anticipated many developments of the 1980s' (Kennedy, 1996, p. 75).

At one level, of course, Kennedy's, apparent, unwillingness to analyse the work of Machlup is perfectly understandable. After all, Machlup's work was published in 1962, and was based upon empirical materials gathered in the US during the 1950s. Thus Kennedy's unwillingness to analyse Machlup's work, in detail, may, in part, be based upon the calculation that his analysis has been overtaken by circumstances, such that *The*

*Production and Distribution of Knowledge in the United States,* now has signifi-cance as a historical document, rather than as a tool to assist contemporary analysis. Likewise, and while still considering motives for disregarding or downplaying Machlup's (1962) analysis, it is worth observing that, in comparison to the works of the 'gurus' quoted by Kennedy, Machlup has a rather tortured and, at times, pedantic style of writing, which offers the management reader few incentives for persistence. Thus, in selecting texts for her analysis of management's 'gurus', Kennedy may have consid-ered Machlup's work to be too dated, and too pedestrian, for her management readers, and so, may have chosen to focus upon Drucker, as a 'prescient' and pacy writer, more suitable for her elucidation of know-ledge work, and the associated problems of working with and through knowledge workers.

Yet, while we can acknowledge that there is an element of wisdom in the choice-making behaviour of Kennedy (as I have interpreted and recon-structed this), it is important, when analysing 'knowledge work' to confirm Machlup's role *and* to return to his work, because (1) to do otherwise would be to allow convenience and laziness to get in the way of good scholar-ship, and (2) because Machlup's careful, if pedestrian, analysis raises matters for consideration which, as we shall see, remain central to a 'critical-practical' account of knowledge work.

## Machlup on Knowledge

Machlup's (1962) analysis of the production and distribution of knowledge in the United States looked out on an American economy in transition. The manufacturing and metal-bashing industries which had made America an economic and military superpower, Machlup argued, were being surpassed by a new engine of economic development. Indeed Machlup argued that in previous decades American industry had grown and had attained predominance, because it had used knowledge to produce phys-ical outputs, and to enhance material prosperity. Yet, looking out on the America of the 1960s, Machlup argued that America stood on the threshold of a new productive era. Thus, Machlup argued that knowledge was no longer a primary resource in American industry. Instead, he contended, knowledge had become America's primary output.

This transition, from a knowledge-using, industrial economy, to an economy where knowledge represents America's primary resource and its most important output, Machlup argued, had a range of possible outcomes, which would need to be managed with care. Indeed, in his analysis Machlup was keen to stress that the development of the knowledge economy would pose challenges for academic analysis, as well as for public policy-making.

As Machlup introduces his study of the production and distribution of knowledge, therefore, he is keen to stress that as a field of study, economics, among other disciplines, had been slow to catch on to the important implications associated with the development of knowledge as a product, and as a sphere of production. This, tardiness, he argued was a matter for regret since, as he saw it, there were, at least, eleven good reasons for analysing the production and distribution of knowledge from an economist's standpoint:

1   Increasing shares of the US national budget, Machlup noted, writing in 1962, were being allocated to knowledge production.
2   Much of the US national expenditure on knowledge production he argued is financed by governmental spending and is dependent upon continuing political support to ensure the appropriation of funding (for a more up-to-date account relating to the information super high-way, see Giddens, (1999)). Reflecting upon these political matters, Machlup noted, for example, that much of the expenditure on know-ledge production and distribution was financed by government, thanks to governmental funding of educational programmes (such as the GI Bill, which guaranteed college funding to military veterans), and to governmental spending with the military–industrial complex.
3   Expenditure on knowledge production (for example through the subsidies attached to education) Machlup suggested, should be financed by the public purse, since investments in knowledge would tend to develop social benefits above and beyond the private benefits accruing to the recipients of knowledge (such as students).
4   Knowledge production may well be limited by deficiencies in the supply of qualified labour. Noting the knock-on benefits of knowledge produc-tion and distribution (mentioned above), Machlup argued that these labour market issues raised important questions, regarding public policy and the public acquisition and distribution of funds for such things as training, education and development.
5   Part of the costs of knowledge production, Machlup noted, is met (via taxation, for example) by those who will not use that knowledge directly. Again, while recognizing the wider, social benefits associated with investments in knowledge, Machlup argued that this spectre of inequality and uneven benefit raised larger questions for policy-making and government investment.
6   Changes in knowledge in one subject discipline, Machlup's analysis suggested, may cause changes in many spheres of knowledge produc-tion. Thus Machlup's analysis makes us aware that while knowledge economies tend to develop specialists, these specialists, if they are to benefit from advances in knowledge, should retain an open-minded, if not a more generalist approach to their work. The development of the mathematics of chaos and the influence of this new mathematics on many subject disciplines such as physics, economics and organi-zation theorizing more generally, would be a contemporary example

of the sort of change and development which Machlup seems to have had in mind here (see Grint, 1997a).

7  Machlup suggested that the experience of working might change quite profoundly as the production and distribution of knowledge progressed. Indeed he suggested that it would be fair to hypothesize that key changes would be experienced as we moved from being 'physical' labourers to become 'brain' labourers.

8  Machlup argued that empirical analysis suggested that more and more of the labour force would be employed in knowledge production as employees moved from various forms of industrial and physical toil to become 'brain labourers'.

9  While celebrating the development of the knowledge economy, Machlup also suggested that there was room for the suspicion that knowledge production may well be inefficient. However, he also noted that such technical inefficiencies in the production of knowledge might actually be inescapable since, he warns us, those forms of activity considered wasteful in a manufacturing environment might actually be central to the processes of producing knowledge.

10  While noting that certain 'inefficiencies' might be inescapable in the production of knowledge, Machlup was fearful that other forms of inefficiency, not central to the processes of knowledge production might also be tolerated. Thus Machlup was fearful that more and more administrators would be hired to manage knowledge production, adding unnecessarily to the 'inefficiencies' built into knowledge production.

11  In spite of the requisite and non-requisite inefficiencies of knowledge production, Machlup argued that a switch from physical to brain production would be associated with improvements in productivity and prosperity.

Overall, then, and in spite of what some might regard as a pedestrian approach to the analysis of knowledge, Machlup offers us a rich, thoughtful and far-reaching approach to the analysis of knowledge production and distribution, which goes far beyond the normal boundaries of the organization. Furthermore, we should note that Machlup's approach to the production and distribution of knowledge in America transcends the normal bounds of management and 'guru' thinking, to embrace something akin to a political economy of knowledge.

Thus, Machlup's analysis demonstrates the roles which state bodies tend to play in the production and distribution of knowledge (for example, through governmental spending on such things as defence, health and education). In addition, Machlup also demonstrates the difficulties which policy-makers have in allocating both costs and benefits when accounting for such expenditure on knowledge. Similarly, we should note that Machlup draws our attention to the fact that much of the production and distribution of knowledge is priced at less than full cost (being subsidized by a variety of state transfers), and so he highlights a range of larger and often intractable policy issues within the discussion of knowledge management, which remain both pertinent and problematic (see, for example, the survey of universities offered by *The Economist*, 04/10/97. See also the many problems associated with attempts to change towards what might be termed a 'fuller-cost' system of education in Britain: *The Sunday Times*, 11/01/98). Finally, in this discussion of the continuing relevance of Machlup's analysis, it is also worth acknowledging that, in drawing our attention to the problems within the opportunities of knowledge production, Machlup offers a sanguine form of analysis which many of management's 'gurus' would do well to study.

With this account of Machlup fresh in our minds, let us return to Kennedy's preferred agenda and timetable, to examine the 'gurus' and their accounts of knowledge work. Let us examine Drucker's account of the production and distribution of knowledge.

## Drucker on Knowledge

Like Machlup's work, much of Drucker's work on management is concerned with the problems and pitfalls associated with moves towards a knowledge producing economy. Indeed, questions pertaining to the management of knowledge, and to the management of knowledge workers, as an educated, occupational elite represent one of the key and recurrent themes in Drucker's huge collection of writings. We will select just three pieces from Drucker's many works to illustrate this point: a piece from the 1970s (Drucker, 1969), a piece from the 1980s (Drucker, 1981) and a piece from the 1990s (Drucker, 1993).

In *The Age of Discontinuity*, Drucker (1969) discusses the economic problems associated with, as he sees it, the moves from a goods-producing, to a knowledge-producing economy. While discussing these economic changes, Drucker is keen to pursue the managerial problems of controlling and motivating the new, highly skilled, highly mobile 'knowledge workers' who will be central to the, new, knowledge economy. Thus, in *The Age of Discontinuity*, Drucker observed that, while knowledge workers, as a highly skilled, highly mobile elite would still occupy, formally, the role of employees, the highly marketable nature of their skills would make them quite unlike most other employees, and quite immune to the normal practices and technologies of management normally used to discipline and to control employees in the industrial era. Drucker argued, therefore, that managers in the knowledge age would confront a paradox. Managers, he argued, would become, increasingly, dependent upon the skills and talents of a key occupational grouping. Yet, thanks to changes in the economic basis of society, the knowledge elite, central to managerial aims and ambitions, would tend to become less and less amenable to managerial control.

Drucker argued, therefore, that the knowledge age would necessitate a revolution in management thought and practice designed to allow managers to work with, and through, this talented grouping.

Writing more than a decade later, at the start of the 1980s, Drucker (1981) again chose to discuss the problems associated with the management of a knowledge elite in some depth. Thus, in *Managing in Turbulent Times*, Drucker argued that managers would have to learn new skills and new techniques. These new skills and techniques would be required to allow organizations to manage the special skills and talents of knowledge workers. Somewhat ironically, therefore, Drucker's analysis suggests that knowledge workers, as a group, represent both the cause and the outcome of the turbulence and complexity which, as he saw it, managers in the 1980s would have to face.

A little more than a decade later, and some forty years since he had first coined the term 'knowledge worker' (Drucker, 1993), Drucker, again, found it necessary to return to the question of managing knowledge. Thus, in *Post-capitalist Society*, Drucker, devotes a considerable part of his analysis to the issues of knowledge production and distribution, and to the impacts of these issues on our daily lives.

Drucker's book, *Post-capitalist Society*, begins with an account of the world we are leaving behind. We are, Drucker warns us, leaving the capitalist mode of production behind. Where we are heading, he tells us, however, is not yet clear to see. Indeed he suggests that we will be caught in 'the muddle of transformation' for some 20 to 30 years, hence his book defines the new form of society in terms of what/where we are moving *from*, rather than attempting to define what/where we are moving to. However, and with the collapse of the soviet bloc, and the destruction of the Berlin wall still fresh in his mind, Drucker (1993) argues that post-capitalist society will *not* be, as had been assumed for many years, a Marxist society.

Where Marxist societies transform capitalism by rejecting it, Drucker argues that post-capitalist society is to be regarded as extending, yet, at the same time, transforming capitalism. In presenting a non-Marxist, yet transformed, capitalistic future, therefore, Drucker argues that post-capitalist society will sweep away all that we had assumed would persist as truth.

It is worth examining this discussion of post-capitalist society in a little more depth.

### Post-capitalism?

Post-capitalist society, Drucker (1993) suggests is an outcome of the development of the knowledge economy. Comparing capitalist with post-capitalist society, Drucker argues that, whereas capitalism is a society where power and influence turn upon the ownership and control of productive resources, power and influence in post-capitalist society will depend upon access to a qualitatively different form of economic resource. Thus, Drucker argues that while the likes of Carnegie and Ford, in America, Vickers in Britain, and Krupp in Germany, built fortunes and became powerful because they exercised control over capital resources – factories, finance and furnaces – the economic elite of the post-capitalist economy will be both powerful and influential thanks to its privileged access to knowledge, and its ability to realize value through the application of knowledge.

Drucker is keen to stress, however, that post-capitalist society is not non-capitalist. Indeed he suggests that Marxism, as the traditional template for a post-capitalist future, represents a flawed utopianism which is now in retreat (for a dissenting view, see Hobsbawm's discussion in *The Guardian*, 20/10/98). Keen to stress the capitalist roots of post-capitalism, therefore, Drucker might be viewed as vaunting and celebrating what might be termed the architecture of capitalism, as he discusses the manner in which the knowledge elite will work with, and within, free market economies to realize value. Yet, while noting the operation of the free market and other, essentially capitalist methods of resource allocation, within the knowledge economy, Drucker argues that this new, and emergent society represents, not simply an extension of industrial capitalism, but the transformation of this form of capitalism. Hence he suggests that we should consider the knowledge economy, with its new resources and its new elites as being 'post-capitalist'.

In common with Machlup's analysis of knowledge production and distribution, Drucker argues that post-capitalist society poses a range of economic and social challenges. The economic challenge, he suggests, will be a productivity challenge. Thus, Drucker notes that the methods and manners of industrial management – as expressed in Taylorism and Fordism, for example – represent an inappropriate template for the management of a highly skilled and mobile elite, whose commitment is the key to productivity, and to added value.

The social challenge of the knowledge economy, on the other hand, reflects the problems of managing the new, and emergent, social dichotomy evident in knowledge society. Thus Drucker argues that, just as capitalist society divides the world, crudely, into two camps, (1) those who own and control, key, productive resources, and (2) those employed by the owners of the factories, finance-houses and furnaces, so post-capitalist society will be divided into two, (1) an educated elite who will deploy/employ knowledge to enhance productivity and innovation, and (2) a lesser educated grouping (a group Drucker, sometimes, refers to as service workers) who will constitute the majority of the population, yet will lack the productive resources (the education) to become knowledge workers.

These social and economic challenges have also occupied the mind of perhaps Britain's foremost management commentator, Charles Handy.

# Handy on Knowledge

Introducing *The Future of Work*, Handy (1984) notes eight key changes in work and society. In common with the writings of Machlup (1962) and those of Drucker, noted above, Handy's account of work, and working, suggests the need for a range of changes in both the economy and the polity. Thus, as Handy muses on the passing of industrial capitalism as the predominant sphere of production, he sees eight key changes/ movements which, he argues, will serve to shape the future of work:

1   The development of a part-time employment future as compared to our historical expectation regarding employment as a full-time activity.
2   The development of knowledge work, as distinct from manual toil, as the primary form of economic activity.
3   The decline of industrial employment as compared to the increasing scale of service employment.
4   The development of new forms of organizing, to meet the expectations of knowledge workers, and the challenge of managing employees in the knowledge economy. Thus, in common with Drucker, Handy suggests the development of more co-operative and collegiate forms of organizing – such as networks and matrix structures – as opposed to the more traditional, centralist, bureaucratic structures associated with industrial capitalism.
5   The end of the traditional career, and 'job for life', as knowledge workers exercise the opportunities for mobility which their marketable skills allow.
6   The development of a more productive and fulfilling 'third age' as those approaching statutory retirement age (65 in Britain), refuse to become 'inactive', economically, or otherwise.
7   A challenge to sexual stereotyping, at work and at home, in part, as people become valued for their skills and knowledge, rather than devalued for their gender.
8   The emergence of a new geographical division-of-labour as traditional forms of industrial labour, and some forms of knowledge work, migrate southwards.

Handy argues that any one of these eight changes, taken in isolation, could be managed and accommodated within familiar policies, procedures and structures. However, taken *en masse* he tells us, these developments call forth far-reaching changes in social, fiscal and political management, which cannot easily be accommodated within existing ideas an assumptions. For example, Handy suggests (perhaps speaking autobiographically – see Handy (1997)) that we may have to become less fixated upon work and careers, and will have to stop defining ourselves, and others, in terms of the economic activity we perform for reward, as we face up to an era where the notion of the career, and of continuous economic activity is less meaningful. Similarly, Handy suggests that the educational system and the provision of educational services, more generally, will have to be rethought and redesigned, since, he warns us, an educational system geared to producing an industrial working class, will be, singularly, unsuited to the post-industrial, (or as Drucker would have it, post-capitalist), knowledge age.

## Summary

From the discussion above, it should be clear that a range of managerial authors concerned with economic change and with the management of social and economic development have crafted remarkably similar accounts of our futures within an emergent post-capitalist or post-industrial, knowledge economy. We have seen, for example, how both Drucker and Handy share a view of society, and of working, which hinges around knowledge as *the* primary productive resource in society. Indeed both of these authors, in common with Bell (1980, 1987), as we shall see in a moment, agree that the development of knowledge as the primary economic resource, upsets and transforms the traditional class basis of society. Similarly, we also observed that the advent of a knowledge elite is said to lead to transformations in both the nature of management and in systems of managerial control. Again, as we shall see, this focus upon the changing nature and scope of management is a feature which the works of Handy and Drucker share in common with the work of Bell. This is not to say, of course, that the works of Handy and Drucker are identical in all respects. In fact there exist tensions and conflicts between these two authors.

On the question of managing our emerging futures, for example, Handy (1984) sees an enhanced role for the state in matters of education, training and resource redistribution. Drucker (1993), however, seems highly suspicious of state planning and intervention, and in comparison to Handy, seems to advocate more of a free-market approach to the management of our post-capitalist futures.

Yet, and in spite of these questions concerning the best way to manage our futures, both Handy and Drucker – in common with 'futurologists' such as Toffler (1983) – are agreed that we are entering a new era in human and economic history, a post-industrial or post-capitalist era which will restructure the class basis of society, such that the elite of the industrial era, the owners of factories, finance and furnaces will be supplanted by a new elite who enjoy privileged access to the new, and primary, economic resource – knowledge.

But does this line of argument make sense? Do these representations of working and managing bear empirical scrutiny? Do they make sense when compared to your experiences of working? Do the arguments invoked in the name of knowledge work fit the historical evidence of economic and social development? Can we delineate, reliably and safely, a new knowledge elite? Is there really *a need to transform* the practices of managing to accommodate the model of working, which Drucker is keen to promote?

In an attempt to analyse these questions we will examine Bell's (1980, 1987) account of post-industrial society, together with Kumar's (1981) critical commentary on the concept of post-industrialism.

## The Post-industrial Age?

In spite of the fact that Kennedy has identified Machlup (1962) as the father of the knowledge work debate, and Drucker as the prescient prophet of knowledge work, Kumar (1981), argues that the work of Daniel Bell (1980, 1987) represents, perhaps, the main intellectual springboard for the current discussions of 'knowledge work' and the 'knowledge age' (see also, Webster, 1994). Kumar (1981), of course, acknowledges that a wide variety of commentators and analysts have discussed a range of visions for a post-industrial age. However, he argues that Bell's work, since it is probably the most sociological in orientation (in that it begins from a discussion of the nature of industrial society) represents the prime source of reference for the analysis of the post-industrial literature. Accordingly, Kumar bases his critique of post-industrial society on a reading of Bell's work. Whether or not the work of Bell does represent the primary reference for the discussion of knowledge work is, perhaps, a moot point. Nonetheless, in the section that follows we will use Bell as the vehicle for our analysis and critique of post-industrialism since this will facilitate our critical discussion, while allowing us to examine another managerial contribution to the discussion of knowledge work.

## Bell on Knowledge

Discussing the changing nature of capitalism, Bell argues that humanity is entering a new phase of evolution, which will move human society from an industrial form to a post-industrial form. In common with Machlup (1962), Drucker (1969, 1981, 1993), Handy (1984) and Toffler (1983), Bell argues that this move from industrial to post-industrial society represents a basic change in economic activity: the move from a goods producing economy to a service economy; and from blue-collar to white-collar employment. In addition Bell argues that the post-industrial age is marked by an increasing predominance of professional, scientific and technician groups. Indeed Bell foresees a combination of economic and technical advance as leading to a change in class structure, since, he argues, the growing information handling requirements of business, the development of information products, and the primacy of scientific research will call forth a new and powerful class of (knowledge) workers. In this way, Bell, in common with Drucker, with Handy and with Machlup, argues that post-industrial society will be based, not on the ownership of private property but on the basis of professional skill.

Kumar, however, is highly sceptical of these predictions, and of the intellectual framework which underpins them. He offers a powerful critique which, for economy of presentation, may be grouped under four headings (see also Webster, 1994, for a useful sociological account and critique of Bell).

## A Sociological Critique

The four key areas of criticism discussed by Kumar relate to:

*   Questions concerning the extent to which the growth of the tertiary (service) sector implies that society is moving from an industrial base to a post-industrial form of society.
*   Questions as to the nature of service sector employment.
*   Questions as to the validity of the term 'professional'.
*   Questions as to the extent to which post-industrial hinges upon codification and the use of scientific knowledge by scientists within large-scale employment concerns.

Let us deal with each of these briefly.

### The Service Sector

On the first point, Bell argues that post-industrial society represents a decisive break from industrial forms. He contends that we may glean the extent of this change from the decline in manufacturing employment and the switch to service sector employment. However, Kumar notes that, if anything, the service sector grows at the expense of the agricultural sector, and so, he argues that, if the development of the service sector indicates anything, it is the decline of agricultural employment, rather than the decline of the industrial economy. Hence, Kumar argues that the growth of the service sector represents not so much the move to post-industrial society, as a move towards a post-agrarian society.

Kumar, to be fair, does acknowledge that the figures describing sectoral changes in employment are, perhaps, more supportive of the post-industrialism thesis, when applied to the case of England. Yet, he notes that in having a large manufacturing sector England was in fact atypical, and so, could hardly be considered as representative of a more generalized, post-industrial trend.

With these caveats in mind, therefore, Kumar argues that one of the key tenets of post-industrial thinking – that the growth of the service sector represents a decisive shift from manufacturing – is unfounded.

## The Nature of Service Employment

On our second point, Kumar notes the need to question some of the assumptions which post-industrial thinkers tend to build into their models of service sector work. Examining the assumptions, variously, built into, or hidden within the discussions of our post-industrial futures, Kumar notes that the advocates of post-industrialism tend to imply that the enlargement of the service sector, and the move towards service sector employment leads to improvements in the terms and conditions of employment, for those who transfer into this line of work. Kumar, however, is sceptical of these assumptions (see also, Webster, 1994; Gershuny, 1978). Indeed, he suggests that it is wrong to think of the service sector as a meaningful category of work, within which all employees share common experiences of work, power and authority. Instead, Kumar argues that what is commonly termed the service sector, and what many of us assume to be a meaningful aggregation of workers with experiences in common, is more properly thought of as a residual category of employment, and quite a large and diverse one at that.

The rather rosy view of the experience of service sector employment, presented by Bell, by Drucker and by Handy, therefore, must be at best an exaggeration. Indeed, Wood (1992) in his analysis of the hotel and catering industry demonstrates that accounts of service work often fail to acknowledge the size of the 'service sector' and the diverse practices found within it. Furthermore, Wood argues that accounts of service sector work, often, tend to focus upon the high skills end of the market, and so, fail to understand the extent of managerial control and the relative poverty endured by many of those who work in 'services'.

## The Management of Professionals?

Kumar's third critique of post-industrial thinking relates to the discussion of professionalization, which is implicit in the treatment of the service sector, and in the discussion of the growing predominance of scientific knowledge. Bell implies that post-industrial society is marked by a growth in the professional workforce who form a new elite class. For Kumar, however, this growth is a result of 'a sociological sleight of hand' (Kumar, 1981, p. 215) which fails to acknowledge the extent to which professional employment is socially constructed and contested.

Kumar notes, for example, that Bell's new 'professional' groups are accorded few of the rights and benefits of the longer established professional groups, and he notes too, that in contrast to Bell's vision of elitism, contentment and motivation these new 'professionals' are increasingly disaffected and militant. Thus the vision of affluence, collegiality and contentment, assumed within the discussion of post-industrial society appears somewhat chimerical.

### Knowledge, Science and Training?

Kumar's final criticism of Bell's post-industrial schema invites us to take issue with the basic contention that post-industrial society is built upon science and on the codification of theoretical knowledge. Kumar notes, as does Bannock (Bannock, 1973), that, in spite of Bell's faith in the power and prestige of the scientific academies, much 'scientific' innovation is undertaken by amateurs and dabblers.

As Bannock (1973) notes, independent innovation (as distinct from the academic scientific-technical model of innovation, assumed in the post-industrial literature), has been, and continues to be, the dominant mode of innovation. Thus, in contrast to the post-industrial account of scientific research and innovation, Bannock reminds us that many of the important scientific developments of our age have been produced by individuals who lack a formal scientific training. Casting an eye over a catalogue of devices and developments, he notes that:

> The inventor of the dial telephone was an undertaker, that of the ball-point pen a sculptor, painter and journalist. The inventor of the Hovercraft, Sir Christopher Cockerell, was an electronic engineer turned boat-builder and he proved the principle of the air cushion with two coffee tins, tubing, a hair dryer and some kitchen scales.
>
> (Bannock, 1973, pp. 183–184)

Pressing this point home, Bannock also reminds us that Moulton's revolutionary suspension system, Wankel's rotary engine, the study and treatment of rhesus-haemolytic disease, photo-typesetting, and the refinement of the computer, were all the outcomes of independent innovation which was neither sponsored by business, nor conducted under the auspices of the scientific academies.

Similarly, and again disputing the idea that the development of a scientific, knowledge, elite is central to, and necessary for invention and innovation, Sterling (Sterling, 1992) notes that in the field of computing and hacking, 'phreakers' are so far ahead of their corporate counterparts, that large corporations, and indeed the CIA, are all forced to 'subscribe' to the underground publications which they produce. Similarly, and perhaps more telling, Kumar also argues that calculation and rationalism are as much a feature of the industrial age as of any post-industrial vision. This, final point of critique, of course, has been well documented by Braverman (1974).

Based on this four-part critique, which attacks post-industrialism both conceptually and empirically, Kumar concludes that post-industrial forms of analysis are unconvincing. Indeed, he argues that the concept of post-industrial society is naive and 'intellectually conservative' (Kumar, 1981, p. 235)

One might have thought (or even hoped) that this form of debate would, therefore, have been laid to rest some time ago. Yet it appears that it has not, since, as we saw in our analysis of Drucker, and as we shall see below, the debates and problems of post-industrial thinking are with us once more. Recognizing the currency of this debate we will attempt to look critically at the concept of knowledge work which underpins the current run of the post-industrial performance.

## The Knowledge Worker?

In an attempt to look critically at 'knowledge work' and at 'knowledge workers', as these are defined by the advocates of post-industrialism, one could, as we have seen, select from among a huge variety of papers and discussions. In this section, and reflecting the origins of this chapter, we will begin the next stage of our critical inquiry into knowledge work, and its managerial consequences, by analysing the definition(s) of knowledge work as presented in the work of Despres and Hiltrop (1995). Following this analysis of the work of Despres and Hiltrop, we will, then, widen our discussion to include a larger range of contemporary studies and definitions of knowledge work.

Despres' and Hiltrop's (1995) discussion of knowledge work and the knowledge age, revolves around a consideration of the problems of managing, motivating and rewarding 'knowledge workers'. As such, their paper is couched as a call to action for management; in particular, those working in the sphere of human resource management.

In broad terms the thesis of Despres and Hiltrop reflects the concerns of Bell's (and the other advocates of post-industrialism). Thus, Despres and Hiltrop argue that societies and work organizations stand on the brink of a new technological age which, inevitably, will lead to disruptions in work patterns, work rhythms and ultimately to changes in class structure. Although they never quite tell us when this age will begin, or indeed if it has already begun, Despres and Hiltrop are confident enough in their analysis to generate a range of imperatives which they argue, human resource management practitioners must address, if they are to manage and motivate the, new, knowledge elite.

Yet, Despres and Hiltrop appear to have some difficulty in deciding upon the nature of this resource. Indeed, and mirroring the definitional and conceptual problems which dog the post-industrial schema, Despres and Hiltrop seem to have tremendous difficulty in actually defining knowledge work.

Ultimately they settle for a definition by proxy. Using the UNESCO definition of research and development activity, they tell us that this is a useful proxy definition for knowledge work. Thus quoting a UNESCO publication (UNESCO, 1993) they define knowledge work as:

'any creative systematic activity undertaken in order to increase the stock of knowledge of man, culture and society, and the use of this knowledge to devise new applications. It includes fundamental research . . . applied research . . . and experimental development work leading to new devices, products of processes'.

(Despres and Hiltrop, 1995, p. 14)

Yet we all know, and as an analysis of the post-industrial literature confirms, anything which can only be defined by proxy will tend to be very slippery, conceptually, and weak empirically. Indeed the concept of 'knowledge work' (like service work, or professional work – see Pritchard, 1996) is so slippery that the authors apparently feel the need to generate two, additional, definitions to supplement the UNESCO definition of research and development which, we had been told, represented their, chosen, working definition. Thus in a rather tautological fashion, Despres and Hiltrop, tell us that:

It is possible . . . to define knowledge work as systematic activity that traffics in data, manipulates information and develops knowledge. The work may be theoretical and directed at no immediate practical purpose, or pragmatic and aimed at devising new applications, devices, products or processes.

(Despres and Hiltrop, 1995, p. 12)

Yet, just a little later, Despres and Hiltrop offer an analysis of work which, in attempting to wrestle with the conceptual ambiguities of 'knowledge work', tries to analyse the orientations of their knowledge workers as opposed to the intrinsic task requirements of the jobs these workers perform. Thus Despres' and Hiltrop's third attempt at definition moves further from a concentration on the invention and refinement of devices to focus upon the orchestration of symbols and the importance of communication in knowledge work. In their third attempt to define/refine the nature of knowledge work, therefore, Despres and Hiltrop assert that: 'Knowledge workers manipulate and orchestrate symbols and concepts, identify more strongly with their peers and professions than their organizations, have more rapid skill obsolescence and are more critical to the long-term success of the organization' (Despres and Hiltrop, 1995, p. 13).

Let us test these attempts at definition. Let us examine the extent to which these definitions assist in the analysis of knowledge work. Let us see to what extent they clarify our analysis. Our key question, then, is this: just who are these 'knowledge workers'?

Or putting this another way, we might note that if we are to separate knowledge work as a distinctive form of work, different from more familiar forms of manual toil, we must have some reliable means of describing and delineating knowledge workers. Thus we have the right to ask: who belongs in this special category?

Perhaps these knowledge workers include groups such as medical doctors, as in the UNESCO definition? Perhaps marketing professionals, thanks to their involvement in the development of new devices and products, should also be included as knowledge workers? Indeed, and since Despres' and Hiltrop's primary definition of knowledge work includes all those who add to the stock of knowledge concerning man, culture and society; perhaps we would do well to widen our definition of (knowledge) work and employment to include artists, poets and philosophers of all kinds, both religious and secular?

A case, I suppose, could be made for the inclusion of all of these 'workers'. However, as we move to examine Despres' and Hiltrop's first, supplementary, definition of knowledge work, the scene becomes even more fuzzy and confused. Thus, far from refining knowledge work, this first, supplementary, definition seems to open a new branch of knowledge work for inspection. In their second attempt to define knowledge work, therefore, Despres and Hiltrop seem to abandon the esoteric, in favour of the instrumental. Thus in this second definition we seem to leave behind our concern with humanity, culture and society, to focus upon the trafficking of data and the tracking of information. So, if we follow this second attempt at definition; who are our knowledge workers now?

Stockbrokers and currency dealers track information and traffick in data (Lewis, 1989); so perhaps these groups are our knowledge workers now? Similarly, recognizing the importance of information technology in the prosecution of modern warfare, perhaps we should also include military strategists within this second definition of knowledge work?

However, as we move to examine the implications for analysis of Despres' and Hiltrop's second, supplementary, definition, we seem to leave information technology and information tracking to one side, as we turn to examine a more traditional form of working akin to that associated with 'the professions' (Pritchard, 1996).

So, just who are these knowledge workers now? Whom among these various occupational and professional groupings are we to regard as knowledge workers? Perhaps surprisingly it appears that they are none of these groups, since we are told that: 'new types of work are now being performed by new types of worker' (Despres and Hiltrop, 1995, p. 12). And again just a little later this is confirmed when we are told that: 'the nature of knowledge-based work is *fundamentally different from that known previously*' (Despres and Hiltrop, 1995, p. 12, emphasis added).

Thus Despres' and Hiltrop's knowledge worker would appear to be both everyone yet no one. The grouping seems to include all those who invent or refine devices, all those who engage in scientific endeavour, all those who manipulate data and symbols, yet it is a form of work like no currently existing forms of work!

In spite of their (various) efforts to define knowledge work, therefore, Despres and Hiltrop do little to clarify or to promote the analysis of the future of work. Indeed, noting that Despres' and Hiltrop's paper is couched as a 'wake-up' call to HRM, we might wonder what the managerial outcomes of such a confused form of analysis might be.

However, we should not seek to victimize Despres and Hiltrop over their treatment of 'knowledge work', since they are by no means alone in suffering from these problems. Indeed, in encountering these definitional and conceptual difficulties they are rubbing shoulders with Bell and contemporaries of Bell such as Touraine (Touraine, 1974) and Dahrendorf (Dahrendorf, 1959). In the section that follows, therefore, we will examine a range of contemporary contributions to the 'knowledge work' debate and we will, in addition, indulge a little speculation as to the longevity of this frankly rather limited line of analysis.

## Varieties of Knowledge Work

In attempting to explain the longevity of the post-industrial/post-capitalist schema, we might wish to speculate that when academics supportive of such notions of post-industrialism and knowledge work turn their attention to knowledge workers their judgement becomes clouded. Perry (Perry, 1993) and Ackroyd (Ackroyd, 1993), for example, note that theorizing is both a social and a cognitive activity. In this way, both Perry and Ackroyd suggest that, in part, the academic models and frameworks we deploy in our analyses have been selected from among the host of available models and frameworks for personal and social reasons. Perry and Ackroyd argue, therefore, that academics, as other actors, do not think, act and theorize in a vacuum, or in an entirely dispassionate fashion. Instead, they tell us, thinking and theorizing must be considered to be, both, a mental and a social process, such that academics should be viewed as actors who *choose* certain forms of thinking. In this sense, Perry and Ackroyd remind us that academics tend to choose to make use of certain constructs and models when/where these models satisfy certain theoretical conditions (the need for rigour and theoretical reliability), as well as certain social conditions (the need for the theoretical constructs to resonate, sympathetically, with the actor's experiences and orientations).

Thus, in modelling knowledge work we might indulge the speculation that management academics and educators are, perhaps, thinking, too much 'socially', and not enough 'cognitively'. After all, in analysing knowledge workers, however, loosely defined, academics are, in fact, studying a group of people with whom they apparently have much in common. Both groupings, for example, possess skills which, having been acquired over a prolonged period, are valued. Additionally the skills, which both groupings possess, are looked upon as allowing both knowledge workers and academics considerable discretion in the tasks they choose, and how these tasks are managed to completion.

This apparent similarity between subject and investigator may go some way to explaining the diversity, and the fuzziness of definitions of 'knowledge work', since we could argue that the majority of knowledge workers that appear in discussions of post-industrial/post-capitalist society, reflect the self-image academics would like to see in the mirror (and would like others to share), and as such represent rather personal and self-referential viewpoints. The problem is, of course, that most often, these personal and narrow views fail to capture the diverse management practices associated with 'knowledge work'.

Within the academic sphere, for example, Perry (1993) notes the distinctive approaches to management adopted by academic departments in the UK and the USA. Perry tells us that in the UK, academic research in the social sciences has followed an artisan type of approach, where relatively independent craft workers have pursued their own projects largely free from interference. However, analysing the nature and processes of academic toil in the USA, Perry tells us that academics, or if you like, 'knowledge workers', operate in a more formal, more hierarchical and a rather more Taylorized set-up, and so, are more directly under the gaze and control of management.

It seems clear, then, that it would be dangerous to generalize about, or attempt to universalize the management of a diverse group of workers, whether academics, marketers, doctors, soldiers or clerics, since it is plain to see, that the management policies and practices under which these knowledge workers labour, will tend to be the outcome of, often *ad hoc*, local accommodations, negotiations and historical traditions which would tend to confuse and befuddle any exercise in rationalization or prediction. Indeed, when we look beyond the work of Despres and Hiltrop to the contributions of their contemporaries in this knowledge work debate, the conceptual and empirical problems multiply.

## In Search of the Knowledge Worker

Nomikos, in his discussion of the problems of managing knowledge workers, adopts a definition of knowledge work, which seems to conflict directly with the analysis of Despres and Hiltrop. While Despres and Hiltrop argue that knowledge work is like no hitherto existing form of work, for Nomikos, knowledge workers are rather familiar and are 'a group that includes scientists, engineers, professors, attorneys, physicians and accountants' (Nomikos, 1989, p. 165).

Drucker, in contrast offers a far wider definition. In fact it is so wide that, at times, he seems to collapse knowledge work into the service sector. He tells us that:

> Knowledge and service workers range from research scientists and cardiac surgeons through draftswomen and store managers to 16 year

olds who flip hamburgers in fast food restaurants on Saturday afternoons. Their ranks also include people whose work makes them 'machine operators': dishwashers, janitors, data entry operators.

(Drucker, 1991, p. 71)

In fairness to Drucker we should note that, in this discussion, he does note some differences between knowledge and service workers. These differences we are told, reflect 'diversity in knowledge, skill, responsibility, social status and pay' (p. 71). But, as in our discussion of the management of academic departments, we have to wonder whether these differences are to be looked upon as differences in degree, or in kind, since we are never told where to draw a boundary around the knowledge work group. Clearly, the burger flipper is not a knowledge worker in Drucker's eyes but what of the draftswoman or store manager?

We should note too, that if the indices of knowledge work are, indeed, responsibility and social status, then there is the possibility that we are not gauging the knowledge worker or anything intrinsic about the task they perform. Instead, we may well be drawing attention to differences in management style between organizations, or differences in localized labour markets which affect the responsibilities, status and rewards accorded.

Kelley, in his discussion of knowledge workers, takes a slightly different tack which, in attempting to pick up on some of these less tangible aspects has similarities to, at least, one of the definitions offered by Despres and Hiltrop. Kelley tells us:

One change in the workforce that necessitates a new approach to management style is the emergence of gold collar, or knowledge workers. These workers are hired for their problem solving abilities, creativity, talent and intelligence.

(Kelley, 1990, p. 109)

Unlike the work of Nomikos, therefore, Kelley's approach does not seem so strongly wedded to formal qualifications, since he notes the necessity of key personal attributes which knowledge workers will require, such as creativity. However, we should note that creativity is a term reserved for socially sanctioned activity and like the term 'knowledge work', disguises a range of factors, which intervene in the judgement of such issues. Thus waiting tables, mixing cocktails, hewing wood and drawing water might all be regarded as highly creative forms of endeavour. Equally, acts of hacking, sabotage and other forms of crime made possible by information technology (Sterling, 1992) might also be regarded as creative and imaginative, but I doubt that many of these would count as knowledge work in Kelley's judgement.

However, just as in the post-industrial debates the diversity of the category of knowledge work, as revealed in these definitions, does not seem to trouble the various commentators. Perhaps these authors think *too socially*, and as a consequence have become blinded by their own reflection. Perhaps the need to address the problems of managing knowledge workers is so pressing that action is required over reflection.

No matter the reason, it is clear that in spite of the diverse definitions offered, the common conviction exists, that this, new, knowledge elite must receive concessions at work and must be managed in new and enlightened ways. No matter what he or she might look like, all seem agreed that knowledge workers are destined to be the new core of a happy, productive and committed workforce.

Yet these pronouncements must be treated with caution. Surely the competition between definitions, disguised within the espoused policies for knowledge work, makes such notions poor templates for action (and doubtful concepts in education). In fact, given the previous rehearsals of these issues, and given the limited analysis and reflection upon the concept of knowledge, which is at the heart of the debate, it should be of no surprise that the limited empirical work built upon this foundation demonstrates, only, that it is quite easy to mould the structural 'evidence' to fit your preferred policy outcome. A colleague of mine; an economist by training, assures me that: *if you interrogate data for long enough it will confess to anything.* As an illustration of this manipulation of evidence, we could do worse than examine Kanter's end of bureaucracy thesis (Kanter, 1991) since this has clear affinities to the concept of 'knowledge work'.

Kanter tells us that bureaucracy and large-scale corporations, as we understand them, are things of the past. They are, she tells us, unresponsive and anti-dynamic, and so, are badly suited to the modern environment of business. However, the empirical evidence Kanter offers to substantiate her claims as to the demise of bureaucracy, is weak. In fact her 'death of bureaucracy' thesis turns out to be based largely on a decline in the number of white-collar employees (which is in itself a fairly arbitrary categorization), rather than any real examination of the supposed bureaucratic nature of corporations – their modes of operation and the manner of reporting relationships prevalent (Perrow, 1979).

The problem common to analyses of post-industrialism and the 'knowledge age', as our brief critique of Kanter's work highlights, therefore, is that the categorization and future forecasts concerning work, are based upon vague and dubious notions as regards the nature of work, the processes of work and the processes of management in general.

In the section that follows, while acknowledging the existence of some important truths within the 'knowledge work' literature, we will attempt to demonstrate the ways in which the managerialist discussion of knowledge work misrepresents the nature and processes of managing. Indeed, we will argue that the current focus on 'knowledge work' is a distraction, which decontextualizes the experience of work and removes questions of control from the analysis. Using this analysis, we will attempt to show that what is basically an optimistic prognosis for 'knowledge work' – a form of analysis which assumes that levels of worker skill and discretion are bound to improve – often fails to comprehend what really happens to work, and to workers, when management takes an active interest in 'knowledge'.

## From Knowledge Work to Working Knowledge

Leaving aside the critique offered by Kumar, probably the simplest way to dash the variously competitive notions of 'knowledge work' as a new and elite form of activity, would be to make the general observation that knowledge workers cannot be a new, specialist or minority group. No matter what we do we are all, in some form or other, *knowledge workers*. To accomplish even the simplest of tasks requires some kind of working knowledge, acquired both formally and informally from supervisors, friends and co-workers. For example, Bendix (1956) in his historical study of management and management attitudes, reminds us of the importance of working knowledge and of the potency of 'working to rule'. He notes:

> Beyond what commands can effect and supervision can control, beyond what incentives can induce and penalties prevent, there exists an exercise of discretion important in relatively menial jobs, which managers of economic enterprises seek to enlist for the achievement of managerial ends.
>
> (Bendix, 1956, p. 256)

Kusterer (1978) also notes that even under Taylorist principles of work organization, 'unskilled workers must acquire a substantial body of knowledge to survive and succeed on their jobs – despite mechanization and automation, despite bureaucratization and the ever narrower division of labour' (Kusterer, 1991, preface).

In a similar fashion, Sennett (1998) discussing, perhaps, the exemplar of modern, unskilled labour; the McDonald's counter server, reminds us that studies of these workers, reveal them to be quite different to the unskilled, unsophisticated automata of popular imagination. Indeed, he warns us of the dangers of stereotyping when he notes that a study of servers in McDonald's restaurants: 'found that supposedly unskilled workers suddenly spring to mental attention and deploy all manner of improvised skills to keep the operation going when faced with [some unforeseen event such as] a mechanical crisis' (Sennett, 1998, p. 72). However, while these discussions and quotations offer a powerful rebuttal to the notion of knowledge work, they do not explain why such distractions should be so persistent, nor do they really offer insight into what, actually, tends to happen when management begins to take a real interest in the activities and skills of subordinates.

## A Persistent Folly?

Leaving to one side our discussion of management academia and its vanities and preoccupations, perhaps the easiest way to rationalize the managerial interest in knowledge work and in post-industrial society would be to acknowledge that, in many ways, the world of work has changed quite markedly. Equally, based on the earlier argument that theorizing is both a cognitive and a social activity we might, as Keat and Abercrombie (1991) do, and as Huczynski does (Huczynski, 1993), locate the rather optimistic and managerialist agenda of the 'knowledge worker' debate within a discussion of shifting economic and political agendas in Britain and the US during the 1980s (see chapter 5).

Alternatively, in attempting to speculate on the persistence of the folly which is the knowledge work debate, we might wish to speculate on the personal mission of these management academics, as say Baritz (Baritz, 1965) might have, had he observed the resurgence of a confident managerialist discourse in the 1980s and 1990s. Thus, following Baritz, we might wish to argue that management academics often seem to care little for theoretical elegance and vitality, because they have abandoned the manners and mores of the academy and have, instead, come to share the preoccupations of management's practitioners. As such, Baritz's analysis would suggest that management academia should be considered part of the technology of management control, and so, should be evaluated in a fashion which gauges the extent to which management academia refines and/or extends management's control over the labour process. Thus, at one level, Baritz's analysis would suggest that when we harangue the advocates of post-industrialism over their failure to develop robust models and definitions of knowledge work, we misunderstand their aims, since these actors do not seek to explain the world of work, rather, they seek to control the world of work, and are keen to market their ability to perform this task for management.

However, these discussions are a little outwith the scope of this particular chapter, and so we will confine our attention to the first line of analysis offered above, and will offer a brief sketch of the changing experience of (physical) work.

## The Changing Experience of Work

Reflecting upon the nature of work, and of the changing experiences, both of working and of managerial control, Zuboff (1989) in her study of the *smart machine* notes how, in earlier periods, the experience of work for the majority of the population revolved around extremes of physical effort. Historically, she tells us, work was something which was enacted upon the body. Indeed, she reminds us that in the processes of working the body was, quite literally, expended. Orwell (1978) notes, for example, the physical effort which coal miners had to endure simply to reach their place of work, at the coal face. Similarly Zuboff makes us, rather painfully, aware of the extreme physical toil associated even with apparently gentle pursuits such as candy making. She offers a quotation, which observes:

> 'The whole process . . . requires great skill in the manipulation and it also requires the most severe and continuous muscular labour. We know, indeed of no other kind of labour that requires more. Not a muscle or joint of the whole body remains inactive. It has quite a marvelous effect in taking down superfluous fat. It is well known that a stout man taken perhaps from lozenge making, and put to work on the hot pan, becomes in six weeks converted into a living skeleton.'
>
> (Zuboff, 1989, p. 38)

Discussing the working conditions of 'puddlers', a group of skilled furnace men, she notes: '"Few puddlers, it was said, lived beyond the age of 50"' (Zuboff, 1989, p. 39). Zuboff argues that as mechanization and automation have advanced, so work has become, less and less, an activity enacted upon the body. Indeed, she notes that in an era marked by the development of information technology, the act of working has, for many, become more remote; distant from the five senses, which we routinely use to orientate ourselves. In her analysis of the automation of a paper mill, for example, Zuboff communicates, clearly, the sense of loss and disorientation experienced by operatives. She notes that, previously, workers had been accustomed to monitoring the production of paper by handling, squeezing and physically testing its 'feel'. However, following the automation of the mill, workers became isolated from the product of their labours by a new computer controlled system. Zuboff notes that following the implementation of the new technology, the workers were forced to attempt to control the, once familiar process using the abstract and disembodied symbols which the new IT system made available to them. However, she warns us that this new system designed to control the process of paper-making served to deskill workers, and, furthermore, served only to place the paper-making process beyond effective control.

In his discussion of the forms and processes of work in a modern, computerized, bakery, Sennett (1998) makes a similar point. Indeed, in common, with Zuboff, Sennett, manages to communicate, (1) the sense of loss which is felt by the 'bakers', and (2) the limited and fallible nature of this, supposed, smart technology. Thus Sennett argues:

> Computerized baking has profoundly changed the balletic physical activities of the shop floor. Now the bakers make no physical contact with the materials or the loaves of bread, monitoring the entire process via on-screen icons which depict, for instance, images of bread color

derived from data about the temperature and baking time of the ovens; few bakers actually see the loaves of bread they make. Their working screens are organized in the familiar Windows way; in one icons for many more different kinds of bread appear than had been prepared in the past – Russian, Italian, French loaves all possible by touching the screen. Bread had become a screen representation.

As a result of working in this way, the bakers now no longer actually know how to bake bread. Automated bread is no marvel of technological perfection; the machines frequently tell the wrong story about the loaves rising within, for instance, failing to gauge accurately the strength of the rising yeast, or the actual color of the loaf. The workers can fool with the screen to correct somewhat for these defects; what they can't do is fix the machines, or more important, actually bake bread by manual control when the machines all too often go down. Program-dependent laborers, they can have no hands-on knowledge. The work is no longer legible to them, in the sense of understanding what they are doing.

(Sennett, 1998, p. 68)

At one level, then, we can rationalize the interest in knowledge work, and in the manifest interest, in the manipulation of data and symbols, as reflecting a clear understanding that, in certain ways, the experience of work has changed quite profoundly. Thus we may rationalize the focus upon knowledge work as a recognition of changes in the physical experience of labour.

However, we should also acknowledge that, in spite of the growing use of information technology, and in spite of the changing physical aspects of working, in other ways work has remained little changed. In places Zuboff demonstrates this quite well. For example in her analysis of the paper mill workers, Zuboff draws our attention to the fact that these 'knowledge workers' share an experience of working, common to many work contexts – both historical and contemporary. Thus Zuboff communicates the continued and indeed, growing, sense of alienation and disaffection among the workers in the paper mill.

Sennett (1998), again also observes a similar package of change and degradation. Discussing the case of the bread makers – they could hardly be considered bakers – he notes:

in the bakery, I caught sight of a terrible paradox. In this high-tech, flexible workplace where everything is user-friendly, the workers felt personally demeaned by the way they work. In this bakers' paradise, that reaction to their work is something they do not themselves understand. Operationally, everything is so clear; emotionally, so illegible.

(Sennett, 1998, p. 68)

We should note, however, that these experiences of work are not peculiar to factory environments. Lest we should think that these negative accounts of work and working are confined to a few groups of employees, whom the 'gurus' observed might be left behind by the march of knowledge work, Zuboff offers us an analysis of clerical work. In her study of white-collar work, Zuboff demonstrates the enlarged potential for remote, management supervision which can be enacted upon 'white collar factory' workers (Simon, 1976). Indeed making use of the work of Bentham and Foucault (1991) she argues that knowledge work, and the 'information age' carry with them, not liberation, but the threat that management, and perhaps the state, will use technology to invade more and more of the space previously claimed by workers and citizens for unsupervised, discretionary activity (Wooley, 1993).

Taken together with our concerns regarding the robustness and vitality of the concepts of knowledge work and post-industrial society, these questions of control and alienation; and the obvious control activity enacted upon knowledge workers, suggests that we would do well to abandon the notion of 'knowledge work' in favour of the concept of working knowledge. Thus, as compared to the essentially conservative account of knowledge work, the concept of working knowledge serves to remind us of the important skills – the day-to day, working knowledge which unskilled workers possess and must exercise. Indeed, in comparison to notions of 'knowledge work', the concept of working knowledge serves to remind us of the basic facts of paid employment (Terkel, 1985) and pinpoints too, significant continuities in the experience of the labour process, which management writers would prefer to dismiss as the prehistory of the industrial age (Thompson and McHugh, 1990).

Thus instead of rushing to embrace the collegiate, empowering and harmonious visions of the future, laid out before us, we would instead, do well to examine the lessons of history. Even if knowledge (however construed), is becoming more important in the workplace, even if the physical experience of labour is changing, all the lessons of history tell us that when management becomes interested in (appropriating) the knowledge which workers have with regard to work skills and processes, the conditions under which we work tend to deteriorate. Fucini and Fucini (1990) demonstrate this for the automobile industry (see also Graham, 1994, and Parker and Slaughter, 1988). Similarly, Sewell and Wilkinson (1992) demonstrate the importance of supervision and surveillance in the electronics industry.

In their case study of an organization concerned with the manufacture of electronics goods, Sewell and Wilkinson show that while this type of workplace is often vaunted and celebrated by the 'gurus' as representative of the new knowledge age – where knowledge as the primary economic resource serves to bind management and workers in a co-operative embrace – the management group they studied had developed a range of control initiatives which seem to conflict with the collegiate image of knowledge work. Indeed, Sewell and Wilkinson report that the organization they studied had, in effect, reintroduced an older system of workplace surveillance and control, known as the 'silent monitor'. This system, we should note, was developed in the nineteenth century to discipline and control a working population which was so 'given to drunkenness, improvidence and prolific conception out of wedlock' (Gatrell, 1970, p. 39) that it could not be trusted to work without detailed supervision. So much for trust and collaboration!

Zuboff, in her account of work, autonomy and control offers us a, similarly, stark contrast to the visions of collegiate harmony promoted by the 'gurus' of knowledge work. Indeed, she demonstrates that detailed supervision and control are not just features of factory work. Indeed, contrary to the accounts of Drucker and Bell, Zuboff argues that detailed forms of managerial control may also be found in clerical workplaces, and in the work environs of 'professional' groups. Analysing the habits and work patterns of a range of workers, employed to track information, and to traffic in data, Zuboff attempts to analyse the implications for working life, of the management strategies and practices designed to facilitate the use of novel information systems.

In order to probe the implications, for work and for work skills and interaction, of management's use of information technology, Zuboff asked her respondents to draw, for her, a series of sketches depicting the 'old' and the 'new' systems of working. Typically, these sketches are notable because they present a picture of change at work, which is far from the up-skilling, harmonious and professionalized account of knowledge work presented by the 'gurus' of management. Indeed, the sketches presented by Zuboff convey a strong sense of loss, disaffection and dissatisfaction with the nature of the work; and with the nature and extent of supervision.

If we move from the office back to the plant, and compare a contemporary discussion of the system of work in a car factory; namely the Mazda factory studied by the Fucinis, with what for a variety of reasons (see Collins, 1995), might be regarded as a classic contribution to industrial sociology, namely Beynon's *Working for Ford* (Beynon, 1979), one cannot help but be struck by the increased pace of work and the deterioration in work experience which the knowledge appropriating policies of empowerment (see chapter 7), just-in-time production (JIT) and *kaizen* (a strategy of continuous improvement in products and in work processes) seem to bring with them.

In *Working for Ford*, Beynon presents a grim view of a deskilled form of work, taking place in an environment where work is often degrading, and where mutual distrust between workers and managers is the order of the day. Yet, within this account, the work groups studied by Beynon are regularly reported as modifying their pace of working in order to allow them to vary the rhythm of work. Beynon, for example, notes how groups of workers would decide amongst themselves to increase their pace for a short period so that they could 'work up the line' and enjoy an unscheduled break – perhaps to allow the employees to smoke a cigarette.

However, in the Mazda plant reported by the Fucinis, a plant which celebrates its post-Taylorist credentials, and which promises the empowerment of workers, such teamwork and endeavour would not be rewarded by a cigarette break. Instead the ability to work up the line would be called '*kaizen-ing*' and would tend to result, not in an *ad hoc* benefit enjoyed by a particular work group, but in a generalised increase in the pace of work for all employees. Viewed in these terms, the so-called post-Taylorist, knowledge work, environment seems to offer less scope for discretion, and offers workers fewer opportunities to control and to shape their work rhythms, when compared to the Taylorized environment discussed by Beynon!

However, it is worth noting that it is doubtful whether anyone could find the reserves of strength to work up the line in the Mazda plant discussed by the Fucinis. In comparison to previous (pre-knowledge work?) times when workers might have expected to work 43 seconds per minute, the empowered knowledge elite of the Mazda plant can expect only 3 seconds respite per minute.

It seems, then that in spite of the rhetoric of 'knowledge work', employees in the auto industry, in the electronics industry, in clerical work and in the professions are being driven to work smarter, harder *and* for longer. And so, if we truly stand on the threshold of a new age of work, there may be little cause for celebration. Indeed, given the implications for work, skill and worker autonomy, which we have uncovered, it seems appropriate to suggest that the knowledge age, and its associated intellectual and political baggage should be regarded as a cause for concern.

## Summary

In this chapter we have argued that the concepts of 'knowledge work' and the 'knowledge age' serve as a brake on academic analysis. While some of the ideas and arguments associated with knowledge work have a plausible ring, the potency of these arguments tends to become very much weakened when we examine the ambiguity and confusion which surrounds these terms. Indeed, the arguments marshalled by the 'gurus', as they attempt to build their preferred model of the future of work, tend to become very much weakened when we place 'knowledge work' in context. When we pause to look, critically, at where knowledge work will be performed and when we look critically at the organizations which play host to the ideal of knowledge workers our futures tend to look less than alluring.

Yet we need not remain tied to the concept of post-industrial society. Nor need we tie ourselves to the social and intellectual conservatism of this debate. We can, if we choose to make the effort, develop and use concepts for quite different ends. Why not, instead of bandying around terms such as knowledge work, begin from the understanding that all workers are knowledge(able) workers, and that all have skills and working knowledge, rather than claim knowledge in work as the possession of a minority group.

If we are to regard workers as key resources, why begin from an initial assumption which implies that many have only the most limited resources at their disposal? How much better it would be if, instead of levering buzz-words into currently popular models and ways of thinking about management and organizations, we attempted to develop and apply concepts which could engender different ways of thinking about problems and innovations within organizations.

In this way we could turn the debate on its head. In the case of working knowledge – my preferred alternative to 'knowledge work' – we could begin from an analytical standpoint which would argue/remember that all have knowledge, but that in seeking to appropriate this knowledge, the rhetoric which management commentators apply, and which they encourage others to apply, serves to deny the existence and value of this knowledge in all but a few. From this understanding a range of different projects and research agendas could be spawned – not least of which might be a critical analysis of the nature of management education.

# 11  Globalization

## Introduction

The world of management is, by any definition of the term, a crazy place; a place where pools of common knowledge have a tendency to evaporate. During the 1960s and 1970s, for example, 'common knowledge' advised managers that success, size and efficiency went hand-in-hand. To succeed, organizations had to dominate. Hence, organizations all across Europe and America expanded and grew by conglomeration. ITT, for example, grew from being a telephone and telegraph company to become a complex holding company; the owner of a wide range of businesses, including a hotel chain, a car rental business and a bread-making process (Geneen and Moscow, 1986). Similarly, Ford, which had always been a vertically integrated company, expanded its operations during the 1960s and 1970s to acquire a diverse range of businesses including electronics companies, defence contractors and aeroplane manufacturers, in an attempt to become big and strong.

During the 1980s, however, Peters and Waterman (1982), together with other colleagues at McKinsey (see Pascale and Athos, 1986), began to argue that the big, strong conglomerates had succeeded in only part of their ambition. They had become big, but their size and their muscle, it was argued, had made them surly. The conglomerate corporations of the 1970s had set out to dominate markets but had come to dominate their customers. Accordingly, American corporations had become big, but weak, because a range of 'excellent' organizations, focused upon a core of business, and upon the needs of their customers, had found ways to out-compete the big businesses, which common knowledge had assumed would be both, big and strong.

By the mid-1980s, however the excellence pool of common knowledge was beginning to look a little like a damp stain. A range of Peters' and Waterman's, 'excellent' companies, it was noted, were failing (Guest, 1992). In the light of these events, it seemed the 'new' excellence exemplar might be just as flawed as the 'old' big business exemplar. Reflecting upon this, Peters and Austin (1985) argued that, while the concept of 'excellence' was robust, the conduct of the organizations, which had been labelled as excellent, did not always live up to the ideals of business excellence. Thus Peters and Austin argued that organizations would have to rethink, and would have to refine, the concept of excellence.

Imparting to the argument of Peters and Austin, perhaps more eloquence than it truly deserves we could summarize the position as follows: to become excellent, organizations have to shake off the assumptions, which under-pinned the conduct of American business in earlier eras. Thus Peters and Austin have argued that excellent organizations will have to abandon the assumption that big is best, and will have to abandon the assumption that they can, somehow, dominate, or come to a peaceful accommodation with the business environment.

Reflecting upon the apparent failure of their excellent companies, there-fore, Peters and Austin argued that the decline of these businesses could be explained in terms of the persistence of out-moded business assump-tions. Excellent organizations would fail, and would continue to fail, they warned, so long as these organizations continued to think of excellence as a structure which could be achieved, or as something which would pacify a capricious environment. The environment of business, Peters and Austin argued, was not about to settle down to a stable and familiar pattern. It would continue to change and, like customers would not be dominated. Accordingly, organizations would have to stop talking about being 'excel-lent'. Instead, they would have to recognize that excellence is a destination that cannot be reached. Organizations, Peters and Austin argued, would always and forever, be in the process of *becoming* excellent. In the parlance of the 'gurus', therefore, excellence is to be regarded as a 'mind-set', and not a structural attribute.

Since the 1990s a range of different commentators (see Huczynski, 1993) have put forward a bewildering array of concepts and techniques which, in essence, detail the path or paths (Hilmer and Donaldson, 1996) to becom-ing excellent. A range of these ideas and techniques have been analysed and criticized in the preceding chapters of this book. We have noted, for exam-ple, the ways in which organizations have, variously, been urged to embrace cultural change; to downsize (and embrace cultural change); to re-engineer (and embrace cultural change); to empower employees, and so on.

In this chapter, I wish to look more closely at one of the more recent ideas which has occupied the hands and minds (sadly, not the minds and hands!) of management which, so far, we have not had an opportunity to discuss in detail. Accordingly, this chapter will examine the concept of globalization.

## Exploring Globalization

The notion of globalization, as we shall see, encompasses a loose, diverse and, at times, contradictory package of ideas. Waters (1998) notes, for

example, a basic dispute between academic commentators who view globalization as a 'modern' phenomenon, associated with the development of
capitalism, and other commentators who view globalization as a postmodern phenomenon, which challenges our definition of work, society,
geography, distance and mobility.

In the business world, the concept of globalization seems both to reject,
and to build from a range of earlier ideas and assumptions. In the book,
*World Class,* for example, Kanter (1995) suggests that globalizing processes have given birth to new forms of competition and new modes of
organizing, yet she uses a familiar variant of contingency analysis (see
McLoughlin and Clark, 1994; Woodward, 1970) to convey her thesis.
Thus Kanter argues that changes in the environment and structure of
business, and in forms and processes of technology, will force all organizations (no matter their size) to change their structures and processes.
Indeed, Kanter argues that globalizing imperatives will force organizations
to source materials, to compete for business, and to sell to customers on
a world stage. Building upon an eclectic mix of management theorizing,
(see Collins, 1998), therefore, Kanter insists that 'world class' organizations need to be the right size: excellent but not complacent, customer,
not product-focused, lean but not mean, organized yet disorganized, if
they are to thrive within an environment of business which is global in,
both, scale and scope. Thus Kanter notes:

> Globalization is surely one of the most powerful and pervasive influ-
> ences on nations, businesses, workplaces, communities and lives at the
> end of the twentieth century.
>     Information technology, communication, travel, and trade that link
> the world are revolutionary in their impact. Global economic forces
> – and desires – are causing regimes to topple, enemies to bury the
> political hatchet in a common quest for foreign investment, large corpo-
> rations to rethink their strategies and structures, governments to scale
> back and privatize services, consumers to see the whole planet as their
> shopping mall, and communities to compete with cities worldwide for
> prominence as international centers that attract the best companies
> and jobs.
>
> (Kanter, 1995, p. 11)

In a similar fashion, Ohmae's (1994) account of 'the borderless world',
that is, the global economy, portrays a picture of economic change and
turbulence which, of necessity, will require action from a range of decision-makers. Thus, he argues that the process of globalization will require
a new mode of economic theorizing, and new modes of social organization which, in turn, will draw on the skills of politicians, and the skills of
the business community, to construct a new order. In addition Ohmae
also argues that these changes will require action from 'bureaucrats – a

faceless grouping (of course) whom he seems to despise. In this sense Ohmae's book, like Kanter's, should be regarded as an attempt to construct a particular representation of globalization. This representation, in common with the other buzzwords we have analysed, builds from a 'grammar' of imperatives to present a particular account of management and organization in the post-cold war, borderless world.

Ohmae, of course, is a management consultant, not a social theorist. It should not surprise us to learn, therefore, that much of his analysis – his reading of political movements and events – is driven by an understanding of consumers and consumer behaviour. Thus he tells us:

> people are global when as consumers they have access to information about goods and services from around the world. But these same people could support protectionist representatives if all they read is rhetoric based upon archaic nationalistic sentiments. Students, even today, are learning old economic theories that do not work in the ILE [the inter-linked economy which is the term Ohmae uses to highlight the extent of mutual trade activity within and across the economic 'triad' which includes the US, Europe and Japan]. Most of these theories were created at the turn of the century when the national model – the closed economy – was *the* model. Most statistics are still gathered based on this old framework, and hence macroeconomic analyses tell little about what is happening or what will happen in the world, or even in a country.
>
> It is time for us to look at the real economy of an interlinked world.
>                                 (Ohmae, 1994, p. xiii, original emphasis)

But how are we to accomplish this? What is the 'real' economy? What are we looking for? How should we look?

These are important areas for consideration since we cannot hope to make sense of globalization until such issues have been considered. As Bauman (1998) warns:

> 'Globalization' is on everybody's lips; a fad word fast turning into a shibboleth, a magic incantation, a pass key meant to unlock the gates to all present and future mysteries. For some 'globalization' is what we are bound to do if we wish to be happy; for others 'globalization' is the cause of our unhappiness. For everybody, though, 'globalization' is the intractable fate of the world, an irreversible process; it is also a process which affects us all in the same measure and in the same way. We are all being 'globalized' – and being 'globalized' means much the same to all who 'globalized' are.
>
> All vogue words tend to share a similar fate: the more experiences they pretend to make transparent, the more they themselves become opaque. The more numerous are the orthodox truths they elbow out

and supplant, the faster they turn into no-questions-asked canons. Such human practices as the concept tried originally to grasp recede from view, and it is now the 'facts of the matter, the quality of the 'world out there' which the term seems to 'get straight' and which it invokes to claim its own immunity to questioning. 'Globalization' is no exception to that rule.

(Bauman, 1998, p. 1)

Reflecting Bauman's concerns and the misgivings he has, regarding the concept of globalization, we will attempt to offer a 'critical-practical' account of this contested phenomenon. This chapter, therefore, will seek to offer a readily digestible account of globalization, which recognizes that this concept is a complex and contested representation of social processes. In presenting globalization in these terms, I hope to resist the temptation to descend into the reductionist mode of analysis preferred by the 'gurus' of management.

Globalization, as we shall see, has become a management buzzword. In the name of globalization a number of commentators have suggested that far-reaching changes *will have to be* engineered at home, at work, and in our communities, if we are to prosper in the new age, which we are assured, awaits those who are ready to adjust their expectations. Viewed in these terms the globalization buzzword (as articulated by the 'gurus') clearly achieves its force and significance from a grammar of imperatives, which will countenance no objection or dissent concerning the 'facts' of globalization as a force which cannot be opposed. In keeping with the approach we have adopted throughout this book, however, this chapter will seek to challenge and undermine the 'guru' discussion of globalization. Indeed, we will attempt to show how the 'gurus' contrive to disguise the contest and controversy, which surround the concept of globalization. In an attempt to reveal globalization as a contested representation of social change, therefore, we will seek to undermine the 'grammar' which the 'gurus' have invoked to give this buzzword its force and immediacy. Accordingly, this chapter is structured as follows.

We begin by offering a discussion of globalization as put forward by management's 'gurus'. As we shall see, globalization is a concept, which appears in the works of all management's key 'gurus'. Indeed, we might say, in keeping with our earlier metaphorical exposition, that the concept of globalization is, currently, one of the biggest fish in management's pool of common knowledge. Yet, we should not assume that all of management's commentators, necessarily, share a common understanding of globalization. The managerial commentators, of course, do share a common 'grammar', which is invoked in an attempt to express the significance of globalization as a business process driven by the imperatives of competition and technological change. However, it would be unwise to assume that management's key writers share a common vocabulary designed for, and dedicated to the analysis of globalization. Indeed, we would do well to note that the widespread usage, and common-sense acceptance of the term 'globalization' as an issue *requiring urgent action*, often serves to disguise a subtle, yet fundamental contest within the ranks of management's 'gurus'.

Thus among the 'gurus' discussing globalization we may identify two main camps: a grouping which analyses globalization as a market phenomenon, and so, implies that tendencies towards globalization *will* change the operation of markets such that organizations *will have to rethink* their competitive strategies and their approach to 'overseas' business (see Ohmae, 1994) *versus* a second grouping which analyses globalization as having consequence for markets *and* products, such that globalization is interpreted as an imperative to produce standardized, 'global products', designed to meet the demands of a singular, global market (Levitt, 1983; Enis and Cox, 1991).

Reflecting this basic tension at the heart of the 'guru' discussions of globalization we will offer an analysis of management's 'gurus' which will acknowledge, both, the commonalties which unite, and the contests which tend to divide these commentators. Having accomplished this analysis of the 'gurus' and their accounts of globalization, we will turn from our focus upon market imperatives, in order to embrace a larger and more sociological form of debate. This, more sociological form of debate, as we shall see, is rooted in a different form of 'grammar'. As opposed to the 'guru' analyses which derive their force and meaning from a 'grammar' of imperatives, our more sociological form of analysis builds from 'subjunctive' or 'imperfect' grammar, and so, seeks to show those ways in which globalizing forces may be mediated and/or deflected. Our alternative account of globalization, therefore, is an attempt to transcend the narrow and limiting concerns of business, in order to analyse, more fully, the human consequences of (the terms of the) globalization (debate). Thus, we will invoke our 'critical-practical' line of analysis so that we might throw off the imperative-determinist arguments of management's 'gurus'. Through this analysis I hope to encourage readers to consider the human possibilities, rather than the business and organizational consequences of globalization.

In this sense, the chapter developed here might be considered as an attempt to explore the terrain of the globalization discussion, while attempting to expose the limits and blind alleys which are part of its geography. In keeping with the preceding chapters of this work, therefore, I hope to provide a form of analysis which is designed to allow readers to locate, and to understand, the debates over globalization, so that they might offer more thoughtful voices amid the clamour of the available management commentaries. Yet, as we shall see in the section that follows, the achievement of this 'critical-practical' form of analysis is not unproblematic.

## Once More from the Top?

A key problem confronts any attempt to offer a thoughtful yet economical account and summary of the management 'gurus' and their ideas. There are, I am afraid, so many commentators active in the field of management that any attempt to offer a summary briefing becomes a fraught and dangerous pursuit. Indeed, any attempt to offer an economical analysis of management's 'gurus' is, in truth, a gift to hostile reviewers, since any summary review of this subject is bound to be incomplete and, in any sense of the term, partial (see Collins, 1998).

In previous chapters we have employed a number of different devices, designed to facilitate an economical account of the 'gurus'. For example, in discussing Total Quality Management (TQM) we were able to subdivide the 'guru' world according to expertise and speciality. Indeed, we were able to highlight a select band of quality 'gurus' with relative ease (see chapter 6). Likewise in our discussion of re-engineering (see chapter 8) we were able to isolate, with comparative ease, the important commentaries prepared for managers. Yet, any attempt to isolate those 'gurus' concerned with globalization is more problematic, and will tend to be somewhat arbitrary since, in a variety of ways – whether as a spectre or as a fully formed analytical concern – the concept of globalization tends to appear in all, contemporary 'guru' discussions of management. It is, after all, but a small step from the familiar argument: the competitive imperative makes all markets and processes vulnerable to competitors, and forces all organizations to get close to the customer (by whatever means), to make the amendment; of course these competitors are global in scope and reach.

Yet, while recognizing the perils and pitfalls associated with any attempt to classify, or to sub-divide the 'gurus' of management, we must try to isolate a group of commentators, and/or some accounts of globalization from the larger 'boast' (my preferred collective noun) of 'gurus', if we are to have any hope of producing a digestible account of this phenomenon. Accordingly, and mindful of the problems and pitfalls of selecting from among the boast of 'gurus', our analysis of the managerial account of globalization begins with a brief account of Levitt's seminal discussion of *The Globalization of Markets* (Levitt, 1983) before proceeding to analyse three, recent and influential, managerial texts which have taken globalization as their central analytical theme. Thus, following our analysis of Levitt's paper, we will turn our attention to Kanter's (1995) *World Class*, Ghoshal's and Bartlett's (1998) *Managing Across Borders* and to Ohmae's (1994) *Borderless World*. Through this analysis I hope to show those facets which unite, and the words which tend to divide the 'gurus' in their explorations of globalization.

# The Globalization of Markets

In keeping with the, now familiar, leitmotif of management's 'gurus', Levitt locates globalization as a product of changes in technology and consumption. Indeed, he argues that the process of globalization amounts to the production of a singular, global market for the standardized goods and services which organizations will find it sensible, and viable to produce in the new global era of business. He argues:

> A powerful force drives the world toward a converging commonality, and that force is technology. It has proletarianized communication, transport and travel. It has made isolated places and impoverished peoples eager for modernity's allurements. Almost everyone wants all the things they have heard about, seen, or experienced via the new technologies.
>
> The result is a new commercial reality – the emergence of global markets for standardized consumer products on a previously unimagined scale of magnitude. Corporations geared to this new reality benefit from enormous economies of scale in production, distribution, marketing and management. By translating these benefits into reduced world prices, they can decimate competitors that still live in the disabling grip of old assumptions about how the world works.
>
> (Reproduced in Enis and Cox (eds), 1991, p. 528)

Levitt argues, therefore, that all across the globe there are now markets, opportunities and *sotto voce*, competitors hungry for 'modernity's allurements' (see Enis and Cox, 1991, p. 528). But what are these old and disabling assumptions which globalization seems set to rip from the text-books of management?

Reflecting upon an era prior to the globalization of markets, Levitt argues that globalization signals the death-knell of the multi-national corporations which, in the post-World War II era, rose to occupy a privileged position in economic matters. These multi-national corporations, Levitt warns us, conduct business using tired assumptions which, in the global era, make for an out-moded and unsustainable approach to commerce, because they still conceive of the world in multi-national terms; as a range of different national segments each with its own tastes and preferences. The global corporation, he warns us, acts quite differently. In an illuminating passage (which could, equally have been penned by a radical critic of big business (see Collins, 1998) he argues that, unlike multi-national businesses, the global corporation:

> treats the world as composed of few standardized markets rather than many customized markets. It actively seeks and vigorously

works toward global convergence. Its mission is modernity and its mode, price competition, even when it sells top-of-the-line, high-end products.

(Reproduced in Enis and Cox (eds), 1991, p. 532)

For Levitt, then, globalization has key implications for the production and marketing of products, such that the entire globe should be regarded as a single market, or as converging towards a single market. Perhaps unsurprisingly, given the magnitude of the change envisaged, Levitt also suggests that the process of globalization will have key implications for the nature of organizations and for the conduct of management. As we shall see, Kanter seems to endorse much of Levitt's analysis of globalization.

## World Class

In common with Levitt, Kanter argues that globalization is a process driven by technological change and market imperatives. Like Levitt's analysis, however, Kanter's discussion of globalization does not begin and end with a discussion of market imperatives. Instead, Kanter is keen to trace the manner in which changes in markets and technology work to enforce wider changes within organizations. In common with Levitt, therefore, Kanter argues that the forces of globalization, facilitated by technological change, will cause changes in markets such that organizations will have to modify the products and services they offer, while changing their mode of organizing.

Unlike the work of Levitt, however, Kanter seems less assured as to the validity and viability of a global product strategy. Thus where Levitt extols the virtues of global products, designed and produced with a single global market in mind, Kanter's work, the case of the aircraft industry aside, maintains a quieter, more low-key approach to this issue.

Those hostile to the work of Kanter might be tempted to venture that, on the subject of global products, Kanter has attempted to evade a key, yet problematic issue. In fairness to Kanter, therefore, we should point out that, while her analysis does not pursue the issue of global products, her discussion of globalization, in other ways, goes beyond Levitt's analysis, since unlike Levitt, she is keen to step outside the immediate environs of the workplace to study the impact of the processes of globalization on the lives we must lead outside work.

Thus, while noting the organizational and market consequences of globalization as key areas for analysis, much of Kanter's text is focused upon the implications for community politics, and for local economies, of globalization. Indeed Kanter is keen to stress that globalization, as a pervasive force for change, will touch every community and every home, as well as every workplace. She argues:

Four broad processes are associated with globalization: mobility, simultaneity, bypass and pluralism. Together they help put more choices in the hands of individual consumers and organizational customers, which, in turn, generates a 'globalization cascade' – mutually reinforcing feedback loops that strengthen and accelerate globalizing forces.

(Kanter, 1995, p. 41)

It is worth looking a little more closely at these four processes.

## Mobility

Kanter argues that capital, people and ideas are increasingly mobile. Organizations in the global era of business, she argues, will be forced to source and sell resources, not according to some regional policy, and not with reference to the 'home-base' of the organization. Instead, she argues that organizations will operate globally and will be mobile in their attempts to pursue the economic advantages which mobility allows.

## Simultaneity

In the days when multi-national corporations reigned supreme, products would be produced, marketed and sold in a phased manner. The US market might receive the product in 1956, Britain and Europe might receive the version of the product designed for their markets in 1957, Australia in 1958 and Africa much later, if at all.

Yet, this picture has changed quite fundamentally. Now, Kanter tells us, products become available in all corners of the world simultaneously. Indeed, and carrying echoes of Levitt's discussion of global products, she notes: 'The newer the technology or application, the more likely it is to be designed with the whole world in mind' (Kanter, 1995, p. 44).

## Bypass

Kanter argues that globalization is facilitated by the presence of alternatives. Technological change, deregulation and the privatization of government monopolies, she argues, all make it easier for entrepreneurs and innovators to bypass problems, or to overcome deficiencies, and so, allow business to be transacted in areas where logistics or politics had previously made commerce problematic.

## Pluralism

The fourth of Kanter's processes of globalization describes a tendency, which is supported and facilitated by the three globalizing processes noted above. Put plainly, the notion of pluralism, in this context, suggests a process where mobility, bypass and simultaneity, 'de-centre' power structures by making local action (which, for Kanter implies, among other things, action out of the gaze of national headquarters), both unavoidable and attractive. Thus the concept of pluralism suggests that while the activities of global businesses shape local policies, global business, itself, will be shaped by local considerations.

Reflecting upon these four processes of change and the problems and opportunities these throw up, Kanter argues that *both* work organizations, and the communities which play host to these businesses, will have to embark upon change programmes designed to make them competitive in the globalized world. Kanter argues, therefore, that global organizations will have to compete for business and will have to be prepared to produce, source and market their goods according to the rules of competition (as opposed to the whim of national politics and nationalist sentiment).

In tandem with this programme of change Kanter also argues that the communities we inhabit will have to adopt a similar approach to the problem of globalization. Thus Kanter argues that communities need world class organizations if they are to thrive and survive. She suggests, therefore, that communities will have to compete to play host to world class organizations, and so must be prepared to accommodate their needs. Those organizations and communities, which achieve competitiveness on a global scale, Kanter describes in metaphorical terms as being 'world class'.

## World Class Communities

Pursuing her notion of 'world class' communities (as the necessary adjuncts to 'world class' organizations), Kanter argues that communities can become world class, and so, can become worthy to host world class work organizations by pursuing one of three strategies. To become world class, communities must structure themselves as either:

- *Thinkers*: geared to defining, refining and improving concepts.
- *Makers*: geared to offering 'exceptional competence'.
- *Traders*: forging, maintaining and profiting from the ability to make connections.

For a community to be world class, therefore, Kanter argues that it must endeavour to 'become' a global centre for research and development; a global centre for production and manufacture; or a global centre for trading and arbitrage.

How are communities to achieve this? By developing the skills of the population, by improving infrastructure, by being willing to change, and, perhaps most importantly, by being willing to work with business leaders, whom, it is said should be allowed to lead our communities through the requisite change process. All of this sounds highly plausible. But, we have the right to ask a few more questions of this analysis.

- Is it true that communities can only achieve the requisite level of competence in one of the three areas of capability identified?
- How did Kanter happen upon her preferred agenda for change?
- How did she decide upon this agenda as the only sustainable mode and pattern of change?
- On what basis, and for what reason, did she select her preferred model of community change and development?
- Will this top–down model of change suit all contextual settings?
- Why does she promote a top–down model of change for the US when this society is notable for its grass-roots democracy (Freedland, 1998)?

## World Class Research?

In the opening discussions which frame the analysis of this book we observed that 'guru' commentaries are, often, very poor pieces of scholarship. Indeed, citing Burnes (1998) we noted how the 'gurus' of management have, often, attempted to pass 'opinion' as 'truth', and their *ad hoc* reflections as valid research. So when Kanter – a recognized business 'guru' – offers us the new 'facts' of community and business life, we have the right to inquire about the manner in which these facts have been acquired and formed.

Kanter's work begins with grand assumptions. It assumes that globalization is a fact (rather than a contested and controversial representation (Waters, 1998)), and as an adjunct to this, her work assumes that the process of globalization acts upon organizations and communities with the force of an imperative for change. The research which flows from these assumptions, we are told, is an attempt to analyse the implications for communities of the globalizing imperatives of business. This programme of research revolves around three key activities/instruments. First, Kanter tells us that she and her team analysed questionnaire returns from over 2,650 organizational 'leaders'. We should note, however, that Kanter fails to define this notion of 'leader'. Furthermore, we would do well to note that the technical appendix of *World Class* reveals the true figure to be 2,655 questionnaires which, equals only a 13.2 per cent rate of return from a mail-shot of 20,070.

This group of business leaders (13.2 per cent of the original *ad hoc* grouping, which had been pursued) represents, we are told, a new, highly skilled, highly mobile elite. Using the metaphor 'world class', now, in a slightly different manner, Kanter ventures that this elite might be considered to be *the* world class, because her analysis suggests that they are leading, directing and shaping the process of economic convergence which will lead, inexorably, to a global economy. However, Kanter does not confine her research activity to the analysis of 'the world class', in isolation.

The second stage of Kanter's research, we are told made use of 'focus groups'. Indeed, Kanter tells us that she supplemented her questionnaire analysis with the opinions and ideas of around 300 'ordinary' people who took part in 40 'focus groups', which were arranged in a variety of different locations. But, again this summary is not quite accurate. In the technical appendix to her text, Kanter tells us that these, 40 focus groups, typically, involved groups of 5, 6 or 7 participants. Thus, simple arithmetic reveals the number of focus group participants to be somewhat less than 300. Indeed the simplest of calculations yields a minimum number of 200 participants and a maximum number of only 280 respondents to Kanter's focus group work.

What is a focus group? How were these activities planned? How were these ordinary folk selected for focus group activities? We do not, and cannot know the answer to these questions since Kanter offers no real account of her focus group activity, and offers no account of the manner in which these activities were arranged. Nor, we should note, does she offer an account of the manner in which these focus group responses were processed and interpreted. It seems, then, that Kanter's research is to be taken on trust. Indeed, it seems that we are required to have trust in Kanter as a venerable 'guru', since she offers us no means of gauging whether her focus group activity offers an objective means of collecting and analysing data.

Together with the results of the questionnaire analysis and the focus group activity, which we are to assume was conducted rigorously and scientifically, Kanter tells us that she also made use of a third source of information. Thus she tells us that she has incorporated the 'results' of a number of (more) *ad hoc* conversations, incidents and meetings with a variety of ordinary and, more or less, extraordinary people. These meetings and incidents, it seems, are offered in an attempt to provide her analysis with pathos (Collins, 1998).

But who are Kanter's ordinary people? Kanter never shares her definition of 'the ordinary' with us, but we have a right to ask. Clearly, 'ordinary people' are not part of 'the world class' – so we can rule out 20,070 members of the US population – but beyond this we are offered no means of locating John and Jane Q Public. It is worth noting, however, that 'ordinariness' seems to extend in to the ranks of senior management, since we are told (Kanter, 1995, p. 161) that a 'senior manager' was involved in one of the focus groups.

So does Kanter's research activity offer us a valid base for action? Does this research offer a useful basis for thinking about, and for planning the futures of our schools, for our future industrial training, and for our future mode of political action and representation? Since a lack of information limits our ability to form judgements on the process of this research, let us address these questions by considering the outputs of Kanter's research activity.

## An Agenda for Change?

Kanter's notion of world class businesses, and of the need for world class communities dedicated to supporting global business concerns presents a familiar (it is, in part the agenda of Blair's Labour government in Britain) yet a curious model of political and community life. Indeed, Kanter offers a vision of community action, which is full of tension and contradiction. It is a vision of community politics where the electorate is encouraged to adopt policies designed to be supportive of (subservient to?) business concerns. Yet Kanter seems to ignore the contradiction built into this, her preferred mode of community action, since she ignores the fact that, in being truly global, world class corporations, must by definition, refuse to reciprocate.

Kanter's globalizing imperative requires that communities commit to the needs of organizations, yet her definition of world class business is built upon the understanding that globalized corporations will have to refuse to commit to the needs and goals of any particular community. Yet, in spite of the absence of mutual commitment and social reciprocity, Kanter's vision of community action accords a key role to a group of 'cosmopolitan' members of 'the world class', whom it is argued, should be allowed to play a primary role in shaping and re-shaping 'world class' communities. Thus Kanter argues that world class organizations – corporations which must be loyal to customers, not locations, corporations which must be mobile in pursuit of market advantage – should shape our schools, highways and colleges, among other structures, to ensure that these meet the requirements of business. Clearly, then, there is an important, yet ignored, tension at the heart of Kanter's prescription for change.

In an attempt to strengthen her case (through the artifice of pathos), Kanter contrasts this cosmopolitan grouping of business leaders, with a grouping whom, it seems, are as yet unconvinced by her model of economic (and political) convergence. This group of laggards and doubters, Kanter dubs 'isolates'. However, she does not define this term, nor does she analyse in any real depth the ideas and orientations of what we are to regard as a more-or-less cohesive group. It is clear, however, that Kanter feels some degree of pity for this grouping, since she has chosen to invoke a concept normally used in the study of group dynamics to refer to individuals who lead rather lonely and disaffected lives within otherwise vital social arrangements (Buchanan and Huczynski, 1997). Thus Kanter suggests that her 'isolates' should be regarded as individuals who make and receive no choices, because they hold to beliefs about global business, which Kanter clearly regards as misguided, parochial and, at times, xenophobic.

But are all those who would disagree with Kanter and her vision for change 'isolates' as Kanter seems to describe these? Michael Moore (1997), for example, is anything but a parochial, racist. He clearly holds opinions, and he clearly makes choices. Yet, he has real misgivings concerning the idea that corporations should be given an enlarged role in the engineering of community life, since his experience of life and work suggests that globalizing corporations in America stand prominent among those factors which have despoiled community life. Indeed, in an incisive, yet humorous attack on 'the world class' (which owes much to the work of Chomsky (see Herman and Chomsky, 1988), Moore produces a range of 'cut out and keep', corporate crook cards (modelled on baseball cards), designed to show the real nature of many of the business–community partnerships which Kanter is keen to promote.

In keeping with the currently popular business-political agenda, therefore, Moore argues that we should tackle welfare dependency. He notes:

> I HATE WELFARE mothers. Lazy, shiftless, always trying to get something for nothing. They expect the rest of us to take care of them instead of getting off their collective ass and taking care of themselves. Always looking for a handout, they simply expect us average, hard-working decent taxpayers to underwrite their illicit behaviour as they churn 'em out, one after the other. How long are we going to tolerate Big Business acting this way?
>
> Each year, freeloading corporations grab nearly $170 billion in tax-funded federal handouts to help them do the things they should be paying for themselves (and that doesn't count all the corporate welfare they're getting from state and local governments). That's $1,388 from each of us going to provide welfare to the rich!
>
> (Moore, 1997, p. 43)

To remedy the problem of 'corporate welfare dependence' and community subservience, Moore advocates, not parochialism, and not isolationism, but a form of inclusive social democracy where citizens, state government and local politicians, recognizing the wanderlust of 'world class' organizations, take steps to resist, and to discipline, those corporations, which have learned to demand concessions from communities (see, for example, the essay, 'Why Doesn't GM Sell Crack?': Moore, 1997). Of course, Moore does not imply that all corporations are 'welfare mothers'. However, he is clear that a properly, accountable form of democratic politics should be used to frame, and to control, both community life and corporate activities. What, then, of Kanter's approach to the problems and processes of globalization?

In a nutshell Kanter's research represents the opposite agenda to that outlined by Moore. Kanter's work, her experience, and her drive to be a modern business 'guru' leads her to a vision of the future where key business leaders – elected by no one, and so, answerable to no one in the local community – will 'help' politicians to run communities. Through this assistance, Kanter argues that communities will be able to embark upon the changes necessary to allow them to to become global centres, renowned for the possession of a skill prized by world class corporations. Such a policy, she argues, will secure life in communities by providing income and employment; the foundations for the ongoing reproduction of family and community life.

Leaving to one side Kanter's attempt to subvert local democracy, we should note that, in order to claim this agenda for change as useful and valid, we need some reassurance that, given the questions asked, and given the research process which was conducted, there might be some prospect that Kanter *would not* happen upon this agenda for change.

Ask the senior members, the world class of the tobacco industry if smoking kills. Now ask the world class of medicine and surgery if smoking kills. When asked for their opinions and ideas, different groups often venture quite different responses. On the question of smoking and mortality, for example, tobacco industry insiders have consistently offered an opinion quite different to that held by general medical practitioners.

Being aware that different groupings tend to hold different ideas, good researchers normally take steps, systematically, to solicit ideas and information from a broad variety of sources, in order to avoid the problem of bias. Yet, when we look at Kanter's sample what do we find? A perfunctory attempt to solicit the opinion of 'ordinary' people (how condescending!), and a willingness to accept, uncritically, the opinions of 2,655 members of the 'world class'; and only 13.2 per cent of the original sample pursued. Where, might we ask, are the community groups? Where are the environmental groups? The Public Affairs Committees (Freedland, 1998)? The unions? The Sheriff's Department? The 'civic organizers' (Freedland, 1998)? The real community researchers? Why did no one, systematically, seek the ideas and opinions of these groups? What purpose is served by silencing the community in the name of community development and change?

Until we receive satisfactory answers to these questions, Kanter's analysis of globalization, and its impact upon life and work must be regarded as flawed, partial and misleading, because in spite of its supposed community focus, this work cares little for community democracy and decision-making. Indeed, we should note that Kanter's prescription would tend to destroy that which she seeks to protect and sustain – the American way of life (Kanter, 1989). She argues, as we have seen, that communities must be world class to survive – to maintain the American way of life – in the globalized world of business, yet her process for becoming world class, effectively kills off the American way of life she is keen to maintain, since, in spite of its liberal rhetoric of markets and opportunities, Kanter's approach to the problems and processes of globalization is founded upon a peculiar process of 'reverse corporatism', which celebrates the corporate control of civic politics!

With this judgement of Kanter's work in mind, let us move on to examine the second of our selected 'guru' works on globalization: Ghoshal's and Bartlett's *Managing Across Borders*.

## Across Borders

Ghoshal's and Bartlett's (1998) *Managing Across Borders* is a revised and updated edition of the, earlier, *Managing Across Borders*, which had been produced by these two authors (billed as Bartlett and Ghoshal) in 1989.

Like Kanter's *World Class*, this Ghoshal and Bartlett text attempts to examine, empirically, the problems and potential of globalization. However, where Kanter and her team attempt to analyse the impact which globalization will have upon the economics and politics of community life, Ghoshal and Bartlett offer a dedicated analysis of the impact of globalization on the structure and functioning of work organizations. In this sense, Ghoshal's and Bartlett's analysis should be viewed as an attempt to analyse modes of business organizing. The political and community implications of these modes, consequently, are little discussed and represent, what might be termed an episode of silence in their work (Berry, 1993).

Basing their analysis and recommendations on a five year study of 236 managers, in nine employing organizations, Ghoshal and Bartlett argue that their attempts to study emerging organizational issues, and their attempts to develop frameworks for analysis, and change, in the light of globalization, suggest that organizational deficiencies lie at the heart of managerial failures to harness the potential of globalization. In fact, Ghoshal and Bartlett suggest that the rash of fads and buzzwords experienced by managers since the 1980s are indicative of the, often, fumbling attempts which managers have made to develop the new, and emergent corporate model, which globalization seems to call forth.

The new corporate model, analysed and promoted by Ghoshal and Bartlett is labelled as 'the transnational solution' by the authors. It is worth examining this model, and the alternative frameworks, which it seems set to displace, in some depth, since unlike Kanter's metaphorical explorations, Ghoshal and Bartlett are keen to point out that their 'transnational solution' is but one of four modes of organizing, designed to allow organizations to manage across borders, (a convenient form of phrasing which, as we shall see, relieves us of some of the analytical tensions which arise when we are forced to choose between terms such as global, international and multinational business).

# The Transnational Solution

Making a case for their, preferred, transnational solution to the problems of globalized business, Ghoshal and Bartlett argue that organizations have, historically, tended to adopt one of three uni-dimensional approaches to strategy and structure when confronted with the problem of selling goods and services abroad. Thus, we are told that organizations, when managing across borders, have tended to adopt one of the following approaches to strategy and structure:

• a multinational approach
• a global approach
• an international approach.

## *A Multinational Approach*

Companies adopting a multinational approach to business are those organizations which, we are told, 'have developed a strategic posture and organizational capability that allows them to be very sensitive and responsive to differences in national environments around the world' (Ghoshal and Bartlett, 1998 p. 16). In these terms, a multinational approach to managing and organizing is a response to the problems of managing across borders which recognizes differences in markets, technologies and tastes in different parts of the world, and so, attempts to design a structure and a strategic response, which can deliver the product differentiation demanded by different nations and/or market segments. Thus, a multinational approach to managing across borders describes a situation where a corporation, in the name of flexibility and market responsiveness, runs, not so much a single business entity, as a 'portfolio of multiple national entities' (Ghoshal and Bartlett, 1998, p. 16), each geared to serving the needs of a particular national market or market segment.

This multinational approach to business, Ghoshal and Bartlett argue, offers benefits under particular market conditions. For example, where differentiation is at a premium, or where companies confront markedly different political situations in different market segments, it may be sensible, and economically advantageous, to adopt a multinational approach to business. Yet, under different circumstances – where the rewards accruing to differentiation and segmentation are poor – it may make sense to adopt a quite different approach to managing across borders which the authors have dubbed, a 'global approach'.

## *A Global Approach*

What Ghoshal and Bartlett label a 'global approach' to business, describes those circumstances which Levitt's analysis of the globalization of markets

(Levitt, 1983) assumed would be the single, and predominant model for managing across borders. Levitt's analysis, which in many ways is framed as a reaction to the nationally tailored mode of managing, typical among 'multinational organizations', suggests that managers should view the world, not as a myriad of markets, but as one market. Thus, where multinationals seek to tailor their products, and their approach to management, in order to reflect the peculiarities of different markets, and of different national conditions, a 'global' approach views customer demand as a worldwide, standardized phenomenon, and so, offers standardized goods designed for a unitary, 'world market'.

To maintain this global strategy, global organizations, we are told, make use of centralized structures, designed to allow co-ordination, and to enhance efficiency across the globe. In turn, this 'global' mode of organizing might be contrasted with Ghoshal's and Bartlett's 'international' mode of organizing.

## An International Approach

'International' organizations, Ghoshal and Bartlett tell us, tend to adopt a parent-overseas mode of operation. Whereas multinational businesses operate in a fashion that attempts to balance the needs of the various (national) businesses, which make up the multinational corporation, the 'international' corporation adopts a different form of power structure, which eschews balance in favour of dependence. Thus, under an international mode of managing and organizing, 'overseas' organizations are set up to exploit the skills and technology of the parent organization, yet remain dependent upon the parent for strategic direction, and for future development.

Under an 'international' mode of operation, therefore, the parent organization tends to adopt an incremental approach to markets, and to market penetration. Thus, as distinct from both the multinational and the global approach to managing across borders, companies adopting an international approach to business tend to 'roll-out' technology, ideas and expertise from a strong parent, to weaker and dependent 'overseas' operations which are not expected to engage in innovation and development activities. Under this mode of operation, goods and services radiate from a primary market to a range of secondary and tertiary markets until worldwide coverage is eventually achieved. Thus an international approach to business, demands that customers overseas from the parent corporation must be willing to wait for the allurements of modernity (Levitt, 1983).

Ghoshal and Bartlett argue, however, that consumers and customers are no longer willing to wait in line for the roll-out of products. With this in mind, they argue that an international approach to managing across borders is now, no longer tenable. Reflecting upon the market for video cassette recorders, and for colour televisions, (each of which demonstrates an ongoing compression in the roll-out phase of technology), they argue that the roll-out period is now so compressed that organizations must be able to satisfy primary, secondary and tertiary markets simultaneously.

So, if the international mode of organizing is inadequate, should organizations reject the international model of business in favour of the global mode? Apparently not, since while global organizations *might* be able to supply all markets simultaneously, the global mode of operation is, we are warned, unable, fully, to reflect the complexities of market demand since it is unresponsive to consumer and customer demands for goods and services, tailored to reflect different tastes.

So does this, ongoing requirement for differentiation, and for tailoring imply that the solution to managing across borders is to be found in a multinational approach? Apparently not, since Ghoshal and Bartlett argue that a multinational approach to business is also unsuited to the current competitive environment. Indeed, they warn us that multinational organizations, in comparison to the global and international modes of organization, tend to suffer a cost disadvantage, because, in offering tailored solutions to different national markets, they tend to duplicate services such as marketing, and research and development, which might, otherwise, be centralized in the name of efficiency. Furthermore, we are warned that the willingness of multinational corporations to grant significant levels of autonomy to their various federated national organizations has tended to delay decision-making, and has tended to hinder the adoption of new forms of technology, and the new forms of technological architecture vital for many modern products. Thus Ghoshal and Bartlett dismiss the multinational mode, the global mode, and the international mode of conducting business across borders as flawed, and as inappropriate for the current environment of business. Instead, they urge managers to adopt their 'transnational solution'.

## A Transnational Solution

Cataloguing the methods and mores traditionally adopted by organizations in their dealings with 'foreigners', Ghoshal and Bartlett note that while the multinational mode of business is responsive to different and changing requirements, while the global mode of business is efficient, and while the international mode of business is able to diffuse innovation worldwide, changes in technology and changes in consumer preferences no longer reward companies who adopt one-dimensional strategies. Ghoshal and Bartlett argue, therefore, that organizations will have to adopt a 'transnational' approach to business, since changes in patterns of demand and technology both require and facilitate the pursuit of a flexible and multi-dimensional approach to competition.

Summarizing this position, and mirroring Kanter's account of globalization to some degree, Ghoshal and Bartlett argue that organizations must strive simultaneously to be responsive to market changes, yet cost effective. Furthermore, they warn us that organizations must be able to spread their products and their innovations, worldwide. They argue:

> Today, no firm can succeed with a relatively unidimensional strategic capability that emphasizes only efficiency, or responsiveness, or leveraging of parent company knowledge and competencies. To win, a company must now achieve all three goals at the same time. With their multidimensional strategic requirements, these business have become *transnational industries*.
>
> (Ghoshal and Bartlett, 1998, p. 29, original emphasis)

Reflecting upon the process of becoming transnational, Ghoshal and Bartlett argue that organizations which truly wish to be transnational in their approach to business will have to rethink the assumptions which guide their strategic capability. In a rich, historical and contextual study (contextual and historical forms of analysis being rare treasures in 'guru' works), the authors suggest that the structural and political 'heritage' left by the historical pursuit of uni-dimensional strategies will for some time to come tend to mitigate against the development of transnational approaches to business.

Indeed, it is a concern with the enduring legacy of prior approaches to business which leads Ghoshal and Bartlett to argue that organizations will have to rethink the assumptions which guide their approach to business. Thus, (and mirroring Peter's and Austin's concern with *becoming* excellent) the authors suggest that organizations will have to drop their quest for strategic fit, and will have to give up their hopes of attaining a symmetry between market conditions and organizational structure if they are to be transnational in their thinking and in their mode of operation. The transnational solution as outlined by Ghoshal and Bartlett, therefore, suggests that organizations will have to move away from traditional models of strategy and planning, which focus upon the need for symmetry and strategic fit (since market conditions change too quickly to allow a stable congruence) in order to focus upon 'capability'.

Let us look more closely at their notion of capability and its role in the 'transnational solution'.

## Capability

Ghoshal and Bartlett argue that, at least since the advent of 'contingency' approaches to management (McLoughlin and Clark, 1994; Woodward, 1970), organizations have been encouraged to seek a fit between market conditions and organizational functioning. Organizations facing stable market and technological conditions, therefore, have tended to develop mechanistic management and production systems, designed to meet the needs of a high volume, mass market. Meanwhile, organizations facing environmental turbulence have tended to adopt more organic structures designed to promote innovation and responsiveness.

The question which Ghoshal and Bartlett pose, however, is this: what structure should organizations adopt when they face both volatile and stable markets? How should managers react to meet the myriad of market conditions evident both within and across borders?

The traditional response to this question might be to adopt a multinational approach. Yet, as we have seen, this would be an inadequate structure for Ghoshal and Bartlett, since this mode of operation would achieve only one of the business goals which, they argue, must be attained. Indeed we are warned that the multinational mode of organizing tends to achieve its key goal at the expense of the two remaining goals (cost-effectiveness and 'simultaneity') which cannot be ignored. So which structure and strategy should managers adopt?

## The Myth of Fit

Ghoshal's and Bartlett's response to this question is that managers must stop thinking in terms of structures. The notion of structural fit, they tell us, is an out-moded idea. The quest for symmetry (between market conditions and the organization's structure), they warn us, is based upon an assumption that no longer holds; the assumption of stable and enduring market conditions. Indeed, they warn us that a focus upon structural matters tends to make managers, if not hostages to fortune, then prisoners of history and organizational heritage. Thus, they argue that managers must be wrenched from a focus upon structural matters, in order to concentrate on the question of 'capability'. In this sense, organizations are to be judged, not on how they look, but on their capacity to meet the, three, competitive imperatives of managing across borders.

'Capability', then, as an organizational attribute, comes not from changing structures, but from changing assumptions. In this sense, the notion of organizational capability demands that managers commit to the three imperatives of transnational management, and commit to an understanding that the environment of business is capricious and fast-changing. Thus Ghoshal and Bartlett argue that while multinationals, effectively, operate independent businesses, and while 'global' and 'international' forms of organization, manage (overseas) dependent units, transnational forms of organization are notable for the *interdependence*, which characterizes relations between business operations. Indeed, Ghoshal and Bartlett are keen to stress that transnational organizations do not have 'home' and 'overseas' businesses. Instead, they warn us that transnational organizations simply have business dealings, and no qualification of residence is required to judge their contribution.

Transnational organizations, then, in comparison to their forebears, are complex and interdependent forms of business designed to maximize overall business success. To maintain this business focus amid the requisite complexity, we are told that (a new form of) transnational management will be required. This form of management, it seems, will turn upon vision and values. In short, the transnational solution as this applies to the conduct of management is, in many ways, the familiar cultural solution which we analysed in chapter 4. This is a pity really, since in chapter 4 we highlighted the limited appeal of this managerialist metaphor; arguing that as an explanatory tool, it tends to make opaque that which it promises to make transparent.

Indeed, it is worth observing that while Ghoshal and Bartlett offer a rich, historical and contextual account of business, politics and economics as experienced by the forebears of the transnational organization, their concern with 'visions' and with mind-sets, and their impatience with structural forms of analysis does little to explore, or to reveal, the complex inner workings of their transnational firms. We should note, therefore, that in spite of their commitment to a cultural resolution of the problems of transnational management, their discussion offers little guidance on the inner workings of their transnational firms. There is, then, a certain irony in a book which promotes a cultural-metaphorical examination of everyday life, as a powerful tool designed to inform and to underpin management action, yet would abstract action from the very structures which give these human endeavours meaning and effect. It is difficult to avoid the conclusion, therefore, that the transnational solution promoted by Ghoshal and Bartlett works to disembed action from context, and so fails to investigate how people, real, living breathing people (Sims *et al.*, 1993; Ackroyd and Thompson, 1999; Burrell, 1997), conduct their lives and live out their ambitions within organizations.

Once again it seems that the 'guru' taste for prescription has overwritten and blighted the need for description, and the need for analysis. While conceding that Ghoshal and Bartlett offer a rich and, often insightful history of the problems, and pitfalls of managing across borders, therefore, we part company with the authors and their analysis, when they announce their resolution of the key paradox of transnational management, since, as we saw in chapter 4, their cultural solution to the problems of management is, in many ways, just another means of stating a problem, while pretending to have the imagination and the technology to control, and to resolve that which makes managing problematic.

With this (mixed review) fresh in our minds, let us turn to examine Ohmae's (1994) problem-statement and preferred solution. Let us examine Ohmae's *Borderless World*.

# The Borderless World

At face value, Ohmae's (1994) text, like the texts of Kanter (1995) and Ghoshal and Bartlett (1998) offers a discussion of globalization. Given the complex vocabulary that circumscribes and divides this domain, however, we would do well to note that Ohmae offers a discussion, which focuses upon the problems and opportunities associated with managing across borders. Yet Ohmae's text offers more (less?) than this. Ohmae's work is not a simple discussion of globalization. It is, as we shall see, a rhapsody on the 'free market' and a funeral oration for market intervention.

In common with the other contributions to globalization already examined, Ohmae locates his discussion of managing the 'borderless world' (his preferred metaphor to describe the process of globalization) within an analysis of markets and technologies. However, unlike Kanter (1995), and unlike Ghoshal and Bartlett, Ohmae does not (quite) view globalization as an imperative; enforcing itself upon humanity to redefine our modes of organizing. Instead, he argues that, in the face of globalizing trade movements we have a choice to make.

Ohmae notes that we may choose to resist globalization – as some 'bureaucrats' urge us to – opting instead for protectionist trade policies. Alternatively, he notes, we can embrace the problems and opportunities of managing the new global movements in trade, in finance and in ideas. Ohmae, however, dismisses the first of these two choices. The second 'choice', he argues is the only feasible means of managing the potential of the global market. Hence it might be argued that, disguised as choice, Ohmae presents us with a globalizing imperative by the back door!

Indeed, discussing the first of the two 'choices' which is quickly discarded, Ohmae tells us that the adoption of protectionist trade policies as a means of coping with globalization would be a grave mistake. Trade protection policies, as attempts to insulate domestic producers from the vagaries of world competition, he tells us, serve, only, 'slack' organizations and, it seems, slack-jawed 'bureaucrats'. In fact, taking issue with those, such as Kanter's 'isolates', who harbour protectionist sentiments, Ohmae asks, what would we protect, and from whom?

Recognizing that the process of globalization will link organizations and economies together in a complex and tangled fashion, Ohmae raises an extremely pertinent and problematic question. He asks us to consider the following: what is an American product? What counts as an American car? Viewing the world from Japan, a viewpoint increasingly informed by American calls to institute protectionist measures against Japanese corporations and their products, he notes:

> Is IBM an American or a Japanese company? Its work force of 20,000 is Japanese, but its equity holders are American. Even so, over the past decade IBM Japan has provided, on average, three times more

tax revenue to the Japanese government than has Fujitsu. What is its nationality? Or what about Honda's operation in Ohio? Or Texas Instruments' memory-chip activities in Japan? Are they 'American' products? If so, what about the cellular phones sold in Tokyo that contain components made in the United States by American workers who are employed by the US division of a Japanese company. Sony has facilities in Dotham, Alabama, from which it sends audiotapes and video-tapes to Europe. What is the nationality of these products or of the operation that makes them?

(Ohmae, 1994, p. 10)

Clearly, then, Ohmae finds protectionism to be problematic both politically and analytically. Accordingly, he finds calls for nationalist-inspired protectionism unconvincing and unpalatable.

He remains, similarly, unconvinced by 'one-market', globalizing arguments. Indeed he seems positively hostile to Levitt's notion of the 'global product'. He argues:

Contemporary global corporations ... have to serve the needs of customer segments. Instead of educating the 'barbarians' to drink Coke or eat cornflakes, they have to discover the basic drinking and eating needs of people and serve these needs. Sometimes they come up with entirely new products and services that headquarters never dreamed of. Coca-Cola's success in Japan was due to the establishment of its route sales force, but also to its rapid introduction of products unique to Japan. In Japan Mr. Donut's changed everything about its product/ service, except for the logo.

(Ohmae, 1994, p. 9)

This is a point echoed by Micklethwait and Wooldridge (1997). In a passage worth quoting at length, they argue that:

The idea that you can sell identical products nearly everywhere in the same way has been thoroughly rubbished. True there are a few big ticket items – jumbo jets, for instance – where there is a global market, though anybody who visits Boeing's factory in Seattle will be given a long lecture about the way that every aircraft is made differently in order to satisfy its customers. True, also, there are a few niche products that appeal to broadly the same people in the same way around the world: one invariably cited by harassed globalists in interviews is *The Economist*. However, in the broad consumer market, survey after survey has shown that there are only a few truly global brands, such as Coca-Cola, McDonald's and Marlboro, and even this select handful certainly do not mean the same thing in, say, Beijing (where they are all status symbols), as they do in Baltimore.

Indeed, a close look at Coca-Cola's strategy shows that, for all the ubiquitous 'Always Coca-Cola' advertisements, the Atlanta company exploits rather than ignores national differences. It uses independent local bottlers to get its products to local markets. It also tweaks the product's recipe from country to country – and sometimes within them. In Japan, the southern Japanese like their Coca-Cola slightly sweeter than people in Tokyo, and the company obliges. And when it comes to selling other drinks, Coke adopts a very local strategy. Two-thirds of Coca-Cola's Japanese products are made specifically for the local market; Georgia Coffee, for example, can be seen everywhere in Tokyo but is unknown in Coca-Cola's Georgia home.

(Micklethwait and Wooldridge, 1997, p. 248)

On one key issue, however, Ohmae is convinced. Echoing Ghoshal's and Bartlett's discussion of the transnational firm, Ohmae argues that global corporations must learn to serve customers rather than locations. Indeed, he warns us that the global corporation (what Ghoshal and Bartlett term the transnational corporation) 'serves its customers in all key markets with equal dedication' (Ohmae, 1994 p. 90). Indeed, echoing the unfolding logic used to explain and to explore Ghoshal's and Bartlett's preferred transnational solution, Ohmae continues:

It does not shade things with one group to benefit another. It does not enter individual markets for the soul purpose of exploiting their profit potential. Its value system is universal, not dominated by home-country dogma, and it applies everywhere. In an information-linked world where consumers, no matter where they live, know which products are the best and cheapest, the power to choose or refuse lies in the hands, not in the back pockets of sleepy privileged monopolies like the earlier multinationals.

(Ohmae, 1994, p. 90)

Ohmae warns his managerial audience, however, that they should not expect to 'go global', or to attain this transnational mode of organizing over-night. Indeed he suggests a five stage process of globalization.

## The Process of Globalization?

- *Stage One*: characterized by the arm's length export of goods and services, where 'foreign' producers link with domestic dealer networks to distribute goods and services.
- *Stage Two*: where 'foreign' companies take over the responsibility for the management and control of what, from the perspective of the supplying corporation, amounts to overseas distribution.

- *Stage Three*: where the responsibility for manufacturing, for marketing and for sales is transferred abroad from the home, parent corporation to the overseas arm of the corporation.
- *Stage Four*: where support functions, previously retained as domestic responsibilities – personnel management and finance, for example, are moved overseas to support the devolved manufacturing and marketing functions.
- *Stage Five*: characterized by the development of a denationalized system and mode of operation which is 'company neutral', such that, in Kanter's terms, the now global (that is, the transnational) corporation sources materials, competes for business, sells to customers, and nurtures ideas on a world stage, unhindered by notions of nationality and nationalism.

However, two key questions are suggested by this discussion of Ohmae's. How will global organizations be maintained and reproduced? And perhaps more importantly, what steps has Ohmae taken to establish the validity of his, globalizing, free-market account of the internationalization of trade?

On the first of these two questions, Ohmae stands stiffly to attention within the ranks of the 'gurus'. His response is that globalized corporations should be managed and controlled through the medium of an independent, country-neutral, corporate culture. However, we noted in chapter 4 that such accounts of cultural management grossly over-estimate the capacity of managers to understand, isolate, massage and manage cultures, and for this reason Ohmae's solution to managing global business concerns seems glib and superficial. Indeed, we should note that Ohmae's account of cultural management – and the need to develop global business cultures – causes tensions for his own analysis, since it seems to argue that organizations, unable to supply global products might, successfully, develop a cultural form that would float free from all the anchors of race, gender, ethnicity and history!

Ohame's solution to the managerial problem of globalization, then, is unconvincing. But how did he arrive at this solution? How does Ohmae know what he believes?

Reflecting upon the requirements of global businesses, Kanter chose to interrogate her chums; important business leaders. Reflecting upon company history and the (imagined) future of organization, Ghoshal and Bartlett trawled documentary materials and spent five years studying nine organizations. While Ghoshal and Bartlett, as we have seen, have done little to improve our understanding of these organizations as cultural formations, we must, in fairness, concede that they do offer a rich, and often sensitive account of business strategy. So how did Ohmae arrive at his opinion? What research design; what process of scholarly endeavour underpins his analysis?

Sadly, it seems that no systematic form of research activity underpins Ohame's work. Indeed, while we must concede that Ohmae's work offers us insights into the politico-economic context of Sino-American trade, we must also point out that it is, singularly, untroubled, and distinctly untrammelled by the norms and practices of social scientific research, such that time after time, Ohmae offers ideas without substantiation and opinion as fact.

For example, discussing the problems of building and maintaining alliances (an issue central to globalized business) he offers this: 'Nine times out of ten you will want to stay in the alliance' (Ohmae, 1994 p. 129). However, he offers no indication as to the origins of this, 90 per cent certain judgement. On managing the tensions across organizations he offers this, sagely, advice: 'Top managers are always slow to point the finger of responsibility at headquarters or at themselves' (Ohmae, 1994, p. 86).

On this issue Ohmae speaks with 100 per cent certainty – managers *always* – and he may be accurate in his judgement of politics and blame, but again, he gives us no reason to regard his opinion as valid, because he gives us no opportunity to test whether his logic and 'research' is robust.

We could offer yet more examples of this kind of scholarship, but there is no real reason to labour the point: Ohmae's analysis of trade, and of the globalized future, which awaits us, is convincing only for those who already share his world view. Since he offers me no means to test, or to gauge, the validity of his key pronouncements, I choose to remain unconvinced by his partial analysis.

Of course, Ohmae and his supporters will protest that, as Japan's most prominent McKinsey-ite, this discussion of globalization, and the borderless world, benefits from Ohmae's knowledge and consulting experience such that I should bow to his training, experience and status to accept his judgement as an informed and experienced insider.

This (anticipated) rejoinder deserves two forms of response:

1 That the 'research' track record of other McKinsey-ites (see chapter 5) does little to inspire confidence.
2 That no other 'academy' with scientific pretensions is prepared to let reputation and seniority stand in the stead of normal scientific practices.

Accordingly, we might do well to regard Ohmae's analysis as a political eulogy, rather than as a business commentary underpinned by the normal conventions of social scientific research. We may, therefore, treat Ohmae's work as we would treat similar, political manifestos.

## Packing Up

Our analysis of the three 'guru' accounts of business and globalization, selected as vehicles for our analysis of 'managing across borders', reveals three rather different approaches to the issue of globalization, which in an (almost) uncanny fashion, happen upon the same vision-led, culturally managed, type of solution. We have been critical of this 'solution', however, and have attacked it as glib; and in the light of our previous discussions (see chapter 4), as arrogant and over-socialized. Yet, we have not confined our attention to the outputs of these works alone. Indeed, reviewing the works of Kanter and Ohmae, in particular, we argued that the inputs to these analyses – the research design and the research process (in Kanter's case), and the absence of research or some other means of validation (in Ohmae's case) – have served to construct partial and limiting accounts of work, organization and management in the context of trade flows which are, increasingly, global in their nature and scope.

Yet, we need not confine an analysis of globalization to such organizational (or in Kanter's case, organizationally coupled) issues. We can, if we choose to make the effort, undertake a qualitatively different form of analysis.

Rather than discuss globalization with 'the organization' in the foreground, and with 'organizational needs' as our central concern, we might learn more, and we might understand more fully, the processes and problems of globalization, if we make the effort to analyse those things which the 'gurus' tend to push to the background in their haste to serve organizational needs. In the section that follows, therefore, we will attempt to retrieve the 'background', so that we might push into full focus the human, the socio-political, consequences of globalization.

## A Human Face for Globalization?

Friedman writing in *The Sunday Times* (28/03/99) captures the necessity of this endeavour rather well. Acknowledging the business and economic impacts of globalization, and so, conceding a measure of ground to the 'gurus' and their preoccupations, Friedman, nevertheless, chooses to foreground those issues which tend to become obscured by a focus upon organizational matters, and on the needs of the organization. Thus while Kanter, Ohmae and Ghoshal and Bartlett discuss globalization as a market phenomenon with consequences for organizations, and in Levitt's (1983) case with consequences for the nature of competitive products, Friedman defines globalization quite differently. Perhaps mindful of the debt crisis which afflicts a range of African states, and which puts the allurements of modernity, such as clean water, education and health care beyond the reach of the majority of the population, Friedman highlights the potential backlash consequent upon continued and continuing exclusion from modernity.

Reflecting upon the change, upheaval and dislocation associated with the development of a, truly, global form of international trade, he tells us:

I DEFINE globalisation as the integration of finance, markets, nation states and technologies to a degree never witnessed before – in a way that is enabling individualism, corporations and nation states to reach around the world further, faster, deeper and cheaper than ever before, and in a way that is producing a powerful backlash from those brutalised or left behind.

*(The Sunday Times,* 28/03/99)

Fouskas (1998), reflecting a similar humanist form of concern, shows the same disdain for the 'gurus', and for their up-beat account of globalization. Indeed he argues against the concept of globalization, and against the 'guru'-populist elaboration of globalization on three counts:

1　That discussions of globalization are ideological, inasmuch as they camouflage choices and policy-making (and brutalism, dependency and third world debt) as the outcome of iron laws and imperatives.
2　That globalization is presented as a new departure when evidence suggests it is the continuation of an established socio-economic trend.
3　That the 'guru' discussion of globalization builds from an impoverished form of scholarship, since it presents a 'convergent' model of economic change and development which, unwarrantedly, assumes that all economies are converging on a common form, and towards a common mode of operation.

Let us examine these issues and ideas in a little more depth. For ease of exposition, however, and because our 'grammar' allows us to make valid choices, we will examine this analysis in a slightly different order to that adopted by Fouskas. Thus we shall examine Fouskas' second point of criticism as a prelude to the examination of points one and three.

## A New Departure?

For the 'gurus', globalization is a process of socio-economic convergence facilitated by changes in information technologies. As such, globalization is to be regarded as a feature of late twentieth-century life. The 'gurus' argue, as we have seen, that as distinct from earlier decades, products and technologies now become available more or less simultaneously in all regions of the globe. In part, we are told, this 'simultaneity' (Kanter, 1995) has occurred because organizations have changed (or are changing) their modes of organizing in order to source materials, ideas and technologies worldwide. This is, of course, to be regarded as a departure from earlier modes of organizing which, it is claimed, tended to guard certain responsibilities as the birthright of the 'home' based arm of some multi-national organization.

However, not everyone on the planet is willing to accept this 'guru' product. Indeed, Fouskas argues that the notion of a new globalized world, distinct from historical trends, and representative of a new era in world trade is little more than the effluent waste of an affluent industry which, itself, has global pretensions (see also Waters, 1998). Thus he argues that the concept of globalization is so much, 'guru'-inspired nonsense.

For Fouskas, globalization – or as he terms it, trade internationalization – is not, primarily, a product of late twentieth-century capitalism. Indeed, Fouskas argues that the process of trade internationalization is a nineteenth-century phenomenon, familiar to, and discussed by scholars such as Marx (1908) and Lenin (1982).

Hammer's biography (Hammer with Lyndon, 1988), for example, shows the existence of corporations, such as Occidental, with a worldwide reach, and with political and economic clout on a global-international scale in the early years of the twentieth century. Similarly, in their account of the Singer corporation, Ballantine *et al.* (1989) show, well, the size and scope of Singer's operations during the Victorian era. Discussing one of Singer's satellite operations – their works in Clydebank, Glasgow, they note:

> Singer was one of the world's earliest multinational manufacturing companies. From their American base they expanded to Scotland, starting assembly of sewing machines at a small factory near John Street in Glasgow in 1867–8. With growing demand came expansion . . . By 1911, the works had expanded to employ 12,000 [workers who were engaged in ] . . . producing the component parts and assembling the completed sewing machines, most of which were destined for export.
>
> (Ballantine *et al.*, 1989, p. 13)

Giddens (1999), however, rejects this form of continuity-inspired argument. The globalized era of international trade, he argues, does represent a discontinuous, step-change, from the experience of earlier eras. Waters (1998) shares this view of globalization to some degree. He argues that globalization might be defined as: '*A social process in which the constraints of geography on social and cultural arrangements recede and in which people become increasingly aware that they are receding*' (Waters, 1998, p. 3, original emphasis).

Waters argues that this understanding of globalization has important implications, both practically and academically. At an academic level, Waters argues that the process of globalization poses a challenge for sociological theorizing since, at an analytical level, it undermines the role and status of the nation-state as one of the central analytical components of sociological theorizing. Thus Waters suggests that sociological theorizing will have to adjust its mode of thinking as changes in our social and cultural lives modify the standing of the nation-state. At a more practical level Waters argues that the widespread changes in our social and cultural lives, which are suggested and promoted by changes in our modes of organizing demonstrate the distinctiveness of our current period of history.

He argues, therefore, that the process of globalization is recent and accelerated. Indeed, he contends that this accelerated process of change and development is likely to bring upheaval and uncertainty into our lives, since the processes of globalization have a janus potential.

Reflecting upon the janus of globalization, he notes, for example the different trajectories which this process suggests for different forms of social organization. Indeed, he suggests that while the processes of globalization will liberate aspects of production and consumption from the limiting factors of geography and nationality, the bulk of humanity will tend to remain located within, if not tied to, certain states or regions. Waters seems to suggest, therefore, that the (global) liberation of capital may imply the subordination of states and communities, which unlike business concerns will remain tied to the restricting concerns of geography and nationality. With this in mind, he contrasts the economic status and low mobility of families and communities, with the more than $2 trillion of 'stateless' money, which circulates the globe in search of advantage.

Neither Giddens nor Waters would seek to deny, however, the extent of international trade in earlier eras. Indeed, both readily acknowledge that the existence of a high volume of international trade and exchange pre-dates the late twentieth century. However, they argue that the current era of globalization is distinctive from the Victorian era, which Fouskas harks back to. For Giddens, therefore, the process of globalization builds upon, yet is distinctive from previous periods of capitalism. The process of globalization, he tells us, accelerates yet redefines, these previous trends. As distinct from earlier eras, therefore, Giddens argues that trade flows, today, are massive and bilateral in nature. Reflecting upon flows of capital, for example, he argues that the value of 'institutionally managed money' has risen by 1,100 per cent worldwide since 1970. This change in the size and scope of international business, he argues, will suggest and promote a battery of wider changes, which make globalization, as a process, distinctive from earlier colonial, or imperialist capitalist modes of organization. Contradicting Fouskas, therefore, Giddens and Waters argue that the concept of globalization represents a useful means of summarizing and analysing *recent* movements in production, consumption and politics. Yet, this does not put Giddens and Waters with the 'gurus' of globalization. Instead, both warn us from taking the path of 'guru' analysis.

Indeed, contrary to the imperative-based argument of the 'gurus', Giddens reminds us of the potential social and political impacts of globalization which both build from our actions, yet demand further choices from us. He notes:

> the idea of globalization is misunderstood if it is only applied to connections that are literally world-wide and if it is treated as only or even primarily, economic. Globalization . . . is not only, or even primarily, about economic interdependence, but about the transformation of time

and space in our lives. Distant events, whether economic or not, affect us more directly and immediately than ever before. Conversely, decisions we take as individuals are often global in their implications. The dietary habits individuals have, for example, are consequential for food producers, who might live on the other side of the world.

(Giddens, 1999, pp. 30–31)

Contrary to Fouskas' analysis, therefore, both Giddens and Waters argue that the concept of globalization represents a useful means of exploring and summarizing the contemporary movements and social processes which make this era distinctive from earlier phases of capitalist production (and reproduction). In common with Fouskas, however, both Giddens and Waters argue that a focus upon globalization as a business and economic imperative is short sighted, since this view fails to grasp the full implications of globalization and the choices which exist within such large and seemingly impersonal movements.

With this rebuke of the 'gurus' and their preferred analytical approach fresh in our minds, let us turn to examine Fouskas' concern that globalization is, at root, an ideological concept, invoked to construct, and to facilitate forms of change which reflect the self-interested concerns of certain, powerful, socio-economic elites.

## Ideology

Hobsbawm writing for *The Guardian* (20/10/98) suggests that much of what is said on, and written about globalization is marred by confusion and conflation. Reflecting our concern with the 'grammar' of imperatives, which gives force and meaning to management's fads and buzzwords, Hobsbawm suggests that the concept of globalization is often discussed in narrowly ideological terms. Thus Hobsbawm argues that commentators on globalization tend to conflate the 'free market'; the neo-liberal ideal of unhindered markets free from regulation (Gray, 1999), with the notion of globalization. In this way, he warns us that, often, 'the global market' is assumed to be, *de facto*, a free market, which it would be folly to attempt to control – hence the tendency of the 'gurus' to see globalization as an imperative.

However, Hobsbawm argues that this conflation confuses the key issue at hand because it presents the outcome of planned and engineered forms of human activity *as if* these were natural, spontaneous phenomena. Giddens (1999), for example, while conceding the extent and the complexity of international trade – in the first of his Reith lectures, he notes that global trade in currency, alone, now stands at more than one trillion dollars each day – argues that although:

> Globalization is quite often spoken of as if it were a force of nature ... it is not. States, business corporations and other groups have

actively promoted its advance. Much of the research that helped create satellite communications was funded by governments, as more recently were the early phases of what has become the internet. Governments have contributed to the expansion of world financial markets through the bonds they have issued to raise money for their domestic commitments. Liberalization and privatization policies have contributed to the intensifying of world trade and economic exchange . . . Globalization, in sum, is a complex range of processes, driven by a mixture of political and economic influences.

(Giddens, 1999, p. 33)

Giddens, in common with Hobsbawm and Friedman, therefore, gives us some reason to view the conflated, 'guru' account of globalization as an ideological construct, since his analysis of globalization reveals that this process is a product of human choice-making activity, which has become mystified and disguised as a disembodied force, apparently beyond human control and human comprehension (Waters, 1998). Thus, while the 'gurus', acting as ciphers for the so-called needs of business present globalization as an imperative which will crush anyone with the temerity to question either the logic or the momentum of international-ization, Giddens, Hobsbawm and Moore (Moore, 1997) remind us that, in spite of the huge flow of international trade, and in spite of the wealth of certain corporations and individuals (see Bauman, 1998), we should not consider ourselves as impotent in the face of globalizing processes. We need not, meekly, accept the precarious futures the 'gurus' foretell for us, and we would be wrong to view the nation-state, or commu-nity politics as victims or as spent forces, slapped down by the free hand of the global market.

Indeed, reflecting upon the changing nature of the state, and the poor *choices* made by the governments of Britain, America and new Zealand, Gray (1999) argues that corporations – whether these be multinational, global, international or transnational in nature – depend upon the contin-uing presence and vitality of the apparatus of the state. Where states are weak, for example as in the case of Russia, the conduct of business becomes problematic. Thus, reflecting upon the mobile, globalized opportunities of capital, Gray reminds us that:

If it is true that corporations can shop around the world for the tax and regulatory regime that they want, it is also true that political risks have increased in many parts of the world. Where states are fragile it is harder to regulate the mobile production and capital; but it is also harder for business to stitch up enduring corporatist relationships with governments. That is a limitation on the power of both states and corporations.

(Gray, 1999, p. 69)

Of course, this analysis should not be taken as a suggestion that, for the economy and polity, globalization means business as usual. It does not (Waters, 1998). Yet, by the same token, globalization does not imply the end of the nation-state as Ohmae suggests, nor need it imply the development of communities impotent in the face of transnational corporations, and so subservient to the needs of these corporations, as Kanter implies.

Contrary to these perspectives, both Giddens and Waters argue that, even though economies are becoming more and more inter-connected and interdependent (de-localized in Gray's (1999) terms) governmental structures retain their importance. However, Giddens warns us that, as actors within a political framework, we may have to adjust our thinking about government. Indeed, rather than conceiving of government as an entity bounded by national borders – as *our* government, or as *the* government – he warns us that we may need to think of the apparatus of the state in the absence of the definite article. Thus Giddens suggest that we may need to embrace the notion of governance, to encompass the changes in governmental function and process associated with the developing importance of transnational forms of non-governmental organization, which play an enlarging role in administrative and regulatory matters. However, Giddens warns us against the assumption that government will 'go global', either to meet, or to serve transnational organizations. Reflecting this understanding, Waters suggests that within the process of globalization, there are simultaneous tendencies to de-localize and to (re)localize the apparatus of the state. In fact, as I draft this chapter the new parliaments of Scotland and Wales are convening to swear in their elected members, and are trying to come to terms with the prospect of a coalition government (in Scotland), and a minority government (in Wales).

In spite of the 'guru' commitment to notions of globalization as a competitive imperative, which reshapes communities and politics as a downstream result of organizational restructuring, the analyses noted above suggest the persistence of a range of valid choices both about, and within globalization. As distinct from the 'guru', change or die, *pliable or perishable*, argument, therefore, it is clear that we are not bound to be slaves to, nor victims of globalization, as an irresistible (natural) force.

Thus, while Giddens and Gray acknowledge that the process of globalization will shape our lives, they also argue that, through a more reflexive and informed kind of action (a 'critical-practical' approach!), we may play a meaningful role in shaping globalization.

This, as we shall see, has implications for the notion of convergence, which underpins 'guru' accounts of globalization.

## Convergence

'Guru' analyses of globalization tend to be driven by a model of convergence. Convergent models of development and change assert, or assume, that state formations and organizational forms have a tendency to converge upon a common, uniform model. Ghoshal and Bartlett (1998), for example, in their discussion of globalization, promise their readers '*the* transnational solution', and while it is true that the authors warn us that this transnational solution should not be considered in structural terms, the notion of a singular solution to the challenge of globalization clearly suggests a convergent-type approach.

Perhaps the clearest account of convergence is offered by Levitt (1983) in his account of the globalization of markets. Presenting a vision of a (future) world full of products, standardized to meet the needs of a single, global market, Levitt argues: 'The earth is round, but for most purposes it's sensible to treat it as flat' (Enis and Cox, 1991, p. 540). However, other groups of scholars would tend to argue against convergent forms of analysis, primarily because historical records and empirical analyses have, time after time, mocked the assumptions and ideals of convergence thinking.

Frank (1967), for example, has criticized Wallerstein (1979) for his assertion that 'under-developed' economies will/should follow a western path of development such that all the economies of the world will tend to converge on one, westernized economic form. Rejecting this kind of analysis, Frank argues that this is folly. The economies of Africa, he warns us, cannot follow the developmental path taken by western economies precisely because these routes to economic development have already been exploited. Thus, contrary to the ideas and assertions of convergence thinking, Frank suggests that *divergence* represents the only viable approach to economic development for the 'under-developed' world. Endorsing this form of analysis, Rodney (1983) suggests that convergence models of development lead only to under-development and to the construction of dependent, satellite, economies in areas such as Africa.

Placing these discussions of convergence and development within the context of our analysis of globalization, we can see that, in spite of the 'guru' commitment to a convergent, global economic form, and in spite of their commitment to the development of a single, dominant mode of organizing, we would do well to remember that capitalism may take many different forms (Gray, 1999), such that we might expect to find a range of different capitalisms engaged in the internationalization of trade. Indeed, Gray notes key differences, for example, between the deregulated, Anglo-Saxon capitalism of the USA, much celebrated by the 'gurus', the regulated 'Rhine' capitalism of Germany, and the 'anarcho-capitalism (which Burrell, 1997, refers to as a 'kleptocracy') of Russia.

With these examples of alternative and (more-or-less) viable capitalisms in mind, Gray suggests that our western notions of convergence should be regarded as being little more than narrow, pragmatic and ego-centric (Burrell, 1997) statements of self-interest and vanity, which fly in the face of the realities of economic life, and of economic development and change.

Taking issue with the conflation of the 'free market', and the global-ized market to expose the delusion of economic convergence, as the extension of free-market, Anglo-Saxon capitalism, Gray notes:

> A global free market presupposes that economic modernization means the same thing everywhere. It interprets the globalization of the economy – the spread of industrial production into interconnected market economies throughout the world – as the inexorable advance of a singular type of western capitalism: the American free market.
>
> The real history of our time is nearer the opposite. Economic modernization does not replicate the American free market system throughout the world. It works against the free market. It spawns indigenous types of capitalism that owe little to any western model.
>
> The market economies of east Asia diverge deeply from one another, with those of China and Japan exemplifying different varieties of capi-talism. Equally, Russian capitalism differs fundamentally from capitalism in China. All that these new species of capitalism have in common is that they are not converging on any western model.
>
> The emergence of a truly global economy does not imply the exten-sion of western values and institutions to the rest of humankind. It means the end of the epoch of western global supremacy. The orig-inal modern economies in England, western Europe and north America are not models for the new types of capitalism created by global markets. Most countries which try to refashion their economies on the model of Anglo-Saxon free markets will not achieve a sustainable modernity.
>
> (Gray, 1999, pp. 3–4)

In spite of the 'grammar' of imperatives which has been invoked in an attempt to give force and meaning to the buzzword of globalization, there-fore, our critical-practical analysis reveals globalization to be a contested concept whose processes are controversial, contestable and subject to both mediation and human intervention. Our analysis of globalization, there-fore, suggests the need for a 'subjunctive' or 'imperfect' grammar.

As we work towards our summary discussion of the 'gurus' and global-ization, therefore, it is worth pointing out a potential, subsidiary benefit of our 'critical-practical' account of globalization. Gray's analysis, as we have seen, debunks the idea of a single, viable approach to business, since it explores a range of successful, and less-than-successful capitalisms. Indeed, Gray suggests that among these choices, the Anglo-Saxon free-market familiar to, and vaunted by the 'gurus', represents a non-viable approach to globalization (see also Giddens, 1999). If this is, indeed, true, we may be able to look forward to a future less polluted by eulogies on the free market, and a future less cluttered by the (Anglo-Saxon) 'guru' arrogance and triumphalism to which we are all currently subjected.

Indeed, with 'guru' arrogance and triumphalism in mind, we might do well to remind ourselves of the peculiarity of what the 'gurus' hold to be *natural*. Thus, having braced ourselves for the 'new millennium' visions of managements that, doubtless, the 'gurus' will produce (with Fukuyama, 1999, leading the pack), we could do worse than reflect upon the fact that: 'Today the Jewish, Bhuddist and Moslem systems of dating still hold sway in their own cultures, where 2,000 A.D is numbered as 5760, 2544 and 1420 respectively' (Lacey and Danziger, 1999, p. 195).

## Summary

This chapter has attempted to offer a 'critical-practical' analysis of the popular, managerial concept of globalization. However, the chapter has attempted to go beyond the normal confines of 'guru' analysis to offer an account of globalization, which locates the concept as a socio-economic phenomenon, and so, seeks to understand its human consequences.

In an attempt to explain globalization as a managerial concept, three, key, 'guru' texts on international trade and organization were selected for analysis. Following a critical review of these texts, a review which examined the inputs to, and the outputs of these studies, we, then, offered an alternative form of analysis designed (1) to challenge the 'grammar' of the 'gurus', in order to show (2) the human choices within the process of globalization, and (3) the potential human consequences of failing to analyse globalization, fully and properly. Thus, in opposition to the forms of analysis preferred by the 'gurus', the chapter concluded by arguing that it is wrong to see globalization as an imperative, enforcing itself upon us to reshape our lives. Instead, we argued that globalization is a result of human choice-making activity, within which, alternative, yet viable, futures might be pursued. Thus, noting the variety of alternative forms of capitalism currently active across the globe, we concluded by observing that since our globalized futures are not yet written, and since viable choices remain within globalization, we should reject the simplistic, intellectually conservative, and imperative-driven ideas of the 'gurus'.

Let us hope, then that the new millennium will offer a true jubilee; freedom from the 'gurus' and their 'grammar' of imperatives.

# 12  Concluding Comments

## Introduction

This text has attempted to offer a 'critical-practical' analysis of management's 'guru' industry, and has attempted to offer an engaging, yet critical analysis of the fads and buzzwords propagated by the 'gurus' of management. The book, as you will recall, is structured around a hub of four sections. These sections – our introduction, together with chapters 1, 2 and 3 – have been designed to explore the nature of the 'guru' industry, and to explain the need for an alternative, 'critical-practical' form of analysis. Building out from our central hub, chapters 4–11 incorporate the ideas and analysis of our opening four sections, in order to offer an in-depth account of a range of management's fads and buzzwords. These chapters offer an account of the fads and buzzwords of management, designed to allow readers to locate, to understand, to critique, and so, escape the limiting confines of 'guru' analysis, and the management policies which this inspires/justifies.

Given the structure of this work, it seems inappropriate to offer conclusions in the form of a summary. Instead, in these, brief, concluding comments, I would like to do two things. First, I would like to return to the initial account of the 'gurus' of management which was offered in the hub of this book, in an attempt to encourage readers to reflect, once more, upon the limitations which 'guru' analyses impose upon our lives, and upon our world views. Following this, we will conclude our attempts to 'manage change' within the 'guru' industry, by suggesting an alternative vocabulary of buzzwords, which might be pursued within our alternative analytical framework.

## The Sociological Imagination

Writing originally in 1959, C. Wright-Mills offers an account of the nature and form of a branch of sociological theorizing which, he argued, restricts the ability of men (this was before PC) to define, and to escape their troubles. Thus, *The Sociological Imagination* begins as follows:

> Nowadays men often feel that their private lives are a series of traps. They sense that within their everyday worlds, they cannot overcome their troubles, and in this feeling they are often quite correct: what ordinary men are directly aware of and what they try to do are bounded by the private orbits in which they live; their visions and their power are limited to the close-up scenes of job, family, neighbourhood; in other milieux, they move vicariously and remain spectators. And the more aware they become, however vaguely of ambitions and of threats which transcend their immediate locales, the more trapped they seem to feel.
>
> (Wright-Mills, 1973, p. 9)

Moving on from this initial statement, Wright-Mills argues that a form of social theorizing, which he dubs 'technician sociology', acts to confine men (and women) within their domestic afflictions and experiences. In an attempt to loose these traps and bonds, Wright-Mills encourages his readers to exercise their sociological imaginations. Indeed, Wright-Mills argues that the sociological imagination is vital to any attempt to escape the traps, which scar the terrain of life and living. He warns us that while the 'technician sociologist' engages with large projects, and in grand theory, technician sociology, by nature, is confining. It confines us because it is unable to provide the form of analysis necessary to allow individuals to locate their own, domestic concerns and afflictions, within a larger account of social movements and crises.

Forms of analysis built upon the exercise of the sociological imagination, Wright-Mills argues, hold the key to the traps which would, otherwise, contain us, because they have a reflexive quality which sees through, and so, attempts to overcome the limitations accepted and, often compounded by those 'technicians' engaged in the mindless crunching of data sets.

Wright-Mills' comments, of course, were not directed at management's 'guru' industry, as we now understand it. However, his analysis of elements of the sociological academy might just as well have been written about management's 'gurus' because his comments capture, so well, the nature and form of their preferred analytical approach, as well as the problems associated with this mode of thinking. Indeed, it is worth pointing out the salient aspects of Wright-Mills' work, for our 'critical-practical' analysis of management.

## The Perils of Domesticity?

Wright-Mills argues that the men and women of the late 1950s – and this holds true today, more than forty years on – often felt so entrapped by 'domestic' ideas and afflictions that they were forced to experience the world beyond their domestic attachments in a vicarious way. Our attempts to provide a 'critical-practical' analysis of the 'gurus' of management confirms this sense of entrapment, and, furthermore, suggests that, in the field of management, it is the 'gurus' who, time and again, spring the traps, tight-shut.

But how can the forms of analysis preferred by the 'gurus' of management, confine us? After all, do the 'gurus' not exist to provide cogent analyses and useful resolutions of the problems, which threaten to swamp us/management? No, nothing could be further from the truth.

Chia (1996), as we have seen, argues that mainstream discussions of management, such as those offered by management's 'gurus', provide a 'ready-made' science of management (Latour, 1987) which simplifies that which is inherently complex. Reflecting upon the problems of the ready-made science of management, Chia argues that this form of analysis confronts the user with a seductive yet simplistic account of management. This analysis of management, he warns us, limits our ability to forge linkages between the domestic and the public, the private and the political, because it resists, or denies, the virtues of theoretical deconstruction.

When we elect to use 'guru' theory, therefore, we, in essence, sign up to a catalogue of terms and conditions which shape our thinking and guide our action, even though we may not be aware, fully, of their force and effect. Notably, the ready-made science of management demands our allegiance, while denying the value of our lived experience. In this way, the ideas and assumptions which are part-and-parcel of 'guru' models of work and organization, maroon each of us on an island of ideas and understanding which is alien to us, yet demands from us both faith and conformity. Little wonder, then, that Wright-Mills argues that, away from the most mundane of our domestic afflictions we experience life 'vicariously' as a deathly-pale simulation of our own lived experience which is presented to us as 'reality' (Chia, 1996).

In an attempt to overcome the arrogance of the 'gurus', and the limitations of their analyses – which are, at best, a variant of 'technician sociology' – this text has adopted a mode of analysis quite different to that preferred by the 'gurus'. In the hub of the book we spelled out the need to embrace a reflexive, theoretical mode of analysis, designed to prise open the 'encased' concepts, and the ready-made science of the 'gurus', so that the outputs from, and the inputs to, 'guru' theory might be exposed to public scrutiny. This process of scrutineering has been informed by Wright-Mills' concerns, regarding what might be termed the entrapments of domesticity, and the vicarious experience of the workplace.

Recognizing that 'guru' analyses silence dissent (Jackson and Carter, 1998) because they deny the reality (and the validity) of our day-to-day experiences (Burrell, 1997), this text has, self-consciously, sought to reunite the domestic and the public realm; the patterns of life and the course of history, so that readers might be more able to locate, to understand, to critique, and so, escape the traps set by the 'gurus'.

For example, when discussing the notion of culture change, I have deployed elements of my own (domestic) biography as a challenge to the models of social action put forward by the 'gurus'. Similarly, the chapter on 'downsizing', and the concerns it articulates, stem directly from my late father's experience of redundancy, and my consequent inability to stomach the anti-social, anti-community models of downsizing operationalized by the 'gurus'. Offering just one more example of my attempts to move between levels of analysis, and my attempts to wriggle free of the traps inherent in 'guru' analyses, it is worth pointing out that my rejection of 'knowledge work' (an elitist and empirically unconvincing notion), and my preference for the concept of 'working knowledge' is informed, as much by my personal biography, as by a sociological training.

Indeed, my concerns over the concept of 'knowledge work' have their well-spring in my personal biography, and reflect my preference for an egalitarian mode of thinking which recognizes and celebrates both the formal and the tacit abilities of my family, friends and elders, who work with skill and imagination, in spite of (or because of) the absence of a formal scientific training, endorsed and accredited by the academies. Furthermore, my preference for the concept of 'working knowledge' is a direct reflection of my childhood fascination with mechanical devices, and the romantic attachment I retain for dabblers and inventors of all kinds.

Of course, my concern to link levels of analysis should not be interpreted as an attempt to place the (*ad hoc*) experiences of life, prior to a more coherent body of theorizing. It is, instead, an attempt to encourage a more useful and reflexive mode of *coherent* theorizing which, because it does not deny the validity, nor the vitality of lived experience, might help each of us to navigate, more fruitfully, the path of our own existence. Thus, through a 'critical-practical' analysis which draws on my own biography, I hope readers might be encouraged to reclaim their voice (Jackson and Carter, 1998), and to demand the validity of their biographies and experiences, since as Wright-Mills makes clear:

> The first fruit of [the sociological] imagination – and the first lessons of the social science that embodies it – is the idea that the individual can understand his own experiences and gauge his own fate only by locating himself within his period, that he can know his own chances in life only by becoming aware of those of all individuals in his circumstances. In many ways it is a terrible lesson; in many ways a magnificent one. We do not know the limits of man's capacities for supreme effort or willing degradation, for agony or glee, for pleasurable brutality or the sweetness of reason. But in our time we have come to know that the limits of 'human nature' are frighteningly broad. We have come to know that every individual lives, from one generation to the next, in some society; that he lives out a biography, and that he lives it out

within some historical sequence. By the fact of his living he contributes, however minutely, to the shaping of this society and to the course of its history, even as he is made by society and by its historical push and shove.

(Wright-Mills, 1973, p. 12)

Let us turn now to consider the second theme of our concluding discussion: the aim to offer an alternative vocabulary of management buzzwords, which might grow as organ and tool (C. Collins, 1998) as we attempt to promote a 'critical-practical' form of analysis

## An Alternative Vocabulary

The lexicon of management, as we have seen, is now based upon a collection of terms which have been labelled as fads and buzzwords. To articulate the lexicon of management, a grammar based upon commands and imperatives has been developed which will not, and cannot, countenance dissent. We have attempted to challenge this grammar, by questioning the imperatives of management. Indeed, our challenge to the (so-called) imperatives of management has been built upon an attempt to demonstrate, both the political, choice-making behaviour of managers, and the variety of organizational forms which persist within, and in spite of, the attempts made by 'Handy pocket theory' (Burrell, 1997) to enforce a totalizing logic, and a universal model upon our complex and varied experiences.

Having sought to undermine the nature of 'guru' theorizing, and the grammar invoked to communicate this, it seems sensible to suggest an alternative vocabulary; an alternative array of terms and concepts which might serve as focal points for alternative, and more meaningful, 'critical-practical' forms of analysis.

The first term in our new vocabulary we have already examined. In an attempt to deflect the elitist and anti-social form of analysis proffered by the advocates of 'knowledge work', we suggested 'working knowledge' as a useful counter-balance, in part, because it returns voice, capability and dignity to the workers silenced and belittled by the advocates of 'knowledge work'. Building from the example set by our analysis of 'working knowledge', the terms below are suggested as potential buzzwords, which invite deconstruction and reflexive action.

The following terms should be thought of as an initial attempt to construct an alternative, and supplementary, vocabulary of management investigation which, it is hoped, might allow managers and other interested readers, to locate their experiences, and to loose the bonds of 'guru' theorizing.

On the basis of this (re)location of experience, I hope others might be prepared to add their voices (and additional terms) to the discourse suggested by:

- *Disempowerment*
- *Organizational misbehaviour*
- *Workers' rights*
- *Sexism*
- *Trade unions*
- *Racism*
- *Power . . .*

# Bibliography

Abrahamson, E. (1991) 'Managerial Fads and Fashions: The Diffusion and Rejection of Innovations', *Academy of Management Review*, Vol. 16, No. 3 (pp. 586–612).

Abrahamson, E. (1996) 'Management Fashion', *Academy of Management Review*, Vol. 21, No. 1 (pp. 254–285).

Ackroyd, S. (1993) 'Paradigms Lost: Paradigms Regained', in Reed, M. and Hughes, M. (eds), *Rethinking Organisations: New Directions in Organisation Theory and Analysis*, Sage, London.

Ackroyd, S. and Crowdy, P. (1990) 'Working with Raw Material: The Case of the English Slaughterhouse Workers', *Personnel Review*, Vol. 19, No. 5 (pp. 3–13).

Ackroyd, S. and Thompson, P. (1999) *Organizational Misbehaviour*, Sage, London.

Alvesson, M. (1993) 'Organization as Rhetoric: Knowledge Intensive Firms and the Struggle with Ambiguity', *Journal of Management Studies*, Vol. 30, No. 6 (pp. 997–1015).

American Management Association (1994) *1994 AMA Survey on Downsizing: Summary of Key Findings*, American Management Association, New York.

Anthony, P. D. (1977) *The Ideology of Work*, Tavistock Publications, London.

Anthony, P. D. (1987) 'In Defence of the Inappropriate', *Management Education and Development*, Vol. 18, No. 4, (pp. 255–259).

Appelbaum, S. H., Everard, A. and Hung, T. S. (1999) 'Strategic Downsizing: Critical Success Factors', *Management Decision*, Vol. 37, No. 7 (pp. 535–552).

Atkins, J. (1971) *George Orwell: A Literary Study*, John Calder Publishing, London.

Ayto, J. (1999) *20th Century Words*, Oxford University Press, Oxford.

Ballantine, I., Collins, C., Forster, L., Maguiness, H., McIvor, A., Savage, H. and Tuach, L. (1989) *The Singer Strike: Clydebank, 1911*, Clydebank District Library, Glasgow.

Bank, J. (1992) *The Essence of Total Quality Management*, Prentice-Hall, London.

Banks, I. (1995) *The Crow Road*, Abacus, London.

Bannock, G. (1973) *The Juggernauts: The Age of the Big Corporation*, Penguin, Harmondsworth.

Baring-Gould, S. A. (1914) *The Lives of the Saints*, John Grant, Edinburgh.

Baritz, L. (1965) *The Servants of Power*, Wiley, New York.

Barley, S. R. and Kunda, G. (1992) 'Design and Devotion', *Administrative Science Quarterly*, Vol. 37 (pp. 363–399).

Barnard, C. I. (1938) *The Functions of the Executive*, Harvard University Press, Boston, MA.

Baruch, Y. (1998) 'Applying Empowerment: Organizational Model', *Career Development International*, Vol. 3, No. 2 (pp. 82–87).

Baruch, Y. and Hind, P. (1997) 'Survivor Syndrome: A Management Myth?', paper presented to the 8th European Congress of Work and Organizational Psychology, Verona, Italy.

Baskerville, S. and Willett, R. (eds) (1985) *Nothing Else to Fear: New Perspectives on America in the Thirties*, Manchester University Press, Manchester.

Bateson, G. (1972) *Steps to an Ecology of Mind*, Ballantine Books, New York.

Bauman, Z. (1998) *Globalization: The Human Consequences*, Polity Press, Cambridge.

Beale, D. (1994) *Driven by Nissan?* Lawrence and Wishart, London.

Bean, R. (1986) *Comparative Industrial Relations: An Introduction to Cross-national Perspectives*, Croom Helm, London.

Beaumont, P. B. (1993) *Human Resource Management: Key Concepts and Skills*, Sage, London.

Beaumont, P. B. (1995) *The Future of Employment Relations*, Sage, London.

Beckford, J. (1998) *Quality: A Critical Introduction*, Routledge, London.

Bell, D. (1980) *Sociological Journeys: Essays 1960–1980*, Heinemann, New York.

Bell, D. (1987) 'The Post-industrial Society: A Conceptual Schema', in Cawkell, A. E. (ed.), *Evolution of an Information Society*, Aslib, London.

Belous, R. S. (1989) *The Contingent Economy*, National Planning Association, Washington.

Bendix, R. (1956) *Work and Authority in Industry*, Wiley, New York.

Bennington, J. and Taylor, M. (1992) 'The Renewal of Quality in the Political Process', in Sanderson, I. (ed.), *Management of Quality in Local Government*, Longman, Harlow.

Berry, T. (1993) 'Book Review', *British Journal of Management*, Vol. 4, No. 4 (pp. 277–299).

Best, S. and Kellner, D. (1991) *Postmodern Theory: Critical Interrogations*, Guildford Press, New York.

Beynon, H. (1979) *Working for Ford*, E. P. Publishing, Wakefield.

Blanchard, K. and Johnson, S. (1983) *The One Minute Manager*, Fontana/Collins, Glasgow.

Blauner, R. (1973) *Alienation and Freedom: The Factory Worker and His Industry*, University of Chicago Press, Chicago.

Block, P. (1986) *The Empowered Manager*, Jossey-Bass, San Francisco.

Blyton, P. and Turnbull, P. (1994) *The Dynamics of Employee Relations*, Macmillan, London.

Boje, D. (1998) 'Amos Tuck's Post-sweat Nike Spin Story', paper presented to The International Association of Business Disciplines, San Francisco.

Boreham, P. (1992) 'The Myth of Post-Fordist Management: Work Organization and Employee Discretion in Seven Countries', *Employee Relations*, Vol. 14, No. 2 (pp. 13–24).

Bowen, D. and Lawler, E. (1992) 'The Empowerment of Service Workers: What, Why, How and When', *Sloan Management Review*, Vol. 33, No. 3 (pp. 31–39).

Boyle, J. (1977) *A Sense of Freedom*, Pan Books, London.

Brannen, P., Batstone, E., Fatchett, D. and White, P. (1976) *The Worker Directors: A Sociology of Participation*, Hutchinson, London.

Bratton, J. (1991) 'Japanization at Work: The Case of Engineering Plants in Leeds', *Work, Employment and Society*, Vol. 5, No. 3 (pp. 377–395).

Braverman, H. (1974) *Labor and Monopoly Capital*, Free Press, New York.

Brockner, J. (1988) 'The Effects of Work Lay-offs on Survivors: Research Theory and Practice', in Staw, B. M. and Cummings, L. L. (eds), *Research in Organizational Behaviour*, JAI Press, Greenwich, CT.

Brockner, J. (1992) 'Managing the Effects of Lay-offs on Survivors', *California Management Review*, Vol. 34, No. 2 (pp. 9–28).

Brown, A. (1998) *Organizational Culture*, Pitman, London.

Bryant, A. (1998) 'Beyond BPR: Confronting the Organizational Legacy', *Management Decision*, Vol. 36, No. 1 (pp. 25–30).

Bryant, A. and Chan, D. (1996a) 'BPR: To Redesign or Not To Redesign', *Business Change and Reengineering*, Vol. 3, No. 2 (pp. 52–61).

Bryant, A. and Chan, D. (1996b) 'Goal Directed Development: Confronting the Organizational Legacy', paper presented at Business Information Technology (BIT) 96, University of Manchester Institute of Science and Technology (UMIST), November.

Bryant, D. and Vanhoenacker, J. (1999) 'Deriving a Methodological Perspective for Business Process Management and Business Process Change', paper presented to Information Resources Management Association (IRMA).

Buchanan, D. and Huczynski, A. A. (1997) *Organizational Behaviour*, Prentice-Hall London, 3rd edition.

Burawoy, M. (1982) *Manufacturing Consent: Changes in the Labour Process Under Monopoly Capitalism*, University of Chicago Press, Chicago.

Burkitt, B. (1981) 'Excessive Trade Union Power: Existing Reality or Contemporary Myth?', *Industrial Relations Journal*, Vol. 12, No. 3 (pp. 65–71).

Burnes, B. (1996) *Managing Change: A Strategic Approach to Organisational Dynamics*, Pitman, London.

Burnes, B. (1998) 'Recipes for Organizational Effectiveness: Mad, Bad or Just Dangerous to Know?', *Career Development International*, Vol. 3, No. 3, (pp. 100–106).

Burrell, G. (1997) *Pandemonium*, Sage, London.

Burrell, G. and Morgan, G. (1979) *Sociological Paradigms and Organisational Analysis*, Heinemann, Oxford.

Burton, J. (1982) 'The Varieties of Monetarism and Their Policy Implications', *The Three Banks Review*, No. 134, June (pp. 14–31).

Calas, M. B. and Smircich, L. (1996) 'Not Ahead of Her Time: Reflections on Mary Parker Follett as Prophet of Management', *Organization*, Vol. 3, No. 1 (pp. 147–152).

Callaghan, P. and Hartmann, H. (1991) *Contingent Work*, Economic Policy Institute, Washington.

Campbell, A. and Tawadey, K. (1990) *Mission and Business Philosophy*, Heinemann, Oxford.

Cappelli, P. (1995) 'Rethinking Employment', *British Journal of Industrial Relations*, Vol. 33, No. 4 (pp. 563–602).

Cappelli, P., Bassi, L., Katz, H., Knoke, D., Osterman, P. and Useem, M. (1997) *Change at Work: How American Industry and Workers are Coping with Corporate Restructuring and What Workers Must Do to Take Charge of Their Own Careers*, Oxford University Press, Oxford.

Carrol, L. (1989) *Through the Looking Glass*, in *The Complete Illustrated Works of Lewis Carrol*, Chancellor Press, London.

Cascio, W. F. (1993) 'Downsizing: What Do We Know? What Have We Learned?', *Academy of Management Executives*, Vol. 7, No. 1 (pp. 95–104).

Casey, B. (1995) *Redundancy in Britain: Findings from the Labour Force Survey*, Department for Employment Research Series, No. 62, London.

Chia, R. (1996) 'Teaching Paradigm Shifting in Management Education: University Business Schools and the Entrepreneurial Imagination, *Journal of Management Studies*, Vol. 33, No. 4 (pp. 409–428).

Chia, R. (ed.) (1998) *In the Realm of Organization: Essays for Robert Cooper*, Routledge, London.

Chia, R. (ed.) (1998a) *Organized Worlds: Explorations in Technology and Organization with Robert Cooper*, Routledge, London.

Child, J. (1981) *The Challenge to Management Control*, Kogan Page, London.

Clark, P. (2000) *Organisations in Action: Competition between Contexts*, Routledge, London.

Clark, T. and Salaman, G. (1996) 'The Management Guru as Organizational Witchdoctor', *Organization*, Vol. 3, No. 1 (pp. 85–107).

Clark, T. and Salaman, G. (1998) 'Telling Tales: Management Gurus and the Construction of Managerial Identity', *Journal of Management Studies*, Vol. 35, No. 2 (pp. 137–161).

Clegg, H. A. (1975) 'Pluralism in Industrial Relations', *British Journal of Industrial Relations*, Vol. 13, No. 3 (pp. 297–314).

Clegg, S. (1993) *Modern Organizations: Organization Studies in the Postmodern World*, Sage, London.

Clutterbuck, D. and Kernaghan, S. (1994) *The Power of Empowerment*, Book Club Associates, London.

Cockburn, C. (1983) *Brothers: Male Dominance and Technological Change*, Pluto Press, London.

Cockerham, J. (1994) 'Redundancies in Great Britain: Results from the Spring 1992 to Spring 1993 Labour Force Surveys', *Employment Gazette*, January (pp. 11–20).

Cole, R. E. (1999) *Managing Quality Fads: How American Business Learned to Play the Quality Game*, Oxford University Press, Oxford.

Collins, C. (1999) *Language, Ideology and Social Consciousness: Developing a Sociohistorical Approach*, Ashgate, Aldershot.

Collins, D. (1994) 'The Disempowering Logic of Empowerment', *Empowerment in Organizations*, Vol. 2, No. 2, (pp. 14–21).

Collins, D. (1995) 'Review Article: The Nissan Enigma', *Personnel Review*, Vol. 24, No. 1 (pp. 67–71).

Collins, D. (1995a) 'Rooting for Empowerment?', *Empowerment in Organizations*, Vol. 3, No. 1 (pp. 25–33).

Collins, D. (1996) '*No Such Thing As . . .* A Practical Approach to Management', *Management Decision*, Vol. 34, No. 1, (pp. 66–71).

Collins, D. (1996a) 'Control and Isolation in the Management of Empowerment, *Empowerment in Organizations*, Vol. 4, No. 2 (pp. 29–39).

Collins, D. (1997) ' "Knowledge Work" or Working Knowledge: Ambiguity and Confusion in the Analysis of the "Knowledge Age" ', *Employee Relations*, Vol. 19, No. 1 (pp. 38–50).

Collins, D. (1998) *Organizational Change: Sociological Perspectives*, Routledge, London.

Collins, D. (1998a) 'Is Empowerment Just a Fad? Process, Power and Culture in the Management of Empowerment', *Systemist*, Vol. 20, No. 1 (pp. 53–68).

Collins, D. (1998b) 'Applying Empowerment: A Reply in the Form of a Corrective', *Career Development International*, Vol. 3, No. 2 (pp. 88–92).

Collins, D. (1998c) 'Il a commencé à penser avant d'avoir rien appris: A Processual View of the Construction of Empowerment', *Employee Relations*, Vol. 20, No. 6 (pp. 594–609).

Collins, D. (1999) 'Born to Fail? Empowerment, Ambiguity and Set Overlap', *Personnel Review*, Vol. 28, No. 3 (pp. 208–221).

Coulson-Thomas, C. (1991) 'IT and New Forms of Organization for Knowledge Workers: Opportunity and Implementation, *Employee Relations*, Vol. 13, No. 4 (pp. 22–32).

Covey, S. (1989) *The Seven Habits of Highly Successful People*, Simon and Schuster, New York.

Crainer, S. (1998) 'In Search of the Real Author', *Management Today*, May (pp. 50–54).

Crainer, S. (1998a) *The Ultimate Business Guru Book: 50 Thinkers Who Made Management*, Capstone, Oxford.

Cressey, P. and MacInnes, J. (1980) 'Voting for Ford: Industrial Democracy and the Control of Labour', *Capital and Class*, Vol. 11, No. 1 (pp. 5–33)

Crosby, P. (1979) *Quality is Free*, Mentor, New York.

Crosby, R. P. (1992) *Walking the Empowerment Tightrope: Balancing Management Authority and Employee Influence*, Organization Design and Development Inc., New York.

Cross, M. (ed.) (1985) *Managing Workforce Reduction*, Croom Helm Beckenham.

Crouch, C. (1982) *The Politics of Industrial Relations*, Fontana, London.

Cruise O'Brien, R. and Voss, C. (1992) *In Search of Quality*, London Business School Working Paper.

Cunningham, I., Hyman, J. and Baldry, C. (1996) 'Empowerment: The Power to Do What?', *Industrial Relations Journal*, Vol. 27, No. 2, (pp. 143–154).

Dahrendorf, R. (1959) *Class and Conflict in Industrial Societies*, Routledge and Kegan Paul, London.

Daniel, W. W. (1985) 'The United Kingdom', in Cross, M. (ed.) *Managing Workforce Reduction*, Croom Helm, Beckenham.

Dawson, P. (1994) *Organizational Change: A Processual Approach*, Paul Chapman Publishing, London.

De Burgundy, J. (1995) 'Working Daze: Uncertainty and Ambiguity in Consulting', *Management Decision*, Vol. 33, No. 8 (pp. 51–55).

De Cock, C. and Hipkin, I. (1997) 'TQM and BPR: Beyond the Myth', *Journal of Management Studies*, Vol. 34, No. 5 (pp. 659–675).

Deal, T. E. and Kennedy, A. A. (1982) *Corporate Cultures*, Penguin, Harmondsworth.

Debo, A. (1993) *Geronimo: The Man, His Time, His Place*, Pimlico, London.

Delbridge, R., Turnbull, P. and Wilkinson, B. (1992) 'Pushing Back the Frontiers: Management Control and Work Intensification under JIT/TQM Factory Regimes', *New Technology, Work and Employment*, Vol. 7, No. 2 (pp. 97–106).

Deming, W. E. (1986) *Out of the Crisis*, Press Syndicate, Cambridge.

Despres, C. and Hiltrop, J. M. (1995) 'Human Resource Management in the Knowledge Age: Current Practice and Perspectives on the Future', *Employee Relations*, Vol. 17, No. 1 (pp. 9–23).

Donaldson, L. (1985) *In Defence of Organization Theory: A Reply to the Critics*, Cambridge University Press, Cambridge.

Donaldson, L. (1996) *American Anti-management Theories of Organization: A Critique of Paradigm Proliferation*, Cambridge University Press, Cambridge.

Dore, R. (1973) *British Factory–Japanese Factory*, Allen and Unwin, London.

Drucker, P. (1969) *The Age of Discontinuity*, Heinemann, London.

Drucker, P. (1981) *Managing in Turbulent Times*, Pan Books, London.

Drucker, P. (1991) 'The New Productivity Challenge', *Harvard Business Review*, Nov.–Dec. (pp. 69–79).

Drucker, P. (1992) *Managing for the Future*, Heinemann, London.

Drucker, P. (1993) *Post-capitalist Society*, Butterworth–Heinemann, Oxford.

Drummond, H. (2000) *Introduction to Organizational Behaviour*, Oxford University Press, Oxford.

Du Gay, P. and Salaman, G. (1992) 'The Cult(ure) of the Customer', *Journal of Management Studies*, Vol. 29, No. 5 (pp. 615–633).

Eco, U. (1983) *The Name of the Rose*, trans. William Weaver, Harcourt Brace, London.

Economist Intelligence Unit (1992) *Making Quality Work: Lessons from Europe's Leading Companies*, EIU, London.

Edwards, P. (ed.) (1995) *Industrial Relations: Theory and Practice in Britain*, Blackwell, Oxford.

Edwards, P. K. (1986) *Conflict at Work*, Blackwell, Oxford.

Eldridge, J. E. T. (1983) Review of Wood, S. (ed.), *The Degradation of Work?* and Littler, C., *The Development of the Labour Process in Capitalist Society*, *British Journal of Industrial Relations*, Vol. 21, No. 3 (pp. 418–420)

Emery, F. E. and Trist, E. L. (1969) in Emery, F. E. (ed.), *Systems Thinking*, Penguin Harmondsworth.

Enis, B. and Cox, K. (eds) (1991) *Marketing Classics: A Selection of Influential articles*, Allyn and Bacon, London.

Evans-Pritchard, E. E. (1983) *Witchcraft, Oracles and Magic among the Azande*, Clarendon Press, Oxford.

Fayol, H. (1949) *General and Industrial Management*, Pitman, London.

Feigenbaum, A. V. (1986) *Total Quality Control*, McGraw-Hill, New York.

Feldman, S. P. (1986) 'Management in Context: An Essay on the Relevance of Culture to the Understanding of Organizational Change', *Journal of Management Studies*, Vol. 23, No. 6, (pp. 587–607).

Feldman, S. P. (1989) 'The Broken Wheel: The Inseparability of Autonomy and Control in Innovation within Organizations, *Journal of Management Studies*, Vol. 26, No. 2 (pp. 83–102).

Field, K. (1997) 'Redundancies in Great Britain', *Labour Market Trends*, April (pp. 135–142).

Fincham, R. and Rhodes, P. (1999) *Principles of Organizational Behaviour*, Oxford University Press, Oxford.

Fisher, J. (1991) *New Management Techniques*, TGWU Education Document, quoted in Tuckman, A. (1998).

Flanders, A. (1970) *Management and Unions*, Faber and Faber, London.

Follett, M. P. (1941) *Dynamic Administration*, Metcalf, H. C. and Urwick, L. F. (eds), Pitman, London.

Forrest, D. (1984) 'Self-destructive HRD', *Training and Development Journal*, December, (pp. 53–57).

Foucault, M. (1991) *Discipline and Punish*, Penguin, Harmondsworth.

Fouskas, V. (1998) *The Internationalisation of Economic Relations and the State*, University of Hertfordshire Working Papers, Politics Paper 5 (UHBS 1998: 20).

Fox, A. (1985) *Man Mismanagement*, Hutchinson, London.

Foy, N. (1994) *Empowering People at Work*, Gower, Aldershot.

Hatch, M. J. (1997) *Organization Theory: Modern, Symbolic and Postmodern Perspectives*, Oxford University Press, Oxford.

Hayek, F. (1978) *A Tiger by the Tail: The Keynesian Legacy of Inflation*, Institute of Economic Affairs, London.

Heller, R. (1972) *The Naked Manager*, Barrie and Jenkins, London,

Henderson, S. (1998) 'No Such Thing As . . . Market Orientation: A Call for No More Papers', *Management Decision*, Vol. 36, No. 9 (pp. 598–609).

Herman, S. and Chomsky, N. (1988) *Counter Revolutionary Violence*, Warner, New York.

Hill, S. (1991) 'Why Quality Circles Failed but Total Quality Management Might Succeed, *British Journal of Industrial Relations*, Vol. 29, No. 4 (pp. 541–568).

Hill, S. (1998) 'From Quality Circles to Total Quality Management', in Wilkinson, A. and Wilmott, H. (eds) (1998) *Making Quality Critical: New Perspectives on Organizational Change*, International Thomson Business Press, London.

Hill, S. and Wilkinson, A. (1995) 'In Search of TQM', *Employee Relations*, Vol. 17, No. 3 (pp. 8–25).

Hilmer, F. and Donaldson, L. (1996) *Management Redeemed: Debunking the Fads that Undermine Our Corporations*, Free Press, New York.

Hobsbawm, E. (1998) 'Markets, Meltdown and Marx', *The Guardian* (20/10/98).

Hofstede, G. (1986) 'The Usefulness of the Organization Culture Concept', *Journal of Management Studies*, Vol. 23, No. 3 (pp. 253–257).

Hofstede, G. (1991) *Cultures and Organizations: Software of the Mind*, McGraw-Hill, Maidenhead.

Homans, G. C. (1968) *The Human Group*, Routledge, London.

Hopfl, H. (1992) 'Death of a Snake-oil Salesman: The Demise of the Corporate Life-lie, paper presented to British Academy of Management, Cardiff.

Hopfl, H. (1994) 'Empowerment and the Managerial Prerogative', *Empowerment in Organizations*, Vol. 2, No. 3, (pp. 39–44).

Huczynski, A. A. (1993) *Management Gurus: What Makes Them and How to Become One*, Routledge, London.

Hughes, R. (1993) *Culture of Complaint: The Fraying of America*, Harvill, London.

Hutton, W. (1996) *The State We're In*, Vintage, London.

Iacocca, L. with Novak, W. (1986) *Iacocca*, Bantam Books, London.

Ishikawa, K. (1985) *What is Total Quality Control? The Japanese Way*, Prentice-Hall, London.

Jackson, B. G. (1996) 'Re-engineering the Sense of Self: The Manager and the Management Guru', *Journal of Management Studies*, Vol. 33, No. 5 (pp. 571–590).

Jackson, N. and Carter, P. (1998) 'Management Gurus: What Are We to Make of Them?', in Hassard, J. and Holliday, R. (eds), (1998) *Organization-Representation: Work and Organization in Popular Culture*, Sage, London.

Jackson, T. (1996) 'Management: Now It's a Case of Dumbsizing', *The Financial Times* (20/05/96).

Juran, J. (1988) *Juran on Planning for Quality*, Free Press, New York.

Kahn, H. (1970) *The Emerging Japanese Superstate*, Harper and Row, London.

Kahn, H. and Pepper, T. (1978) *The Japanese Challenge: The Success and Failure of Economic Success*, Harper and Row, London.

Kamata, S. (1983) *Japan in the Passing Lane: An Insider's Account of Life Inside a Japanese Auto Factory*, Allen and Unwin, London.

Kanter, R. M. (1977) *Men and Women of the Corporation*, Free Press, New York.

Kanter, R. M. (1985) *Change Masters: Corporate Entrepreneurs at Work*, Allen and Unwin, London.

Kanter, R. M. (1989) *When Giants Learn to Dance*, Simon and Schuster, London.

Kanter, R. M. (1991) 'The Future of Bureaucracy and Hierarchy in Organizational Theory: A Report from the Field', in Bourdieu, P. and Coleman, J. S. (eds), *Social Theory for a Changing Society*, Westview Press, Boulder, CO.

Kanter, R. M. (1995) *World Class*, Simon and Schuster, New York.

Kearney, A. T. in association with *TQM Magazine* (1992) *Total Quality: Time to Take off the Rose Tinted Spectacles*, a report, IFS Publications, Kempston.

Keat, R. and Abercrombie, N. (eds) (1991) *Enterprise Culture*, Routledge, London.

Keenoy, T. (1993) *Invitation to Industrial Relations*, Blackwell, Oxford.

Keenoy, T. and Anthony, P. (1992) 'HRM: Metaphor, Meaning and Reality', in Blyton, P. and Turnbull, P. (eds), *Reassessing Human Resource Management*, Sage, London.

Kelley, R. E. (1990) 'Managing the New Work Force', *Machine Design*, 10 May (pp. 109–113).

Kelly, J. (1982) *Scientific Management, Job Redesign and Work Performance*, Academic Press, London.

Kelly, J. (1998) *Rethinking Industrial Relations*, Routledge, London.

Kennedy, C. (1996) *Managing with the Gurus: Top Level Guidance on 20 Management Techniques*, Century Books, London.

Kennedy, C. (1998) *Guide to the Management Gurus. Shortcuts to the Leading Ideas of Leading Management Thinkers*, Century, London, 2nd edition.

Kessler, I. and Purcell, J. (1995) 'Performance Related Pay: Objectives and Applications', *Human Resource Management Journal*, Vol. 2, No. 3 (pp. 34–59).

Kessler, S. and Bayliss, F. (1992) *Contemporary British Industrial Relations*, Macmillan, London.

Kondratieff, N. D. (1935) 'The Long Waves in Economic Life', *Review of Economic Statistics*, No. 17 (pp. 105–115).

Kotter, J. (1982) *The General Managers*, Free Press, New York.

Kuhn, T. (1970) *The Structure of Scientific Revolutions*, University of Chicago Press, Chicago, IL.

Kumar, K. (1981) *Prophecy and Progress*, Pelican, Harmondsworth.

Kuper, A. (1993) *Anthropology and Anthropologists: The Modern British School*, Routledge, London.

Kusterer, K. C. (1978) *Know-How on the Job: The Important Working Knowledge of 'Unskilled' Workers*, Westview Press, Boulder, CO.

*Labour Market Trends*, July 1999, Government Statistical Services, London.

Lacey, R. and Danziger, D. (1999) *The Year 1000*, Little Brown and Company, London.

Latour, B. (1987) *Science in Action*, Open University Press, London.

Leadbetter, C. (1996) 'How Fat Cats Rock the Boat', *The Independent on Sunday* (03/11/96).

Lee, R. (1987) 'The Use of "Appropriate theory" in Management Education', *Management Education and Development*, Vol. 18, No. 4 (pp. 247–254).

Legge, K. (1995) *Human Resource Management: Rhetorics and Realities*, Macmillan, London.

Lenin, V. (1982) *Imperialism: The Highest Stage of Capitalism*, Progress Publishers, Moscow.

Levitt, T. (1983) 'The Globalization of Markets', *Harvard Business Review*, May–June (pp. 92–102).

Lewin, K. (1958) 'Group Decisions and Social Change', in Swanson, G. E., Newcomb, T. M. and Hartley, T. L. (eds), *Readings in Social Psychology*, Holt, Rhinehart and Winston, New York.

Lewis, M. (1989) *Liar's Poker*, Corgi, London.

Littler, C. (1982) *The Development of the Labour Process in Capitalist Societies*, Heinemann, London.

Lockyer, C. (1992) 'Pay, Performance and Reward', in Towers, B. (ed.), *The Handbook of Human Resource Management*, Blackwell, Oxford.

Lukes, S. (1974) *Power: A Radical View*, Macmillan, London.

Luthans, F. and Davis, T. (1980) 'Managers in Action: A New Look at their Behaviour and Operating Modes', *Organizational Dynamics*, summer (pp. 64–80).

Mabey, C. and Mayon-White, B. (1993) *Managing Change*, Open University Press, Milton Keynes.

MacGregor, I. (1986) *The Enemy Within*, Collins, London.

Machlup, F. (1962) *The Production and Distribution of Knowledge in the US*, Princeton University Press, Princeton, NJ.

MacInnes, J. (1989) *Thatcherism at Work*, Open University Press, Milton Keynes.

Malone, T. W. (1997) 'Is Empowerment Just a Fad? Control, Decision Making and IT', *Sloan Management Review*, winter (pp. 23–35).

Marchington, M. (1995) 'Employee Relations', in Tyson, S. (ed.) (1995) *Strategic Prospects for HRM*, Institute of Personnel and Development, London.

Marchington, M., Wilkinson, A., Ackers, P. and Goodman, J. (1992) *New Developments in Employee Involvement*, Employment Department Research Paper, No. 2.

Marglin, S. (1976) 'What Do Bosses Do? The Origins and Functions of Hierarchy in Capitalist Production', in Gorz, A. (ed.), *The Division of Labour*, Harvester Press, Sussex.

Martin, J. (1992) *Cultures in Organizations: Three Perspectives*, Oxford University Press, Oxford.

Martinez-Lucio, M. and Weston, S. (1992) 'Human Resource Management and Trade Union Responses: Bringing the Politics of the Workplace Back into the Debate', in Blyton, P. and Turnbull, P. (eds), *Reassessing Human Resource Management*, Sage, London.

Marx, K. (1908) *Capital*, Sonnenschein, London.

McArdle, L., Rowlinson, M., Procter, S., Hassard, J. and Forrester, P. (1998) 'Total Quality Management and Participation: Employee Empowerment or the Enhancement of Exploitation', in Wilkinson, A. and Wilmott, H. (eds), *Making Quality Critical: New Perspectives on Organizational Change*, International Thomson Business Press, London.

McCrone, D. (1992) *Understanding Scotland: The Sociology of a Stateless Nation*, Routledge, London.

McLoughlin, I. and Clark, J. (1994) *Technological Change at Work*, Open University Press, Milton Keynes.

Melvern, L. (1986) *The End of the Street*, Methuen, London.

Merquior, J. G. (1985) *Foucault*, Fontana Modern Masters, London.

Meyer, S. (1981) *The Five Dollar Day: Labor Management and Social Control in the Ford Motor Company, 1908–1921*, State University of New York Press, NY.

Micklethwait, J. and Wooldridge, A. (1997) *The Witch Doctors: What the Management Gurus are Saying, and How to Make Sense of It*, Mandarin, London.

Millward, N. (1994) *The New Industrial Relations?*, PSI Publishing, London.

Minford, P. (1982) 'Trade Unions Destroy a Million Jobs', *Journal of Economic Affairs*, No. 2, January (pp. 73–79).

Mink, O. G. (1992) 'Creating New Organizational Paradigms for Change', *International Journal of Quality and Reliability Management*, Vol. 9, No. 3 (pp. 21–35).

Mintzberg, H. (1973) *The Nature of Managerial Work*, Harper and Row, New York.

Mitchell-Stewart, A. (1994) *Empowering People*, Pitman, London.

Monk, R. (1990) *Ludwig Wittgenstein: The Duty of Genius*, Penguin, London.

Moore, M. (1997) *Downsize This! Random Thoughts from an Unarmed American*, Boxtree, London.

Morgan, G. (1986) *Images of Organization*, Sage, London.

Mukherjee, S. (1973) *Through No Fault of Their Own: Systems for Handling Redundancy in Britain, France and Germany*, MacDonald, London.

Mullins, L. (1996) *Management and Organisational Behaviour*, Pitman, London, 3rd edition.

Munro, R. (1998) 'Governing the New Provence of Quality: Autonomy, Accounting and the Dissemination of Accountability', in Wilkinson, A. and Wilmott, H. (eds), *Making Quality Critical: New Perspectives on Organizational Change*, International Thomson Business Press, London.

Newman, K. S. (1988) *Falling from Grace: The Experience of Downward Mobility in the American Middle Class*, Random House, New York.

Nomikos, G. E. (1989) 'Managing Knowledge Workers for Productivity', *National Productivity Review*, Vol. 8, No. 2 (pp. 165–174).

Noon, M. and Blyton, P. (1997) *The Realities of Work*, Macmillan, London.

O'Rourke, P. J. (1998) *Eat the Rich: A Treatise on Economics*, Picador, London.

Oakland, J. (1993) *Total Quality Management*, Butterworth–Heinemann, Oxford.

Ogbonna, E. and Wilkinson, B. (1988) 'Corporate Strategy and Corporate Culture: The Management of Change in the UK Supermarket Industry', *Personnel Review*, Vol. 7, No. 6 (pp. 10–14).

Ohmae, K. (1994) *The Borderless World: Power and Strategy in the Global Marketplace*, HarperCollins, London.

Oppenheim, C. (1997) 'The Growth of Poverty and Inequality', in Walker, A. and Walker, C. (eds), *Britain Divided: The Growth of Social Exclusion in the 1980s and 1990s*, Child Poverty Action Group (CPAG), London.

Oram, M. (1998) 'Re-engineering's Fragile Promise: HRM Prospects for Delivery', in Sparrow, P. and Marchington, M. (eds), *Human Resource Management: The New Agenda*, Pitman, London.

Oren, H. and Bell, C. R. (1995) 'Is Wile E. Coyote in Your Office?', *Management Review*, Vol. 84, No. 5 (pp. 57–61).

Orr, S., Millen, R. A. and McCarthy, D. (1999) 'Beyond Downsizing; Recreating Australia', *Management Decision*, Vol. 37, No. 8 (pp. 657–670).

Orwell, G. (1978) 'Down the Mine', in *Inside the Whale and Other Essays*, Penguin, Harmondsworth.

Ott, S. J. (1989) *Classic Readings in Organizational Behavior*, Brooks/Cole Publishing, Pacific Grove, CA.

Ouchi, W. (1981) *Theory Z*, Addison-Wesley, Reading, MA.

Paddon, M. (1992) 'Quality in an Enabling Context', in Sanderson, I. (ed.),

*Management of Quality in Local Government*, Longman, Harlow.

Parker, M. and Slaughter, J. (1988) 'Management by Stress', *Technology Review*, Vol. 91, No. 7 (pp. 36–44).

Parker, T. (1993) *May the Lord in His Mercy Be Kind to Belfast*, Jonathan Cape, London.

Pascale, R. T. and Athos, A. G. (1986) *The Art of Japanese Management*, Sidgwick and Jackson, London.

Pastor, J. (1996) 'Empowerment: What It Is and What It Is Not', *Empowerment in Organizations*, Vol. 4, No. 2 (pp. 5–7).

Pateman, C. (1970) *Participation and Democratic Theory*, Cambridge University Press, Cambridge.

Pattison, S. (1997) *The Faith of the Managers: When Management Becomes Religion*, Cassell, London.

Paxman, J. (1998) 'The Joy of Thuggery', *The Sunday Times, News Review* (11/10/98).

Pearn, M., Mulrooney, C. and Payne, T. (1998) *Ending the Blame Culture*, Gower, Aldershot.

Perrow, C. (1979) *Complex Organizations: A Critical Essay*, Scott Foresman, Illinois.

Perry, N. (1993) 'Putting Theory in Its Place: The Social Organization of Organizational Theorizing', in Reed, M. and Hughes, M. (eds), *Rethinking Organisations: New Directions in Organization Theory and Analysis*, Sage, London.

Peters, T. (1988) *Thriving on Chaos: Handbook for a Management Revolution*, Pan Books, London.

Peters, T. (1993) *Liberation Management: Necessary Disorganization for the Nanosecond Nineties*, Pan Books, London.

Peters, T. (1994) *The Tom Peters Seminar: Crazy Times Call for Crazy Organizations*, Macmillan, London.

Peters, T. (1995) *The Pursuit of Wow! Every Person's Guide to Topsy Turvy Times*, Macmillan, London.

Peters, T. (1997) *The Circle of Innovation: You Can't Shrink Your Way to Greatness*, Hodder and Stoughton, London.

Peters, T. and Austin, N. (1985) *A Passion for Excellence: The Leadership Difference*, Fontana, London.

Peters, T. and Waterman, R. (1982) *In Search of Excellence: Lessons from America's Best Run Companies*, Harper and Row, New York.

Peterson, W. C. (1995) *The Silent Depression: The Fate of the American Dream*, W. W. Norton and Co., London.

Pettigrew, A. (1985) *Awakening Giant: Continuity and Change in ICI*, Blackwell, Oxford.

Pettigrew, A. (1987) 'Context and Action in the Transformation of the Firm', *Journal of Management Studies*, Vol. 24, No. 6 (pp. 649–670).

Plunkett, L. C. and Fournier, R. (1991) *Participative Management: Implementing Empowerment*, John Wiley and Sons, Chichester.

Pocock, D. (1988) *Social Anthropology*, Sheed and Ward, London.

Poole, M. (1986) *Industrial Relations: Origins and Patterns of National Diversity*, Routledge, London.

Porter, M. (1985) *Competitive Advantage: Creating and Sustaining Superior Performance*, Free Press, London.

Pritchard, J. (1996) 'Acting Professionally: Something That Business Organizations and Individuals Both Desire?', in Davies, P. W. F. (ed.), *Current Issues in Business Ethics*, Routledge, London.

Pugh, D. (ed.) (1990) *Organization Theory*, Penguin, London.

Pugh, D. and Hickson, D. J. (1996) *Writers on Organizations*, Penguin, London.

Ramsay, H. (1977) 'Cycles of Control, *Sociology*, Vol. 11, No. 3 (pp. 481–506).

Ramsay, H. (1997) 'Fool's Gold? European Works Councils and Workplace Democracy', *Industrial Relations Journal*, Vol. 28, No. 4 (pp. 314–322).

Reed, M. (1992) *The Sociology of Organizations*, Harvester-Wheatsheaf, Hemel Hempstead.

Rees, W. D. (1996) *The Skills of Management*, International Thomson Business Press, London.

Rose, N. (1990) *Governing the Soul: The Shaping of the Private Self*, Gower, Aldershot.

Rodney, W. (1983) *How Europe Underdeveloped Africa*, Bogle L'ouverture Publications, London.

Roy, D. F. (1960) 'Banana Time: Job Satisfaction and Informal Interaction', in Ott, S. J. (ed.), (1989) *Classic Readings in Organizational Behaviour*, Brooks/Cole Publishing, Pacific Grove, CA.

Sadler, P. (1992) 'Leaders: Born or Bred', in Syrett, M. (ed.), *Frontiers of Leadership*, Blackwell, Oxford.

Sadler, P. (1993) *Managing Talent*, Economist Books, London.

Sayles, L. R. (1964) *Managerial Behaviour*,McGraw-Hill, New York.

Schein, E. (1985) *Organizational Culture and Leadership*, Jossey-Bass, San Francisco.

Scott, A. (1994) *Willing Slaves? British Workers under HRM*, Cambridge University Press, Cambridge.

Scott, J. C. (1990) *Domination and the Arts of Resistance*, Yale University Press, New Haven.

Seaton, M. (1995) 'All Work But No Point', *The Independent* (10/12/95).

Semler, R. (1994) *Maverick: The Success Story behind the World's Most Unusual Workplace*, Arrow Books, London.

Senge, P. (1990) *The Fifth Discipline*, Doubleday, New York.

Sennett, R. (1998) *The Corrosion of Character: The Personal Consequences of Work in the New Capitalism*, Norton, New York.

Sethi, S. P., Namiki, N. and Swanson, C. L. (1984) *The False Promise of the Japanese Miracle: Illusions and Realities of the Japanese Management System*, Pitman, London.

Sewell, G. and Wilkinson, B. (1992) 'Empowerment or Emasculation: Shopfloor Surveillance in a Total Quality Organization', in Blyton, P. and Turnbull, P. (eds), *Reassessing Human Resource Management*, Sage, London.

Shapiro, E. (1998) *Fad Surfing in the Boardroom: Reclaiming the Courage to Manage in the Age of Instant Answers*, Capstone, Oxford.

Sheldrake, J. (1996) *Management Theory: From Taylorism to Japanization*, International Thomson Business Press, London.

Shingo, S. (1987) *The Sayings of Shingo Shingo*, trans. A. P. Dillon, Productivity Press, New York.

Simon, H. (1976) *New Science of Management Decision*, Prentice-Hall, Hemel Hempstead.

Sims, D., Gabriel, Y. and Fineman, S. (1993) *Organizing and Organizations: An Introduction*, Sage, London.

Sinclair, J. and Collins, D. (1994) 'Towards a Quality Culture?', *International Journal of Quality and Reliability Management*, Vol. 11, No. 5 (pp. 19–29).

Sirs, B. (1985) *Hard Labour*, Sidgwick and Jackson, London.

Slater, R. (1998) *Jack Welch and the GE Way*, McGraw-Hill, London.

Sly, F., Price, A. and Risdon, A. (1997) 'Women in the Labour Market: Results from the Spring 1996 Labour Force Survey', *Labour Market Trends*, March (pp. 99–120).

Smelser, N. J. (1994) 'Sociological Theories', *International Social Science Journal*, Vol. 139, February (pp. 1–14).

Smircich, L. (1983) 'Concepts of Culture and Organizational Analysis', *Administrative Science Quarterly*, Vol. 28, No. 3 (pp. 339–358).

Snape, E., Wilkinson, A., Marchington, M. and Redman, T. (1995) 'Managing Human Resources for TQM: Possibilities and Pitfalls', *Employee Relations*, Vol. 17, No. 3 (pp. 42–51).

St George, A. (1994) 'Working Life: Downsizing Seeks New Employment', *The Financial Times* (15/09/94).

Starkey, K. and McKinlay, A. (1993) *Strategy and the Human Resource: Ford and the Search for Competitive Advantage*, Blackwell, Oxford.

Steinbeck, J. (1939) *The Grapes of Wrath*, Heinemann, London.

Steinbeck, J. (1988) *The Harvest Gypsies: On the Road to the Grapes of Wrath*, Heyday Books, Berkeley, CA.

Steiner, R. (1998) 'Prufrock' Diary, *The Sunday Times* (28/06/98).

Steiner, R. (1998) 'Prufrock' Diary, *The Sunday Times* (29/11/98).

Sterling, B. (1992) *The Hacker Crackdown: Law and Disorder on the Electronic Frontier*, Penguin, Harmondsworth.

Stewart, R. (1976) *Contrasts in Management*, McGraw-Hill, Maidenhead.

Storey, J. (ed.) (1991) *New Perspectives on Human Resource Management*, Routledge, London.

Strassman, P. A. (1994) 'The Hocus-Pocus of Reengineering', *Across the Board*, Vol. 34, No. 6 (pp. 35–38).

Sweet, M. L. (1985) 'The United States of America and Canada', in Cross, M. (ed.), *Managing Workforce Reduction*, Croom Helm, Beckenham.

Taguchi, G. (1987) *Systems of Experimental Design*, Unipub/Kraus International Publications, New York.

Taylor, F. W. (1911) *The Principles of Scientific Management*, Harper and Row, New York.

Terkel, S. (1985) *Working*, Penguin, Harmondsworth.

Thackray, J. (1993) 'Fads, Fixes and Fictions', *Management Today*, June (pp. 40–42).

Thomas, A. B. (1993) *Controversies in Management*, International Thomson Business Press, London.

Thompson, E. P. (1972) *The Making of the English Working Class*, Pelican, Harmondsworth.

Thompson, P. and McHugh, D. (1990) *Work Organisations: A Critical Introduction*, Macmillan, London.

Thompson, P. and McHugh, D. (1995) *Work Organisations: A Critical Introduction*, Macmillan, London.

Toffler, A. (1983) *The Third Wave*, Pan Books, London.

Tomaney, J. (1990) 'The Reality of Workplace Flexibility', *Capital and Class*, No. 40, spring (pp. 29–60).

Tooher, P. (1996) 'The Boss is Demoralised, Downsized and Delayerd Too', *The Independent* (16/09/96).

Torrington, J. (1996) *The Devil's Carousel*, Secker and Warburg, London.

Touraine, A. (1974) *The Post-industrial Society*, Butler and Tanner, London.

Treneman, A. (1998) 'Empire Britannia', *The Independent, Weekend Review*, (25/07/98).

Tsoukas, H. (1995) 'Introduction: From Social Engineering to Reflective Action in Organizational Behaviour', in Haridimos, H. (ed.), *New Thinking in Organizational Behaviour*, Butterworth–Heinemann, London.

Tucker, R. C. (ed.) (1978) *The Marx–Engels Reader*, W. W. Norton and Co., New York, 2nd edition.

Tuckman, A. (1998) 'Ideology, Quality and TQM', in Wilkinson, A. and Wilmott, H. (eds), *Making Quality Critical: New Perspectives on Organizational Change*, International Thomson Business Press, London.

UNESCO (1993) *Statistical Yearbook*, UNESCO, Paris.

Ungoed-Thomas, J. (1998) 'A Nation of Thieves', *The Sunday Times* (11/01/98).

Veblen, T. (1994) *The Theory of the Leisure Class*, Dover Publications, Don Mills, Toronto, Ontario.

Vonnegut, K. (1973) *Breakfast of Champions, or Goodbye Monday*, Delacorte Press, New York.

Waddington, J. and Whitson, C. (1996) 'Empowerment Versus Intensification: Union Perspectives of Change at the Workplace', in Ackers, P., Smith, C. and Smith, P. (eds), *The New Workplace and Trade Unionism: Critical Perspectives on Work and Organization*, Routledge, London.

Walker, A. and Walker, C. (eds) (1997) *Britain Divided: The Growth of Social Exclusion in the 1980s and 1990s*, CPAG, London.

Wallerstein, I. (1974) *The Modern World System: Capitalist Agriculture and the Origins of the European World-Economy in the Sixteenth Century*, Academic Press, New York.

Walsh, K. (1998) 'Quality Through Markets: The New Public Service Management', in Wilkinson, A. and Wilmott, H. (eds), *Making Quality Critical: New Perspectives on Organizational Change*, International Thomson Business Press, London.

Waters, M. (1998) *Globalization*, Routledge, London.

Webb, J. (1998) 'Quality Management and the Management of Quality', in Wilkinson, A. and Wilmott, H. (eds), *Making Quality Critical: New Perspectives on Organizational Change*, International Thomson Business Press, London.

Weber, M. (1958) *The Protestant Ethic and the Spirit of Capitalism*, Harper and Row, New York.

Webster, F. (1994) *Theories of the Information Society*, Routledge, London.

Wedderburn, R. K. (1986) *The Worker and the Law*, Pelican, Harmondsworth.

Weick, K. (1995) *Sensemaking in Organizations*, Sage, London.

Whittington, R. (1993) *What is Strategy and Does it Matter?* Routledge, London.

Wickens, P. (1987) *The Road to Nissan*, Macmillan, London.

Wilkinson, A. (1994) 'Managing Human Resources for Quality', in Dale, B. G. (ed.), *Managing Quality*, Prentice-Hall, London.

Wilkinson, A. (1998) 'Empowerment: Theory and Practice', *Personnel Review*, Vol. 27, No. 1 (pp. 40 56).

Wilkinson, A. and Wilmott, H. (1995) 'Total Quality: Asking Critical Questions', *Academy of Management Review*, Vol. 20, No. 4 (pp. 789–791).

Wilkinson, A., Allen, P. and Snape, E. (1991) 'TQM and the Management of Labour', *Employee Relations*, Vol. 13, No. 1 (pp. 24–31).

Wilkinson, A., Godfrey, G. and Marchington, M. (1997) 'Bouquets, Brickbats and Blinkers: Total Quality Management and Employee Involvement', *Organization Studies*, Vol. 18, No. 5 (pp. 799–819).

Wilkinson, A., Redman, T. and Snape, E. (1993) *Quality and the Manager: An IM Report*, Institute of Management, Corby.

Wilkinson, A., Marchington, M., Goodman, J. and Ackers, P. (1992) 'Total Quality Management and Employee Involvement', *Human Resource Management Journal*, Vol. 2, No. 4 (pp. 1–20).

Wilkinson, A., Redman, T., Snape, E. and Marchington, M. (1998) *Managing with Total Quality Management: Theory and Practice*, Macmillan, London.

Wilkinson, B. (1983) *The Shopfloor Politics of New Technology*, Heinemann, London.

Wilmott, H. (1994) 'Business Process Re-engineering and Human Resource Management', *Personnel Review*, Vol. 23, No. 3 (pp. 34–46).

Wilmott, H. and Wray-Bliss, H. (1996) 'Process Reengineering, Information Technology and the Transformation of Accountability: The Remaindering of the Human Resource', in Orlikowski, W. J., Walsham, G., Jones, M. R. and DeGross, J. I. (eds), *Information Technology and Changes in Organizational Work*, Chapman and Hall, London.

Winfield, I. (1994) 'Toyota UK Ltd: Model HRM Practices?', *Employee Relations*, Vol. 16, No. 1 (pp. 41–53).

Witcher, B. and Whyte, J. (1992) *The Adoption of Total Quality Management in Northern England*, Durham University Business School Occasional Paper Series.

Wolfe, T. (1979) *The Right Stuff*, Jonathan Cape, London.

Wolfe, T. (1994) *The Pump House Gang*, Black Swan, London.

Wood, R. C. (1992) *Working in Hotels and Catering*, Routledge, London.

Woodward, J. (1970) *Industrial Organization: Theory and Practice*, Oxford University Press, Oxford.

Wooley, B. (1993) *Virtual Worlds*, Penguin, Harmondsworth.

Wright, P. (1980) *On a Clear Day You Can See General Motors*, Sidgwick and Jackson, London.

Wright, S. (ed.) (1994) *Anthropology of Organizations*, Routledge, London.

Wright-Mills, C. (1973) *The Sociological Imagination*, Pelican, Harmondsworth Middlesex.

Wyatt Company (1993) *Wyatt's 1993 Survey of Company Restructuring – Best Practices in Corporate Restructuring*, Wyatt Company, New York.

Zairi, M., Letza, S. and Oakland, J. (1994) 'Does TQM Impact on Bottom Line Results?', *TQM Magazine*, Vol. 6, No. 1 (pp. 38–43).

Zuboff, S. (1989) *In the Age of the Smart Machine*, Heinemann, New York.

# Index